GLOBAL CULTURE

GLOBAL CULTURE

Media, Arts, Policy, and Globalization

Edited by

Diana Crane, Nobuko Kawashima,
and Ken'ichi Kawasaki

JAY
Routledge
New York   London

The chapters by Toepler and Zimmer, Lindsay, and Iwabuchi appeared in somewhat different form in the following publications:

StefanToepler And Annette Zimmer (1999) The subsidized muse: government and the arts in Western Europe and the United States," *Journal of Cultural Economics*, 23, 1–2: 33–49.

Jennifer Lindsay (1995) Cultural policy and the performing arts, *Bijdragen*, 151-IV: 655–671. Printed with permission from Koninklijk Instituut voor Taal-, Land- en Volkenkunde (Royal Institute of Linguistics and Anthropology), Leiden, The Netherlands.

Koichi Iwabuchi (1998) Marketing 'Japan': Japanese cultural presence under a global gaze, *Japanese Studies*, 18,2: 165–180. For more information about Taylor & Francis Ltd. Journals see: http://www.tandf.co.uk.

Cover of "Killah Babe" spring/summer 1999 catalog courtesy of SIXTY S.p.A., Via Piaggio, 35, Chieti 66013 (Italy)

Front and back cover of music CD "Xche' Si!" by Articolo 31 courtesy of BMG Ricordi, S.p.A., Via Berchet, 2, 20121 Milano (Italy)

Published in 2002 by

Routledge
29 West 35th Street
New York, NY 10001

Published in Great Britain by

Routledge
11 New Fetter Lane
London EC4P 4EE

Routledge is an imprint of the Taylor & Francis Group.

Library of Congress Cataloging-in-Publication Data
Global culture : media, arts, policy, and globalization /
edited by Diana Crane, Nobuko Kawashima, and Ken'ichi Kawasaki.
        p.   cm.
    Includes bibliographical references and index.
    ISBN 0-415-93229-7   —   ISBN 0-415-93230-0 (pbk.)
    1. Mass media and culture.   2. Mass media—Social aspects.
    3. Cultural policy.   I. Crane, Diana, 1933–
    II. Kawashima, Nobuko.   III. Kawasaki, Ken'ichi.

    P94.6 .G57   2002
    302.23—dc21   2001049113

4126102   a4995676

Contents

PART II. REGENERATING CULTURAL RESOURCES: URBAN AND ORGANIZATIONAL STRATEGIES

PART III. REFRAMING URBAN CULTURES FOR LOCAL AND GLOBAL CONSUMPTION

PART IV. REFRAMING MEDIA CULTURES FOR GLOBAL CONSUMPTION

Acknowledgments

We thank the Japanese Ministry of Education and Science for a Grant-in-Aid for Scientific Research (1997–2000) which permitted our international group of researchers (including, in addition to ourselves, Sachiko Kanno, Kian-Woon Kwok, Kee-Hong Low, Rosanne Martorella, and Keniyuki Tomooka) to meet in a number of "global" cities, including Tokyo, Singapore, Barcelona, Birmingham, and New York, where we were able to discuss, learn, and present preliminary drafts of papers on issues related to international cultural policy and globalization. These sessions generated perspectives that were useful in developing this volume. We are also grateful to the other authors of the essays in this volume, who constitute with us a "global" group representing nine countries. We appreciate their willingness to respond patiently to numerous requests during the two years in which this book was in progress. We also thank the Department of Sociology at the University of Pennsylvania for secretarial assistance. Finally, we are very grateful to Ilene Kalish at Routledge for her confidence in us and in this book.

The chapters by Crane and Ballé appeared in a somewhat different form in the following publications:

Diana Crane, As culturas nacionas na era de globalização cultural. *Sociedade e Estado*, XV, Janeiro-Junho, 2000: 33–51. (translated by João Gabriel L. C. Teixeira).

Catherine Ballé, Le public: un enjeu des musées contemporains. In *Analyser le musée. Travaux du Centre de recherches semiologiques*. août, 1996: 49–58.

Diana Crane
Nobuko Kawashima
Ken'ichi Kawasaki
May, 2001

1

Culture and Globalization

Theoretical Models and Emerging Trends

Diana Crane

Globalization has become an immensely popular topic among social scientists despite the fact that it is poorly defined and difficult to research systematically. In this volume, cultural globalization—as opposed to economic, political, or technological globalization—refers to the transmission or diffusion across national borders of various forms of media and the arts.[1] Generally the circulation of cultural products or artifacts occurs among advanced or advancing countries, particularly those that constitute desirable markets for media or that possess sufficient levels of revenue for investment in the arts and in arts institutions. It is important to realize that cultural globalization is no longer conceptualized in terms of the emergence of a homogenized global culture corresponding to Marshall McLuhan's global village. Instead, cultural globalization is recognized as a complex and diverse phenomenon consisting of global cultures, originating from many different nations and regions.

Assuming that all forms of culture construct and deconstruct social identities and social relations, cultural globalization raises important and controversial issues concerning its effects on national and local cultures and their responses to it. Do global cultures differ in important ways from national or local cultures? Does the existence of global cultures imply homogeneity in the tastes of publics located in different countries? What policies, if any, should national governments undertake in order to adjust, adapt, or resist the effects of global cultures? Understanding cultural globalization requires an examination of economic organizations and political institutions that contribute to it or attempt to respond to it. What are the implications of changes in the character and ownership of international media conglomerates, of the roles of regional and national cultures in relation to global cultures, and in the complexity of the public's responses to global cultures?

My objectives in this chapter are: (1) to review the principal theoretical models that have been used to explain or interpret cultural globalization; (2) to propose an

1

additional model; and (3) to discuss the status of these models in relation to recent literature on globalization. Cultural globalization is sufficiently complex that no single theory can be expected to explain it adequately. The four models I will discuss are the following: the cultural imperialism thesis, the cultural flows or network model, reception theory, and a model of national and urban strategies toward cultural globalization (see fig. 1.1). The first three models have been undergoing substantial revision as new information becomes available and as factors driving cultural globalization change. As a result, these models are substantially different from what they were when first proposed. In the chapters that follow, the authors have been guided, implicitly or explicitly, by these approaches in developing their arguments or conducting their studies.

Theoretical Models of Cultural Globalization

The best known model of cultural globalization is cultural imperialism theory. This theory emerged in the 1960s as part of a Marxist critique of advanced capitalist cultures, including their emphasis on consumerism and mass communications. Building on ideas from world-systems theory, the theory argues that the global economic system

Figure 1.1   Models of Cultural Globalization

Model	Process of Cultural Transmission	Principal Actors, Sites	Possible Consequences
Cultural imperialism Media imperialism	Center-periphery	Global media conglomerates	Homogenization of culture
Cultural flows/ networks	Two-way flows	Regional and national conglomerates and corporations	Hybridization of culture
Reception theory	Center-periphery; multidirectional	Audiences, publics, cultural entrepreneurs, gatekeepers	Negotiation, resistance
Cultural policy strategies e.g., preservation, resistance, reframing, glocalization	Framing of national cultures	Global cities, museums, heritage sites, cultural memory, media, ministries of culture and trade	Competition, negotiation

is dominated by a core of advanced countries while Third World countries remain at the periphery of the system with little control over their economic and political development (Tomlinson 1991:37). Multinational or transnational corporations are key actors in this system, producing goods, controlling markets, and disseminating products, using similar techniques. The theory is similar to ideas developed by the Frankfurt School in Germany insofar as it presupposes a relatively homogenous mass culture that is accepted passively and uncritically by mass audiences.

The strong version of cultural imperialism theory refers to the imposition upon other countries of a particular nation's beliefs, values, knowledge, behavioral norms, and style of life (Salwen 1991). Cultural imperialism is defined as a kind of cultural domination by powerful nations over weaker nations. It is viewed as purposeful and intentional because it corresponds to the political interests of the United States and other powerful capitalist societies. The effects of this type of cultural domination, reflecting the attitudes and values of Western, particularly American, capitalist societies, are viewed as extremely pervasive and as leading to the homogenization of global culture, as suggested by the following comment by an Australian scholar (White 1983): "The Americanization process becomes far more formidable when the fundamental concepts of a society's national identity are remodeled in the American image" (pp. 120–21).

The concept of cultural imperialism is inherently vague and implies a negative evaluation of the behavior and intentions of advanced countries, particularly the United States, toward other advanced countries and toward poorer countries. Critics have argued that the term "imperialism," which can be seen as the imposition of power from rich to poor, from powerful to weak, implies a degree of political control by powerful countries that no longer exists. According to John Tomlinson (1991), "The idea of imperialism contains . . . the notion of a purposeful project: the *intended* spread of a social system from one center of power across the globe." He contrasts imperialism with the concept of "globalization," which suggests "interconnection and interdependency of all global areas" happening "in a far less purposeful way" (p. 175).

Despite its weaknesses, cultural imperialism, reconceptualized as media imperialism (see below), remains a useful perspective because it can be used to analyze the extent to which some national actors have more impact than others on global culture, and therefore are shaping and reshaping cultural values, identities, and perceptions. Since the scope and influence of global cultures are rapidly expanding, these are important issues.

In contrast to cultural imperialism theory in which the source of cultural influence is Western civilization, with non-Western and less developed countries viewed as being on the periphery—as the receivers of cultural influences—the cultural flows or network model offers an alternative conception of the transmission process, as influences that do not necessarily originate in the same place or flow in the same direction. Receivers may also be originators. In this model, cultural globalization corresponds to a network with no clearly defined center or periphery (see, for example, Appadurai 1990). Globalization as an aggregation of cultural flows or networks is a less coherent and unitary process than cultural imperialism and one in which cultural influences move in many different directions. The effect of these cultural flows, which Arjun

Appadurai identifies as consisting of media, technology, ideologies, and ethnicities on recipient nations is likely to be cultural hybridization rather than homogenization.[2]

A third model, reception theory, has been used to explain responses to cultural globalization by publics in different countries. This theory hypothesizes that audiences respond actively rather than passively to mass-mediated news and entertainment and that different national, ethnic, and racial groups interpret the same materials differently. This model does not view globally disseminated culture as a threat to national or local identities. Multiculturalism rather than cultural imperialism is perceived as the dominant trend. Critics of reception theory argue that audience response has little effect on global media conglomerates or cultural policy. Media conglomerates treat audiences as undifferentiated consumers of their products rather than as citizens with distinct rights and preferences.

A fourth approach, which I propose, focuses on the strategies used by nations, global cities, and cultural organizations to cope with, counter, or promote cultural globalization. Specifically, nations, global cities, and cultural organizations engage in strategies for preserving and protecting inherited cultures, strategies for rejuvenating traditional cultures, strategies for resisting cultural globalization, and strategies for altering or transforming local and national cultures for global consumption. From this perspective, cultural globalization is a process that involves competition and negotiation as organizations and countries attempt to preserve, position, or project their cultures in global space. Countries vary in their emphasis upon preservation as opposed to production of culture for exportation. In this approach, cultural globalization is seen as a disorderly process, fraught with tension, competition, and conflict.

In the following sections, I will review the current status of these models to show how they are being adapted to changes in our understanding of the level and character of cultural globalization.

From Cultural Imperialism to Global Capitalism and Media Imperialism

Major forces leading to cultural globalization are economic and organizational. Cultural globalization requires an organizational infrastructure. One form of globalization occurs as a result of the activities in advanced countries of news and entertainment media that produce films, television programs, and popular music and distribute them to countries all over the world. Dominance of a particular country in the global media marketplace is more a function of economic than cultural factors. American corporations particularly have benefited from the size of their national market and the availability of funds for investment.

A small number of media conglomerates, based in a few Western countries, dominate the production and global distribution of film, television, popular music, and book publishing. Robert W. McChesney (1999) has documented the existence of a global media market that has developed as a result of new technologies and the deregulation of national media industries. This market is oligopolistic. Because of high production and distribution costs, the level of investment required to enter this market is very high. These vertically integrated corporations make huge profits by selling the same product in different media. For example, a film may be shown in movie theaters and on pay cable television and sold in the form of a CD-ROM, a book, or as comics. A spin-off may be used for a television series. Merchandise based on the film generates additional profits. According to McChesney, corporations without access to this type of "synergy" are incapable of competing in the global marketplace.

Though some of the global media conglomerates are European, American media products continue to dominate in global markets. Foreign conglomerate owners invest heavily in American media companies. Several major American film studios have recently been bought by foreign companies, but this has had little effect on the nature of the Hollywood film product. Australian-American media magnate Rupert Murdoch owns more American television stations than anyone else. He has also created a successful television network (Fox) that competes with the three major American television networks. A German conglomerate (Bertelsmann) purchased the largest American book publishing company.

Because of the huge audience for films in the United States, American companies producing and distributing films earn enormous profits in their own country. As a result, American producers can afford to make more expensive films than their competitors in other countries, and this in turn increases profits. The more expensive a film is to produce, the more money it is likely to make. Blockbusters attract the largest international audiences (Phillips 1982). These expensive films represent a type of homogenous, uniform culture permeated by Western capitalistic values. They are full of elaborate technical effects and concentrate on stunts, action, and violence rather than character and emotion. Action films are more easily understood in diverse, non-English-speaking cultures than other types of films. Given the enormous cultural diversity among the potential audiences for globally marketed films, filmmakers have to find common denominators that are universal in a weak sense and will attract audiences in different countries.

Hollywood has dominated the international market for films for several decades because American film companies have been more successful in creating film distribution networks in other countries than local film companies have been. Film industries in many other countries have declined. Two exceptions are India, with its huge internal market, and France, which has heavily subsidized this form of popular culture. India is the leading producer of fiction films in the world, but, with few exceptions, they circulate entirely within Indian Asia and Indian Africa (Straubhaar 1997:289).

The United States also predominates in the production and sale of television programs (Barker 1997:50) for reasons that have more to do with economic factors than with cultural attitudes and values. Hoskins and Mirus (1990) argue that the success of American television programs in the international market is largely a result of the conditions under which they are produced. Again, the size and wealth of the country means that successful programs are extremely lucrative. Consequently, the high costs of television production (more than $1 million per episode) can be recouped locally. Programs can be sold for export at substantially lower prices than indigenous producers can offer. In Latin America, for example, American companies have been accused of flooding the media scene by "dumping" old movies and television shows (Sreberny-Mohammadi 1991:128). In some countries, U.S. television represents about 50 percent of the programs, although in many European countries the figure is less than one-third (Curran 1998). Many other countries are unable to invest at the American level in television programming because they cannot meet the costs of production through distribution in their own countries, and they cannot afford distributing and marketing costs in other countries. The cost of an imported television drama can be less than one-tenth of the cost of creating an original production (Curran 1998). Nevertheless, Mexico's Televisa is the largest single exporter of television programming in the world (Hallin 1998).

Changes in the availability of technology in developing countries have led to an increase in transnational dissemination of television programs and in expansion of world demand for programming (Straubhaar 1991:47). International satellite delivery systems have been very important in disseminating television programs from advanced countries to less advanced countries (Sinclair 1996:52–53). In Latin America, increases in the availability of VCRs, cable TV, and direct satellite reception have expanded audiences for U.S. and European television. In countries where the availability of media has been severely limited or restricted, the arrival of foreign programming may greatly increase the range of cultural choices.[3] In countries that have the resources to produce their own media, foreign programming disseminated by powerful media conglomerates may reduce the profitability of national programming and consequently limit the range of cultural choices. However, there are still many less developed countries that have few media resources of their own and lack the resources to receive media. According to Peter Golding (1998:145), the developed world has nearly six times as many radios per capita as the developing world and nearly nine times as many television sets. The level of communication in many poor countries is indicated by the fact that approximately half the people in the world have never made a telephone call (Golding 1998:145–46).

Global musical culture disseminated by media conglomerates generally concentrates upon artists from English-speaking countries and excludes artists from other countries, particularly those who do not speak English (Negus 1996:184–85). The international repertoires of major record companies have increasingly focused on a small number of international stars and excluded local artists. The American cable company MTV, which specializes in music videos and which has aggressively marketed its products in Europe, Asia, and Latin America, includes primarily artists from the United States and the United Kingdom, particularly those being distributed by major music conglomerates, and pays little attention to artists from other countries (Banks 1996). For example, MTV Europe plays mainly American and British artists. Jack Banks states: "The spotlight on U.S. and U.K. acts reinforces the dominance of these acts throughout the continent, consigning indigenous artists to the margins of popular culture even within their own countries" (p. 91). A vehicle for American advertisers, MTV glorifies a consumer lifestyle that is often inappropriate for audiences in less developed countries and that has been accused of subverting traditional values.

The influence of American television as a form of global culture can be seen in the media products of some countries whose populations have been heavily exposed to these shows. In these countries locally produced television programs have been described as "pale copies of Western genres" (Nain 1996:173). The Brazilian telenovela which has been touted as one of the great successes of Third World media resembles American soap operas in its strong emphasis on consumer values as seen in the merchandizing of products in the story lines (Sreberny-Mohammadi 1991: 128; B-iltereyst and Meers 2000). Similar criticisms have been made of Peruvian media.

As these developments indicate, cultural imperialism with political motives has been replaced by media imperialism based on global capitalism, although some media industries fit this model more than others. A small·number of media conglomerates based in a few countries (the United States, Germany, France, and Great Britain) have continually extended their control over the television, film, music, and publishing industries and hence the global reach of their products. Douglas Kellner (1999) identifies a new postindustrial form of "techno-capitalism . . . characterized by a decline in the power of the state and increased power of the market" (p. 246). He states that mergers of major entertainment and information conglomerates have produced "the most extensive concentration and conglomeration of information and entertainment industries in history" (p. 243). However, this model does not explain all the dimensions of cultural globalization.

Cultural Globalization as Network Flows

Two contradictory trends are operating in the phenomenon of cultural globalization. On the one hand, international media conglomerates are extending their influence and control over certain types of global culture. On the other hand, the increasing importance of regions as producers of and markets for their own media provides support for a network model of cultural globalization. Regions exhibit subnetworks of denser connections within the global network but are also linked less strongly to other areas. Jan Nederveen Pieterse (1995) states: "What globalization means in structural terms is the increase in available modes of organization: transnational, international, macro-regional, national, micro-regional, municipal, local" (p. 50).

The numbers of producers of media content and of countries producing such content are steadily increasing, contributing to the diversification of global culture. The influence of Western global cultures is being offset by the development of regional cultures within global cultures. Some scholars claim that world television is not so much global as regional (Sinclair et al. 1996), consisting of several distinct regions in which television programming circulates. Regional cultures represent shared communities of language and culture. Each major region, Asia, Middle East, and Latin America, is dominated by one or two countries that are centers of audiovisual production, such as Mexico and Brazil in Latin America, Hong Kong and Taiwan in Chinese Asia, and India in Indian Asia and Indian Africa. A Francophone market links France to its former colonies, and an Arab market links the Arab-speaking countries. The decreasing cost and increased flexibility of television production technology have led to an expansion of television production in these countries. A few developing countries (e.g.,

Brazil, Egypt, India, and Mexico) have become exporters of film and television programming (Sreberny-Mohammadi 1991:121; Straubhaar 1997).

Each region has its own dynamic. Mexican television has benefited from the existence of a large Spanish-speaking population in the United States, as a lucrative market for its programming. The most successful television genre in Latin America is the telenovela, which is produced in several countries, including Brazil, Colombia, Mexico, and Venezuela, and which attracts more viewers in the region than American soap operas. The major Brazilian television network exports telenovelas to more than 100 countries.

Each region draws its audiences from within and outside its area, including migrants now living in other regions. For example, Zee TV in India claims to be "the world's largest Asian television network, covering Asia, Europe, the United States, and Africa, catering to the 24 million-strong Indian diaspora who live outside the region but retain their linguistic and cultural links with the subcontinent" (Thussu 1998:279). In Asia, three major countries, China, Singapore, and Malaysia, have exercised tight control over their television programming, but other countries in the region have benefited from the development of Pan-Asian satellite services that bring in programming from other Asian countries.

Consequently, Joseph Straubhaar (1991) argues that television industries in developing countries are moving away from simple dependency on the American industry and toward "a greater but still asymmetrical interdependency" (p. 55). Regional markets are developing as well as increasing interdependence of the world television market, as seen by the fact that Latin American countries import television series from Asia as well as the United States. Television in European countries is becoming increasingly regional as well (McAnany and Wilkinson 1992:732). Straubhaar (1991) states: "Although the United States still dominates world media sales and flows, national and regional cultural industries are consolidating a relatively more interdependent position in the world television market" (p. 56).

The popular music industry also fits the network model of cultural globalization in some respects. The American share of the global music market has changed in the past decade. The relatively low cost of making recordings (compared to television programs and film) and the ways in which new music is created (which frequently occurs outside the huge corporations that market it), make it possible for new music to develop in many different countries and at times to compete with the American product. Today only one of the top five record companies in the global market is owned by an American conglomerate. According to one scholar:

> To the extent that the United States is identified as the main imperialist culprit in the export of pop and rock, it must be noted that the U.S. is no longer the main beneficiary of the profits. The economic foundation of the cultural imperialism thesis has shifted so radically as to require a wholly new formulation. (Garofalo 1995:29)

Popular music is less identified with dominant American culture than film or television in the sense that it draws from numerous ethnic cultures, both in the U.S. and elsewhere (p. 33). Reebee Garofalo says, "There is a strong interaction between international pop and indigenous music that simply doesn't exist with other mass cultural forms." In Brazil, sales of American music are declining while Brazilian music constitutes about 80 percent of recordings broadcast on radio (see Mendonça, chap. 7 in this volume). Even the multinational recording companies become involved in recording local music in the countries in which they have branches. A scholar who has written extensively about the popular music industry claims that "globally successful sounds may now come from anywhere" (Frith 1996:172). However, international, if not American, global musical culture constitutes a major point of reference for local music. Simon Frith (cited in Mitchell, 1993) referring to local music originating in non-Anglo-Saxon countries outside the World Music commercial circuit, states:

> All countries' popular musics are shaped these days by international influences and institutions, by multinational capital and technology, by global popular norms and values. Even the most nationalistic sounds—carefully cultivated "folk" songs, angry local dialect punk, preserved (for the tourist) traditional dance—are determined by a critique of international entertainment. (p. 311)

Nevertheless, this does not necessarily mean that popular music in other countries is purely an imitation of genres disseminated internationally. Mendonça, for example, studied rock bands in a Brazilian city, and found that they blended rock music and traditional local music with African and Iberian roots. Dave Laing (1997) identified three principal regional or linguistic-based production centers for popular music that are beginning to compete with Anglo-American music: Mandarin and Cantonese Chinese in Asia, Spanish-speaking regions in the Americas and Europe, and Continental Europe.

The extent to which cultural products emanating from a specific country or region dominate international markets varies by media industry and even by the nature of the product within a particular cultural industry. Some forms of media are so widely disseminated that they appear to constitute a homogenous global culture. At the same time the availability of diverse cultural forms and styles is steadily increasing. Globalization is said to "pluralize the world by recognizing the value of cultural niches and local abilities" (Waters 1995:136). James Curran and Myung-Jin Park (2000) state that "minorities too small to be catered for in national contexts are aggregated into viable global markets. Globalization selects elements of neatly partitioned national cultures, and remixes them in new ways for an international public" (p. 8). To summarize, the network model views globalization as "a process that is increasing international dialogue, empowering minorities, and building progressive solidarity" (Curran and Park, 2000:10). Further research is required to determine the relative importance that should be attributed to this model in comparison with the previous model.

Cultural Globalization and Reception Theory

Unlike the previous models, which focus on the creators and organizations that disseminate global cultures, reception theory concentrates on the responses of audiences and publics. On the one hand, reception theory looks at people's responses to specific cultural products. On the other hand, it theorizes the long-term effects of cultural products on national and cultural identity. Theories of globalization have stressed two major consequences of globalization, homogenization of cultures and hybridization of cultures (Nederveen Pieterse 1995; Robertson 1995). The first concept suggests that all national cultures will absorb a homogenous global culture and will become increasingly similar; the second concept suggests that national cultures will assimilate aspects of many other cultures and become more diverse. Global cultures may render traditional identities less salient or produce hybridized identities as local cultures absorb and respond to these influences.

In contrast to theories of the mass audience and of ideological indoctrination by the media, reception theory views the audience as capable of interpreting media texts in different ways. Members of the audience may or may not interpret texts in terms of dominant ideologies as the producers of the texts intended (Hall 1981). Variations in the ways in which texts are interpreted depend on the context and on the social characteristics of the receiver (class, gender, race, and age). For example, studies have found that gender roles affect responses to Western television programs (Salwen 1991). One of the most elaborate studies of cross-cultural differences in responses to television programs is Liebes and Katz's (1990) analysis of the American television program *Dallas*. They found that different aspects of the program were salient to different ethnic groups in Israel and in the United States.

A number of factors offset the dominant role of Western and specifically American products in global culture. The first is the attitude of consumers toward globally disseminated television programs. Audiences generally prefer local programs, because they find it easier to identify with the style, values, attitudes, and behaviors expressed (Biltereyst 1991, 1995; Chadha and Kavoori 2000). This is known as the "cultural discount." Consequently, national programs tend to be shown during prime-time hours and American imports in off-hours (Straubhaar 1991:50). In some countries, studies have found that the preference for national material is related to social class. Lower-middle-class, working-class, and poor viewers tend to prefer national and local culture, which reinforces their regional and ethnic identities. Upper-middle- and upper-class viewers, who are better educated, tend to prefer American programs (Straubhaar 1991:51).

Certain countries, among them Japan, are said to be particularly resistant to American television programs. In the 1950s and 1960s, Japan relied heavily on Hollywood for its television programs. Now only 5 percent of television broadcasts in Japan originate in the United States, much lower than in European countries (Iwabuchi, chap. 15 in this volume). MTV has also been relatively unsuccessful in Japan, in part because of competition from Japanese music video programs and the fact that MTV Japan emphasized American artists while Japanese viewers tend to prefer Japanese artists (Banks 1996). [4]

One of the most difficult questions to study is how foreign programs affect national and cultural identity. Recent theories (Hall 1992) have stressed the problematic aspects of the concepts of national and cultural identity. The idea of homogenous national cultures that confer specific identities and values on all its citizens, to the exclusion of others, is no longer tenable; nations are becoming increasingly multicultural. One author states that "real concerns arise as to whether 'national' media cultures adequately represent ethnic, religious, political and other kinds of diversity" (Sreberny-Mohammadi 1991:129).

Consequently, national identities are not necessarily unitary but may be perceived in different ways depending upon race and ethnicity. Cultural identities often transcend national boundaries. Transnational programming performs an important role in creating a sense of cultural identity that crosscuts nationality. For example, regional programs in the form of telenovelas have redefined national identity for viewers in some Latin American countries and created a new sense of cultural identification with other Spanish-speaking countries for Hispanic viewers in the United States (Lopez 1995). Aihwa Ong (1997) explains the significance of regional programming in Asia as follows:

> Ethnic Chinese, like other people, are inhabitants of a diversity of communities, and defined by a plurality of discourses that situate them in different subject positions. . . . As Chinese cultural identity becomes destabilized, fragmented, and blurred outside of nationalist definitions, the mass media has [sic] become an extremely important realm for reworking subjectivity. (p. 196)

Koichi Iwabuchi (see chap. 15 in this volume) discusses the emergence of a new sense of regional identity among affluent young Asian consumers. They look for media products that represent "a common experience of modernity in the region that is based on an ongoing negotiation between the West and the non–West-experiences that American popular culture cannot represent."

To summarize, audience responses to global programming are highly differentiated, depending in part on levels of exposure to national, regional, and global fare and in part on the social characteristics of specific publics. Availability of foreign programming, even if it is widely watched, does not necessarily imply that its values and ideological content are accepted uncritically. On the other hand, provided that cultural imports are widely consumed, audience resistance has little significance for media conglomerates in charge of programming.

Some new studies suggest that further understanding of reception can be gleaned from studies of cultural innovators in countries on the receiving end of global culture. These individuals act as cultural gatekeepers, translating global products into local idioms and assimilating them with ideas of their own. For example, Richard L. Kaplan (chap. 12 in this volume) undertakes to explain the "pervasive presence of American blacks in the Italian 'mediascape.'" While availability of American media products in Italy can be explained in terms of agreements between Italian media conglomerates and American media conglomerates, the high level of enthusiasm for certain American media products has to be understood in other ways. He points out that with respect to entertainment involving blacks and black themes the two countries share a long history of depictions of blacks in minstrelsy in the United States and in marionette puppetry in Italy. In fact Italian black marionettes were one of the sources for American minstrelsy in the nineteenth century. In this sense, the two cultures were not distinct but "cross-pollinating and feeding off one another." Today, local industries in Italy selling fashion and popular music mediate between the two cultures in order to market specific elements of American media culture, based on their own selections, emphases, and biases. Cultural entrepreneurs draw on black American styles in order to define what is hip and cool for the youth scene.

Arguing that rock music contains an aesthetic that constitutes "a global cultural component with which contemporary local and national styles of popular music are constructed," Motti Regev (1997:131–136; see also Bennett 1999) develops a typology of uses and appropriations of rock by musicians and audiences in different countries. Rock music may be used in its original Anglo-American versions, imitated through the creation of original rock music with lyrics in the local language, or hybridized through adaptation and mixture with traditional music of a specific country or region. All three types may coexist in a particular country.

In other words, the study of reception of global cultures needs to expand beyond the examination of audience reactions to specific globalized media products in order to include artists, promoters, and distributors who market those products and who also create new products based on particularly salient themes and images. Reception cannot be explained in terms of content alone but needs to be supplemented by an analysis of "the mediating role of 'gatekeepers' in creating a reception context" (Cunningham and Jacka 1997:308). This is particularly true for imports from peripheral countries. Such studies also reveal the ways in which the influence of global media products extends beyond the consumption of the product itself and contributes to the production of new media products in the receiver country.

National, Organizational, and Urban Strategies toward Cultural Globalization

Cultural policy can be viewed as the stage where power struggles are waged on the national and international levels to set global policies and priorities for cultural globalization and to resist threats to the dissemination of national or regional media. Cultural policy is a political instrument that countries use in an attempt to control the types of channels and types of content that enter and leave their territory. A country's success in responding to the pressures of cultural globalization has major consequences for the future of the country's culture.

The outcomes of these power struggles have implications for the preservation of cultural heritage and cultural memory, the survival of public as opposed to private broadcasting, for the roles of members of global publics as consumers or as citizens, and for the existence of transnational public spheres as compared to free trade zones for media products.

The capacity of national governments to control the dissemination of culture within their borders has been greatly diminished by recent technological developments, such as satellite broadcasting, and international trade policies favoring deregulation and privatization that have increased market penetration by foreign companies (Richards and French 1996:41). According to John Street (1997), "As more television is transmitted by satellite, the less significance attaches to national borders and the presumption of national control" (p. 78).

Nevertheless, strategies are available to national governments, urban governments, and cultural organizations for preserving, protecting, and enhancing their cultural resources. On the international level, three goals of cultural policy can be identified: (1) *Protecting the country's culture* from domination by the cultural achievements of other countries and from encroachments by the media industries of other countries; (2) *Creating and maintaining international images* of the country or of a region or city within the country; and (3) *Developing and protecting international markets and venues* for the country's international "exports." To what extent does the country project consistent or inconsistent cultural images? What aspects of the culture are chosen, either deliberately or by market forces, to represent the country's culture on the international scene? Cultural policy is not exclusively the domain of national governments. Regional and local governments pursue such policies in an attempt to obtain economic benefits and to provide satisfying environments for residents. The so-called global city performs a major role in increasing awareness of a country's culture in other countries (Zukin 1995; Trasforini, chap. 11 in this volume; Kwok and Low, chap. 10 in this volume). Cultural images of certain cities are widely disseminated globally, drawing both producers and consumers of culture to those cities, which in turn leads to the reinforcement of local cultural policies.

In a sense, cultural policy provides a frame for a country's culture, indicating how the country's leaders perceive the culture and the value they place on different aspects of it. In the United States, a cultural policy that provides minimal resources for high culture signifies the ambivalence of lawmakers toward this type of culture, their fear of being viewed as supporting elitist institutions, and their distrust of culture creators who might challenge traditional views of what the country stands for. At the same time, lawmakers provide financial incentives for investing in high culture to the rich and the powerful. The government's protection of media conglomerates reflects the importance of media culture in the country's economy and as a major component of its exports to other countries.

Strategies that countries, cultural organizations, and global cities use to preserve, protect, and enhance their cultural resources include the following:

(1) *Preserving and protecting national and local cultures.* In countries that are increasingly being exposed to global culture, traditional and classical cultures may be the object of concerted efforts for preservation and protection. In some countries, such as Japan, preservation and protection have been the major focus of cultural policies and have constituted these countries' primary responses to cultural globalization (Tomooka, Kanno, and Kobayashi, chap. 3 in this volume). Southeast Asian countries view the arts as an expression of their social and national identities (Lindsay, chap. 4 in this volume). Government support is a form of patronage in which, for example, performing artists are commissioned to perform because of their contribution to the maintenance of national identity and a strong commitment to protecting indigenous cultural heritage. Their governments exert considerable control over artistic content

and performance. In the past three decades, many European governments have redefined the museum as a major repository of cultural heritage and cultural memory and
therefore as an essential resource for the public and for society as a whole (Ballé, chap.
9 in this volume). Exhibitions of museum art collections that travel from country to
country have become an important form of globally disseminated culture. Museums
perform significant roles in sustaining and transmitting global cultural alternatives to
commercial culture.

The role of culture in urban regeneration has been widely discussed (Bianchini
and Parkinson 1993). Regeneration of cultural resources involves the increasingly
important role of certain cities as global cultural actors. For example, in response to
economic, political, and cultural pressures engendered by various forms of globalization, certain forms of culture, both local and global, have been used to rejuvenate
urban neighborhoods and local cultures. J. Pedro Lorente (chap. 6 in this volume)
explains how depressed neighborhoods in cities that have suffered economically from
economic globalization have been revived and transformed through strategic construction of museums in their midst. Luciana Mendonça (chap. 7 in this volume) shows
how local ethnic musical traditions in a Brazilian city have been reinvigorated as a
result of the success of local rock bands influenced by globally disseminated music.
Traditional local organizations that created and performed music for Carnival parades
and had been in danger of disappearing more than quadrupled in number during the
1990s, in large part as a result of the increased recognition for popular music and culture that stemmed from the success of local rock bands.

(2) *Resisting global culture.* Understanding national strategies toward cultural globalization requires an understanding of various aspects of resistance to global cultures. Using
taxes, tariffs, and subsidies, many governments attempt to control channels for the dissemination of imported culture to preserve national cultural sovereignty and national
cultural diversity. Advanced and developing countries alike have resorted to strategies
for resisting global media cultures. Television and film have been subject to import
quotas. Brazil, India, and Iran have placed limits on the amount of imported programming (Sreberny-Mohammadi 1991:127; Chadha and Kavoori 2000). France subsidizes its
film industry and has a system of quotas for non-French films and television programs.
Fifty percent of the content of cable channels must be European (Hedges 1995:153).
Other European countries have similar policies (Curran 1998). Australia has also had
media content requirements and has subsidized its film industry (Cunningham and
Flew, 2000). The European Commission recently took steps to curb American film
companies' control over distribution of films in Europe on the grounds that their system
discriminates against European films (Andrews 1998). A few countries have taken even
more stringent measures. Some developing countries in which Islamic fundamentalists
are in control have totally banned foreign news and entertainment media.

Popular music is another area where some countries have resorted to protectionism
and various forms of state assistance to musicians and music industries. In 1986, the
French government mandated that public radio stations must devote more than half
their musical programs to French popular music (Crane 1992:154). The goal of the pol-

icy was to prevent French radio stations from becoming waste bins for American popular music that had failed in the United States. The Canadian government has developed policies for curbing American influence in music video. It requires Canadian video cable services to program a proportion of Canadian music (Banks 1996:111). National television channels in developing countries such as Nigeria and Jamaica also have policies supporting indigenous music (Banks 1996:112). Governments of countries including France, Denmark, Sweden, The Netherlands, New Zealand, Australia, and Canada, have implemented policies for assisting musicians and bands in producing, distributing, and performing both nationally and internationally (Negus 1996:185) in order to resist the emphasis placed on Anglo-American repertoires by the international music industry (Negus 1997).

These forms of resistance lead to political conflicts with countries that are major exporters of commercial culture as well as with multinational organizations that are concerned with profit rather than the public interest (Beale, chap. 5 in this volume). However, protectionism is becoming less effective because the United States is able to obtain rulings from the World Trade Organization to overturn such legislation.

The American government has strenuously opposed regulations designed to limit access of American cultural products to foreign markets. It is unwilling to concede that other nations might be justified in attempting to protect their cultural identities and generally views such measures as nothing more than protectionism (Sinclair 1996:51). American arguments against protectionism center on issues of free speech and free trade (Munro 1990:526). From the American perspective, culture can be traded like any other commodity (Boddy 1994). Ironically, the United States itself is remarkably resistant to imported cultural products, but not through protectionist measures. Instead, tight control by media conglomerates over film distribution systems and cable and broadcasting networks in the United States effectively restricts the availability of foreign films and foreign television programs in the American market. One of the few exceptions are the programs produced by the British BBC, which are heavily used by American public television channels. Significantly, the United States retains the right to limit foreign investment in the media and broadcasting areas and to administer direct grants, tax incentives, and other forms of subsidy (Beale, chap. 5).

Negotiations concerning international trade agreements often pit these two orientations toward policy against one another (French and Richards 1996; McAnany and Wilkinson 1996). Countries that favor protectionist policies have attempted to exclude the media from international trade agreements in the name of national cultural sovereignty. A recent strategy has been to argue for protectionism in the name of cultural diversity rather than national cultural sovereignty. Using this approach, some countries have lobbied for cultural trade protections for minority cultures that are ill served by national public media and the mainstream press instead of the traditional protectionist approach that was directed toward cultural industries (see Beale, chap. 5).

(3) *Globalizing national or local cultures.* Understanding the process of cultural globalization requires an understanding of how national and local cultures are transformed in order to make them more attractive and meaningful to foreign visitors or foreign

consumers. This type of activity takes several forms. The first three strategies transform cultural sites within a particular country in order to project new images of the country's culture to the outside world. The fourth and fifth types of strategies involve creating or re-creating national cultural items for global export.

The first three strategies of national or local transformation are processes of *reframing*. For example, *retooling* is a type of policy in urban neighborhoods and historical sites that provides more activities for tourists and more commercial outlets to serve them (Zukin 1995). Traditional arts and performances may be reframed to make them more interesting and understandable for tourists. Kian-Woon Kwok and Kee-Hong Low (chap. 10 in this volume) show how turning Singapore into a "global city for the arts" affected the preservation of cultural memory through historic sites and the identity of the city-state itself. In Singapore, historic sites and traditional neighborhoods have been simulated and replicated rather than conserved, replacing chaotic, disorderly areas with sanitized substitutes.

Another form that reframing takes is *Disneyfication*, influenced by the Disney theme parks and Walt Disney's vision of a utopian city. For example, a city's historic sites will be categorized and publicized in terms of specific themes that lead the citizen or tourist to view them from a particular perspective. Kwok and Low examine the consequences of Disneyfication for the types of cultural images that Singapore projects.

An alternative and less frequently used strategy for reframing local culture is *postmodern upscaling*. This strategy attempts to use the arts to attract elite international audiences to major events featuring artistic celebrities. Trasforini (chapter 2 in this volume) discusses the advantages and disadvantages of this strategy for an urban economy and for traditional arts groups that may be excluded from this process. Trasforini shows that a particular type of artistic event, the so-called Great Event that draws audiences from outside the region, tends to displace other types of artistic performance and productions that are directed toward local publics.

Two other strategies are used in preparing cultural products for global markets. *Negotiated modification* is an important phenomenon, but it is almost invisible to those outside the entertainment industry. Carefully selected national cultural products, such as television series, are globalized by editing or revising them to suit the tastes of consumers in other countries (Bielby and Harrington, chap. 13 in this volume). Details of these negotiated modifications are worked out at annual sales meetings where media companies present their wares for purchase on the international market. Co-productions in which companies from different countries jointly produce television series and films are an important site in which cultural products are adapted or modified to suit the needs of consumers in different countries (Hubka, chap. 14 in this volume). Conglomerates selling recorded music target countries and regions with different types of repertoires, such as international, regional, and domestic, depending on feedback from these areas based on sales and other types of information (Negus 1996). Considerable importance is placed on audiovisual exports by many countries, including those that are less developed:

> These are fostered both as a form of cultural diplomacy, and for intrinsic economic reasons. . . . In the case of the Middle East, one commentator has observed that the popu-

larity of Egyptian television exports in the Arab states has a number of cultural and even political "multiplier effects" . . . and carries with it a potential acceptance and recognition of Egyptian accents and performers that can operate as a "soft-sell commercial for Egyptian values" which is then translated into indirect political leverage. (Cunningham, Jacka, and Sinclair 1998:188)

Another approach to preparing cultural products for global markets is referred to as *global localization* or *glocalization*. Robertson (1995:28) discusses the ways in which global genres are adapted for local audiences so that the global blends with the local. This process does not lead to global homogenization but to a situation in which cultural forms that originated in the West and that diffuse globally, such as soap operas, are adapted to local conditions and primarily carry messages about local cultures (Straubhaar 1997:288). Audiences often prefer local imitations of American popular culture to American popular culture itself.

In some cases, this process completely eliminates traces of the country of origin, by framing the items as having originated in the countries to which they are being marketed (Iwabuchi, chapter 15 in this volume; Robertson 1995). In this situation, cultural forms being marketed outside the country assimilate aspects of the local cultures in the receiving country in a process that challenges the binary opposition between global and local. The Japanese, with their long experience of assimilating foreign influences, are particularly adept in this area. They create culturally neutral products for sale in other parts of Asia, including animated films in which physical, racial, and ethnic differences have been erased or softened. They also export popular music that listeners in other Asian countries think is a local product but actually consists of cover versions of Japanese songs. What the Japanese attempt to create in these products is not an authentic traditional Asian identity but a kind of combination of Asian and Western culture. This strategy results in hybrid products that are a combination of the foreign and the indigenous. Japanese "glocalized" popular culture has been very successful in Asia.

As this discussion suggests, national governments, cultural organizations, and global cities have responded to cultural globalization in various ways. Cultural globalization can be seen as a major threat to national identities or at the very least as contributing to a decline in people's identification with nation-states. While national governments and cultural organizations are losing their power to completely control the dissemination of global cultures within their borders, they can and do resort to a number of strategies for preserving or reframing their cultures or for positioning their cultures in the global marketplace.

Conclusion

What can one conclude about the relevance of these four models for understanding the nature and effects of globally disseminated cultures? First, the cultural imperialism model has been reconceptualized as the media imperialism model in which the motivation for dissemination is economic rather than political. As such, it is evident that global media culture is dominated by, and in the future will increasingly be dominated by, media conglomerates with huge holdings in all forms of popular culture. Though ownership of these conglomerates was largely American in the past, recently some of these organizations have been bought by companies based in other major industrial countries. However, the content of the global culture transmitted by these organizations, whether American or non-American, remains heavily influenced by American media industries (music, film, television). A more accurate term for this type of culture might be transnational culture rather than global culture since many less developed countries are not perceived as attractive markets.

It is important to keep in mind that the factors that ensure the dominance of a particular type of global culture are constantly changing. American dominance today is based on economic and technological advantages that are probably diminishing as a result of technological changes and of changes in other countries. At the beginning of the twenty-first century, the media are on the verge of the digital revolution, which will merge communications, broadcasting, and computer industries. The speed and variety of communications will increase enormously. These changes will have important effects on cultural globalization. They will increase access to all forms of media and reduce the impact of powerful organizations, such as those based in the United States. Specifically, it will reduce their power as distributors of global culture because distribution will become freer and cheaper. Some experts predict that in the future the impact of American programming will be primarily in North America, Europe, and Australia. In other words, its impact will be confined to a specific region, defined more in terms of shared culture than geography. However, the digital revolution will also increase the value of American companies' stocks of existing films and TV programs, because there will be an enormous demand for cultural materials and for experienced creators of cultural products, such as those based in Los Angeles.

At the same time, the digital revolution will make it more difficult to control the circulation of media across borders. Cultural policies based on restricting imports of American media will face losing battles. The increasingly rapid dissemination of all types of media will pose problems for the maintenance of national identities as cultures undergo increasing hybridization.

The second model, the cultural flows or network model, is useful for understanding the roles of regional cultures. They tend to be more multicultural and diverse than global cultures and, in some areas of the globe, tend to perform more important roles. They generally have more links to Third World national cultures. They are, however, heavily influenced by international media conglomerates that often invest in specific regions and perform important roles in creating regional cultures. The combination of transnational culture and regional culture is closer to the network model, as regions begin to send cultural products to other regions. In the future, the network model should be increasingly relevant to the study of cultural globalization as more regions and more countries produce various forms of media culture and send them to other countries. A truly global media culture that mingles cultural traditions and social values from many different countries has yet to emerge.

The third model, reception theory, requires modification to be useful in today's complex global environment. Understanding the public's responses to global culture in different countries and in different settings within those countries necessitates a broader conceptualization of reception theory, one that goes beyond focusing entirely on the audience itself and instead examines the relationships between the imported culture and the national culture, as well as the roles of cultural entrepreneurs.

Finally, the fourth model shows that the various strategies that are open to national governments, global cities, and cultural organizations for coping with and responding to influences from global and regional cultures need to be better understood. Although national governments are sometimes presented as being relatively powerless in the face of these influences, the relative weight and influence of global cultures in comparison with regional, local, and national cultures is an issue that requires more empirical research. In some cases, the cultures of global cities are as visible to global publics as those of nations and perform important roles in disseminating national culture.

By contrast, opportunities for local cultures representing diverse ethnic, religious, and political groups within particular countries to influence national, regional, and global cultures are different in each media industry. Popular music, in which recording costs are relatively low, offers the most opportunity for local cultures; film and television, in which production costs are generally much higher, offer the least opportunity for local cultures.

To conclude, each of these four models is useful for explaining specific aspects of the phenomenon of cultural globalization. Since cultural globalization is not static but an ongoing process with dimensions that are continually evolving and consequences that are difficult to predict, we can expect that new models will emerge.

Overview of the Volume

The studies in this book reveal the importance of examining closely how countries, cities, and cultural organizations are actually producing and responding to global cultures. The articles in part I of the volume reveal the similarities and differences among cultural policies in Europe, the United States, and Asia. The first chapter compares national cultural policies of three countries. Stefan Toepler and Annette Zimmer provide an overview of developments in national cultural policies since World War II and identify three models of cultural policy, as exemplified by the French top-down bureaucratic model, the Swedish corporatist approach, which permits private organizations to influence public policy, and the American "third-party" approach, which relies on private organizations to implement federal programs. Toepler and Zimmer's analysis reveals the influence of historical traditions in the evolution of national cultural policies and the importance placed on preserving and enhancing such legacies.

In the second chapter, Kuniyuki Tomooka, Sachiko Kanno, and Mari Kobayashi trace the evolution of Japanese cultural policy, showing how the country's policymakers have responded to cultural influences from the West and how the country's arrangements for funding the arts and for providing culture to its citizens have developed distinctive characteristics related to the historical and social context of Japan. In the second half of the nineteenth century, when Japan was adapting to Western cultural, social, and economic influences, cultural policy performed an important role in the dissemination of Western arts and culture to the Japanese people. By the second half of the twentieth century, cultural policy had been relegated to a relatively minor role, that of preserving rather than renewing the country's cultural heritage.

Jennifer Lindsay shows a similar pattern in several countries in Southeast Asia. She examines the impact of national policies, administrative structures, and public support on performing arts organizations in Southeast Asia, where the performing arts have become a major repository of national identity and cultural memory. She shows that governments in these countries have a strong commitment to protecting their indigenous cultural heritage. She also finds that cultural policies in these countries are converging, presumably as a result of what might be considered a subcategory of globalization—"regionalization"—and of increasing awareness of mutual identity among countries located in the same region.

A central thesis of this volume is that cultural policy is always conducted on an international stage. Alison Beale's chapter highlights the tensions between national policies for the arts and the globalization of media organizations and industries. Beale shows why national policies for media industries are so frequently a subject of international debate, contention, and controversy.

The subject of part II of the volume is the regeneration of cultural resources in cities and cultural organizations. Culture and cultural policy contribute to gentrification in run-down areas of cities through, for example, the creation of new museums and other attractions for the public, while improving the image of these cities in global culture. J. Pedro Lorente discusses the role of museums and other arts organizations in the gentrification of poor neighborhoods in Liverpool, Marseilles, and Barcelona. Specifically, Lorente examines how the strategic location of museums initiates a series of changes in such neighborhoods that lead to urban regeneration.

Considerable debate has been devoted to the effects of global media on local media organizations. Whether these effects are negative or positive varies broadly with the type of media and local conditions. Media that are very expensive to produce, such as film and television entertainment, tend to be hurt by global competition with international media conglomerates, while popular music, which is less costly to create, is more likely to benefit when musicians are exposed to foreign musical influences. Luciana Ferreira Moura Mendonça focuses on the impact of musicians on cultural life in Recife in Brazil. The success of local rock bands in the global music industry led to renewed interest in traditional music in the city and to increased appreciation of the role of popular music and popular musicians among policymakers and citizens alike.

Rosanne Martorella analyzes cultural organizations and cultural policy in New York in terms of their contributions and benefits to the local economy. In the case of New York, cultural organizations are important components of the urban economy and also contribute to the city's role as a site for global tourism.

Catherine Ballé traces the evolution of museums, particularly in Europe, from the pinnacle of their success in the nineteenth century to their decline in the early twentieth century and their eventual renewal in the late twentieth century. Museums in different countries have evolved in similar ways, disseminating their own form of global culture and facing similar problems in communicating this type of culture to the public.

A major goal of cultural policy is to influence the way a country's culture is viewed and esteemed by relevant actors in other countries at a similar or more advanced stage of development. The subject of part III is the ways in which cultural policies have led to the reframing of urban cultures and the transformation of urban images. As Kian-Woon Kwok and Kee-Hong Low discuss in their chapter, cultural policy has performed a crucial role in the definition of the city-state, Singapore. Cultural policy has redefined the city's history and reshaped the meaning of the city. A major goal of Singapore's cultural policy has been to position Singapore as a world city in which culture and the arts contribute to and enhance the city's economic potential and political image.

Maria Antonietta Trasforini analyzes the effects of reframing a city as a center of postmodernity dedicated to cultural events and performances for global audiences. She examines the remarkable development of cultural policy for the arts in the small Italian city of Ferrara, which was bypassed by the Industrial Revolution but which is highly successful as a postmodern, postindustrial center for the arts and media culture. These changes raise the question of how the traditional role of the arts in the city as a repository of collective memory has been affected by the city's commitment to Great Events that draw audiences from outside the region.

Richard Kaplan examines the reception of one country's culture in another country. Specifically, he looks at the sources of the attraction of elements of African American popular culture for Italian youth and the ways in which this culture has been "reframed" in the Italian context. His analysis helps to elucidate the conditions that foster transnational communication.

Little is known about the process of marketing television programs for international distribution. The findings of two studies described in part IV challenge the long-standing assumption that American media products can simply be "imposed" upon foreign audiences, regardless of the content of the products and the cultural climate of countries at the receiving end. Denise Bielby and C. Lee Harrington examine how perceptions of foreign audiences and their tastes influence the selection of American television series for export and lead to important modifications in these exports to increase their salability. David Hubka discusses barriers to the international dissemination of television programming and shows how these barriers have been overcome in children's animated television programs through international co-productions and dubbing.

Finally, Koichi Iwabuchi's analysis shows that Japanese strategies for producing popular culture for export to other Asian countries are entirely different from the strategies used by American media industries. The Japanese attempt to conceal their presence in the international media markets while the Americans use every channel of publicity and advertising to call attention to their cultural exports. At the same time, while Japanese cultural products are often adaptations of Western genres, these genres are increasingly used as containers for Asian cultural repertoires.

Notes

An earlier version of this chapter was presented at the Cultural Dynamics Conference, Princeton University, Princeton, March 30, 2001.

1. This term could also refer to "ways of life," religions, and popular attitudes. These are excluded from discussion for reasons of space.

2. Appadurai also includes financial flows in his discussion.

3. One example is the case of Turkey in the early 1990s, where the introduction of a satellite television service completely changed the formerly monopolistic television industry, providing not only a wider range of entertainment options but uncensored news and talk programs (Sahin and Aksoy, 1993).

4. MTV claims to present programming that reflects the culture of its audience but given the number of countries and languages it serves, the results are bound to be superficial (Banks, 1996: 100).

References

Andrews, E.L. (1998) 'European Commission may revoke exemption for U.S. movie studios,' *New York Times*, February 9, p. D7.

Appadurai, A. (1990) 'Disjuncture and difference in the global cultural economy,' *Public Culture*, 2: 1–24.

Banks, J. (1996) *Monopoly Television: MTV's Quest to Control the Music*, Boulder, CO: Westview Press.

Barker, C. (1997) *Global Television: An Introduction*, Oxford, UK: Blackwell.

Bennett, A. (1999) 'Hip hop am Main: the localization of rap music and hip hop culture,' *Media, Culture and Society*, 21: 77–91.

Bianchini, F. and Parkinson, M. (eds.) (1993) *Cultural Policy and Urban Regeneration: the West European Experience*, Manchester: Manchester University Press.

Bitereyst, D. (1991) 'Resisting American hegemony: a comparative analysis of the reception of domestic and US fiction,' *European Journal of Communication*, 6: 469–497.

Bitereyst, D. (1995) 'European audiovisual policy and the cross-border circulation of fiction: a follow-up flow study,' *Cultural Policy*, 2: 3–24.

Bitereyst, D. and Meers, P. (2000) 'The international telenovela debate and the contra-flow argument: a reappraisal,' *Media, Culture and Society*, 22: 393–413.

Boddy, W. (1994) 'U.S. television abroad: market power and national introspection,' *Quarterly Review of Film and Video*, 15: 45–55.

Chadha, K. and Kavoori, A. (2000) 'Media imperialism revisited: some findings from the Asian case,' *Media, Culture and Society*, 22: 415–432.

Crane, D. (1992) *The Production of Culture: Media and Urban Arts*, Newbury Park: Sage.

Cunningham, S. and Jacka, E., (1997) 'Neighborly relations? Cross-cultural reception analysis and Australian soaps in Britain,' pp. 299–310 in A. Sreberny-Mohammadi, D. Winseck, J. McKenna, and O. Boyd-Barrett (eds.) *Media in Global Context: A Reader*, London: Arnold.

Cunningham, S., Jacka, E., and Sinclair, J. (1998) 'Global and regional dynamics of international television flows,' pp. 177–192 in D. K. Thussu (ed.) *Electronic Empires: Global Media and Local Resistance*, London: Arnold.

Cunningham, S. and Flew, T. (2000) 'De-Westernizing Australia? Media systems and cultural coordinates,' pp. 237–248 in J. Curran and M.J. Park (eds.) *De-Westernizing Media Studies*, London: Routledge.

Curran, J. (1998) 'Crisis of public communication: a reappraisal,' pp. 175–202 in T. Liebes and J. Curran (eds.) *Media, Ritual and Identity*, London: Routledge.

Curran, J. and Park, M..-J. (2000) 'Beyond globalization theory,' pp. 3–18 in J. Curran and M.-J. Park (eds.) *De-Westernizing Media Studies*. New York and London: Routledge.

French, D. and Richards, M. (1996) 'Open markets and the future of television—Fiction and fact: GATT, GATS and the World Trade Organization,' pp. 343-358 in D. French and M. Richards (eds.) *Contemporary Television: Eastern Perspectives*, New Delhi: Sage Publications.

Frith, S. (1996) 'Entertainment,' in J. Curran and M. Gurevitch (eds.) *Mass Media and Society*, 2nd edition. London: Arnold.

Garofalo, R. (1995) 'Whose world, what beat? The transnational media industry, identity and cultural imperialism,' *Radical America*, 25: 25–38.

Golding, P. (1998) 'Worldwide wedge: division and contradiction in the global information infrastructure,' pp. 135–147 in D. K. Thussu (ed.) *Electronic Empires: Global Media and Local Resistance*, London: Arnold.

Hall, S. (1981) 'Encoding/decoding,' pp. 128–138 in S. Hall et al. *Culture, Media, Language*, London: Hutchinson.

Hall, S. (1992) 'The question of cultural identity,' in S. Hall, D. Held, and T. McGrew (eds.) *Modernity and Its Futures*, Cambridge, UK: Polity Press.

Hallin, D. C. (1998) 'Broadcasting in the Third World: From national development to civil society,' pp. 153–174 in T. Liebes and J. Curran (eds.) *Media, Ritual and Identity*, London: Routledge.

Hedges, I. (1995) 'Transnational corporate culture and cultural resistance,' *Socialism and Democracy*, 9: 151–164.

Hoskins, C. and Mirus, R. (1990) 'Television fiction made in U.S.A,' pp. 83–90 in P. Lauren (ed.) *Import/Export: International Flow of Television Fiction*, Paris: UNESCO.

Kellner, D. (1999) 'New technologies, the welfare state, and the prospects for democratization,' pp. 239–256 in A. Calabrese and J.-C. Burgelman (eds.) *Communication, Citizenship and Social Policy: Rethinking the Limits of the Welfare State*, New York: Rowman and Littlefield Publishers, Inc.

Laing, D. (1997) 'Rock anxieties and new music networks,' pp. 116–132 in A. McRobbie (ed.) *Back to Reality: Social Experience and Cultural Studies*, Manchester: Manchester University Press.

Liebes, T. and Katz, E. (1990) *The Export of Meaning: Cross-cultural Readings of Dallas*, New York: Oxford University Press.

Lopez, A. (1995) 'Our welcomed guests . . . telenovelas in Latin America,' pp. 256–275 in R. Allen (ed.) *To Be Continued . . . Soap Opera Around the World*, New York: Routledge.

McAnany, E. G. and Wilkinson, K. T. (1992) 'From cultural imperialists to takeover victims? Questions on Hollywood's buyouts from the critical tradition,' *Communication Research*, 19: 724–748.

McAnany, E. G. and Wilkinson, K. T. (1996) 'Introduction,' pp. 3–27 in E. G. McAnany and K. T. Wilkinson (eds.) *Mass Media and Free Trade: NAFTA and the Cultural Industries*, Austin: University of Texas Press.

McChesney, R. (1999) *Rich Media, Poor Democracy*, Urbana: University of Illinois Press.

Mitchell, T. (1993) 'World music and the popular music industry: an Australian view,' *Ethnomusicology*, 37: 309–338.

Munro, J. R. (1990) 'Good-bye to Hollywood: cultural imperialism and the new protectionism,' *Vital Speeches*, 56 (June 15): 524–527.

Nain, Z. (1996) 'The impact of the international marketplace on the organization of Malaysian television,' pp. 157–180 in David French and Michael Richards (eds.) *Contemporary Television; Eastern Perspectives*, New Delhi: Sage Publications.

Nederveen Pieterse, J. (1995) 'Globalization as hybridization,' pp. 45–68 in M. Featherstone *et al.* (eds.) *Global Modernities*, Newbury Park, CA: Sage.

Negus, K. (1996) 'Globalization and the music of the public spheres,' pp. 179–195 in S. Braman and A. Sreberny-Mohammadi (eds.) *Globalization, Communication and Transnational Civil Society*, Cresskill, NJ: Hampton Press.

Negus, K. (1997) 'Global harmonies and local discords: transnational policies and practices in the European recording industry,' pp. 270–283 in A. Sreberny-Mohammadi, D. Winseck, J. McKenna, and O. Boyd-Barrett (eds.) *Media in Global Context: A Reader*, London: Arnold.

Ong, A. (1997) '"A better tomorrow?" The struggle for global visibility,' *Sojourn*, 12: 192–225.

Phillips, J. D. (1982) 'Film conglomerate blockbusters: international appeal and product homogenization,' pp. 325–335 in G. Kindem (ed.) *The American Movie Industry*, Carbondale: Southern Illinois University Press.

Regev, M. (1997) 'Rock aesthetics and musics of the world,' *Theory, Culture, and Society*, 14, 3: 125–142.

Richards, M, and French, D. (1996) 'From global development to global culture?' pp. 22–48 in D. French and M. Richards (eds.) *Contemporary Television: Eastern Perspectives*, New Delhi: Sage Publications.

Robertson, R. (1995) 'Globalization: time-space and homogeneity-heterogeneity,' pp. 25–43 in M. Featherstone *et al.* (eds.) *Global Modernities*, Newbury Park, CA: Sage.

Sahin, H. and Aksoy, A. (1993) 'Global media and cultural identity in Turkey,' *Journal of Communication*, 43 (2): 31–40.

Salwen, M. B. (1991) 'Cultural imperialism: a media effects approach,' *Critical Studies in Mass Communication*, 8: 29–38.

Sinclair, J., Jacka, E., and Cunningham, S. (eds.) (1996) *New Patterns in Global Television: Peripheral Vision*, Oxford: Oxford University Press.

Sinclair, J. (1996) 'Culture and trade: some theoretical and practical considerations,' pp. 30–60 in E. G. McAnany and K. T. Wilkinson (eds.) *Mass Media and Free Trade: NAFTA and the Cultural Industries*, Austin: University of Texas Press.

Sreberny-Mohammadi, A. (1991) 'The global and the local in international communications,' pp. 118–138 in J. Curran and M. Gurevitch (eds.) *Mass Media and Society*, London: Edward Arnold.

Straubhaar, J. D. (1991) 'Beyond media imperialism: asymmetrical interdependence and cultural proximity,' *Critical Studies in Mass Communication*, 8: 39–59.

Straubhaar, J. D. (1997) 'Distinguishing the global, regional and national levels of world tele-vision,' pp. 284–298 in A. Sreberny-Mohammadi, D. Winseck, J. McKenna, and O. Boyd-Barrett (eds.) *Media in Global Context: A Reader*, London: Arnold.

Street, J. (1997) 'Across the universe: the limits of global popular culture,' pp. 75–89 in A. Scott (ed.) *The Limits of Globalization: Cases and Arguments*, London: Routledge.

Thussu, D. K. (1998) 'Localising the global: Zee TV in India,' pp. 273–294 in D. K. Thussu (ed.) *Electronic Empires: Global Media and Local Resistance*, London: Arnold.

Tomlinson, J. (1991) *Cultural Imperialism: A Critical Introduction*, Baltimore, MD: The Johns Hopkins University Press.

Waters, M. (1995) *Globalisation*, London: Routledge.

White, R. (1983) 'A backwater awash: The Australian experience of Americanisation,' *Theory, Culture and Society*, 1: 108–122.

Zukin, S. (1995) *The Cultures of Cities*, Oxford, UK: Blackwell.

Part I

CULTURAL POLICY AND NATIONAL CULTURES

*Preserving Tradition and
Resisting Media Imperialism*

2

Subsidizing the Arts

Government and the Arts in Western Europe and the United States

Stefan Toepler and Annette Zimmer

In the immediate post–World War II period, a lively, vibrant, and innovative cultural scene began to emerge in both Western Europe and in the United States, and it did so in the absence of any specific government policies toward the arts and culture. Although many countries had a long-standing tradition of nurturing and supporting the arts, arts and culture had not yet been discovered as a public policy arena in the 1950s. This took place during the 1960s and 1970s and was closely connected to the golden era of the welfare state. Today, however, the welfare state concept is in a deep crisis worldwide with the specific consequence that cultural policy as one arena of welfare state policies is searching for new paradigms and rationales as well as new forms of policy implementation.

In this chapter, we will trace the development of cultural policies over the last four decades and consider future directions in the post–welfare-state era. First, we will briefly review some of the key rationales for policy intervention in this field as they have emerged since the 1960s. Second, we will analyze the great variety of cultural policies and variations in institutional contexts for cultural policy implementation, using the example of three countries with very distinct approaches to cultural policy-making: France, Sweden, and the United States. In examining these cases, we will draw on the neoinstitutionalist approach of political science, an approach that has also made significant inroads in other social sciences, such as economics and sociology. The chapter will conclude with a brief discussion of comparative arts policy research and the implications of a perceptible trend toward system convergence and new models of cultural policy implementation.

Cultural Policy Rationales during the Rise of the Welfare State

Among the countries taking the lead in the development of a definite cultural policy was France, which established a Ministry of Culture in 1959 (Wangermée 1991:57). In

Washington, D.C., the National Endowment for the Arts (NEA) was established in 1965. In the same year, Harold Wilson appointed Great Britain's first junior minister with special responsibility for cultural policy and significantly increased the budget of Britain's Arts Council (Ridley 1987:229). Also in 1965, a new Ministry of Culture, Recreation, and Social Work was created in the Netherlands (Dutch Ministry of Welfare, Health, and Cultural Affairs 1994:53). By and large, the emergence of arts and culture as a new policy arena took place during the heyday of social democracy. Under the social democratic doctrine, Western democracies began designing "active cultural policies" to improve the production of arts and culture with a particular emphasis on cultural equality and social equity. Step by step, public support for the arts developed into an integral part of the welfare state doctrine.

Compared to the immediate postwar period, public support for the arts had increased significantly by the late 1970s in almost every country in the Western world, and arts and culture had become an accepted and more or less distinguished field of public policy. For instance, public funds for arts and culture increased by about 10 percent annually in Sweden (Zimmer and Toepler 1996:178); NEA funding in the United States multiplied more than eight times during the 1970s (Heilbrun and Gray 1993:252); and the budget of the French Ministry of Culture expanded sevenfold (Wangermée 1991:97). The same holds true for the Netherlands, where the budget of the Ministry of Culture also increased rapidly during the 1970s (Fenger 1987:128).

Underlying this growth were several strands of policy rationales that either emphasized economic problems of the arts or issues of equality and democracy.[1] Among the economic arguments, the so-called cost disease thesis (Baumol and Bowen 1966) has to be named first and foremost. In their classic volume, William J. Baumol and William B. Bowen argued that long-term economic trends, particularly the lack of (technology-induced) productivity gains to offset rising labor costs, will make government subsidy essential to maintain artistic output and production, especially in the performing arts.

Whereas the productivity problem provides one rationale for public support, economists also refer to other market failures in the arts to justify government subsidies. A key argument has been that the arts exhibit certain "public good" characteristics. If we take the example of large works of public art, such as murals and sculptures, we may indeed find cases of pure public goods. No one can be denied access to such a work; and one person's use does not reduce the next person's utility. However, most arts are impure public goods at best, as the box office can enforce exclusion, and audience congestion might introduce rivalry in consumption.

However, there are other types of market failure as well, such as the "merit goods" argument, under which the market will underprovide the arts, because the consumer does not (yet) recognize their inherent merits and worthiness. According to this line of argument, production and consumption of the arts should be encouraged by public subsidy simply because they are meritorious (Netzer 1978:16). Since the consumer does not know what is good for her, government intervention in this case is legitimate from a public welfare perspective.[2]

Of course, there are also other forms of externalities, such as the fact that goods will be underprovided because the market cannot capture positive or negative spillovers through the price mechanism. On a more practical level, economists argue in favor of public support for the arts, because museums, theaters, and the like are viewed to be an important part of economic life, particularly in larger cities, attracting visitors and keeping the well-to-do attached to the community. Thus cultural institutions generate income for the local service industry, including restaurants, hotels, and even retailers. In other words, for economists, public subsidies for the arts have a positive effect on the economy because they are accompanied by external benefits on behalf of the individual or the local community.

As noted above, the second line of argumentation in favor of public support for the arts was strongly influenced by the social democratic paradigm stressing the importance of economic, social, and cultural equality. In line with the Zeitgeist of the 1970s, equality became the driving force of public policy and the most important rationale for the funding of the arts. Since at that time low income was regarded to be a major barrier to wider enjoyment of the arts, government intervention was viewed as a legitimate tool; without subsidy, ticket prices would be too high relative to the income of most people (Netzer 1978:19). Widespread participation across class and social boundaries became a central feature of cultural policy during the 1970s. Public funding for the arts was therefore regarded as an investment in the social rather than the economic environment.

Finally, the social democratic paradigm obliged governments to provide broader opportunities for all types of cultural experiences. Everybody who wished to do so should be able to develop his or her resources as an active and creative individual. Therefore, cultural policy was no longer restricted to public support of high-culture institutions, such as theaters and museums; popular culture and folk art were also viewed as legitimate recipients of public subsidies.

Moreover, during the 1970s, availability became a prominent issue of cultural policy stressing the importance of decentralization of the production of culture. This line of argumentation was strongly influenced by the work of the French sociologist Pierre Bourdieu, who argued convincingly that "cultural capital" provides an important feature of individual career development. If equality provided the bottom line of cultural policy, government had to assure that everybody has the chance to increase her cultural capital regardless of where she lives.

To summarize, next to economic arguments in favor of public subsidies, the concept of equality provided a widely accepted rationale as to why governments were supporting the arts and culture during the 1970s. However, this did not imply any uniformity with respect to levels of subsidies or types of public support for the arts and culture. On the contrary, the arena of cultural policy stands out for its diversity and variety reflecting national policy styles as well as historical traditions and philosophies.

Accounting for Differences

Though government support in the shape of systematic cultural policies is a very recent development, certain countries have a substantial record of direct expenditures as well as indirect government subsidies for the production and consumption of the arts and culture. From a comparative point of view, the larger countries of Continental

Europe have traditionally been seen as "big spenders," whereas the Anglo-Saxon world has always been very reluctant to subsidize for the arts. To complete the picture, it should be noted that, during the 1970s, Sweden and the other Scandinavian countries, as well as the Netherlands, started to take very active roles in arts policy. In these countries, government expenditures for the arts and culture increased significantly; and some of these newcomers even surpassed the traditional big spenders such as France and Germany.

How do we account for these differences and diverse developments? To put it somewhat pointedly, economic justifications for public support of arts and culture are not much help in understanding these phenomenona. Should we not expect that the arts are the same public goods, produce the same externalities, and are subject to the same market failures everywhere? If so, why does government spending vary so substantially? Is the European median voter more culturally attuned and artistically inclined than the American one? Or are Europeans more in tune than Americans with their hidden "true" preferences so that they vote for the provision of merit goods?

In other words, the economic justifications for arts funding are quite elegant, but they fall short of explaining the substantial differences in arts policies across countries. Unfortunately, there is still a significant lack of sound comparative research on cultural policy. Primarily, we find case or country studies describing the development and current state of affairs elsewhere (Heinrichs 1997). Among the few exceptions are the models of state patronage developed by Milton C. Cummings and Richard S. Katz (1987), the classification of the roles of the state developed by Harry Hillman-Chartrand and Claire McCaughey (1989) and more recently by Kevin Mulcahy (2000). However, these types of classifications for the most part tend to focus on government funding rather than taking a more broadly conceived approach toward cultural policy.

To approach this subject, we will argue that history and institutional arrangements matter more than economics in trying to explain cultural policy. Institutionalism represents a distinctive approach to the study of political phenomena such as public support for the arts and culture (Powell and DiMaggio 1991). Whereas in neoclassical equilibrium economics, state intervention in the production of arts and culture is explained by the objective to correct some kind of market failure or cost disease, neoinstitutionalist theories view public policy as being shaped, mediated, and channeled by the history, tradition, and institutional arrangements of any given country. Neoinstitutionalists focus primarily on differences across countries. However, unlike historians, who are primarily telling informed stories about the development of the institutional underpinnings of specific policies, neoinstitutionalists try to clarify explicit policy patterns or models which can be characterized as ideal types in the Weberian sense. While neoinstitutionalists have not yet discovered cultural policy as a fruitful field of analysis, their approach has already revolutionized welfare state research.

In a tentative way, we tried to utilize Scandinavian social scientist Gösta Esping-Andersen's (1990) approach to welfare state research in our earlier work to explain variations in cultural policy (Zimmer and Toepler 1996). To use the regime approach of Esping-Andersen, we based our analysis of cultural policy on the assumption that government support for the arts and culture is a specific field of welfare state activity and as such subject to the logic of the overall regime. In accordance with Esping-Andersen's welfare state analysis, we therefore understand cultural policy as the interface between the market, the state, and the individual. Taking a neoinstitutionalist perspective, the current configuration and future direction of this interface is not exclusively shaped by the socioeconomic context but also by the prevailing institutional arrangements and the legacy of its historic development. From this vantage point, the cultural policy of today is a result of former public policies and therefore deeply path dependent, leaving little room for variation.

In the following pages, we will briefly sketch out three country case studies in order to identify some core elements of institutional frameworks that might help us better understand cross-national differences (or similarities, for that matter). Though these case studies are intended as ideal types, the analysis could be extended to combine an Esping-Andersen-type regime approach with the families of nations concept developed by Francis G. Castles (1993; 1989). This concept derives from the notion that isomorphism is a driving force of policy development across countries. In contrast to structural functionalism which, in a comparative perspective, is searching for structures performing specific functions, the families of nations concept is based on the assumption that countries learn from each other by adopting others' solutions for certain problems. In accordance with common sense, Castles argues convincingly that transmission and diffusion of policies among nations is fostered by regional proximity. Explicit families of nations are therefore defined in terms of shared geographical, linguistic, cultural and/or historical attributes that lead to distinctive patterns of public policy (Castles 1993: XIV). Clearly, the family of nations concept seems to ring true in the comparative cultural policy area, which has occupied itself for quite some time with the notion that various countries may be grouped under a specific model of government intervention. However, for the purposes of this chapter, we will restrict our analysis to three cases, which are nevertheless likely to represent different types of nations.

Cultural Policies in France, the United States, and Sweden

If we in principle accept the notion that in the Western world there are at least three families of nations with respect to cultural policy, we have to distinguish three distinct public policy patterns that vary significantly in their historical roots, institutional arrangements, and modes and extent of support. Drawing on earlier research, we discuss the United States as an ideal type of the Anglo-Saxon family of cultural policy, Sweden as a prime example of the Scandinavian family, and France as a textbook example of cultural policy in Continental Europe.

The Bureaucratic Top-Down Approach to Cultural Policy: France

In France, the state traditionally plays an important role in the artistic and cultural life of the country. Support to writers and artists can be traced back to the ancien régime (before the French Revolution), as can the creation and public funding of such institutions as the Comédie Française founded in 1680 and the Royal Music Academy, which was to become the Paris Opera House (Andrault and Dressayre 1987:18). During the revolutionary period, the first museums were created by the state. In 1793, the Louvre, the city-palace of the French monarchy, was turned into the "Museum of the Republic," and some *dépendances* or satellites of the Louvre were established in the provinces to be used as places where the "excess" holdings of the Louvre could be stored.

A strong tradition of centralization, or more specifically *parisienisation*, is another very explicit feature of public policy in France. During the sixteenth and seventeenth centuries, French reformers such as Descartes and Richelieu took a very rationalistic approach to the modernization of state and society in France. According to Samuel P. Huntington (1968), the French orientation toward social change can be characterized as a "differentiation of functions and centralization of power." To differentiate the various functions of the maturing modern state, an encompassing bureaucracy was set up in the capital (Paris), and the city therefore developed into the center of political, economic, and intellectual life, depriving not only the French provinces but also traditional intermediary societal organizations and institutions, such as the guilds, of any political power. In the aftermath of the French Revolution, the centralization and *parisienisation* were even intensified, because the Jacobin tradition considered regionalist aspirations as well as intermediary bodies to be reactionary and hostile toward the state. Paris therefore gained an exceptional influence, attracting the elite by providing career possibilities in the state bureaucracy. In cultural terms, the most prestigious and powerful institutions were established in Paris, and these received the lion's share of the state's budget, thus casting a shadow over everything that went on outside the capital (Wangermée 1991:83).

This is not to say that the central state's cultural policies were exclusively directed at the capital in recent history. In fact, André Malraux, France's first Minister of Culture, placed considerable emphasis on increasing broad access to cultural activities throughout the country (with a particular focus on youth and multipurpose cultural centers). Decentralization policies expanded in new directions in the early 1980s under Jack Lang (Archambault 1997:141–142; Girard 1997; Loosely 1997:116). Nevertheless, these initiatives did not originate in the provinces, but were driven by the Ministry of Culture. The decentralization of culture has thus not affected the centrality of Paris for shaping French cultural policy.

To summarize: A top-down approach to modernization, with the state and its bureaucracy being the major force, is typical of the way in which the French have proceeded. This also holds true for the country's economic development. While during the ancien régime, the state and its bureaucracy were the most important entrepreneurs under the doctrine of mercantilism, during the Fifth Republic, the government launched an ambitious and very successful program of economic modernization which was primarily guided by a modified version of central planning or *planification*.

Therefore, it does not come as a surprise that the production and much of the consumption of the arts and culture is highly dominated and regulated by the state in France. Thus, cultural institutions are typically owned by the government—although management responsibilities have increasingly been transferred to private, nonprofit groups since the 1980s (Archambault 1997:140). Most major museums and similar institutions are either directly run by the central cultural bureaucracy in Paris or by local state authorities. French theater companies are also highly dependent on government subsidies. Because of the country's aristocratic tradition, the most prestigious groups, including the Comédie Française are public entities, forming the so-called state theater sector. In contrast to the Anglo-Saxon world, in France private patronage and especially support of the arts and culture by the business community were actively discouraged until the 1980s (Essig and de la Taille Rivero 1993). Estimates of corporate support in the early 1990s range from as little as $58 million (Loosely 1997:130) to $140 million (Essig and de la Taille Rivero 1993:99). Accordingly, Archambault (1997:140) states that "business sponsorship is still almost non-existent in France in contrast to practices in other countries." Whatever private patronage emerged in the 1980s and early 1990s in this country without any such traditions rapidly reached its limits (Marc Nicolas, cited in van Hemel and van der Wielen 1997). Moreover, state intervention has been perceived not as a correction of market failure but as a stronghold for protection of the arts and culture against the devastating effects of *mediatisation*, "an appalling rise in audiovisual *anti-culture*" (Girard 1997:122; italics in original), and cultural mass production, particularly by the North American entertainment industry. Therefore, French movie production is highly subsidized, and public radio programs are highly regulated and obliged to meet quotas concerning the numbers of French *chansons* in relation to English or American popular songs they put on the air.

To complete this picture of a predominantly state-dominated and regulated sector of the arts and culture, we should mention that France is one of the few countries in western Europe that has a centralized Ministry of Culture in charge of the implementation of the country's cultural policy. Many French cultural institutions are public enterprises and therefore under the direct control of the Ministry of Culture, which works with local authorities on a contract basis, thus exerting a strong influence on cultural life in the provinces. A panel of European experts evaluating French cultural policy in 1991 came to the conclusion that cultural policy and politics in France are neither drafted on a broad consultative basis, nor does the parliament play a significant role in this respect (Wangermée 1991:43). The driving force behind French cultural policy is either the minister of culture or the president himself, depending on the personality of the officeholder. Generally, the president is in favor of large-scale endeavors, in an effort to associate his name with a prestigious project in the capital such as the Centre Pompidou or the Grands Travaux of the 1980s.

Last but not least, among the Western European countries, France remains among the big spenders with respect to public funding of the arts. As mentioned earlier, since the Ministry of Culture was founded in 1959, its budget increased sevenfold until the late 1980s. By 1993, "cultural budgetary expenditures . . . nearly reached the mythic threshold of 1 percent of the total public budget" (Archambault 1997:141). The reasons for such a high level of funding are twofold: first, when the Ministry of Culture was founded, cultural institutions were predominantly state run and therefore almost exclusively financed with public monies. In other words, in terms of public support, French cultural policy was relatively high from the very beginning. The remarkable level of per capita spending for the arts and culture of the French government can therefore easily be explained by something akin to path dependency. Where the state and its bureaucracy are the dominant supporters of the arts and culture, public spending tends automatically to be high in comparison to private giving as well as to income at the box office. Second, public spending for the arts and culture increased significantly under the presidency of socialist François Mitterrand—the state's cultural budget effectively doubled (Girard 1997: 116; Archambault 1997: 141)—because, during his era, the social democratic doctrine, which views cultural policy as an investment in human and social capital as well as a specific strategy to modernize society, contracted a fruitful marriage with the specific political culture of the country, which has traditionally regarded the arts and culture as the foundation as well as the expression of its greatness.

The specific features of the Continental European model of cultural policy exemplified by the French case can be summarized as follows:

1. The government plays a dominant role particularly in the production of high culture, resulting in high levels of public spending for the arts and culture.
2. A powerful cultural bureaucracy is responsible for agenda setting as well as implementation of cultural policy with the result that the prestigious cultural institutions, concentrated in Paris, overshadow independent artistic developments in the provinces.
3. Due to the traditional antimarket and antibusiness attitudes of policymakers, private and business patronage of the arts and culture remains underdeveloped.
4. Culture is used as a synonym for nationhood as well as for a specific expression of statehood.
5. Under the socialist doctrine, culture served as a tool to modernize society. To quote François Mitterrand, "Nothing changes which does not change first in people's hearts, brains, and perceptions. It is in this sense that I often declare that socialism is above all a cultural project" (von Beyme 1990:41).

The Corporatist Approach to Cultural Policy: Sweden

Like France, Sweden has a long history of government involvement in arts and culture. A government office for the maintenance of archives and the care of cultural monuments was established as early as the seventeenth century, and in the following century, the Crown founded many cultural institutions in Stockholm, including the opera in 1771, the theater in 1788, and the (national) museum in 1792, primarily serving the sophisticated taste of the nobility (Swedish Ministry 1990:69–71; Kleberg 1987:175). In the late nineteenth century, however, the emerging popular movements, including the labor, temperance, and nonconformist movements, "internally developed their own cultural traditions . . . putting early emphasis on music and singing" (Blomkvist 1982) and "contributed to new political ideas as well as supporting popular education and fine arts for the population" (Kangas and Onsér-Franzén 1996:18). Thus a variety of voluntary associations, such as adult education organizations, amateur theaters, traditional folk music and dance groups and amateur choirs, gradually emerged alongside the institutions of feudal culture and often closely affiliated with the Social Democratic Party, the unions, or the state church. Although some of these private organizations also served political goals, voluntary associations began to dominate the cultural life in smaller communities and rural areas (Myerscough 1990: 128–32) and eventually became eligible for public funding as well.

For these reasons, Sweden features a more varied institutional mix than France. Major Swedish cultural institutions are predominantly state run, although many theaters and museums in Stockholm, as well as in the bigger cities, are semi-independent, quasi-governmental organizations in the legal forms of operating foundations or corporations. In addition, numerous voluntary organizations of folk and popular culture also play a significant role in cultural politics (Irjala 1996) and are generously supported by public grants. The particular role of these groups was already recognized in a 1974 parliamentary resolution that held that such "organizations have greater opportunities than cultural institutions for reaching disadvantaged groups" (Swedish Ministry 1990:74). Therefore, federal and local authorities must provide amateur groups with the money they need. In general, those groups and organizations are part of a specific social milieu, and because of their historical roots, they are, even today, closely tied to political parties and trade unions (Myerscough 1990:128). However, resources channeled through these popular movements remain under the same central influences, which help reinforce the pursuit of consensus and the tendency toward uniformity.

Government support for high culture and popular cultural activities was not guided by specific goals and thus evolved "as the product of ideological conflicts between the state and popular movements" (Kangas and Onsér-Franzén 1996:25) rather than explicit policy. This, however, began to change in the 1960s, when artists' unions complained loudly about insufficient social security and low wages. In reaction, the Social Democratic administration established a commission, headed by Olof Palme, who was then the minister of education and cultural affairs, to investigate the current situation of arts and culture and to make recommendations for improving public support for the arts. Programmatically titled New Cultural Policy (NCP), the commission's report served as basis for the 1974 parliamentary resolution *Den statliga kulturpolitiken*, which was unanimously accepted by all political parties (Kleberg 1987:178). The objectives of the NCP, as laid down in the 1974 resolution, were not conceptualized as specific policy goals, but rather as a broad agenda to influence common values and raise national ambitions with respect to the arts. First and foremost, the NCP should "give people opportunities to engage in creative activities of their own, . . . counteract negative effects of commercialization in the cultural sector, make more allowance for the experiences and needs of disadvantaged groups . . . [and] promote a decentralization of activities and decision-making in the cultural sector" (Swedish Ministry 1990:72; also Kleberg 1987:179). With the 1974 resolution, equal access to culture became no less important than social and economic equality. "The overriding aim (of the 1974 resolution) was the creation of a society in which each and every person has the opportunity to develop his and her capacity for self-expression and the opportunity to experience a broad and enriching life. Cultural democracy is important not only as an expression of social justice, but it contributes to the creation of a society which is strengthened and vitalized by the liberation of human potential" (Swedish Ministry 1990:77).

For the implementation of the NCP, a National Cultural Council (NCC) was established to be closely affiliated with the Ministry of Education and Cultural Affairs. Although different societal strata have a voice in the Council, the NCC is bound by detailed guidelines of the government and the *Riksdag*. The largest share of appropriations, or 75 percent, is earmarked for so-called basic grants to individual arts institutions, partially covering personnel costs. With only partial underwriting of these costs by the NCC, local authorities have an incentive to provide the remainder, thereby decentralizing the support system for the arts but encouraging close cooperation between local governments and the NCC.

Generally, public funding is provided by the NCC, county governments, and municipalities, whereby the latter contribute 58.1 percent of total public support, the counties 9.5 percent, and the federal level another 32.4 percent (Swedish National Council 1994). Whereas federal government allocations for the arts roughly equaled the local outlays in the early 1970s, municipalities became the main funders of arts and culture during the 1980s (Swedish Ministry 1990:99). Since Sweden has a long tradition of local self-rule, local governments are officially encouraged to actively pursue cultural policies, and the significant increases in local arts funding can therefore be regarded as a success of the policy goal of decentralization laid down in the 1974 resolution. However, the basic grant system remains in the decision-making power of the NCC and is unlikely to be delegated to the regional and local levels. Although the actual state contribution to the financing of cultural institutions is relatively small, the national level thus retains a degree of authority in the determination of cultural policy (Irjala 1996:126–27).

The Nordic model so far varies from the French case in the greater institutional variety of the cultural sector (resulting from the intersection of a central, regal tradition with the influence of popular movements' broader grass-roots cultural development) and a pronounced decentralization tendency, mitigated by the central government's general steering function to ensure overall equity and equality. Similar to the French case, however, is the dominance of public funding and rejection of private support and mass marketization.

The dominance of the government in financing the arts derives from a broad consensus among the different political parties, trade unions, and industry that the provision of basic resources for cultural institutions is a public rather than private matter (Swedish Ministry 1990:101). In other words, public support for the arts is considered a statutory government responsibility. In large part, this consensus is based on the assumption that increases in leisure time and disposable income might be "exploited by those who see a chance to earn money on mass-culture products" thus necessitating a "counterweight to the 'junk' culture that is being marketed with slick commercial methods" (Svenson 1982). Accordingly, an important function of public funding is to counteract such negative effects of commercialization, which was also one of the policy goals of the 1974 resolution. Moreover, cultural institutions are neither expected to increase earned income nor to engage in fundraising and thus are further insulated from the market. Swedish theaters, for instance, are among the most heavily subsidized cultural institutions in Europe, with box office income averaging less than 10 percent of revenues (Myerscough 1990:41) despite relatively strong demand. By the same token, Swedish tax law does not have any provision to encourage private individual or corporate support and, although this issue is being discussed, it remains highly unlikely that such provisions will be introduced in the near future (Nerep 1997). Altogether, there is no tradition to promote collaboration between commercial life and culture in Sweden.

The adoption of the public funding imperative brought Sweden to the forefront of governmental arts spending. Immediately following the enactment of the 1974 resolution, public funding for the arts and culture increased significantly. In comparative terms, Sweden ranges among those countries most highly committed to public funding for the arts and culture, roughly at the same level with Germany and the Netherlands in terms of per capita spending (Schuster 1986). However, though public funding increased steadily with annual growth rates around 10 percent during the 1970s, the growth rate slowed down significantly in the 1980s to about 1.5 percent annually. Nevertheless, public funding for arts and culture is still considered to be quite important (Swedish Ministry 1990:89). In the 1990s, a reorientation and revision of public funding and cultural policy were discussed (Myerscough 1990:31), but ultimately not implemented (Irjala 1996).

The Swedish case, as an example of the Nordic cultural policy model, can be summarized as:

1. Government retains exclusive financial responsibility for the arts and culture, and they are well supported.
2. While aiming to maintain a universal, egalitarian approach through encouragement from the central level, the system is largely decentralized, giving regional and local institutions a high degree of control.
3. Corporatist arrangements (cf. Osland and Mangset, as cited in Irjala 1996) provide support not only for high culture, but also a broader network of popular, grass-roots cultural activities.
4. A preponderance of anticommercialization sentiments and lack of incentives for private (financial) support prevails.

Dominance of the Private Sector in Cultural Policy Initiatives: United States

Prior to the mid-1960s, public support for the arts was largely limited to indirect subsidies though tax exemption for arts organizations and relatively generous deductions for benefactors in a system of private policy making. Among the reasons for the traditionally low involvement of government are the lack of feudal-aristocratic heritage of cultural institutions, puritanical beliefs that regarded the arts as unnecessary luxury, and a strong republican tradition of limited government (Toepler 1991). Since arts patronage is widely perceived as a private rather than a public responsibility, cultural venues are usually either commercial or nonprofit. Though for-profit enterprises dominate the cultural industry by and large, nonprofit organizations dominate the provision of high culture (Netzer 1992). All major orchestras and opera companies are nonprofit, and the share of state-run organizations in the institutional mix of cultural institutions is rather small. Moreover, public arts organizations tend to be affiliated with public educational institutions, such as university museums or orchestras (DiMaggio 1987:197).

One of the main reasons for the dominance of nonprofits in the institutional mix of high culture lies in the historical development of the field. Beginning in the second half of the nineteenth century, upper-class elites established arts institutions that were supported mainly by wealthy individuals (DiMaggio 1987). Funding of the arts remained the more or less exclusive domain of private patrons at the local level until the 1950s. A major change took place in 1957. The Ford Foundation, soon to be followed by a few other private foundations, commenced a new comprehensive program designed to revitalize the arts in America and especially the performing arts. In a way the Ford program was a reaction to the rapid growth of the arts sector with new organizations emerging and established institutions expanding their services (Cummings 1991). Ford grants helped to stabilize existing institutions financially and created incentives for the formation of new arts groups. This systematic effort was a clear departure from the scattered and occasional support that foundations had provided to the arts in the past. Moreover, this significant push by the Ford Foundation, and the fact that a few other private foundations soon began to take similar approaches, helped establish the arts as a legitimate recipient of public funds and a relevant policy issue (DiMaggio 1986). Meanwhile, it was becoming obvious that the arts could not be sustained by private sector income alone because of the economic characteristics of the services they produce (Baumol and Bowen 1966), and the "market failure" argument provided a way to justify direct government intervention. These developments, which coincided with a general expansion of the American welfare state, shifted the posture of government toward the arts, culminating in the establishment of the National Endowment for the Arts in 1965.

The original enabling legislation set out a number of very broad goals, including the fostering of artistic excellence, increased accessibility of the arts, and the creation of a decentralized public support system. Although the economic problems endemic to high-culture institutions provided the main rationale for the agency's establishment, the preamble of the National Foundation on the Arts and Humanities explicitly reiterated the preeminence of private and local initiatives (Wyszomirski and Mulcahy 1995:122).

The preeminence of private initiative is reflected in the forms of support that the NEA provides. The NEA—in contrast to state and local arts agencies—does not provide statutory funding, or operating support, for arts institutions. Moreover, projects and programs are only partially underwritten through matching or challenge grants. The most important aspect of the NEA's funding is what is referred to as imprimatur; public grants are perceived as a form of recognition for quality, and therefore bolster the arts organization's fundraising from private foundations, corporations, and individuals.

The NEA's strategy of reaching its other major goal, increasing access to the arts, is to stimulate new public support at the state and local levels. The largest single share of the endowment's budget has therefore traditionally been designated as block grants to state arts agencies (SAAs). In fiscal year 1993, the NEA distributed 27.5 percent of its budget as basic grants to SAAs, with an additional 7.5 percent of budget set aside for state grants for specific project areas (Wyszomirski and Mulcahy 1995:133). The availability of federal funds through the state program nurtured the establishment of SAAs in all states, which in turn generated additional public arts spending at the state and local levels as well as substantially decentralized the public support system. In fact, with an estimated $650 million in direct local government allocations and $265.6 million in state appropriations, the local and state levels outspent the NEA appropriation of $162 million in 1995 (Cobb 1996). Moreover, both state and local arts agencies have shown strong patterns of growth, especially during the 1980s. This holds true even for the 1990s, despite recession-induced declines in legislative appropriations for SAAs and in the budgets of local arts agencies (Institute for Community Development and the Arts 1997).

Although government spending on the arts has at all three levels increased significantly over the past three decades and amounted to $1.1 billion in 1995 (Cobb 1996), it is nonetheless low in comparison to other industrialized countries. Direct per capita expenditures amounted to no more than three dollars in the early 1980s (Schuster as cited in Heilbrun and Gray 1993:232), considerably below the spending of most industrialized nations. Furthermore, federal and state outlays account for no more than 15 percent of total revenues of the arts sector (Mulcahy 1987). Private independent and community foundations alone considerably outspend public sources (Weber and Renz 1993; Zeigler 1995). Moreover, after rapid increases in the NEA appropriations during the 1970s, federal spending stalled in the 1980s and decreased in the 1990s, with significant cuts in 1996.

As a recent study, commissioned by the President's Committee on the Arts and the Humanities (Cobb 1996), demonstrates, the continued decline in public spending on the arts is unlikely to be replaced by comparable increases in donations by individuals, corporations, and foundations.[3] Under this scenario, arts organizations are forced to seek ways to increase the third, and last, major type of revenue: earned income (Stevens 1996). Indeed, the interest in arts marketing techniques and other ways of generating profits has grown considerably over the past decade. Among the arts groups that have become savvy at marketing is the museum community, where commercialization strategies range from expansion and modernization of museum shops and restaurants to off-site retailing and large-scale direct merchandising, although the actual financial effect of increased commercialization remains somewhat doubtful (Anheier and Toepler 1998). Moreover, the creeping marketization of the arts fields is further complemented by the shift of corporate support from philanthropic giving to cause-related marketing and sponsorships, requiring a direct quid pro quo.

The Anglo-Saxon model, characterized by the American case, is distinguished by:

1. A dominance of the private (nonprofit) sector, both in the delivery and financing of arts and culture, with government playing only a supporting role.
2. A decentralized and dispersed net of private and public funding, in which the federal government has performed a stimulating function.

3. The lack of a clear and unambiguous overall agenda for the cultural policy process.
4. The lack of both a high-culture tradition as well as a broad popular base for cultural activities.

Discussion

What have we learned from this brief overview? The most interesting aspects in our view relate to the historical evolution of the institutional contexts and the role that various interest groups have played. In the European context, the state's responsibility for, and commitment to, arts and culture is in many ways a historical legacy. The institutions that the aristocracy built all over the continent practically fell into the hands of the modernized nation-states, which were left with what seems to have been little choice but continuing and preserving the tradition. In the French case, we could argue that the absolutist monarch passed the torch directly to the state bureaucracy. The supremacy of the crown was replaced by the supremacy of the government and its bureaucracy in the cultural arena as in other societal fields. In the later republics, the centralist pattern of absolutism remained in place in France. Clearly, the ancien régime established an institutional pattern that subsequent regimes, though radically different, never discarded. This holds especially true for the socialist era of François Mitterrand, when public support for the arts and culture was viewed to be a tool to democratize and to modernize society. Under Mitterrand's powerful minister of culture, the understanding of what constitutes the cultural sector was broadened to include popular, folk, and community culture, but even Jack Lang was not able to achieve a substantial change in the institutional pattern of cultural policy in France. Today, French cultural policy can be characterized as "business as usual" (Hanimann 1997).

We find similarities in Sweden, where the monarchy of the seventeenth and eighteenth centuries also established a distinct but somewhat less centralized institutional pattern. However, though the modern state continued the monarchical tradition of funding and maintaining high-culture institutions, a powerful new actor emerged in the form of popular movements that broadened the tradition considerably. The social democratic pattern inherent in all Nordic countries can be understood as a result of bargaining processes that took place when "the institutional culture of the state was confronted with the alternative culture of the popular movements" (Kangas and Onsér-Franzén 1996:18). Thus, from a neoinstitutionalist point of view, the high commitment of government to culture in Continental European France and Scandinavian Sweden derives largely from institutional patterns established by the eighteenth century. While France followed the path of continuing the aristocratic legacy without further dilution, Sweden broadened the institutional frame by incorporating a broader, popular base for cultural activities and the support thereof. In contrast to France, Swedish cultural policy is not regarded primarily as a vehicle to symbolize the "grandeur" of the nation, but is closely linked to social policy and therefore serves as a tool for empowerment. However, either case ultimately results in a comparatively high degree of government spending on arts and culture.

Against this background, the American case seems obvious. Shunned as the "inmates of corrupt and despotic courts" in Europe (Verplanck, as cited in Grindhammer 1975:2), the arts did not take a strong foothold in the New World. A limited institutional pattern did not crystallize until the second half of the nineteenth century, when the fine arts were appropriated by urban elites. In contrast to Europe, the urban elites and business communities became the driving force of cultural policy development in the United States, primarily providing funds for high-culture institutions. What is more, not only did the United States lack a basic aristocratic cultural infrastructure, but popular activity in the cultural realm was not associated with any kind of ideology or doctrine as was definitely the case in Sweden and in some other European countries, such as the tradition of *Arbeiterkultur* in Germany. This is not to say that the American population at large did not engage in cultural activities. For example, European immigrant groups imported their cultural traditions, such as singing clubs and contest traditions, which were widespread during the nineteenth century and persisted for a long time (Plotinsky 1994). Because of their diversity, however, these groups did not develop a common ground, which could have been used as the foundation for a political movement that could have furthered their cause, as did similar groups in Scandinavia. From this perspective, it is easily understood why the United States lags significantly behind Europe in terms of government spending on the arts.

Conclusion

The Difficulties of Comparative Arts Policy Research

Comparative cultural policy research, while highly interesting and exciting, is also a veritable intellectual and methodological minefield. In his article "Making Compromises to Make Comparisons in Cross-National Arts Policy Research," Mark Schuster (1987) has pointed to the most significant fallacies of comparative arts policy research, including the substantial problems of drawing proper boundaries of what constitutes arts and culture in different societies and the frequent use of such questionable tools as per capita spending. In this piece, Schuster (pp. 3–8) also clearly states the limitations of many such studies. Often comparative studies are politically motivated, addressing the question "How are we doing?" to gather arguments for increasing public support in a given country. Other studies are essentially "fishing expeditions" trying to address the question "What is being done?" without any further policy implications. A third type of study searches for specific policy models in an effort to find out "What can be done?" The first type of study is too easily corrupted by the "quick fix" needs of the arts advocates who commission them. The second type requires an in-depth understanding of the arts policy contexts and processes in the countries under consideration, which is often lacking. And the third type often suffers from a lack of interest in the unusual features of other countries' policies, which reduces the applicability of such research.

From what we have said before, it should be clear that the first type of study and one of the mainstays of comparative arts research—namely the quest for comparative overall or per capita spending patterns—is methodologically and theoretically flawed (Schuster 1987). Indeed, from a neoinstitutionalist perspective, the fact that country x spends more on the arts than country y has no policy relevance. Although an American politician might be impressed by the high spending levels in Europe in the short term, the very fact that spending patterns vary significantly will not and cannot change the underlying institutional patterns in arts support in the United States.

What we have tried to achieve in this paper is the second type of study, a fishing expedition. In a manner of speaking, we have cast our net over three countries and then focused on what seemed to us the most interesting parts of the "catch." Though we do not claim to have in-depth knowledge of the three countries we have discussed, and we may not completely satisfy the other conditions for sound comparative research that Schuster spelled out, our attempt may be a step in the proper direction.

Nevertheless, our approach points to the faultiness of the third type of study, the quest for interesting (though impracticable) policy models and ideas from other countries. Given the state of overall upheaval in the cultural policy scene in western Europe, the search for new ideas and models seems more urgent than ever and raises the specter of a convergence of formerly distinct policy systems. The final and concluding section of this paper is devoted to a brief discussion of this issue.

The Issue of Convergence

The idea that government can affect and change society was still widely accepted in the 1970s. One of the most important lessons from that period has been that massive government intervention—even in the field of arts and culture—has not produced the desired effect. In fact, the battle for equality and democratization of the arts seems largely lost—according to some observers even in the Nordic states (Kangas and Onsér-Franzén 1996), although some skirmishes are still being fought. What we seem to be witnessing over the past decade and a half is a gradual paradigm shift from the social-democratic doctrine of the 1960s and 1970s to a more liberal doctrine fostering the idea of public-private partnership. The front-runner of this paradigm shift has been the instrumentalization of the arts and culture (for other economic purposes) which took place in the 1980s. The 1990s have seen the increasing importance of issues of privatization/degovernmentalization of arts institutions; greater managerial freedom both for local government arts bureaucrats and organizational administrators; changed revenue mixes (with a greater share of private money) and other public-private partnership initiatives; and a stronger embeddedness of cultural institutions in their local communities in hopes of mobilizing new local resources, be that private donations or increased volunteering.

Are these developments clear indications of the convergence of the European models toward the American system? Since U.S. arts advocates and policymakers have—implicitly or explicitly—hoped for an approximation of the European systems of arts patronage, some of the current trends in Europe—such as privatization, attracting private sponsorship, and searching for volunteers—seem somewhat ironic. However, significant differences between Europe and the United States remain. Privatization in the European context is another word for altering the organizational form of the cultural institution but without substantial concomitant fiscal shifts. The same holds true for models of public-private partnership in terms of funding. Artists and managers of cultural institutions have just begun to discover the private sector, and particularly the business community, as sources of support. However, these funds are regarded as a complement to public funding, not a replacement. Instead of following the American way by handing over the cultural sector to the market, a very different approach is likely to be taken by the European countries viewing cultural policy as an integral part of social investment strategies. In the years to come, lifelong learning and training will become a central issue for policymakers. In this context, an active cultural policy will be regarded as an investment in human and social capital development. However, there is no doubt that the ways to implement this new strategy will significantly differ across countries according to the specific institutional arrangements and policy traditions. As economic historian and Nobel laureate Douglass North (1990) has demonstrated for the economic realm, transplanting the formal institutional constraints of one country to another country with a different institutional context and pattern is bound to fail so long as the informal norms and "subjective models of the actors" do not mesh. And what is true for economics is likely to be true for culture.

Notes

This chapter is based on a paper given at the Plenary Session "How Do Subsidies Affect the Muse?" at the Tenth International Conference on Cultural Economics, Barcelona, Spain, June 16, 1998. A different version of this paper was originally published in the *Journal of Cultural Economics*, 23 (1999): 33–49. The sections on Sweden and the United States draw in part on Zimmer and Toepler (1996).

1. These two lines of argument formed one important basis for the first explicit policy analysis of this new field of public policy: Netzer's *The Subsidized Muse* (1978).
2. Since the merit goods concept violates the consumer sovereignty assumption—a holy cow of neo-classical economics, it is now somewhat discredited in public finance.
3. This is also true in other policy fields, such as human services, education, and health; see Salamon 1997.

References

Andrault, M. and Dressayre, P. (1987) 'Government and the arts in France,' pp. 17–44 in M.C. Cummings, Jr. and R. S. Katz (eds.) (1987) *The Patron State: Government and the Arts in Europe, North America, and Japan*, New York and Oxford: Oxford University Press.

Anheier, H.K. and Toepler, S. (1998) 'Commerce and the muse: are art museums becoming commercial?' pp.233–248 in B.A. Weisbrod (ed.) *To Profit or Not to Profit: The Commercial Transformation of the Nonprofit Sector*, Cambridge and New York: Cambridge University Press.

Archambault, E. (1997) *The Nonprofit Sector in France*, Manchester: Manchester University Press.

Baumol, W. and Bowen, W. (1966) *Performing Arts: The Economic Dilemma*, Cambridge: Twentieth Century Fund.

von Beyme, M. (1990). *Kulturpolitik unter den Sozialisten in Frankreich von 1981 bis 1986*, Frankfurt: Lang-Verlag.

Blomkvist, R. (1982) *Popular Organizations and the Promotion of Cultural Activities in Sweden*, Stockholm: The Swedish Institute.

Castles, F. G. (1993) 'The families of nations concept,' pp. xii–xxiii in F. G. Castles (ed.) *Families of Nations: Patterns of Public Policy in Western Democracies*, Dartmouth: Aldershot.

Castles, F. G. (ed.) (1989) *The Comparative History of Public Policy*, Cambridge: Polity.

Cobb, N. (1996) *Looking Ahead: Private Sector Giving to the Arts and Humanities*, Washington, DC: President's Committee on the Arts and the Humanities.

Cummings, M. C., Jr. (1991) 'Government and the arts: an overview,' pp. 31–79 in S. Benedict (ed.) *Public Money and the Muse*, New York and London: W.W. Norton.

Cummings, M.C., Jr. and Katz, R.S. (eds.) (1987) *The Patron State: Government and the Arts in Europe, North America, and Japan*, New York and Oxford: Oxford University Press.

DiMaggio, P. (1986) 'Support for the arts from independent foundations,' pp. 113–139 in P. DiMaggio (ed.) *Nonprofit Enterprise in the Arts: Studies in Mission and Constraint*, New York and Oxford: Oxford University Press.

DiMaggio, P. (1987) 'Nonprofit organizations in the production and distribution of culture,' pp. 195–220 in W. W. Powell (ed.) *The Nonprofit-Sector: A Research Handbook*, New Haven and London: Yale University Press.

Dutch Ministry of Welfare, Health and Cultural Affairs (1994) *Cultural Policy in the Netherlands* (European Programme for the Evaluation of National Cultural Policies), Strasbourg: Council of Europe.

Esping-Andersen, G. (1990) *The Three Worlds of Welfare Capitalism*, Princeton: Princeton University Press.

Essig, C. and de la Taille Rivero, M. (1993) 'Frankreich und die Kulturförderung heute,' pp. 97–104 in R. Strachwitz and S. Toepler (eds.) *Kulturförderung: Mehr als Sponsoring*, Wiesbaden: Gabler.

Fener, P. (1987) 'Government and the arts: the Netherlands,' pp. 105–135 in M. C. Cummings, Jr. and R. S. Katz (eds.) *The Patron State: Government and the Arts in Europe, North America, and Japan*, New York and Oxford: Oxford University Press.

Girard, A. (1997) 'French cultural policy from André Malraux to Jacques Lang: A tale of modernization,' *International Journal of Cultural Policy*, 4, 1: 107–126.

Grindhammer, L.W. (1975) *Art and the Public: The Democratization of the Fine Arts in the United States, 1830-1860*, Stuttgart: Metzler.

Hanimann, Joseph (1997) 'Ächzen im Palais Royal. Frankreichs Kulturministerin hat den Ton noch nicht gefunden,' *F.A.Z.*, November 19.

Heilbrun, J. and Gray, C.M. (1993) *The Economies of Art and Culture*, Cambridge: Cambridge University Press.

Heinrichs, W. (1997) *Kulturpolitik und Kulturfinanzierung*, München: Beck-Verlag.

van Hemel, A. and van der Wielen, N. (eds.) (1997) *Privatization/Désetatisation and Culture: Limitations or opportunities for cultural development in Europe?* Conference Reader for the Circle Round Table 1997. Amsterdam: Boekman Foundation and Twente University.

Hillman-Chartrand, H. and McCaughey, C. (1989) 'The arm's length principle and the arts: an international perspective-past, present, and future,' pp. 43–80 in M.C. Cummings, Jr. and J.M.D. Schuster (eds.) *Who's to Pay for the Arts? The International Search for Models of Support*, New York: ACA Books.

Huntington, S. P. (1968) *Political Order in Changing Societies*, New Haven: Yale University Press.

Institute for Community Development and the Arts (1997) *Building America's Communities II*. Washington, DC: America for the Arts.

Irjala, A. (1996) '(De)centralisation processes in Nordic cultural policy,' *European Journal of Cultural Policy*, 3, 1: 109–132.

Kangas, A. and Onsér-Franzén, J. (1996) 'Is there a need for a new cultural policy strategy in the Nordic welfare state?' *European Journal of Cultural Policy*, 3, 1: 15–26.

Kleberg, C.-J. (1987) 'Cultural policy in Sweden,' pp. 174–198 in M. C. Cummings, Jr. and R. S. Katz (eds.) *The Patron State: Government and the Arts in Europe, North America, and Japan*, New York and Oxford: Oxford University Press.

Looseley, D. L. (1995) *The Politics of Fun: Cultural Policy and Debate in Contemporary France*, Oxford and New York: Berg.

Mulcahy, K. V. (1987) 'Government and the arts in the United States,' pp. 311–332 in M. C. Cummings, Jr. and R. S. Katz (eds.) *The Patron State: Government and the Arts in Europe, North America, and Japan*, New York and Oxford: Oxford University Press.

Mulcahy, K. (2000) 'The government and cultural patronage: a comparative analysis of cultural patronage in the United States, France, Norway and Canada,' pp. 138–168 in J. Cherbo and M. Wyszomirski (eds.) *The Public Life of the Arts in America*, New Brunswick, NJ: Rutgers University Press.

Myerscough, J. (1990) *National Cultural Policy in Sweden*, Strasbourg: Council of Europe.

Nerep, E. (1997) 'Sweden,' pp. 294–303 in L.M. Salamon (ed.) *The International Guide to Nonprofit Law*, New York, John Wiley.

Netzer, D. (1978) *The Subsidized Muse: Public Support for the Arts in the United States*. Cambridge and New York: Cambridge University Press.

Netzer, D. (1992) 'Arts and culture,' pp. 174–206 in C. T. Clotfelter (ed.) *Who Benefits from the Nonprofit Sector?*, Chicago and London: University of Chicago Press.

North, D. (1990) *Institutions, Institutional Change, and Economic Performance*. Cambridge and New York: Cambridge University Press.

Plotinsky, A. (1994) 'Music as philanthropy: making music and building community in nineteenth-century America,' *Nonprofit and Voluntary Sector Quarterly*, 23, 4: 371–381.

Powell, W. W. and DiMaggio, P. J. (1991) *The New Institutionalism in Organizational Analysis*, Chicago: University of Chicago Press.

Ridley, F. F. (1987) 'Tradition, change and crisis in Great Britain,' pp. 225–275 in M. C. Cummings, Jr. and R.S. Katz (eds.) (1987) *The Patron State: Government and the Arts in Europe, North America, and Japan*, New York and Oxford: Oxford University Press.

Salamon, L. M. (1997) *Holding the Center: America's Nonprofit Sector at a Crossroads*, New York: Nathan Cummings Foundation.

Schuster, J. M. D. (1986) 'Tax incentives as arts policy in Western Europe,' pp. 320–360 in P. DiMaggio (ed.) *Nonprofit Enterprise in the Arts: Studies in Mission and Constraint*, New York and Oxford: Oxford University Press.

Schuster, J. M. D. (1987) 'Making compromises to make comparisons in cross-national arts policy research,' *Journal of Cultural Economics* 11(2): 1–29.

Stevens, L. (1996) 'The earnings shift: the new bottom line paradigm for the arts industry in a market-driven era,' *The Journal of Arts Management, Law and Society*, 26, 2: 101–113.

Svenson, G. (1982) *State Organizations and the Promotion of Cultural Activities in Sweden,* Stockholm: The Swedish Institute.

Swedish Ministry of Education and Cultural Affairs (1990) *Swedish State Cultural Policy: Policy, Objectives, Measures, and Results. A National Report,* Stockholm: Allmänna.

Swedish National Council for Cultural Affairs (1994) *Swedish Cultural Policy,* Göteborg: Kulturradet Distribution.

Toepler, S. (1991) *Kulturfinanzierung - Ein Vergleich USA-Deutschland,* Wiesbaden: Gabler.

Wangermée, R. (1991) *Cultural Policy in France* (European Programme for the Appraisal of Cultural Policies), Strasbourg: Council of Europe.

Weber, N. and Renz, L. (1993) *Arts Funding: A Report on Foundation and Corporate Grantmaking Trends,* New York: The Foundation Center.

Wyszomirski, M.J. and Mulcahy, K.V. (1995) 'The organization of public support for the arts,' pp. 121–143 in K.V. Mulcahy and M.J. Wyszomirski (eds.) *America's Commitment to Culture: Government and the Arts,* Boulder: Westview Press.

Zeigler, J. W. (1995) 'The tiny endowment: radical differences in public and private sectors,' *The Journal of Arts Management, Law, and Society,* 24, 4: 345–352.

Zimmer, A. and Toepler, S. (1996) 'Cultural policies and the welfare state: the cases of Sweden, Germany, and the United States,' *The Journal of Arts Management, Law, and Society,* 26, 3: 167–193.

3

Building National Prestige

Japanese Cultural Policy and the Influence of Western Institutions

Kuniyuki Tomooka, Sachiko Kanno, and Mari Kobayashi

Cultural policies are implemented not so much for the advancement of the arts and the careers of artists, or for the satisfaction of the desires of a small number of arts patrons and consumers, but for concerns of the society as a whole, such as the creation and preservation of values that cannot be reduced to economic interest. Just as individuals use cultural capital to acquire or maintain social distinction (Bourdieu 1984), governments establish cultural policies for similar reasons. Japanese cultural policies were established in the Meiji era (1868 to 1911) to give "distinction" to Japanese society by creating cultural symbols that contributed to national prestige.[1] In other words, cultural policies contribute to the distinction of a society by giving it a refined image and by turning its people into more sophisticated, culturally aware citizens (Bennett 1995, 1998).

The origins of cultural policy in Japan can be traced to the beginning of the modern nation-state in 1868, when the country's new leaders were faced with the problems of assimilating and adapting to Western influences after the Meiji Restoration. Like many other non-Western countries during that period, the Japanese saw Western culture as a reference point for evaluating their own culture. Since Japan was eager to emulate Western modernized countries, the government's industrial policy focused on rapid modernization, and cultural policy was formed and transformed in accordance with this goal. In a sense, the Japanese government's orientation toward culture at that time was based on the goal of promoting national integration and improving the international reputation of the nation.

The specific goals of the Japanese government with respect to cultural policy in the Meiji era led the government to define its role rather narrowly. The private sector, in the form of corporations such as department stores, newspapers, and railways, performed a very important complementary role in making the arts and other forms of Western culture available to the Japanese public (Yoshimi 1992). In general, the government's role in cultural policy in the Meiji era was to "reinvent" and preserve traditional Japanese culture based on the concepts of Western art while new forms of Japanese art were slighted (Kitazawa 1989).

In light of this historical background, one could classify current cultural policies in Japan using the following four categories:[2]

1. *Official recognition of existing works*: Designation, protection, and glorification of cultural properties, and purchase, exhibition, and presentation of existing works at public cultural centers. In this category, public organizations (or semipublic third-sector organizations) select "appropriate" cultural resources and recognize them as public (or semipublic) assets. This "certifies" the values of the final products of these cultural activities as public culture, which serves the interests of the society as a whole.

2. *Provision of sites for official recognition of culture*: Construction and operation of cultural centers. The construction of cultural centers functions to sanction the objects presented or exhibited there as permissible public assets, or to provide them with the value and status of public culture.

3. *Creation of new public values*: Organization of and assistance to art and cultural festivals; subsidizing cultural projects and artists-in-residence programs. The activities in this category concern policies for creating new public cultures. They provide opportunities for presentation of newly created works, and selectively support the activities of particular projects, groups, and artists.

4. *Cultivation and management of cultural resources*: Education and training of artists, training in arts management, provision of information, promotion of research, provision of arts education, provision of incentive taxation systems, protection of copyright, and enactment of laws on culture. The activities in this category promote autonomous activities of expression, and play an indirect role in creating values of public culture.

In Japan, the central government has tended, until very recently, to place the greatest emphasis on the first and second categories. The activities in the third category, as well as nonofficial activities in the fourth category, have been performed primarily by organizations in the private sector. Unlike governments in Western countries, the Japanese government has not supported popular culture, which is a highly developed cultural sector in Japan (see, for example, Martinez 1998). This chapter traces historical changes in priorities in government cultural policies and compares them with cultural programs supported by corporations and local governments. Specifically, it analyzes problematic areas in Japanese cultural policies and the effects of those policies on the production and consumption of the arts.

Historical Background for Cultural Policies in Japan

As we have indicated in the previous section, contemporary cultural policies in Japan should be seen in their historical context. In this section, we will provide a brief review of the history of Japanese cultural policies.

After the Meiji Restoration of 1868, when the nation-state was founded, Japan quickly absorbed the cultures of various Western societies. Concepts that originated in the West such as *culture, visual arts,* and *fine arts* were first imported into Japan at this time. Artistic activities were developed based on the Western model, and, in addition, some existing artifacts in Japanese society were reconceptualized as "art" and "culture" (Sasaki 1995). The main focus of this reconceptualization and reconstruction of national culture was on visual arts and music because these arts were important in Western countries. The goal was to produce culture of an appropriate content and level for a modern nation-state. Schools for training in the visual arts and music were founded on the basis of Western systems, and instructors were brought from Europe and America. In 1886, for example, the government sent to all types of Japanese schools a mandate that required singing Western songs and playing Western musical instruments. At the same time, the central government sent students to Europe to acquire techniques and skills in literature, painting, and other arts.

In the early Meiji period, in order to bring about this radical reform in cultural systems, traditional cultures were at first neglected or devalued. There was a tendency to make direct comparisons based on European aesthetics and methods of expression. As a result, indigenous Japanese works were either discarded as obsolete or labeled as commercial products. Ironically, Japanese antiquities were in great demand in Europe and America during this period and were exported to those countries in large quantities. Belatedly the government became aware of the serious consequences of these exports; at the end of the century, legislation to protect and preserve cultural treasures was gradually put into effect.

Because the early Meiji government realized that Japanese traditional handicrafts had value as commodities, its arts policy was also directed by using these objects to create concrete benefits for the country. The government promoted exports of traditional arts and crafts and constructed art museums as part of a plan to promote Japanese industry. Japanese arts and crafts were also exhibited at major exhibitions in London and other big cities in Europe. The first "art museum" was built as an exhibition hall to display contemporary arts and crafts, along with agriculture, tools, and gardening (Sato 1996:176). In short, those traditional arts and crafts were regarded as commodities rather than art works.

For the Meiji government, culture and the arts were material for building national prestige; there was little interest in the arts and culture for the sake of aesthetic enjoyment. For most people, Western culture during the Meiji era was a new type of spectacle. For them, the term "art" referred to oil painting which was attractive because of its use of realistic techniques and perspective that were lacking in traditional Japanese paintings (Kinoshita 1993). Therefore, from the late Meiji era, department stores, newspaper companies, railways, and other private corporations performed important roles in meeting consumer demands for new and popular cultural items, taking on a role that was complementary to the government's cultural policy. In order to satisfy popular demand, department stores organized art exhibitions. They also founded orchestras, choral groups, and theaters. Newspapers sponsored concerts and art exhibits (Yoshimi 1992). The combination of a national cultural policy that emphasized high culture and private cultural enterprises that responded to consumer tastes is still evident today.

Theater and other popular entertainment were rarely dealt with in cultural policy but were often the subject of regulations as they were considered harmful to public morals. Especially at the beginning of the Meiji era, a movement could be seen by local governments to regulate events, such as spectacles, village plays, and festival dances, that might disturb public morals. As the government was trying to control this kind of "harm," it was simultaneously establishing the Education Agency and trying to figure out how to make use of popular entertainment for instruction and educational activities. Underlying the government's policies was a perception on the part of government officials of America and Europe as the Other, as representing a very different but prestigious culture. In other words, an important problem for the Meiji government was how to develop a general populace that would not be embarrassing when seen by people from "civilized" countries.

To summarize, the cultural policy of the Meiji era was based on the desire to emulate European culture. Cultural policy was intended to develop the nation's reputation among other nation-states. A major focus of this policy encompassed the visual arts, music, and the preservation of cultural properties. In the mid-1890s, this situation changed when the government began to actively use these Japanese works as a means of developing a form of culture that was specifically Japanese. However, little emphasis was placed on artistic creativity, an attitude that stems from the fact that traditional Japanese arts seldom valued innovation for its own sake. Innovation was generally confined to "testing the limits of familiar techniques and concepts, often by bridging native and Western elements" (Havens 1982:71). This suggests the difficulties that arose from trying to place "Japanese culture" within the framework of Western concepts of culture and art. This orientation toward creativity continued throughout most of the twentieth century, leading to stagnation in the production and promotion of contemporary arts. There are relatively few places in Japan where contemporary arts are performed or exhibited.

After World War II, the Japanese government became primarily concerned with the preservation of cultural monuments, artifacts, and techniques. The first epoch-making event in the postwar evolution of cultural policy was the enactment of the Cultural Properties Protection Act in 1950 after the wall paintings of Horyuji Temple were destroyed by fire in 1949. This bill targeted cultural treasures, architectural structures, and handicrafts as material objects; historical locations, scenic spots, and natural wonders as significant locations; theater, music, handicraft techniques, and other immaterial cultural products as intangibles; and folkloric customs, performances, costumes, furniture, and the like as folkloric cultural treasures. Even historic views in the environment that contained valuable works of traditional architecture were grouped into an architectural structures category for preservation.

Cultural policy in the postwar period was slow to develop, in part because of the history of government control of the arts and culture that began in the Meiji period and intensified during the years prior to World War II and during the war itself. Performing arts and the media were regulated and cultural activities were used to mobilize the public for the war effort. Western culture was prohibited. Since the Japanese term for cultural policy before 1945 could be interpreted as "control of culture," the use of the term was avoided for a long time and it was difficult to support the arts on a national level.

In the late 1960s, the Japanese government began a new policy of using culture and the arts to contribute to the public and national interest (Havens 1987). In 1968, the Agency for Cultural Affairs was created with the goals of encouraging artistic innovation and preserving cultural properties. The latter absorbed the majority of the agency's funds, including subsidies for national museums. A much smaller part of the agency's activities were grants to encourage creative activity (for example, only 3 percent of the budget in 1980 was allocated for commissions for creative activity) (p. 337). A large portion of the agency's funds for contemporary arts took the form of subsidies to federations of artists in major art genres rather than to individual artists. The federations in turn distributed the funds to their members. Funds for creative activity also included subsidies for symphony orchestras, opera companies, and ballet companies with the goal of enhancing Japan's standing as a cultured country. A third objective of the agency was to increase access to the arts outside the largest cities. Outreach programs run by the national government attempted to create a public for the arts by bringing exhibitions, concerts, and performing arts productions to local communities all over the country.

Until the 1980s, direct patronage of the arts by the government and by private organizations, such as business corporations, was underdeveloped. Funding for the Agency for Cultural Affairs had the lowest priority in the government's politically weakest ministry (Havens 1987:337). Artists working in traditional and modern genres obtained support for serious music, dance, theater, and visual art through commercial activities: sales of tickets, advertising, recording, radio and television, sales of products and services, and income from teaching (p. 332).

In the following sections, we will briefly review developments in cultural policies in Japan in recent years, based on the categories presented above. What are the factors that have led to changes in cultural policies in Japan? What problems have not changed?

Cultural Policy at the Regional Level

After the war, Japan's cultural policy expanded at the regional rather than the national level. In the 1960s and '70s, cultural administrators in progressive local governments across the country responded to citizens' movements that were attempting to regenerate towns in order to preserve the quality of life. In the context of rapid economic growth in the 1960s, people became alarmed that regional identities and traditions were disappearing. Local governments attempted to build better community environments through beautification projects and cultural activities. The goal was to improve the living standards and the culture of citizens so they would be motivated to stay in these communities for a long time.

A few innovative regions were able to implement structural reforms that made arts of all types available to the public. Culture and the arts became part of a unified administrative effort for the enhancement of the community. When a new public center was being built, a 1 percent tax was added for cultural activities, and an environmental assessment from a cultural standpoint was required. Instead of keeping artworks locked up in galleries and museums, they were used to enliven the community as public art in public places. In these regional movements, a strong official emphasis was placed on the third category of cultural policy, "Creation of new public values," although in fact these movements were also affected by a notion embodied in the first category, "Official recognition of existing works," of recognizing and popularizing in local areas the hitherto centralized "high" cultures (Umesao 1978). However, it should be noted that out of the more than three thousand prefectures, metropolitan districts, counties, cities, and townships, only an extremely small number have implemented this kind of innovative planning.

Construction of cultural centers was promoted because it fit local governments' ideas of cultural administration. In the 1970s and '80s, public cultural centers were constructed one after another. This corresponds to the second category of cultural policy: "Development of sites for official recognition of the arts." It began during a period of economic growth and led to the construction of more than 2,000 public buildings all over the country, ranging from multipurpose halls to specialty venues for concerts and theater, as well as 800 art museums. This building boom was supported, in part, because of its effects on the economy. Most of the public buildings constructed in the 1980s were so-called multipurpose halls, meaning that the policy was an easygoing one that did not judge the value of different types of art. Budgets for constructing public cultural facilities in Japan do not include investment in organizations that would produce or display culture in the buildings. It is often the case that construction itself is considered the principal objective of cultural policy. Such buildings do not establish exclusive agreements with particular theatrical troupes, orchestras, or other art groups. Instead, they are intended for a wide range of cultural activities. In fact, this meant that they were often "purposeless" halls that could not adequately house any cultural activity.

Though such spaces are not heavily used, they do fulfill important roles in providing venues for amateur cultural activities. Japan is, in an extreme sense, a country of the culture of Keiko (learning music, dance, and other cultural activities). Women especially devote a great deal of time to the practice of traditional arts, like haiku poetry and ink brush painting, and classical music. For this reason, the construction of cultural centers was welcomed as places for periodic public exhibition, rehearsal, or performance of these arts by amateurs. Amateur cultural activities are increasing in metropolitan areas.

In the 1990s, the emphasis on construction was severely criticized, while the support of creative activities became more important. People realized that no policies or programs were connected to the buildings that had been constructed. Therefore, the third category of cultural policy, "Creation of new public values," reappeared in a new version. Though the revitalization of communities was emphasized in town planning in the 1970s, the creation of "high-quality" art and culture was emphasized as symbols to be shared in communities in the 1990s. Because of the lack of information among regional government officials about arts administration, the Japan Foundation for Regional Arts was founded in 1994, under the wing of the Ministry of Home Affairs (present Ministry of Public Management, Home Affairs, Posts and Telecommunications) and with funding from the regional governments. Consequently, arts management also became important in the 1990s. This stage represents the fourth category of cultural policy, "Cultivation and management of cultural resources." At the same time, the national Agency for Cultural Affairs realized the need to support regional culture and developed a policy for supporting cultural activities in regional areas. The agency established the "Japan Arts Fund" by adopting the system of the Arts Council of England, and "Arts Plan 21" grants, as a national cultural subsidy policy. This policy provided an unprecedented, extensive subsidy framework for art and cultural projects and groups.[3] It marked the beginning of a shift from funding the construction of buildings for regional arts and cultural activities to funding cultural content.

Cultural Policy at the National Level

Despite these progressive changes, lack of recognition of the importance of art and culture in the central government (symbolized by the subordinate status of the Agency for Cultural Affairs under the Ministry of Education, Culture, Sports, Science, and Technology) continues to affect budget allocation for culture in Japan. The budget of the Agency for Cultural Affairs for 2000 is divided into two parts. Protection of cultural assets accounted for about 70 percent of the total, while promotion of arts and culture amounted to 30 percent (see fig. 3.1). This disparity indicates clearly that the cultural policies of Japan are inclined toward "official recognition of existing works," as in Category 1, and focus on "cultural properties," in particular, for which values are already established. As we have seen, this orientation has predominated in the postwar period.

If the Cultural Agency's budget is compared to the cultural budgets of European countries, the budget of the British Ministry of Culture, Sports, and Media is 11 times larger than Japan's, while that of France's Ministry of Culture and Communication is 14 times as large. If comparisons are made in terms of per capita spending, Japan spends 478 yen per person, while England spends 2,592 yen and France 4,334 yen.

This overview of postwar Japanese cultural policies indicates that the importance attached to various items in cultural policies shifted one after another to compensate for what was lacking. In the 1990s, policymakers started to demonstrate an outlook that was more positive than before for encouraging the arts. However, the priorities of the central government still remained very different from those of the regional and local governments. In 1994, 85 percent of the combined expenditure by all prefectural, metropolitan, and local governments for culture was spent for arts activities, and 15 percent for the preservation of cultural treasures. Of the proportion spent for arts activities, 41 percent went toward arts projects and management of facilities, while 59 percent was spent on the construction of buildings. By contrast, the central government's Agency for Cultural Affairs devoted two-thirds of its funds to the preservation of cultural treasures and one-third to promotion of the arts.

Organizational survival and acquisition of funds from government budgets are very important goals for administrative organizations in general and arts administrative organizations in particular. It cannot be denied that policies tend to be adopted and implemented for these purposes. As mentioned above, cultural centers were constructed in the 1980s, with the emphasis placed on economic benefits, and interest in the creation

Category	FY 2000	FY 2001	Growth rate
Ordinary national accounts	¥84,987.053 billion	¥82,652.379 billion	△2.7%
Ordinary expenditure	¥48,091.352 billion	¥48,658,880 billion	1.2%
Expenditure on national bonds	¥21,965.341 billion	¥17,170.534 billion	△21.8%
Local allocation for grants, etc.	¥14,930.360 billion	¥16,822.965 billion	12.7%
General accounts of the Ministry of Education (A)	¥6,512.920 billion	¥6,578.394 billion	1.0%
Agency for Cultural Affairs (B) (Ratio of B to A)	¥80.933 billion 1.24%	¥90.949 billion 1.38%	12.4%

Breakdown of the ACA's Fiscal 2001 Budget

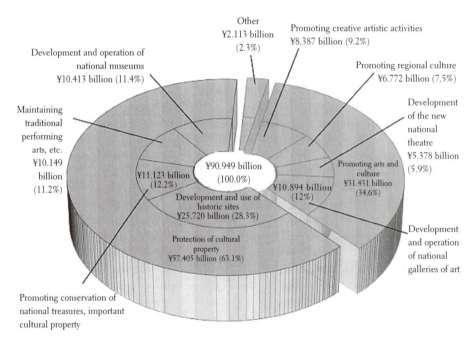

Figure 3.1 Budget of the Agency of Cultural Affairs

of public culture relegated to a secondary position. Currently, the scheme to reorganize the national museum into an independent administrative juridical entity, now in progress, aims to separate its budget from other sources rather than spinning it off as an autonomous operation. In this manner, cultural policies in Japan are often strongly affected by priorities that have little to do with "culture." Although such a tendency may be seen to some degree in any society, the bias toward the protection of cultural assets and construction of buildings indicates its importance in Japan.

One reason why organizational interests affect the implementation of cultural policies is that a precise conception of what contemporary Japanese culture should be like, which could provide a basis for rejecting purely administrative imperatives, has not been established. In other words, questions remain concerning the fundamental purposes of cultural policies and of systems related to such policies. It is not clear what types of cultural policies are needed as Japanese society becomes increasingly diversified.

Support for the Arts from the Private Sector

Corporate sponsorship of arts organizations is well developed in Japan. In the early years of the twentieth century, the first Japanese corporate foundations were established, often influenced by business relationships in the United States that brought corporate leaders into contact with philanthropic activities by wealthy American corporations. Wealthy entrepreneurs established museums that made their extensive collections of art available to the public. Currently, 55 Japanese corporations run their own museums or galleries. Establishing corporate foundations is one of the typical patterns of corporate support for the arts in Japan. Between 1985 and 1989, 79 corporate foundations were established, particularly by companies in industries with rising stock prices. However, only about 20 percent of corporate foundations support the fields of culture, education, and the arts. Many of these foundations have been experiencing financial problems because of low interest rates since 1990.

When the Japanese yen became stronger against the dollar in 1985, Japanese corporations took advantage of the favorable exchange rate and started to build more factories overseas, particularly in the United States. Partly as a result of their experience with the American business environment, Japanese corporations became aware of ideas such as "community relations" and "corporate philanthropy," which were little known in Japanese society. They began to think about what corporations could contribute to the community as "corporate citizens." During the late 1980s, which coincided with the peak of the so-called "bubble economy," corporate philanthropy began to take root in Japan.

The Japanese Federation of Economic Organization (Keidanren), one of the most powerful business organizations in Japan, acted as a go-between for fund-raisers and potential corporate donors, helping to decide the amount of the donation to be given by each company. In a group-oriented society such as Japan, Keidanren's consultation was appreciated in the sense that each company knew how much it was expected to contribute so that it would not lose face with its competitors. During the early years of Japanese corporate philanthropy, the major factors which determined the level of contributions were: (a) the merits of the project; (b) the benefits to the company; and (c) the identity of the fund-raiser. Donations were usually regarded as a way to show gratitude or friendship, and therefore the amounts were not restricted.

Based on American examples of corporations that contribute 1 to 3 percent of their profits to philanthropy, the so-called One-Percent Club was created within the Federation. This club is a voluntary group of federation members who are encouraged to spend 1 percent or more of their profits on philanthropic activities. In 1997, average spending on corporate philanthropy among One-Percent Club members was 2.81 percent of their annual profits. However, only 8.3 percent of their annual spending on philanthropy went to the arts and culture in that year.

In 1990, the formation of the Association for Corporate Support of the Arts played an important role in furthering the notion of corporate philanthropy in the field of the arts. Since its initiation, this association has encouraged business support for the arts by providing consultation services and organizing seminars and workshops in order to close the distance between the business sector and artists. About one-third of the companies that belong to the association have developed their own arts centers, such as concert halls, galleries, museums, and theaters (Association for Corporate Support of the Arts 1996). In 1994, the association received nonprofit foundation status, which meant that art projects approved by the association and funded by corporations have tax-exemption advantages.

In terms of the four categories of cultural spending discussed above, Japanese corporations engage in more than simply providing cultural centers. They also contribute to artistic innovation by supporting new trends in contemporary music, visual art, and theater. A few corporations have shaped urban neighborhoods by building elaborate complexes including theaters, concert halls, art museums, restaurants, and stores. For example, a major international arts complex in Tokyo belongs to a conglomerate of retail, transport, and real estate businesses.

Japanese Cultural Policies: Emerging Trends

In general, two major directions in recent national cultural policies can be identified. One is to support diverse activities in the private sector, as seen in the United States (Zemans and Kleingartner et al. 1999:113–202), and the other is for the government to attempt to address issues of national identity, as seen in France and other European countries (D'Angelo and Vespérini 1998:23). Whichever direction Japan follows regarding cultural policies, Japan will be required to come to terms with the issues of setting priorities for culture and with clarifying the bases for cultural policies.

Japanese cultural policies are still focused on high culture and have not supported popular culture and the culture industries seriously, in contrast to cultural policies in the United States and France. It is ironic that Japanese popular culture, which has been neglected by government policymakers, has been produced and exported very successfully by Japanese cultural industries. On the other hand, high culture in Japan, which is the main objective of government policymakers, is still largely based on Western imports, as it was at the end of the nineteenth century.

Those in charge of making cultural policy have not considered seriously what would be needed to contribute to the advancement of high culture in Japan. That is why Japanese artists (with the exception of a few very successful ones) have been forced to make their living by giving lessons and have developed an apprenticeship system, mutual aid societies, and trade associations to maintain their rights and interests. In other words, cultural organizations that provide support for "art worlds" (Becker 1982) have been ineffective in Japan, and voluntary networks of artists and a handful of patrons have attempted to make up for this weakness. As a result, the art market in Japan is also immature, and activities for the promotion of artists and distribution of artworks are underdeveloped. Cultural policymakers in Japan have not been concerned with the improvement of the creative environment. As a result, Japanese cultural policies are unlikely to contribute to artistic change and the democratization of culture in the sense of increasing its accessibility. In short, they lack a sophisticated strategy for developing *social distinction*.

Although the Agency for Cultural Affairs publishes statistics and references on cultural activities, these are limited to information about its annual budget and the numbers of public cultural centers all over Japan. There are few policy papers on arts and culture, and it is possible to extract only fragmentary information about cultural policy from government reports.

In the United States and other countries, officially subsidized groups have a responsibility to justify their use of funds to the subsidy provider. However, this is not yet the case in Japan. Cultural organizations in Japan have rarely been exposed to public scrutiny in that they are virtually exempt from the responsibility to justify expenses or release financial statements. Few grant programs include provisions for peer review. Such indulgence is being reconsidered, and accountability from governmental bodies is now expected by the public.

Moreover, several new trends in Japanese cultural policy in local communities indicate that stress is being placed on public accountability. In discussions about priorities and in actual policies in recent years, concerns about the needs of the public rather than the quality of the arts and culture have predominated as the bases for decisions about culture. In other words, the promotion of culture on the local level tends to be justified in terms of its benefits for citizens, rather than aiming at the development of art itself. For example, the campaign to construct resident art theaters in communities can be cited as consistent with this directive (Ei 1997). The goal of this campaign is to produce dramas based in particular communities to encourage citizens' participation, and to use theaters as the nodes of new forms of communication in these communities. In this case, the administration for community culture is definitely positioned toward the extension of social policy; art activities are used as a means to bolster the needs of the community; and a key point is exchanges through direct participation in a creative process. According to Ei, cultural policies in communities should subscribe to a theory different from that involved in the promotion of artistic creation: what needs to be guaranteed is the benefits of art and culture for the citizen.

In contrast to this approach, a more "art-oriented" approach has appeared. Its adherents make the radical proposal of contributing to cultural life on the local level by enhancing the aesthetic aspects of cultural activities and seeking citizens' consensus for ignoring their economic utility, thereby paradoxically aiming at the social distinction of communities. This could be seen as an application to groups of the "social distinction" strategy (Bourdieu 1984). There are a few proposals based on this theory. Regarding public art museums in the future, for example, Iwabuchi (1998) proposes an emphasis on art museums as a special type of organization that promotes research on beauty and contributes to the aesthetic needs of communities rather than emphasizing the museum as a place for social education.

While prioritizing artistic creativity in local communities has high potential, it also runs the risk of triggering controversy regarding "freedom of expression" or the appropriateness of the purchase and exhibition of artworks as public goods. A number of controversies have arisen concerning these problems at public art museums in Tochigi (Tomooka 1999) and Toyama (Forum on the Toyama Prefectural Modern Art Museum 1994) prefectures and Tokyo Metropolis.

Still another approach can be found in Fukuoka, a city located in the southern part of Japan, near other Asian countries, which has developed a unique outlook. Since the late 1980s, it has focused on exchanges and trade with Asian countries, while the central government and the rest of Japan have looked toward the West. For example, it has introduced Asian culture to its citizens by facilitating various cultural events such as "Asia Month," "Asia Focus Film Festival," "Fukuoka Asia Award" and so on. It has also constructed buildings for cultural activities such as an "integrated" library that houses a minitheater for showing Asian films and the Fukuoka Asia Museum for exhibiting Asian arts. Fukuoka has established a reputation as the most attractive and active city in Asia.

An important problem remains regarding the nature of cultural policies in communities. Whichever is preferred, art or the interests of citizens, the problem is who has the right to judge cultural quality and needs. In Japan, cultural policies are always talked about in terms of the needs and interests of one's own group. However, most people are not conscious of their cultural needs. Under the banner of egalitarianism in favor of "public culture" and "democratization of culture," power dynamics will potentially reemerge. If so, the political problems implied in the support of public culture are likely to become more salient. It may be necessary to reconsider how groups, societies, publics, and democracy relate to culture.

Conclusion

The evolution of cultural policy in Japan reveals that the central government's role became increasingly restricted during the twentieth century, with private organizations and local governments performing major roles as cultural providers. The absence of a concept of a nonprofit organization (until very recently) has meant that arts activities that had narrow audience appeal and that required the development of new aesthetic tastes received little support. In the 1970s and 1980s, private and local resources were squandered on extensive and ill-defined construction projects for arts buildings. By the last decade of the twentieth century, the need for the central government to take a more directive role in cultural policy had become evident. New legislation permitted the creation of nonprofit organizations that would promote and nurture innovative artistic activities. The central government began to move away from its focus upon "official recognition of existing works" toward "the creation of new public values" and "cultivation and management of cultural resources."

In these initiatives, policymakers faced the problem of overcoming an orientation that had influenced Japanese cultural policy throughout its history, specifically a bias in favor of established aesthetic values, either those of Western culture or those of traditional Japanese culture. The reluctance to fund new artistic initiatives stemmed from an unwillingness to face the uncertainty of aesthetic values that is always inherent in new artistic developments. An emphasis on the construction of buildings and the protection of cultural properties was a means of avoiding the necessity of making difficult aesthetic decisions. This type of attitude among cultural policy makers was also manifested in their reluctance to submit the bases for their decisions to public scrutiny. In the twenty-first century, as Japan, like other industrial nations, becomes both more culturally diversified internally and more heavily targeted by external sources of global media and popular culture, the task of developing government priorities for cultural policy and new directions for the future will become increasingly challenging.

Notes

The authors wish to express their gratitude to Naoko Shimamura, International House of Japan, Inc., for her valuable advice concerning this study and to Ikuya Sato for reading and commenting on an earlier version of the manuscript.

1. As will be explained later, there are variations in cultural policies in this respect.

2. These are, of course, ideal types. Glorification activities and art festivals, for example, are not separable in reality. Buildings for cultural activities have a symbolic aspect that includes the characteristics featured in category 3. The important point here is the goal for which the policy is primarily planned and implemented.

3. The budget for Arts Plan 21 was 3.26 billion yen in 1996 and 4.95 billion yen in 2000.

References

Association for Corporate Support of the Arts (1996) *White Paper on Private Patronage, 1996,* Tokyo: Diamond.

Becker, H. S. (1982) *Art Worlds,* Berkeley: University of California Press.

Bennett, T. (1995) *The Birth of the Museum: History, Theory, Politics,* New York and London: Routledge.

Bennett, T. (1998) *Culture: A Reformer's Science,* London: Allen & Unwin.

Bourdieu, P. (1984) *Distinction: A social critique of the judgment of taste,* Cambridge, MA: Harvard University Press.

D'Angelo, M. and Vespérini, P. (1998) *Cultural Policies in Europe: A Comparative Approach,* Strasbourg: Council of Europe Publishing.

Ei, K. (1997) *Geijutsu Bunka Gyosei To Chiiki Shakai: Rejidento Shiata Eno Dezain (Arts Policy and Community: A Design for Resident Theatre),* Tokyo: Teatoro.

Forum on the Toyama Prefectural Modern Art Museum (ed.) (1994) *The Public Museum and Representation of the Emperor* (in Japanese), Toyama: Katsurashobo.

Havens, T. R. H. (1982) *Artist and Patron in Postwar Japan*. Princeton: Princeton University Press.

Havens, T. R. H. (1987) 'Government and the arts in contemporary Japan,' pp. 333–349 in M. C. Cummings, Jr. and R. S. Katz (eds.) *The Patron State*. New York: Oxford University Press.

Iwabuchi, J. (1998) 'Nihongata Bijutshukan No Kanosei (Potential of Japanese-Style Art Museums),' pp.21–32 in National Institute for Research Advancement, *Arts Management and Cultural Policy: Research on Initiatives for Cultural Policies in Japan* (in Japanese), Tokyo: NIRA.

Kinoshita, N. (1993) *Bijutsu to iu Misemono (Arts as Show)*, Tokyo: Heibonsha.

Kitazawa, N. (1989) *Me no Shinden: "Bijutsu" Juyo-shi Note (Shrine of Eye: Notes on the History of the Reception of "Fine Arts")*, Tokyo: Bijutsushuppansha.

Martinez, D. P. (1998) *The Worlds of Japanese Popular Culture*, Cambridge: Cambridge University Press.

Sasaki, K. (1995) *Bigaku Jiten (Dictionary of Aesthetics)*, Tokyo: Tokyodaigakushuppankai.

Sato, D. (1996) <*Nihon Bijutsu*> *Tanjo (Birth of Japanese Fine Arts)*, Tokyo: Kodansha.

Tomooka, K. (1999) 'Kokyo Bunka Kochiku Ni Okeru Takuetsuka Senryaku (Distinction Strategy for Construction of Public Culture),' *Bunka Keizaigaku (Cultural Economics)*, 6:19–28.

Umesao, T. (1978) 'Chiiki Syakai To Bunka (Community and Culture),' pp. 45–92 in Bunka-cho (the Agency for Cultural Affairs) (eds.) *Nihon Bunka Koza 1* (Lectures on Japanese Culture 1), Tokyo: Gyosei.

Yoshimi, S. (1992) *Hakurankai no Seijigaku (Politics of Exhibition)*, Tokyo: Chuokoronsha.

Zemans, J. and A. Kleingartner with M. J. Wyszomirski, M. Watanabe, and Associates. (1999) *Comparing Cultural Policy: A Study of Japan and the United States*, Thousand Oaks, CA: Altamira Press.

4

A Drama of Change

Cultural Policy and the Performing Arts in Southeast Asia

Jennifer Lindsay

The influence that national government policy and structures for culture exert upon the shape and survival of prenational "traditional" performing arts in Southeast Asia has interested scholars for some time.[1] Given the rapid economic, social, and political change in the region over the past 50 years or so and the emergence from colonial domination of nations that state their new nationhood in cultural terms (against an arbitrary political unity imposed by the previous colonial power), the theater of cultural change that is part of this process is itself a dramatic performance to observe.

Staged before us is a drama of change extending over two or three generations. In all societies, cultural forms are intimately linked to a sense of social and national identity. The latter is both expanding and contracting, for, on the one hand, becoming nationally aware provides a larger consciousness and a place in an international arena, but, on the other hand, national consciousness forces an awareness of one's cultural origins as merely regional or infranational. In the societies of postcolonial Southeast Asia, as their sense of identity shifts with each generation and moves toward a new national reality, so are prenational cultural forms called into question. In this context, what is the purpose of performing arts? What is their meaning as "heritage"? What role had performing arts played previously, and what role do they play now? How do the priorities of nationhood and national identity, and the image the nation wishes to portray of itself internationally all affect the form, status, and support for the performing arts?

The focus of much recent writing has been in two main areas—the redefinition of prenational performing arts into nationally acceptable ideals of "tradition" and "identity," and the role of tourism in redefining and commodifying cultural forms.[2] In both cases, the tendency is to view national cultural policy and government structures as an outside agent of change (usually the major outside agent of change), that forces prenational, regional performance into new forms. The direction is portrayed as entirely top down, with the imposition from above of undesirable requirements forcing undesirable changes. While this top-down process exists and does indeed effect drastic change, homogenization, and even obliteration of previously vibrant cultural variety, it is not the whole story. I would like to suggest a more symbiotic scenario: that we should observe cultural policy as part of cultural expression in Southeast Asia—and that government structures, funding, and policies are not only something superimposed upon indigenous, regional, traditional, infranational cultural forms, but are themselves also formed by the context within which these forms exist.

Cultural policy, legislation, bureaucracy, and education are all part of a context within which cultural forms work and function. Though scholars writing on contemporary cultural policy in Southeast Asia have identified and lamented the situation of government control as effectively altering and destroying traditional performing arts, through either heavy-handed intervention, misguided policies, or neglect, no attention has been given to the symbiotic relationship between cultural policy and cultural context. Without viewing this broader picture we cannot become more informed about why the current situation exists. Why is it, for example, that governments can so easily take on the role of national cultural arbiter, and why is this role so easily accepted, even by artists themselves? Understanding the culture of cultural policy in Southeast Asia is not to promote an apologetic stance in the face of negative aspects of state cultural control, but rather to suggest that a broader understanding of how the situation works may be better preparation for changing it.

Contemporary systems of and ideas about cultural policy in Southeast Asia at a national level have strong links with traditional cultural practices within each country, and also exhibit some strong similarities within the region. With regard to the performing arts, government policies for their development, preservation, or perpetration are grounded in concepts about what performing arts are for, the expectations of both donor and recipient of patronage, and the role of performers and of audiences in society. While national policies may be new and intrusive upon the intrinsic identity of performance forms, the concepts underlying these policies are not necessarily new. Often they appear to be grounded in very "traditional" practices and ideas about the role of performance as art, and of its patrons, performers, and audiences.

In this chapter, I will discuss some of the interrelationships I see as significant between national policy, administrative structure, and support for the performing arts in the region, and the way that performing arts exist and change. I will emphasize how policy, structure, and funding are shaped by ways that people think that the performing arts should exist, do exist, and have existed in the past. I will consider three elements in the performing arts complex: the overall national governmental administrative structure, the performers, and the audience.

Cultural Policy and Government Administrative Structure

Governmental administrative structures for culture and statements of national cultural policy indicate both the social approach to culture and the cultural role of the state.[3] The prominence given to culture in Southeast Asia both socially and in terms of national policy is demonstrated by the fact that all of the countries in the region name culture within a government ministry (or the equivalent of a ministry), and most established a government portfolio for culture very soon after independence.

The speed with which the new postcolonial Southeast Asian nations set up government portfolios specifically for culture indicates the importance placed on culture in establishing nationhood. From the outset, culture was identified as a state-directed tool of national identity. In Indonesia, where the debate about cultural heritage and national identity had been raging long before independence, the government department for culture was established immediately in 1945. In Malaysia, the first full agency for culture at ministerial level was established in 1964, seven years after independence. The Philippines established a culture department within the Department of Education when this department was established in July 1947, the year following independence. In the case of Thailand, the only non-postcolonial nation among those discussed here, the government agency for culture (Department of Fine Arts) was established in 1933 as part of the state's new independence under the constitutional monarchy, the year after the system of absolute monarchy was overthrown, with an emphasis not on the creation of something new, but on turning into public property a cultural heritage that was previously attached to the institution of monarchy (Rutnin 1993:189). In 1942, this department became the Bureau for Culture, and was upgraded to a ministry in 1952.

Most countries in the region have shifted culture among various government portfolios, or restructured the total portfolio of the ministry under which culture falls: Malaysia moved culture from its grouping with Youth and Sports to Culture, Arts, and Tourism, Singapore from Community Development to Information and the Arts, and Vietnam removed sport from its previous Culture, Information, and Sport. Indonesia did not alter its original ministry grouping for culture for 53 years. Culture was linked with education from the ministry's establishment in 1945, initially as the Ministry of Education and Culture, but from 1966 called the Department of Education and Culture. Only in the last cabinet of the Soeharto era in early 1998 was the portfolio split, when a new ministry for "arts" (*seni*) and tourism was named, keeping "culture" (*kebudayaan*) with education. Since then, culture has been progressively removed from the Ministry of Education, and, following the Malaysian model, culture is now linked together with tourism. Only Thailand has had a ministry solely for culture—from 1952 until 1958. After that, culture was subsumed into the Ministry of Education, then to the Department of Religious Affairs, and in 1979 back to the Ministry of Education.

Second, the placement of culture overall within a government ministry suggests both the role that society sees culture to have and the role that the government wishes it to have, and I would contend that the former informs the latter. Therefore, where societies stress an educative role for cultural forms (the arts, language, literature), this translates with ease to a national educative role for culture in forming national identity (including fostering national language, for example). From building the person, or building the kingdom, comes building the nation. Linking education and culture in a government ministry (Philippines, Thailand, and formerly, Indonesia) is a natural progression. The shift to place culture with tourism represents a shift in perception of both what "culture" comprises, and of its role, as the focus moves more to commodification and display. In Indonesia, the recent changes effectively narrow the definition of "culture," as those aspects of culture sharply aligned to national identity—particularly activities for the promotion and maintenance of the national language (Indonesian) which were previously grouped with culture—have been placed in the education portfolio.

Thailand is the only country in the region where culture has been overtly linked with religion through placing them together within one ministry. The more homogeneous structure of Thai society, particularly in terms of religion, makes this possible, but the noncolonial past of Thailand also allows for a broader statement of cultural policy in terms of preserving a heritage that has served it well in the past rather than the more forward-looking definitions of postcolonial nation building, and the Thai heritage is a tight amalgam of monarch, the arts, and religion. Religion-as-culture is encapsulated in the official Thai definition of culture as a "way of life," and expressed in the official policy of preservation and protection of cultural identity that is largely defined through religion. Although culture is again under the Ministry of Education (where it began), there is still close liaison with the Ministry for Religion on policy matters.[4]

Malaysia, like the Philippines and Indonesia, states its cultural policy in terms of building national identity, yet in Malaysia the government culture portfolio has never been part of the Ministry of Education. As in Singapore and Brunei, culture is defined more narrowly in terms of entertainment and community leisure activity, and categories that elsewhere in the region fall under the cultural portfolio (libraries, national language) come in Malaysia under the aegis of a separate Ministry of Education. The role of culture as community activity is shown through culture initially (1953) being placed under "youth activities" within the Ministry of Social Welfare, and later at ministerial level together with youth and sport, and most recently tourism. Since the racial riots of 1969, Malaysia's cultural policy has been articulated in racial and religious terms of Malay culture and Islam. However, perhaps because culture (at least the performing arts) is treated as community activity and entertainment rather than a "way of life" as in Thailand, there is no administrative link between the culture department within the Ministry of Tourism and the Division of Islamic Affairs within the Prime Minister's Department.[5]

In practical terms, what culture is paired with—education, information, or tourism—has implications for levels of funding, priorities for development, and general approach. For example, though the link of culture and education indicates an educative national role for culture, this combination is not necessarily beneficial to the culture partner, for the funds dedicated to it are disproportionately small—tiny—in comparison to education. If linked with information, the line of government control, or the potential for control, seems to be tighter as the links between the administration for culture and government-controlled media are closer (and in both Singapore and Vietnam there is also relatively strict control on the entry of foreign media). Where culture is linked with tourism, or with youth and sport, and culture operates as community activity or entertainment as in the case of Malaysia, this also has far-reaching implications for the legislation regarding imported foreign cultural activity.

The Culture Portfolio

The placement of culture as a portfolio within a government ministry is a matter of administrative practicality, but this indicates a social and cultural emphasis of operation. Though this placement may differ, the activities of the culture departments in Southeast Asia show more similarities than differences.

Within the portfolio for culture, all the countries in the region include performing arts, visual arts, museums, monuments, and shrines—in other words, the material and expressive heritage of the nation. For the arts, the culture departments administer funds for activities and research and support national troupes (where these exist). The responsibility for arts education and training shifts (and is often split) between the portfolios for culture and for education depending on whether culture is itself within a Ministry of Education, and also on the vocational versus academic orientation of the training. Most culture portfolios include language and literature (Brunei, Thailand, Philippines, and, until 2000, Indonesia). Vietnam includes publishing and film. Libraries fall within the cultural portfolio everywhere except Indonesia, where under the National Library they are supervised as an autonomous agency (but this is now under review), and Malaysia, where libraries are under the Ministry of Education.

"Culture" in the culture portfolio is, then, generally synonymous with "arts and heritage," other than in Thailand, where, as we have seen, it refers to a way of life. Indonesia includes "cultural values" within the culture portfolio as part of the heritage of expressive culture. The Philippines has special committees for minority cultures.

Performing Arts

Assistance to performing artists through the government cultural agencies in Southeast Asia is predominantly directed from above rather than applied for from below. State cultural agencies act as patrons bestowing project funds and rewards rather than as service organizations reacting to applications from the artistic community. Artists and troupes do not usually apply for grants for their own projects but are appointed as part of a project devised by a state cultural office (or center) at the national or regional level, and a lucky few may receive awards in recognition of their work. Only the Philippines and Singapore have established a formal advertised system of grants for which individual and independent artists may apply, and where the decision makers for the grants include advisors outside the government. In both cases the infrastructure for this is relatively recent (the National Arts Council in Singapore was set up in 1991, and the National Commission for Culture and the Arts in the Philippines was established in 1992), and the grant amounts are still relatively small.

Elsewhere, government funds for performing arts activities are used to support a government infrastructure of venues, cultural centers, arts councils—the use of which may be given for free or for cheap rental to performing artists as a type of production or venue grant. (In Singapore and the Philippines this earlier system still also applies). To be accepted for such assistance, performers must apply to the local organization that is in charge of the venue. However, the government cultural venues are heavily used for government projects, especially festivals and competitions that are a feature of the performing arts scene in Southeast Asia and absorb a major part of government funding.

Direct assistance to performers is more often in the form of national awards or as a reward for service to the community. In Vietnam, the Department of Performing Arts used to be responsible for the national performance troupes, which once received full government support, but have now had their subsidies cut or removed. In Thailand, the Department of Fine Arts is responsible for the national troupes.

State institutions giving training in the performing arts also fall within the cultural portfolio where those institutions have a strong vocational emphasis. In Vietnam, this refers to all the training institutions; in Thailand it is only the college that is linked to the National Theater; in Malaysia, the National Arts Academy. In Indonesia and the Philippines, the state institutions teaching performing arts come under the aegis of the education portfolio. (Singapore has no state centers of performance training).

Before leaving this section on government administration, a special mention must be made of Singapore—for there, unlike elsewhere, the government agency for culture acts not only as grant giver and policy director but as entrepreneur. In Singapore, the government owns all the major performance venues and rents them out as a commercial enterprise. The National Arts Council also acts in a profit-making mode as presenter of performances, especially imported foreign performances. While unusual in the Southeast Asian setup just outlined, in fact it is perfectly in keeping with Singapore's own identity as an entrepôt, maintained since its establishment by Sir Thomas Stamford Raffles in 1819. The performing arts are treated in a traditional Singaporean manner, namely the same way as any other marketable commodity imported or assembled for sale. Singaporean cultural administration functions within its own specific social setting.

The procedures of cultural funding for the performing arts through the government infrastructures in Southeast Asia strengthen the role of the state as patron and employer (and in Singapore, as merchant-impresario).

The Performers

In all of Southeast Asia, the full-time professional performer is the exception. The great majority of performers (dancers, actors, musicians) work within a system that has long existed, of part-time work as an artist (often in tandem with other unrelated work), being paid per commissioned performance. These performances may be for family celebrations (weddings, circumcisions, births), religious ceremonies (Easter pageants, Buddhist temple festivals), village or urban occasions (blessing a new house or harvest, celebrating the new year), or government events (national holiday, visits of state officials, openings of conferences).

The better the performer, the more popular the group, the higher the commissions and the better chance the performer has of making a living from performing. Even so, most troupes are tied into celebration seasons—the wedding season, the harvest season, and so forth, and times of relatively full employment are interspersed with times of no employment at all. Furthermore, some forms of traditional performing arts have a wider appeal or wider application for a variety of celebrations than others (*wayang kulit*, shadow puppet performance, compared to *tayuban*, popular female dance, for example), so their performers have more chances to get work. Some forms are more limited in opportunities for commission, either because of cost or inappropriateness. A Javanese *bedhaya* (court group female dance) performance could only be "hired" by those of equal status as its place of origin, the palace—such as the government or foreign festivals. Their performers can no longer be specialists in one genre; to find work they must be flexible.

The living of a performer is precarious, and today, as 60 years ago, performers seek out patronage for some stability in employment. Then, those patrons were palaces, temples, wealthy aficionados, and radio stations. Today, they are the government departments and institutions, businesses and corporations, television stations and, of course, still the wealthy aficionados. But while the system of patronage itself is merely perpetuated in a modern setting, the new patrons have new tastes and different reasons for their choice of performances to sponsor, and they also have more power. A traditional patron in a village may choose local musicians to play at his daughter's wedding because of their musical skill, while a government agency acting in a traditional manner as patron will be concerned with ideas of national identity, acceptability, and image.

Opportunities for employment in a full-time government-supported national company are few. Thailand's national theater and dance companies employ about 350 artists as civil servants on salary, and Vietnam still subsidizes artists in some national companies. Elsewhere, government "salaries" are seasonal or consist of honorariums. In the Philippines, the resident companies at the Cultural Center receive seasonal salaries or honorariums. Performers in the National Cultural Center in Kuala Lumpur are also on honorariums (or short-term contracts). But where no single identifiable "national" form of music, theater or dance exists, as in a country like Indonesia, the choice of any one performance form for government sponsorship as a "national" company is not politically viable.

Performers seek access to state funds by aligning themselves with government institutions, venues, government-supported celebrations, projects, festivals, and competitions. In doing so, they are forced to comply with government-determined standards. The funding structure makes it unlikely that government subsidies will be granted to performers who want to mount projects and performances of their own definition. The more usual scenario is for performers to be invited to participate in a performance set up as a government project whether that be a national or regional festival, a tour abroad, research into threatened performance genres, or public performances to celebrate national holidays.

As the government is a powerful potential patron, it pays performers to align themselves with government institutions. National television and radio stations provide an important source of work (especially in Malaysia), but generally the state training centers for the arts are the places to be. These schools provide not only a pool of performers for selection for government-sponsored performances and travel abroad, but a source of government employment as teachers, usually with the status of civil servants (in

Indonesia, Malaysia, Vietnam, and Thailand). In a country like Indonesia, the government employment of performers as bureaucrats-teachers (via the Directorate General of Higher Education) is the major government support given directly to performers.

Business and corporate sponsorship also play a major role in supporting the performing arts in Southeast Asia. Performers request sponsorship from banks, newspapers, oil companies, and other businesses that are generous in their support, either in cash or in kind. It is important for performers to maintain and develop a close personal network with friends who have access to corporate ears; family connections are even better. Apart from cash support, sponsors also provide an alternative physical infrastructure. For example, in Malaysia, the state oil company (Petronas), runs an art gallery and performance space given to selected artists free of charge, and the major newspapers frequently sponsor performances. In Indonesia, the publishing chain of the major weekly journal (*Tempo*) supports a number of small venues used for exhibitions, meetings, rehearsals, and discussions. Other journals and newspapers also spend generously on such sponsorship.

Corporate donations generally are not tax deductible. Only Singapore has formalized a system of tax incentives for donations to the arts. (A system is being set up in the Philippines). In Thailand, arts sponsorship falls into a traditional Buddhist practice of gaining merit through donation. Elsewhere, corporate sponsors in Southeast Asia support the arts to appear as good corporate citizens and indeed to foster a public image as patrons. To be an arts patron is the traditionally expected role of the wealthy. However, the intricate link between business and politics in Southeast Asia, especially in countries like Malaysia, Indonesia, and Singapore (particularly evident at times of oppressive control, such as Indonesia's Soeharto era) also ensures that corporate sponsorship will not be forthcoming for controversial material offensive to the government. Corporate sponsorship is entwined with the overall system of state patronage.

An alternative avenue for performers to obtain government funding as direct assistance is through regional, state, or provincial governments, where funds allotted for expenditure at the discretion of the state minister or governor may be spent on cultural activities, and are often given as assistance to performing groups in financial difficulty, for costumes, musical instruments, the repair of performance venues, and so on. Such support is often at the whim of the state or provincial governor (and his wife). Again, performers must develop good personal connections with state or regional officials to keep open potential channels of assistance.

Performers still gravitate to sources of patronage. Even with rapidly increasing levels of business sponsorship, the government continues to be the most significant source of such patronage. But patronage comes with a price, and that price is loyalty. From the performers' point of view, then, the context of employment—as a dancer in a national dance troupe, a teacher at a state academy, a musician touring abroad on a government-funded cultural mission, or an actor paid by the local arts council to perform in a regional theater festival for a national holiday—is not essentially different from a prenational context of a dancer being taken into the palace as a retainer, a musician being invited to perform in a temple festival, or an acting troupe called in to perform at the house of a noble to entertain his guests.

The government acts in the way a patron is traditionally expected to act—nominating the kind of performance, choosing the performers, vetting undesirable elements, favoring those whose performance pleases, and rejecting those whose performance offends. The performers in return display loyalty and gratitude. For what they have received is not merely money and is not a grant that is seen as an individual artist's right to anonymous public funds; rather they have been given status as those chosen to have noblesse bestowed upon them.[6]

The Audience

A major factor that shapes performing arts in Southeast Asia is the pattern of their consumption. In one sense, the context of performance has changed radically from an overwhelmingly ceremonial or ritual prenational context of many "traditional" performances to a secular postcolonial and contemporary context. However, in another sense, the transformation of context is not radical at all, and the process of commodification is not as thorough as may first appear. For although, in the past, performances were commissioned by individuals, palaces, temples, or communities for a ceremonial event, the pattern of commissioning continues in contemporary national secular ceremonial contexts, with the state and businesses as patrons.[7] The traces of traditional performance context in contemporary official commissioned performances extend beyond the authority of the commissioner. As with performances in a village, the audience is invited, and its members are not anonymous to the host, to the performers, or to each other; the performance itself is expected to have a high level of familiarity for its audience, and is also expected to be both entertaining and contemporary in relating directly to the ceremony or event at hand.

Invited audiences are captive audiences. They have not exercised choice in selecting a type of performance they wish to see. An audience at a state function sees a performance that has been chosen for it. So do people invited to a corporate function, the public at a festival or competition, or guests at a wedding. Until the blossoming of commercial television stations in the 1990s, national television also beamed via a single channel to captive audiences—they could turn off the TV, but not switch to an alternative channel. Captive audiences exist even for national performing companies that sell tickets for admission. In Thailand, for example, the government-subsidized National Theater charges for admission. It performs *khon* (masked drama) and *lakhon* (dance-drama) for the public, and the performances are well attended. However, it is school groups that form the largest proportion of their audience, for the study of classic Thai drama is part of the school curriculum (Rutnin 1993:201). Although the performances are open to the general public, in fact the audience is still a captive one, appointed by the state, and the form of the performances, which are simplified and condensed to make them more accessible to the young audience, is determined by that audience.[8]

Throughout Southeast Asia, performances of traditional performing arts are commissioned for state events. As with traditional ceremonies like weddings, state ceremonies also require some aspect of entertainment as part of the overall ceremonial context. In Malaysia, the need for such performances for national celebrations and for visits of state guests was a rationale for setting up the Ministry of Culture, Youth, and Sport in 1964 (Mohd 1988:278). In Thailand, the National Silapakon (Department of Fine Arts) dance troupe has been used by successive regimes for performances mounted in the same way as the Royal Court (Rutnin 1993:190–93). In Indonesia, the state performing arts colleges virtually serve as training centers for state ceremonies. This was particularly true of the Soeharto era, when they created tailor-made performances for government ceremonies.

The requirements of performances for state celebrations are brevity (the performance is not necessarily the only or the main part of the program), an appropriate formality and display (no scruffy village performers), and accessibility to a mixed audience—men and women, people from various regions. It is important that the performance not be offensive to other ethnic and religious sensibilities, or to a sense of official decorum and respectability, for the audience members are not anonymous individuals—they are invited guests, attend as a group, and are usually known to each other in person or in position. Audiences for state celebrations are not usually attending the performance because of their interest in the performance itself. They are there to be seen and to fulfill obligations, and only a small percentage may have any specialist interest in the actual performance. The performance should be dignified and diverting. Guests should not be offended.

Businesses or corporations sponsoring performances for an invited audience will have the same concerns for their guests. At charity events organized with such sponsorship, people pay to attend—yet here the payment is not for tickets bought anonymously by an audience member. Rather, those who attend are demonstrating their joint support for a cause—they are there so that others may see that they have contributed to a joint effort. The audience are guests—guest donors in this case—and must be presented with a performance that is pleasing and appropriate to the sense of occasion.

State-commissioned performances for display to visiting foreign dignitaries or for display abroad must also fit into a formal framework of image and appropriateness. The ASEAN (Association for South East Asian Nations) festivals function in this way. Artists do not apply to participate, rather, the performances have been selected by the governments that send them. The audiences are made up largely of government officials and invited guests. In the audience expectation of what the type of performance should be, and in the way that the performances operate in such situations, the nations of ASEAN speak to each other—they share the same expectations.

The state supports and maintains a traditional system of presentation of performance. Although the performing arts schools may create new performances, this does not change the way that people actually see them. As a captive audience, they will see them anyway. (What Indonesians would pay to see a condensed *bedhaya*, and are they any more likely to pay because it is condensed?). The point is that a commercial framework for the traditional performing arts has not yet emerged, and where a semicommercial structure did exist, for example for urban popular forms such as *bangsawan* (popular Malay theater) in Malaysia or *wayang wong* (dance drama) in Java, the state has taken up the slack of support and molded these too into its system of patronage, the result being that the more they are subsidized and acquiesce to the demands of their patron, the less likely people are to buy tickets to see them (Tan Sooi Beng 1993).[9]

There are, of course, obvious exceptions to this generalization, both within each country and between countries. In Vietnam, where performing arts used to thrive in state-subsidized venues attended by a ticket-buying public, one could still argue that the performances are not commercial commodities, that attendance is also a national duty, and that in many senses (also through limitations on other forms of entertainment) the audience is a captive one. Nevertheless, overall a system of patronage for the arts is the traditional way the arts have functioned in Southeast Asia, and that way is perpetuated by the state. The traditional role of the audience as invited participants to an event, rather than a conglomeration of individuals purchasing tickets to a performance of their choice, is also perpetuated.

The Role of Subsidy

In Europe, Australia, and to a lesser extent in the United States, government subsidy for culture is grounded in the concept that society recognizes certain cultural forms as more than entertainment, and that because of their educative, moral, heritage, aesthetic, or even spiritual value to society as a whole, these should be supported with public money. More pragmatically, there is also recognition that such subsidy helps to maintain an industry of people working in associated activity. Government subsidy or public money supports cultural forms which are not in themselves fully viable commercially, but these activities are also part of a greater whole. Practically speaking, though, these cultural forms operate (on the whole) within a commercial framework, in the sense of venues used, tickets sold, publishing, and so forth. The way that subsidy works is to cover a loss in the calculation of income and expenditure within a commercial situation that operates in the same way for everyone.

In Southeast Asia, government subsidy for the arts functions differently because the sociopolitical context of the arts is different. In the level of government subsidy, the rationale behind it, the expectations of the public for such subsidy, and the government's demands and expectations in giving it, Southeast Asia differs markedly from European, Australian, or U.S. models. Subsidies are given for reasons of establishing national identity, protection of moral and religious values, and protection of indigenous cultural heritage (material and expressive). In terms of the performing arts, this subsidy functions like patronage because there is no commercial framework within which these performances function. Subsidy is not a payment of the deficit in a calculation of income and expenditure for a performance that operates commercially like any nonsubsidized performance.

In Southeast Asia, government support to artists is in general associated with government control. Government funds are not given—nor (yet) expected—as direct grants to individual artists who determine their own artistic direction and apply for public funds from an anonymous donor called "the government." In Southeast Asia, the government patron has a face. Government control is reflected in the award systems used to give funds to artists, or in the employment of artists as civil servants within the state cultural administration or teaching bureaucracies. Furthermore, subsidy operates within an overall context of government control of cultural expression, for example with the requirement of permits for performance and exhibitions, and censorship.

This nexus of government funding and control also affects the role of subsidy with regard to international cultural promotion in Southeast Asia. Government funds given for cultural promotion abroad are also usually tied to the choice of artists sent. International tours or exhibitions by artists of these countries are in general not seen as something that artists themselves negotiate and for which they request subsidy toward the difference between income and expenditure for an event that will function within a commercial framework—but rather as cultural missions or festivals that are noncommercial and where the cultural image presented abroad is something determined by the government that funds it. This is the way that most inter-ASEAN cultural exchange operates, for example, and it is also the way (or at least the government-preferred way) that Southeast Asian artists are sent abroad.[10]

The concept of government subsidy being tied to government direction and control underlies the fact that in Southeast Asia, with the exception of Singapore, an artificial distinction is drawn between foreign "commercial" and "noncommercial" cultural activity brought into the country, a distinction that could be made only by countries where government subsidy to the arts is not given within an independent commercial framework of presentation. The distinction drawn between "commercial" and "noncommercial" performing arts, for example, has very real implications for the legislation (tax, customs, visas, permits) that affects this activity.

Conclusion

Government control and direction in Southeast Asia is part of an overall "tradition" of the way that the performing arts operate. It is an inherited aspect of patronage, which itself persists in various ways. The issue is not merely that in Southeast Asia, as everywhere, any form of government aid comes with strings attached. As the Mapplethorpe case in the United States has demonstrated, the issue of public accountability of government money given as grants to artists is an ongoing social debate in all societies (Hughes 1992). The difference, though, is that in the European, Australian, and U.S. models, the public feels it has a right—both as a taxpayer (therefore donor), and as a consumer who buys tickets or pays gallery entrance fees—to comment on the value of what the assisted artists produce. The audience pays for a commodity. The arts operate in a fully commercial environment. In Southeast Asia, the performers are commissioned, the audience is invited, and the patron pays, and neither audience nor performer criticizes the patron.

Without a truly commercial context—where performance is a purchased commodity and where both audiences and subsidy givers are anonymous, then government subsidy cannot really function in an independent fashion which would allow the performing arts to develop in their own way. Without an independent commercial framework, it is difficult to see how subsidy and government support can function with less control and less direction.

Ironically, it is precisely because the new patrons and audiences operate in such a traditional way in Southeast Asia that such radical demands are imposed upon the traditional arts; it is not the expectations and basic approach to performance itself that are different, but the fact that the patrons and audiences are different. State cultural bodies directing the shape of traditional performing arts act in a very traditional way as patrons, but because they are not the traditional patrons, their demands are made to meet a different taste and for reasons of national unity and national identity—reasons that are inimical to the very authenticity of those art forms. National audiences for traditional and regional performing arts, especially official audiences, also act in a very traditional way in expecting presentations to be made familiar and pleasing to them and in some way contemporary. However, national audiences are by definition not traditional and not regionally specific, and their expectations of familiarity can only be met with pastiche.

The future of threatened traditional performing arts in Southeast Asia cannot rely merely on salvage efforts directed narrowly at those art forms themselves. The problems lie deeper than this. The future vitality of traditional performance in contemporary Southeast Asia depends on a less traditional manner of watching and a less traditional manner of control. As long as the government structures and support for the performing arts function in a traditional way, governments will play the intrusive traditional role of patron, imposing demands on what those performing arts forms should be, directing their consumption via state events and state television channels, and determining their image to be portrayed abroad. Government structure is not just forcing and molding change; it, too, is molded by concepts of performance, audience, patronage, image. Cultural policy and procedure are part of the performance culture itself.

Notes

1. To mention a few examples: Hatley (1993); Geertz (1990); Hughes-Freeland (1993); Lindsay (1985); Rutnin (1993); Sutton (1991); Tan (1993); Widodo (1995); Zurbuchen (1990). See also Beng-Huat and Kuo (1998) on Singapore.

2. Issues of tourism include the appropriation of ritual as spectacle by the state for local and foreign tourist consumption, and the dressing up of custom as performance. See Acciaioli (1985); Volkman (1990); Sellato (forthcoming); and writing about the Pacific, Keesing (1989).

3. Initial research for this section of the chapter was carried out in 1994 while writing a survey on cultural organization in Southeast Asia commissioned by the Australia Council for the Arts, the Department of Foreign Affairs and Trade, and the Myer Foundation. Please refer to that survey for more detailed information (Lindsay 1994).

4. See further Yos Santasombat (1998) and Chaiwat Satha-Anand (1998) on the relationship of Buddhism and national cultural policy in Thailand.

5. The Traditional Arts Unit of the Ministry of Culture, Arts and Tourism defines its role as "To preserve, promote and develop traditional and indigenous art forms including theater, games and the art of self-defense, for their conservation and upliftment, and encourage wider participation of the masses in such activities."

6. Mention should be made of foreign funding agencies that provide an alternative source of support to artists and that have the advantage of operating in a way that allows them to

apply directly and receive funds directly. The thriving community theater scene in the Philippines is virtually run on foreign support, for example.

7. Volkman, writing on Toraja notes "a ritual that in the past might have been measured in number and value of buffalo and pigs is now measured in terms of number and rank of government representatives" (1990: 107).

8. Rutnin explains: "Since the Ministry of Education prescribes only excerpts from dramatic masterpieces (for Thai literature courses), the National Theater productions present mostly short scenes from these classical plays in the form of variety shows rather than complete plays as in the past" (1993: 197).

9. I am struck with the differences in the way that visual arts operate in Southeast Asia where the approach appears to be the opposite of the situation in the performing arts. Throughout the region, exhibitions of contemporary art have become virtually synonymous with sale. The attachment of a money value to something on display in a gallery is part of the exhibition process. There appears to be little tradition of viewing art objects which are displayed in a gallery-like context for no other reason than display.

10. In Indonesia, for example, there is a complicated legal requirement that performers touring abroad must obtain permission from the department of Art and Tourism and must then make all arrangements with the foreign agent through a local Indonesian agent authorized through that department. The role of the agent is basically to obtain (for a price) the approval from the department for the artists to tour. While the enforcement of regulations such as these has been relaxed in the post-Soeharto era, the actual regulations are still in the process of revision.

References

Acciaioli, G. (1985) 'Culture as art: From practice to spectacle in Indonesia,' *Canberra Anthropology*, 8 (1 & 2): 148–172.

Chua Ben-Huat and Kuo, E. (1998) 'The making of a new nation: cultural construction and national identity in Singapore,' pp.35–68 in V. R. Dominguez (ed.) *From Beijing to Port Moresby: The Politics of National Identity in Cultural Policies*, Amsterdam: Gordon and Breach Publishers.

Geertz, C. (1990) 'Popular art and the Javanese tradition,' *Indonesia* 50: 29–94.

Hatley, B. (1993) 'Constructions of "tradition" in New Order Indonesian theater,' pp. 48–69 in V. M. Hooker (ed.) *Culture and Society in New Order Indonesia*, Kuala Lumpur: Oxford University Press.

Hughes, R. (1992) 'Art, morals and politics,' *New York Review of Books* 23, April: 21–27.

Hughes-Freeland, F. (1993) 'Golek menak and tayuban,' pp. 88–119 in B. Arps (ed.) *Performance in Java and Bali: Studies of narrative, theater, music and dance*, London: School of Oriental and African Studies.

Keesing, R. M. (1989) 'Creating the past; custom and identity in the contemporary Pacific,' *The Contemporary Pacific*, I, 1–2: 19–42.

Lindsay, J. (1985) 'Klasik, kitsch or contemporary: a study of the Javanese performing arts,' PhD thesis, University of Sydney, Australia.

Lindsay, J, (1994) *Cultural Organisation in Southeast Asia*, Sydney: Australia Council, Department of Foreign Affairs and Trade, the Myer Foundation.

Mohd, T. O. (1988) 'The concept of national culture: the Malaysian case,' pp. 273–285 in *Bunga Rampai (Aspects of Malay Culture)*, Kuala Lumpur: Dewan Bahasa dan Pustaka.

Rutnin, M. M. (1993) *Dance, Drama and Theater in Thailand: The Process of Development and Modernization*, Yoyo Bunyo: The Center of East Asian Cultural Studies.

Santasombat, Y. (1998) 'Buddhist cultural tradition and the politics of national identity in Thailand,' pp.305–52 in V. R. Dominguez (ed.) *From Beijing to Port Moresby: The Politics of National Identity in Cultural Policies*, Amsterdam: Gordon and Breach Publishers.

Satha-Anand, C. (1998) 'The politics of cultural citizenship: a second look at Buddhist cultural tradition and the politics of national identity in Thailand,' pp.353–66 in V. R. Dominguez (ed.) *From Beijing to Port Moresby: The Politics of National Identity in Cultural Policies*, Amsterdam: Gordon and Breach Publishers.

Sellato, B. (forthcoming) 'Spatial organization and cultural identity: historical factors and current trends in Kalimantan,' in M. Charras (ed.), *Centers and peripheries in peninsular Southeast Asia*, Paris: CNRS, DEVI.

Sutton, R. A. (1991) *Traditions of Gamelan Music in Java: Musical Pluralism and Regional Identity*, Cambridge: Cambridge University Press.

Tan, Sooi Beng (1993) *Bangsawan: A Social and Stylistic History of Popular Malay Opera*, Singapore: Oxford University Press.

Volkman, T. A. (1990) 'Visions and revisions; Toraja culture and the tourist gaze,' *American Ethnologist*, 17, 1: 91–110.

Widodo, A. (1995) 'The stages of the state: arts of the people and rites of hegemonization,' *Review of Indonesian and Malaysian Affairs*, 29, Winter and Summer: 1–35.

Zurbuchen, M. S. (1990) 'Images of culture and national development in Indonesia: the Cockroach Opera,' *Asian Theater Journal*, 7, 2:127–149.

5

Identifying a Policy Hierarchy

Communication Policy, Media Industries, and Globalization

Alison Beale

In the course of international trade negotiations since World War II, a cultural exemption to liberalized trade has been a regular demand from many participating countries. This chapter considers the cultural exemption strategy, most recently manifested in the failed negotiation of the Multilateral Agreement on Investment (MAI) in 1998 and again in the 1999 World Trade Organization (WTO) talks. I argue that the language of an exemption for culture masks the issues at the heart of the relationship between national cultural policies and international markets. National and regional trade negotiators claim a principled base in their responsibility for "public goods" such as universal access to telephony and telecommunications and for citizens' rights to cultural diversity and development. But this responsibility conflicts with others. The concerns of the national governments and the world-regional markets such as the European Union (EU) represented by the negotiators have been to ensure the flow of capital through the electronic paths of the information highway, and to expand investment in ICTs (information and communication technologies). Not far behind these goals is securing advantage for domestically based cultural industries including television, to which ICTs are increasingly linked via cross-ownership and investment, and technological convergence.

In terms of national priorities, therefore, there is a hierarchy in which policies for the arts and heritage come third after information technology and cultural industries policies. In a related ranking, the public interest, public good, diversity, cultural rights, and cultural development—to list the major citizenship-related concepts much cited but effectively ignored in the context of international trade—come a distant second to the market rationalization euphemized as "consumer sovereignty."

The Cultural Exemption: Europe

The cultural exemption originates in European, especially French resistance to the increasingly one-way flow of trade with the United States in film after World War II, an irritant ever since aggressive American moves to export film began in the 1920s. Two features of this background should be underscored. First, there is the historic importance of secondary markets in providing the high return on investment upon which Hollywood and, after it, the television and recorded music industries have come to depend. These markets have been part and parcel of the long-standing international structure of American cultural industries. Second, these industries have benefited from extensive diplomatic and trade intervention on the part of the American government. During the 1920s, for example, "American films seized over 50 percent of the market in a number of European countries and over 80 percent in Britain and Italy," even as screen quotas were introduced (Nowell-Smith 1998:3). With the assistance of the U.S. Department of State and American embassies in Europe, most of this protective legislation was withdrawn by 1945 (Bernier 1998:109). As one commentator has noted "there is evidence of a concerted strategy between the American government and the Motion Picture Export Association of America (MPAA) to promote the export of American movies not only as earners of foreign currency but as bearers of the American flag" (Nowell-Smith 1998:7). This is pursued to such an extent that the MPAA has the reputation of being "the little State Department" (Wasko 1995:166).

In the post–World War II years European promotion of the film industry and intra-European co-production (instigated by Jean Monnet, the "father" of the European Union) culminated in a series of co-production agreements between European countries, as well as the Blum-Byrnes Agreement regulating competition between the French and American film industries (Nowell-Smith 1998:8). But the American critic Victoria De Grazia has argued against seeing these developments as a successful blending of national interest and pan-European interest. Rather, she argues that there has been a slippage between nationalism and Europeanism at several key junctures in the European cinema; in the Nazi era, in the economic boom of the 1960s, and currently within the new borders and among the diversifying populations of Europe. Despite the problematic nature of this ideological framework for defending a European culture, in the long run it has won legitimacy for national cinema as "a veritable monument to high culture" especially in France (De Grazia 1998:21). Though British cinema is in a somewhat different position, it is art cinemas, rather than commercial cinemas, that are regarded as emblems of the nation and of Europe.

As later developments in the European Union were to prove, commercially oriented cultural products, co-production agreements with the United States that sidestepped "European" interests, and the growing broadcasting and new media technology sectors exacerbated existing differences between countries and cultural sectors. The "cultural exemption" was until recently based on a common cultural front concealing ineffective policy and conflict among European nations in their attempts to join forces against Hollywood. The ambivalence about American influence in such countries as France and Britain, given the participation of European artists and companies in the newer cultural industries of popular music and television, leads to accusations of hypocrisy from American skeptics when Europeans continue to argue for a cultural high ground as the basis for imposing limits on American products (De Grazia 1998; Pells 1997).

The unification of the European Union has not come about through the consolidation of a European audiovisual or cultural space, but through firm foundations built for the European audiovisual and information technology sectors as part of economic integration in the 1980s (Beale 1999a; Humphreys 1996; Raboy 1999). As Caroline Pauwels (1991) has demonstrated, far from being built on "consumer sovereignty" in any meaningful sense, these foundations have been laid using this catchphrase as publicity rather than as the object of policy (p. 71). Private interests brought forward by both national and pan-European representation, rather than national or European citizens' interests, have been the key factors in developing the European telecommunications sector. One analysis concludes, "EU telecommunications policy would not have proceeded so far, so fast, without a significant policy shift among the member states themselves: from polarization between 'liberalizers' and 'protectionists' towards a new liberalizing consensus" (Humphreys and Simpson 1996:118).

Meanwhile, at the Uruguay Round of the General Agreement on Tariffs and Trade (GATT) talks in 1986, the first in the sequence of liberalizing trade agreements this chapter is concerned with, European countries obtained a complete exclusion of audiovisual and cultural goods. Janet Wasko (1995) has called the U.S. cultural defeat at the Uruguay Round "a remake of scenes already played out" (p. 165), but one could argue that, in addition, it was a sideshow. The cultural exemption not only masked the historic differences among European countries and among private interests within their borders; it drew attention away from other routes to economic integration and cultural globalization that were fast developing in telecommunications and ICTs (Winseck 1997; Raboy 1996).

The Cultural Exemption: Canada

"Cultural sovereignty," the key to the MAI debate over culture, is a phrase which has accumulated layered meanings during the history of Canadian cultural policies. Its origins are in the establishment of the CBC/Radio Canada as a cultural defense system against American transborder radio. Through the public broadcaster an ideological association was formed between cultural sovereignty and the public sector, according to the rationale of "the state or the United States." The Canadian state was legitimized in compensating for market failure, reaching a geographically dispersed population, and assuring the coverage of Canadian news and representation of the regions. Following demands for public funding for the film and publishing industries in the 1960s, cultural sovereignty also came to mean public support for Canadian cultural industries, whose existence as providers of Canadian content and Canadian jobs was argued to be essential to providing the glue holding the Canadian polity together. Today, cultural sovereignty is used to represent the idea of cultural sovereignty as national security. Public investment in computer-mediated communication is defended on the basis of cultural sovereignty, because computer networks, innovation, and expertise underpin communications and economic production and must be provided in order to guarantee Canada's continued prosperity and political integrity (Menzies 1998).

Canadian researchers reviewing the history of Canadian cultural policy argue that cultural sovereignty thus became, first, a cultural industries policy (which has also industrialized the organization and subsidy of the arts and heritage) (Beale 1997) and, second, a rationale for significant public support for computer-mediated communication. At the same time, spending on public broadcasting, for example, has decreased (Babe 1996). This analysis suggests to some researchers that opening up cultural policy to economic arguments has been a Pandora's box that results in economic considerations taking priority over cultural ones (Godard 1998). A different argument links the triumph of the economic rationale to the centrality of public spending on communication technology in Canada (Dowler 1996). And another view suggests that in the Canadian context some form of economic rationale—market failure—has always been present, and that the cultural industries model has been a success, contributing to continuing demands for both public investment in and protection for Canadian cultural industries and market expansion in order for Canada-based companies to remain competitive. This argument gives qualified support to the North American Free Trade Agreement (NAFTA) (Dorland 1996) but it also raises the issue of how policy measures are unequal in their impact across cultural industries, and across cultural industries, the arts, and heritage.

By the time of the negotiation of the Free Trade Agreement between Canada and the United States in 1988, Canada was the most important secondary market for cultural exports from the United States. Today, far from being significantly controlled in Canada: "Foreign products or firms account for more than 90 per cent of the drama on English-language television, 81 per cent of consumer magazines on Canadian newsstands, 79 per cent of the revenue for recorded music, and close to 95 per cent of annual screen time at Canadian theatres" (Magder 1999:12). This is despite Canadian controls on investment, and content requirements for television and radio that have not yet been altered by free trade in culture.

Free trade with the United States and Mexico has been the goal of the Canadian business elite and government since the 1980s. Its advocates gave Canadians (who in repeated opinion polls tend not to support free trade, yet vote for governments that do) repeated assurances that the cultural sector, employment standards, the universal public health-care system, and other institutions and regulatory powers of the federal government would not be affected by such agreements. NAFTA (1993) featured a cultural exemption clause for cultural industries. The trade-off was that the exemption is subject to the "notwithstanding" clause which specifies in Article 2005 that "a party" can retaliate with measures of "equivalent commercial effect" and do so using sectors unrelated to culture. Commentators questioned the agreement on both sides of the border. The Canadian cultural community pointed out the vulnerability of Canadian interests to potential retaliation. In the U.S. Congress, the original FTA bill had specified that future administrations would have to seek elimination of the cultural exemption.

After NAFTA came into force, retaliation against Canadian exercise of cultural sovereignty occurred in several high-profile cases. The most famous of these is the landmark *Sports Illustrated* case, that magazine being one of the Canadian "editions" of American publications (U.S. editorial content packaged in Canada with Canadian advertising) on whose Canadian advertising the federal government imposed an excise tax of 80 percent. The purpose of the tax, of course, was to encourage advertisers to spend their dollars in such Canadian magazines as *MacLean's* (the largest-circulation news magazine) and *Chatelaine* (the largest-circulation homemakers magazine). In 1997 a ruling by the World Trade Organization determined that Canada would have to withdraw the tax, a ruling described by Ted Magder (1999) as "a stunning victory for the United States" (p. 12). Eventually a negotiated settlement was reached between Canada and the United States which compromised on some of the more severe implications of the ruling for Canada. However, the Canadian government also lost the right to provide postal subsidies for Canadian magazines, which it had been doing since the nineteenth century (Magder 1999). It later introduced some support measures in the form of grants for Canadian publications, but these were not expected to make up for a projected loss of up to 40 percent of Canadian magazine titles over the next few years as a result of the WTO ruling.

Globalization: Victims or Partners?

Before going on to look at the Multilateral Agreement on Investment, the most recent site of confrontation over the exemption of culture from trade rules, it is important to point out two possible interpretations of the direction of national cultural policies since the 1980s. The *Sports Illustrated* case, for example, appears to suggest that international trade rules as enforced by the GATT, the WTO, and the International Chamber of Commerce are responsible for destroying the ability of national governments to act on behalf of national interests in culture. Even where cultural exemptions are in place, countries are obliged to bring their treatment of national and nonnational cultural enterprises into line in order to avoid internationally sanctioned trade retaliation in other sectors. The result is like libel "chill": it leads to the "voluntary" forfeit of national cultural sovereignty in anticipation of such retaliation.

But a second interpretation would argue that national governments and economic unions such as the EU have played a role in the creation of free trade, in which bringing their national cultural subsidies and institutions into line and reconfiguring the regulation of broadcasting and information technology sectors at the ministerial level have played a substantial part. I share this view and would argue that a singular national or world-regional cultural interest may now be seen for the fiction it is. It is principally national "champions," cultural enterprises that have consolidated their market share since the 1970s, information technology firms, and exporters of programming that benefit from Canadian trade rules, and which in Europe have benefited from the information society policies of the EU. During the 1970s and 1980s Canada invested in the production side of film and television, and concentrated its attention on exportable cultural goods rather than in the more visibly "subsidized" cultural goods consumed at home, such as the performing arts. It also imposed Canadian content quotas in television and radio, which were particularly effective in supporting the recorded music industry. But like the major U.S. and British players, Canadian television producers have found their greatest success outside Canada, to the extent that Canada is now the third highest exporter of television programming in the world.

One of the less obvious features of the *Sports Illustrated* case was that a major beneficiary of Canadian tax on advertising in non-Canadian magazines has been Rogers Communications, Canada's largest cable operator, which owns MacLean-Hunter, the largest English-language magazine group, and its Quebec cable counterpart, Telemedia. Are the business interests of such consortia with their huge market share the equivalent of national cultural interest, or of public interest?

Like other countries, the United States has imposed foreign investment limits in the media and broadcasting areas and has reserved the right to administer direct grants, tax incentives, and other forms of subsidy (Wasko 1995). In a manner consistent with this historic stance, the United States was one of the countries to reserve the right to maintain foreign investment restrictions in the media and broadcasting sectors at the 1998 MAI negotiations. Nonetheless it has always been the U.S. trade negotiators' contention that culture is a tradable commodity like any other. Canadian policy analysts disagree, as indicated in the following quote:

> We are obviously confronted here with a longstanding conflict about what could be termed, for lack of a better expression, the specificity of cultural products envisaged from an international trade perspective. The main actors are few and well-defined. Essentially the request for a totally free and open market in cultural products comes from the United States, while the proponents of some form of cultural exception are to be found in Europe, more particularly in France, and in Canada. (Bernier 1998:110–11)

American commercial law analysts stress the importance of extending conventions on copyright as a means of expanding trade in intellectual property, the key to prosperity. They argue that expanding the recognition of copyright will ultimately be more rewarding to producers than continued national cultural exemptions (Strong 1993:123). What is interesting about this argument is that it assumes the reason for national cultural exemptions to be the protection of national cultural producers. This, rather than cultural sovereignty or a national cultural interest, is clearly the historic U.S. position.

And of course, it may be the Canadian position as well. In the backroom parlance of trade negotiations, Americans seem to have got Canada's number as far as the commitment of our government to a cultural rather than commercial defense of Canadian cultural industries is concerned. An American analyst inquired of the 1994 merger of Rogers Communications and MacLean-Hunter: "Are Canadians protecting their culture or their economy?" (Lehman 1997:211). A defender of Canadian cultural big business, borrowing a line from the national anthem, countered, "'We cannot protect our own turf unless there is someone out there big enough to stand on guard for thee'" (p.211).

The MAI and the Cultural Exemption

The impetus to set up the Multilateral Agreement on Investment came from the U.S. trade representative to the Organization for Economic Cooperation and Development (OECD), from the EU within the WTO, from enthusiastic national governments such as Canada and the financial sector. Negotiations were initiated in 1995, but stalled in 1998. The reason for the MAI's failure was not the lack of consensus on a cultural exemption but disagreement on a number of matters related to the unprecedented scope of the proposed agreement. The MAI's key characteristic was that it was comprehensive; for the first time an international trade agreement was to *include* all sectors not specifically *excluded.*

The MAI was therefore widely described as a Bill of Rights for investors. A major feature was that foreign companies were to receive "national treatment." This meant that any national subsidies in the form of direct payments or tax relief, investment tax credits, content regulations, and so on were to apply equally to national and foreign companies. There were to be no controls on profit repatriation. Most significant was a rule mandating that countries could not apply environmental, minimum wage, or regional or sectoral development controls that could be shown to impair a rate of profit similar to that in the home country of the investor or multinational. This indirect but substantial threat would force member countries to "harmonize" legislation in these areas to the lowest common denominator. The big stick approach to forcing harmonization extended to the speculative realm of potential threats to potential investments. A complaint could be brought against a signatory country that its laws inhibited potential profit taking from potential investors, and they could choose the venue in which to have such complaints adjudicated.

Prior to the 1998 MAI discussions, countries appeared to adopt several strategies toward trade in culture, suggesting various analyses of the effects the agreement might have on culture and different strategies to manage such effects. A majority of countries did not submit position papers that voiced reservations which directly affected culture. The common reason given for not doing so was that they were waiting to see whether a general exemption on culture was accepted. A few countries did submit reservations for the cultural industries, principally the right to maintain foreign investment restrictions: these included the United States, Italy, Turkey, the United Kingdom, and the Netherlands. Australia, Spain, Korea, and Mexico also submitted lists of specific reservations related to broadcasting, film, and book publishing.

Canada, Australia, and Turkey were the only countries to specifically state their assumption that there would be a *general agreement for the cultural industries* (my emphasis). France, in addition, submitted the first draft of a general exemption for "cultural diversity." It is notable that many of the countries that did not support a general exclusion for culture are home to the top audiovisual companies in the world. These countries include the United States, Japan, Germany, the United Kingdom, and the Netherlands.

The riotous World Trade Organization meeting of late 1999 in Seattle picked up some of the same agendas but did not attempt to do so in the umbrella fashion that had alarmed not only opponents but cautious supporters of free trade. Intellectual copyright was a major item on the table, but by then a cultural exemption was not.

The Diversity Strategy

After the failure of the MAI negotiations, several countries, notably France and Canada, began to pursue a concerted strategy for a cultural exemption in future trade talks. The Canadian minister for heritage, the Honorable Sheila Copps, led a group of 22 culture ministers who had first met in Sweden in 1998 at a United Nations Educational, Scientific, and Cultural Organization (UNESCO) Intergovernmental Conference on Cultural Policies for Development. They met in Canada in June 1998 and in September 1999 in Mexico. They called themselves the International Network on Cultural Policy and included Armenia, Brazil, Britain, Canada, China, Egypt, France, Hungary, Malaysia, Mexico, Sweden, and Ukraine, as well as a parallel organization of cultural nongovernmental organizations from these countries.

The work of this group drew on the French-initiated strategy of identifying uncontrolled global trade in culture as a threat to cultural diversity. It was supported by a well-advanced UNESCO program of cultural development that had linked cultural diversity to rights to education and freedom of expression and to the human rights of minorities. The same UNESCO initiative, the "World Decade on Cultural Development" that had culminated in the report *Our Creative Diversity* (World Commission on Culture and Development 1996) also viewed cultural diversity as a potential resource to be exploited for the benefit of cultural copyright holders—the minorities whose cultural rights it was concerned with (Beale 1999b: 452–54). The Council of Europe is now carrying out a related Transversal Study on Cultural Policy and Cultural Diversity, with partners from non-European countries including Canada (Baeker 2000).

The rhetoric of the cultural exemption has evolved from defending national modernities to commercializing local hybridities. The Canadian government and UNESCO are cases in point. Since the 1960s the Canadian government's language and its action have shifted from a protectionist emphasis on Canadian cultural sovereignty and the uniqueness of the Canadian way of life to marketing hybridized Canadian cultural production to both domestic and international markets. This was clearly the agenda of the Canadian government as early as a 1994 foreign policy review highlighting such divergent exports and emblems of Canada as the works of Celine Dion and Michael Ondaatje (Beale 1997).

Diversity is tied to a human-rights agenda that arose in the concept of cultural development. But the means of protecting diversity are cultural sustainability, which may mean self-exploitation in the commodification, branding, copyrighting, and marketing of, especially, minority cultures. The World Commission on Cultural Development, treading carefully to avoid transgressing the principle of national cultural sovereignty, came up with a program to protect cultural diversity against what it implies is global Americanization, to be guaranteed by national governments, international human rights conventions, and through the marketing of intellectual property produced in minority cultures (World Commission on Cultural Development 1996). The capacity of intellectual copyright regimes to be enforced for the benefit of creators rather than owners and distributors remains to be seen.

The Council of Europe's study of cultural diversity appears to have more potential for identifying the ways in which states and international human-rights and trade regimes can come to terms with the complex societies of immigrants that most nations have become, which will entail establishing cultural policy on a footing very different from the nationalist modernism that characterizes so many policies (Baeker 2000). Notwithstanding this advance, the pursuit of diversity meantime provides countries such as France and Canada with a moral high ground that national interest does not provide. It is intended to be an irrefutable proposition that diversity is best secured through trade protections for cultural industries.

And this is where the private sector comes back in. Enthusiastic support for a strategy of cultural diversity has come from a surprising source in Canada, the Cultural Industries Sectoral Advisory Group on International Trade, or SAGIT. In a report to the minister of trade in early 1999, these leaders of the film, broadcasting, and cable industries, including the aforementioned Rogers Cable and MacLean-Hunter, advocated "a new international instrument that sets out rules on what kinds of domestic regulations can be used to promote and protect cultural diversity" (Scoffield 1999). These monopolists, some of whom have fought Canadian content regulation, others of whom tailor their production of Canadian television programs to international markets, see the writing on the wall and know an opportunity when it presents itself.

In theory, the ground that unites advocates for minority cultures and for cultural hybridity with cultural entrepreneurs is the provision of entertainment for diverse populations ill served by national public media, mainstream press and periodicals, and Eurocentric cultural institutions. The researchers involved in the Council of Europe study, and in the diversity initiatives of the Canadian Department of Heritage have identified informal diasporic and some genre and audience hybridizing initiated by private broadcasters as evidence of the potential for innovative approaches to audiences. They also note, however, that the national framework may not be the most appropriate or realistic one in which to pursue this audience development strategy (Baeker 2000). Diversity may be a comfortable strategy for lobbies such as the Sectoral Advisory Group on International Trade (SAGIT) because it comes without specific performance requirements to guarantee diversity. But the real divergence between these companies and proponents of cultural diversity arises where, for example, audiences or publics of particular minorities are too small or scattered to attract private investment or advertisers. Ultimately, what the SAGIT lobby in Canada and other private companies outside the United States hope for is that they will be protected as exemplars of "local" cultures and providers for diverse audiences. This should be seen for what it is: an opportunity to gain business advantage rather than a commitment either to traditional national cultural sovereignty or to cultural diversity.

Conclusion

The role of national governments (including the United States) in cultural globalization and of the private and public interests to which they respond is a difficult issue that has been neglected. The developmental gap between a cultural theory of globalization and a theory of the role of cultural *policy* in globalization is explored in Jan Nederveen Pieterse's formulation of globalization as cultural hybridization. Taking the analysis beyond postmodern identity politics, Nederveen Pieterse (1995) argues that "What globalization means in structural terms . . . is *the increase in the available modes of organization*: transnational, international, macro-regional, municipal, local . . . crisscrossed by functional networks of corporations, international organizations and nongovernmental organizations" (p. 50). While this deeper perspective on the structural foundations of hybrid culture is welcome, Nederveen Pieterse concludes that "essentialism will remain strategic as a mobilisational device as long as the units of nation, state, region, civilization, ethnicity remain strategic." We can see this essentialism strategically alive in the SAGIT report above.

But if some consider the national interest, national culture, or the public sphere as a national space to be among the essentialist concepts still strategically significant, I would argue not only that they are unraveling in the face of cultural hybridization, but that their strategic significance and their mobilizing capacity is and has historically been highly unstable and contextual. By this I mean, first, that it is important to consider whether mobilization in support of "national culture" is a politically necessary posture in many states, unless to conceal the role of the state in further market integration.

Second, it is crucial to note the variability of cultural policy language depending on the context in which it is deployed. Diversity is a concept much bandied about in management discourse, but until recently, at least, it has been in the public sector rather than the private that job equity has been addressed. In the private sector lateral structures, informal work environments, and job mobility are elements of a diversity strategy that is to some extent responsive to the local sites of multinational corporations, enabling them to describe themselves as culturally diverse.

The delinking of communications and information technology networks from the traditional marriage of national public and private sectors and their reemergence as the foundation for global markets is a reality whose fallout on national policies for broadcasting and for the arts and heritage is still being accounted for. In Europe and in Canada, as I have discussed elsewhere (Beale 1999a, 1999b), the relocation of decisionmaking about the ICT sector to trade and finance ministries and intragovernmental bodies has established a hierarchy in which the information technology and communications framework is isolated from accountability.

Marc Raboy (1999) has argued that we must move cultural policy advocacy beyond the national setting, because of the uncoupling of cultural production and distribution networks from nation-states. The oligopoly of information technology companies has become the focus of civil society movements seeking to protect the public resources of communication. The question then, as Raboy puts it, is what meaningful role national governments can play in developing a "socially progressive global regulatory framework for mass media, information, and communication technologies"(p. 305)? Similarly, how well will the multistranded strategy of cultural diversity as conducted by national governments represent the cultural interests of citizens of countries all over the world as economic and political integration proceed?

References

Babe, R. (1996) 'Economics and information: Toward a new (and more sustainable) world-view,' *Canadian Journal of Communication*, 21: 161–178.

Baeker, G. (2000) *Cultural Policy and Cultural Diversity in Canada*, Unpublished Report for the Council of Europe Study on Cultural Policy and Cultural Diversity.

Beale, A. (1997) 'Subjects, citizens or consumers? Changing concepts of citizenship in Canadian cultural policy,' pp.51–65 in A. Seager, L. Evenden, R. Lorimer, and R. Mathews (eds.) *Alternative Frontiers: Voices from the Mountain West*, Montreal: Association for Canadian Studies.

Beale, A. (1999a) 'Development and *désetatisation*: cultural policy in the European Union,' *MIA/Culture and Policy* 90: 91–105.

Beale, A. (1999b) 'From "Sophie's Choice" to consumer choice: framing gender in cultural policy,' *Media, Culture and Society*, 21: 435–458.

Bernier, I. (1998) 'Cultural goods and services in international trade law,' pp.108–154 in D. Browne (ed.) *The Culture/Trade Quandary: Canada's Policy Options*, Ottawa: Centre for Trade Policy and Law.

Burgelman, J.-C.. (1999) 'The future of the welfare state and its challenges for communication policy,' pp. 125–136 in A. Calabrese and J.-C. Burgelman (eds.), *Communication, Citizenship and Social Policy: Rethinking the Limits of the Welfare State*, Lanham, MD: Rowman and Littlefield.

De Grazia, V. (1998) 'European cinema and the idea of Europe (1925–1995),' pp.19–33 in G. Nowell-Smith and S. Ricci (eds.) *Hollywood and Europe: Economics, Culture, National Identity 1945–1995*, London: British Film Institute.

Dorland, M. (ed.) (1996) *The Cultural Industries in Canada: Problems, Policies and Prospects*, Toronto: James Lorimer and Co.

Dowler, K. (1996) 'The cultural industries policy apparatus,' pp. 138–156 in M. Dorland (ed.) *The Cultural Industries in Canada: Problems, Policies and Prospects*, Toronto: James Lorimer and Co.

Godard, B. (1998) 'Feminist speculations on value: culture in the age of downsizing,' pp.43–76 in A. Beale and A. Van Den Bosch (eds.) *Ghosts in the Machine: Women and Cultural Policy in Canada and Australia*, Toronto: Garamond.

Humphreys, P. (1996) *Mass Media and Media Policy in Western Europe*, Manchester: Manchester University Press.

Humphreys, P. and Simpson, S. (1996) 'European telecommunications and globalization,' pp.105–124 in P. Gunnet (ed.) *Globalisation and Public Policy*, Cheltenham, UK and Brookfield, US: Edward Elgar.

Lehman, A. (1997) 'The Canadian Cultural Exemption Clause and the fight to maintain an identity,' *Syracuse Journal of International Law and Commerce*, 23:187–218.

Magder, T. (1999) 'Going global,' *Canadian Forum*, August:11–16.

Menzies, H. (1998) 'Challenging capitalism in cyberspace: the information highway, the postindustrial economy, and people,' pp.87–98 in R. W. McChesney, E. M. Wood, and J. B. Poster (eds.) *Capitalism and the Information Age: The Political Economy of the Global Communication Revolution*, New York: Monthly Review Press.

Nederveen Pieterse, J. (1995) 'Globalization as hybridization,' pp. 45–68 in M. Featherstone, S. Lash, and R. Robertson (eds.) *Global Modernities*, Thousand Oaks, CA: Sage.

Nowell-Smith, G. (1998) 'Introduction,' pp 1–19 in G. Nowell-Smith and S. Ricci (eds.), *Hollywood and Europe: Economics, Culture, National Identity 1945–1995*, London: British Film Institute.

Pauwels, C. (1999) 'From citizenship to consumer sovereignty: the paradigm shift in European Audiovisual Policy,' pp. 65–76 in A. Calabrese and J.-C. Burgelman (eds.) *Communication, Citizenship and Social Policy: Rethinking the Limits of the Welfare State*, Lanham MD: Rowman and Littlefield.

Pells, R. H. (1997) *Not Like Us: How Europeans Have Loved, Hated, and Transformed American culture since World War II*, New York: Basic Books.

Raboy, M. (1996) 'Cultural sovereignty, public participation and democratization of the public sphere: the Canadian debate on the new information infrastructure,' *Communications and Strategies*, 21, 1ST quarter:51–77.

Raboy, M. (1999) 'Communication policy and globalization as a social project,' pp. 293–310 in A. Calabrese and J.-C. Burgelman (eds.) *Communication, Citizenship and Social Policy: Rethinking the Limits of the Welfare State*, Lanham, MD: Rowman and Littlefield.

Scoffield, H. (1999) 'Ottawa urged to push for global culture accord,' *Globe and Mail*, Toronto, February 18.

Strong, S. (1993) 'Banning the cultural exclusion: free trade and copyrighted goods,' *Duke Journal of Comparative and International Law*, 4: 93–123.

Wasko, J. (1995) 'Jurassic Park and the GATT: Hollywood and Europe-an update,' pp. 157–171 in F. Corcoran and P. Preston (eds.) *Democracy and Communication in the New Europe: Change and Continuity in East and West*, Cresskill, NJ: Hampton Press.

World Commission on Culture and Development. (1996) *Our Creative Diversity*, Paris: UNESCO.

Winseck, D. (1997) 'Contradictions in the democratization of international communication,' *Media, Culture and Society*, 19: 219–246.

Part II

REGENERATING CULTURAL RESOURCES

Urban and Organizational Strategies

6

Urban Cultural Policy and Urban Regeneration

The Special Case of Declining Port Cities— Liverpool, Marseilles, Bilbao

J. Pedro Lorente

This chapter explores how some cultural policies shape urban regeneration processes. The special contributions of museums and artists studios have already been featured in comparative studies of urban regeneration through the arts. However, most of the existing literature analyzes their impact as the *culmination* of a long-coveted recuperation of some highlights of our architectural heritage. A few researchers in urban studies have paid tribute to the role of new cultural venues as "flagships" of some processes of image betterment and urban regeneration. My aim here is to point out that some of these investments are not merely the end of a renewal process but also a decisive *catalyst* for the reuse of derelict buildings for art purposes and, in general, for enhancing the local arts scene.[1]

Previous work on this topic has discussed some interesting examples in districts of New York, Baltimore, Paris, Dublin, Barcelona, Berlin, and London. But obviously in such rich and burgeoning cities urban revitalization has been boosted by an array of vested interests, among which the arts sector is just one component—and not necessarily the most consequential. No matter the size and history of the arts presence in particular districts, it seems obvious that any derelict area in the heart of a prosperous city is bound to be revitalized by urban developers anyway. However, the prospects for redevelopment are less likely when the derelict area lies in the middle of a declining city facing economic recession, unemployment, depopulation, social/ethnic unrest, and physical decay. If we can show that, even in such adverse circumstances, arts-led regeneration can prosper, then we will have demonstrated its importance beyond doubt.

Liverpool, Marseilles, and Bilbao are such cases. In these cities, the economy, based on heavy industry related to port activities, had become obsolete in the 1970s when their docks and railway goods' terminals and warehouses were shut down as a result of new methods for the transportation of goods, particularly containerization. The once long and labor-intensive loading and offloading of cargoes was replaced by direct transit of containers between lorries and ships. Thus the old linear docks became redundant along with adjacent warehouses, factories, shipping industries and their urban neighborhoods. Moreover, not only were most port-related activities transferred out of these cities, but the ownership of their merchant, industrial, and food-processing businesses was taken over by international corporations based elsewhere. This hastened the physical decay of these cities, which starkly contrasts with their past situation. In the past, speculation in the building industry and in real estate had been a secure investment for local elites in case of ruinous disasters at sea. Finally, the new political and economic realities in Europe had done the rest: Rotterdam now acts as the main port of Europe, absorbing most maritime commerce in the European Union, and its more peripheral competitors have been condemned to languish in the backwaters. The effects of this are especially manifest in Liverpool, Marseilles, and Bilbao, but can be seen clearly also in Genoa, Vigo, Bristol, Glasgow, Antwerp, and Hamburg. Economic decline, unemployment, crime, depopulation, urban dereliction, political radicalism and social violence have been endemic in these cities since the world economic crisis of 1974—with particular virulence in the early 1980s.

However, the shifting geography of macroeconomics does not explain all the recent misfortunes of Liverpool, Marseilles, and Bilbao. Neighboring towns—Blackpool, Southport, and Chester in the case of Liverpool; Nice, Cannes, and Arles in Marseilles' case; and Santander, San Sebastián, and Pamplona in Bilbao's—enjoy a better fate, which is connected to their popularity as tourist resorts and, increasingly, as retailing centers. But the counterpoint is still more striking when contrasting Liverpool, Marseilles, and Bilbao to their great rivals Manchester, Lyons, and Barcelona,[2] because these traditional hubs of textile manufacturing have successfully overcome their postindustrial crisis to become fashionable for their tertiary sector. Thus, Liverpool, Marseilles, and Bilbao suffer from a bad image, which is to a great extent a problem of poor self-image. Yet, no matter how strong the criticisms, these three cities evoke a high level of personal attachment among both locals and foreigners. They certainly have a special charm; people might find them environmentally degraded, dirty, strident, dangerous, but never unattractive. There is a cultural dimension to this. Liverpool, Marseilles, and Bilbao are vastly proletarian, cosmopolitan, and multicultural cities. Their people are renowned in their respective countries for their vivacity, humor, and strong clans. All this is just commonplace, but is part of their glamor and cultural image. Less celebrated is perhaps another common cultural characteristic that I have chosen to discuss here: Liverpool has now the most notable network of museums in England after London; Marseilles's museums have become in France second only to Paris; and Bilbao features, with the modern Guggenheim and the nearby Museum of Fine Arts, an impressive counterpart to the pair formed in Madrid by the Prado and the Reina Sofía Museums. How have these investments fared as regeneration tools? The responses to this question depend, as often happens, on the observer's point of view. One way to answer this question is in terms of the economic trickle-down model and their contribution to urban economies. The other approach is to examine their contributions as catalysts in the emergence of arts communities which in turn lead to urban revitalization.

The Failure of the Economic Trickle-Down Model

It is increasingly obvious that urban regeneration cannot solely be measured in terms of economic statistics or in terms of architectural revamping and real estate investments. For example, it is highly debatable that a flurry of new building developments always constitutes a success, particularly when building boom pressure quickly transforms historic ports into a jungle of office buildings, commercial stores and hotels, as in the London Docklands, New York's Battery Park City, the harborfront of Toronto, or the port of Tokyo. The "spirit of the place" is better kept (as some European cities like Antwerp, Brest, San Sebastián, or Genoa have learned from the celebrated examples of Boston and Baltimore) when ports become sites for maritime museums, aquariums, and leisure waterfronts (Baudoin and Collin 1992). These help urban sightseers get personal insights into seaside experience while creating jobs for which unemployed local workers qualify very well: they are enthusiastic interpreters of maritime displays, they have firsthand knowledge of many aquatic species, and they are the most proficient in the maneuvering and maintenance of boats. Thus historic preservation of port waterfronts can go beyond merely keeping some old buildings, by rescuing the neighborhood too; saving not only the buildings, but also their utility and the morale of the people.

Yet, it is doubtful that such idealistic thoughts counted much in attracting investments for the regeneration of the port of Liverpool. In the 1980s, at the height of the political rule of Margaret Thatcher, about £30m (approximately U.S. $50 million) was invested in the restoration of Liverpool's Albert Dock[3] where the Tate Gallery of the North opened in May 1988, based on designs of the celebrated Liverpool-trained architect James Stirling. In the United Kingdom those were years of cuts in public budgets and British analysts had to adopt arguments according to the prevailing business mood of the decade, attempting to show the economic importance of the arts (Myerscough 1988; Arts Council of Great Britain 1989): consultancies were required to measure with quantifiable "returns" that money given to arts was not a mere "expenditure" but also a good "investment," which would "trickle down"—a favorite Thatcherite term—leading to jobs creation and economic benefits. In such terms Liverpool's Tate Gallery turned out to be a great disappointment. Too many expectations for economic boosting and tourism attraction were raised on the arrival of a new branch of the Tate to Albert Dock. This led to disappointments and, most dangerously, to a feeling of estrangement between some Liverpudlians and the lavishly converted wharf, which was seen locally as a sort of Trojan horse, sheltering officials sent by the right-wing government in London for the conquest of left-wing Liverpool. As for tourists, they did flow to the Albert Dock in considerable numbers—between 2 million and 3.5 million visitors annually—but typically for daylong visits, which makes a very modest impact on the tertiary sector economy of Liverpool.

A similar example is the case in Marseilles of the reopening of the hospice of La Vieille Charité[4] as a museum complex after a restoration carried out from 1970 to 1986 at a cost of 99 million francs (approximately U.S. $14 million) paid for by the city council and the governments of the nation, the region, and the province (Paire 1991). The complex became home to several university institutions, four galleries for temporary exhibitions, a videotheque, the Museum of Mediterranean Archaeology, and the Museum of African, Oceanian, and American Indian Arts. (The latter seems a particularly happy choice, for the neighbourhood includes many inmigrants from non-European countries.) But the awaited trickle-down effect on the regeneration of the Panier quarter never happened, apart from further investments by the public powers in nearby buildings: the regional government restored another baroque building just in front, a former convent, in which was installed the Fond Régional d'Art Contemporain, whilst the municipality refurbished old derelict houses nearby to open there the Maison de la Poésie, which was closed later on. Here again, the locals, many of them living in total destitution, were alarmed by the great expenditure on this cultural center which, as a matter of fact, has failed to attract tourists in significant numbers, probably because the vicinity is perceived as dangerous for those holding a camera or feeling vulnerable.

The story line in Bilbao is similar again. The site of the Euskalduna shipyards, whose closure in 1988 provoked violent riots, was the place chosen for the inauguration in 1997 of a new branch of the Guggenheim Museum in an impressive building by American architect Frank Gehry. Journalists and short-term analysts publicized the great hopes and the great suspicions raised by the project, looked upon by some as an inminent miracle and by others as a swindle, but none failed to point out that its cost amounted to more than 23.000 million pesetas (approximately U.S. $153 million) financed with matching funds from the Basque government and that of the province of Biscay (Tellitu, Esteban, and González Carrera 1997; Zulaika 1997). The local population of unemployed and working-class people contemplated such expenditure as an extravagance, but the rare political protests came from some left-wing groups who accused the oligarchies of serving spurious real estate interests, cleansing out the only spot of dereliction remaining in the suburban area most favored by the upper classes while part of the old city center or nearby streets would continue decaying and rotting with drug dealing, street prostitution, and social ghettos. On the eve of the museum's innauguration, the terrorist organization ETA manifested its opposition by trying to plant a bomb at the entrance; this was prevented by the intervention of two police officers, one of whom was shot to death by the terrorists. During the first year, adding the lure of novelty to a declared cease-fire in terrorist attacks, the museum received a million and a half visitors; but now figures have plummeted. The Basque Government insists on reporting a honeymoon relationship between the new Guggenheim and the people of Bilbao, and visitors from elsewhere—almost a million per year, of which foreigners amount to 50 percent. However, the museum, in spite of charging the highest entrance fees in Spain, has a considerable annual deficit, that has to be covered by Basque taxpayers. Meanwhile, despite official claims (based on studies commissioned by the Basque Government but never published or explained to the scientific community) that every visitor to the museum spends in the city an average of 27,500 pesetas (about U.S. $140), local business linked to the tourist industry has not thrived as much as was expected, probably because Bilbao tends to be a daystop in the typical tourist package offered by travel agencies, many of which look for hotels outside the troubled Basque region.

Synergistic Effect in the Local Arts Scene

Alternatively, these expensive projects can be evaluated in terms of their contribution to the "synergy" of the local arts community. It has taken considerable effort to normalise relations between the Liverpool's Tate and local citizens. However, with time, this national museum, in which exhibitions are mostly free of charge, has bridged the initial gulf with the local community. In particular, the Tate has upgraded the local art scene, mitigating outmigration of artists to London. Even more, Liverpool is now becoming a new Mecca for artists from other places: the local organizations offering studio spaces for artists have waiting lists. The strength of the local arts scene remains a great asset for the regeneration of the city as seen, since 1992, on the occasion of the *Visionfest Festival*, now replaced by a biennial celebration featuring open studio events and alternative exhibitions arranged by the local community of artists, the North West Arts Board and the city of Liverpool, collaborating with galleries, universities, communities, artists' co-ops, and individuals. As any other biennial or annual arts festival, it works primarily as a public showcase for the latest art; but this one also provides a "hothouse" for innovative creation of art in new places: pubs, billboards, warehouses, alternative galleries, ferries, schools, and so on. Moreover, many small independent art galleries and studios have flourished in the derelict warehouses of the Duke Street area between the Anglican Cathedral and the Albert Dock, now known as "the Creative Quarter." Stirring this artistic hubbub are the Hanover Galleries in the Victorian building of a cap and hat factory, just across the street from The View Gallery, or further uptown, The Liverpool Academy of Arts which doubles as a theater, the Acorn Gallery & Cafe, on the top floor of a former warehouse, and the Ainscough Gallery which also runs a trendy pavement cafe.

This boom in places for art production and consumption in a part of town containing many dilapidated landmarks of the Victorian splendor of Liverpool has had a tremendous appeal for young people. Realizing the potential of it for urban regeneration, the Liverpool City Council, the regional art administration, and private developers have launched publicity campaigns claiming a new image for Liverpool—formerly a city of merchants—as a city of artists. Often, as in the Liverpool Palace, private businesses provide studio spaces for creative people (architects, designers, artists) or, as in Baaba Bar, they arrange temporary art exhibitions on the premises. Their strategy is to nurture a lively artist presence as a means to enhance their establishments with an atmosphere of youth and alternative culture. The most outstanding initiative in this respect has been the opening in a Victorian building of the first great department store (called "Quiggins") for club wear, vintage clothing, and secondhand bric-a-brac. The top floor is used by a group of artists, Merseyside Arts Base, who run an exhibitions gallery and five artists studios. Thus even the private market of urban developers and businesspeople sees that nurturing artists and arts venues can improve the image of an urban area and attract people to it. Hosting art exhibitions, inviting musicians, and using designers is now cheered by artist-friendly developers such as Urban Strategies and mixed-use centers for fashion shopping, including Trading Places and the Cream

Shops. Furthermore, the burgeoning array of new nightlife venues in the area and countless dance and music clubs is making the Creative Quarter Liverpool's "Clubland." Once again popular music is creating the miracle of rejuvenating and regenerating the city center of Liverpool!

In Marseilles, too, many rundown houses around La Vieille Charité have been refurbished and reopened as booming small shops and cafes catering to a fringe culture. Alas, botanical terminology describes too well this phenomenon, since very often such initiatives are short lived. But as soon as one closes down, many others emerge, most of them run by artists doubling as amateur dealers/bartenders. It is also true that, since these modest businesses cannot afford costly architectural repairs, their contribution to urban renewal mostly consists of redecorating the premises. Yet the mere presence of art dealers and artists has greatly enhanced the urban milieu, and the thriving art scene in the Panier is now actively supported by the public powers and is well publicized.[5]

This political generosity to the local arts sector has to be seen within the context of political practices in France, where policymakers are not averse to taxpayer money being spent to support artists and encourage art production.[6] The political upheavals in France have brought some changes in arts spending, but not a significant change in cultural policies—in Marseilles the main promoter of the reuse of redundant buildings by artists remains the city council. First, a number of artists, chosen by established application procedures, can benefit from a free lease of about 23 months of a modern studio in one of the converted buildings administered by the Ateliers d'Artistes de la Ville de Marseilles, a municipal agency created in 1990. Its headquarters are based in a former textile factory in the Lorette district (there is a space for exhibitions on the ground floor, usually featuring works by the tenants above); the other main site the agency owns is a former furniture workshop in the central Panier quarter. Second, the Cultural Affairs Bureau of the Marseilles City Council has, in the last decade, run an ambitious programme of art commissions, some of which have consisted of artistic interventions on derelict sites. Third, the Office de la Culture, a semi-independent body financed by the City Council, seeks the coordination of public patronage of the arts in Marseilles, giving special attention to art developments in derelict or less-favored city areas. Thus, in contrast to the usual situation in Liverpool, it is rare to find in Marseilles inner-city artists associations that have not benefited from public money—usually matching funds from the Ville de Marseille Council, the Conséil Général of the province, the Région Provence-Alpes-Côte d'Azur, and the Ministry of Culture.

Trends in cultural policies in Spain lie somewhere between the unashamed protectionism of the French pattern and the Anglo-American noninterventionist model, concentrating public patronage on cultural infrastructures—museums, exhibitions centers—but abandoning art practice to its own fate (Ribalta 1998). In Bilbao, social programs of art encouragement and subsidies to artists organizations initially experienced cuts as a consequence of the heavy investment required from the Basque government and the local authorities to found the Guggenheim Museum. This immediately raised voices of protest in the arts sector, vigorously expressed in the press and in "alternative" exhibitions organized by artists opposing the arrival of the Guggenheim, often with the complicity of existing Basque museums fearing to see at risk their own budgets for enlargement projects or, indeed, for their day-to-day operations. Sculptor Jorge Oteiza, who had nurtured the project of an arts center in another site in the area of Bilbao, became the leader of a lobby opposing this museum, which was seen by many local artists and intellectuals as an instrument of cultural colonialism—no works by Oteiza and Chillida, the most prestigious names in contemporary Basque art, have entered the Guggenheim. Yet, after such contentious beginnings, the arts sector soon became more enthusiastic about the new situation. First, the other museums now have more visitors. The Museum of Fine Arts of Bilbao has sold about 50 percent more tickets since the Guggenheim opened opposite it. Other cultural amenities in the neighborhood, like the Auditorium and Conference Palace and the Rekalde Exhibition Galleries, have paved the way for a burgeoning of new outlets run by artists organizations, including the alternative theater and dance center, La Fundición, the association Mediaz, the Urazurrutia center, the international project Consonni for art, music, and dance, and other venues animated by grass-root movements. Thus, the presence of highbrow international art and mundane crowds of museum-going tourists has increased the number of restaurants and souvenir shops and is also benefiting the rest of the local arts scene.

A New Approach to the "Knock-On" Effect

What these three cases demonstrate is that the level of success of urban regeneration policies cannot be adequately measured solely in physical or economic terms.[7] Museums and art galleries may be a very successful investment if they become catalysts of further urban regeneration, as when an arts district emerges close by. Obviously this is not a suitable remedy for every city with problems of urban decay, because not every place has the artistic background and the cultural glamour of Liverpool, Marseilles, and Bilbao: a new museum would not necessarily work as a talisman healing urban cultures everywhere. But there are plenty of declining ports whose pedigree as art metropolises qualifies them for a such a "cure," with the expectation of similar results in a noneconomic-oriented research evaluation.[8]

The first conclusion I would draw from the three cases examined here is that, in order to accelerate such knock-on reaction, urban developers should be encouraged in some cases to assure the presence of art professionals. It is useful to create multipurpose public spaces, mixed-use centers with shops, offices, and different kinds of leisure provision, including museums and galleries. It is even better to provide lodgings or, if urban planning regulations do not allow that, working spaces for artists. This gives the area some life after business hours, and attracts a nocturnal *dolce vita*.

Another conclusion to be drawn from this comparative study is the existence of a second pattern of arts-led urban renewal processes, diametrically opposed to the general scheme taken for granted regarding the development of art districts in the inner cities. Examples like Montmartre and Montparnasse in the Paris of the Belle Époque, the SoHo district in New York between 1971 and 1981, or the Temple Bar area of Dublin in the 1980s, have led to the assumption that art districts come into existence in deprived neighborhoods following this typical format. First, some nonestablished artists discover the existence of cheap atelier spaces to rent in derelict unused buildings (the Bateau-Lavoir in Paris, the Victorian warehouses of downtown Manhattan, etc). Then art dealers follow suit, installing their galleries in the area while other private entrepreneurs come with alternative/youth amenities like fashion shops, trendy bars, restaurants, dance clubs, and so on. Eventually, almost inevitably, come the museums, national theaters and public arts centers, and their arrival leads to the "legitimation" of such arts districts. The fatal culmination of this is the installation of apartments for yuppies, while artists gradually move out because rents have become too high.

The typical model underlying this process can therefore be described as one of gentrification: redundant buildings with stagnating rents in a deprived city area are resuscitated thanks to the presence of artists; this attracts developers who transform the district into an arts quarter, which brings in a lot of people, institutions, and money but eventually expels the artists because they cannot afford the increasing rents.[9] I do not refute that scheme or even contradict its final outcome—namely that the arts are victims of their own success and act as instruments of a gentrification process. But I believe that another scheme is possible, one in which museums arrive first as a consequence of a political decision to bring derelict landmarks of city heritage into new life, then, in a knock-on domino effect, other derelict buildings in the district become cultural centers or art galleries, and finally artists move their studios into the areas, creating a lively atmosphere in what used to be a blighted area. Such has been the process, as we have seen, in the cases studied here. One could thus conclude that arts-led urban regeneration is not always a spontaneous process originated by "bohemians" and finally benefiting speculators in the housing market. In some cases the process can start after the political decision to open a museum in a derelict area.

This model has important implications in the realm of contemporary politics. One cannot plan to create an art district in a derelict area simply by counting on the help of artists' collectives because the spirit of independence and revolt inherent in the personality of artists makes them, in general, undomesticated citizens, more often eager to confront politicians and urban developers than to collaborate with them.[10] Nevertheless, politicians and planners do have free hands in deciding where to plant a new museum and this, as we have seen, can entail the mushrooming of a thriving arts scene.

Notes

1. I have developed this perspective after long discussions and interviews with activists and enablers of the respective local arts-scenes, a process which first gathered momentum on the occasion of the one-day symposium 'The Role of Museums and the Arts in the Urban Renewal of Liverpool' (Tate Gallery, Liverpool, 21st October 1995) which was the origin of a book I edited (Lorente 1996). Then, wanting to expand the picture, I looked for other points of comparison: a general review of the situation in several Spanish cities (Lorente 1997). This paper condenses some of the findings discussed in such earlier works, seen now in retrospect and with the benefit of hindsight.

Thus this is not yet another study of the trickle-down economic benefits created by cultural policies in distressed areas, but a plea for art entrepreneurs to aim their investments mainly at cultural targets. In order to emphasize this perspective the title chosen for this essay avoids the term urban renewal, more usually linked to physical change, sporting instead 'urban regeneration' — i.e. revitalizing not just in architectural terms but also in terms of quality of life. Now we know better (on present cultural policies cf. Bianchini 1993; Landry and Greene 1995; Langsted 1990; Remesar 1997). Culture and the related business of the so-called symbolic economy provide many jobs, but they are mostly part-time, insecure or low-wage. It is not with the arts budget that politicians are going to solve the problems of unemployment and poverty!

2. I find particularly interesting this double comparison of Liverpool/Manchester with Marseilles/Lyon; but of course the most natural points of comparison in previous studies have been other port-cities in general. Cf. for example the counterpoint Marseilles-Montreal (Gasquy-Resch 1991), the proceedings of two colloquia held in Marseilles, Merseyside (Judd and Parkinson 1990), Le Havre (Marks 1993 and Dufay 1993), and the special issue of the *Annales de la Recherche Urbaine* on "Grandes Villes et Ports de Mer" (September 1992).

3. The Albert Dock, designed by Jesse Hartley as the first enclosed dock warehouse in the world made entirely out of incombustible materials — cast, iron, brick and granite — had opened in 1846 and closed in 1972 — but it was defunct long before that time (Cockcroft 1994). Its restoration was conducted by the (MDC) Merseyside Development Corporation, one of the urban development corporations created by the government of Margaret Thatcher in 1980 in fierce opposition to some Labor-led local councils (Parkinson and Evans 1992). The riots of 1981 prompted the MDC to seek quickly a highly visible physical regeneration in part of the 865 depopulated acres under their command in Liverpool, Sefton, and the Wirral. Therefore, after largely unsuccessful attempts to redevelop the South Docks for industrial and commercial purposes, they turned toward a tourism and leisure-led strategy in the Albert Dock: a complex of shops and museum displays, prominently the Tate Gallery, the Maritime Museum and the *Beatles Story* .

4. The hospice of the Vieille Charité was built at the heart of the city's most popular district in 1671–1745 based on plans by the local architect, sculptor and painter Pierre Puget. It lost its original function in 1883 and subsequently became military barracks, tenants houses, improvised shelter for the homeless and then finally an empty and derelict space. The building basically consists of a three-store patio with porticoes and, in the middle of it, an oblong chapel crowned by an astonishing dome.

5. Presenting this as a success of urban regeneration might seem debatable, but in previous experiences the municipality of Marseilles has encountered social hostility to other kinds of cultural policies for urban regeneration. When the city commissioned 'L'aventure', a public art work from Richard Baquié, the famous conceptual artist, to be placed in Carter Nord Malpassé, a disadvantaged suburb, they found a resentful response from the local community who tagged and vandalized that expensive art commission, money for which they thought could have been better spent in more useful ways (Ayard 1988). When the city opened a national theater for contemporary plays in the depressed Northern district of Merlan, it found few customers in the neighborhood, while people from richer areas were afraid to use their cars to go there or would have difficulties in finding a taxi-driver prepared to do so by night — not for nothing are theater-performances called '*soirées*'.

6. The Department of Plastic Arts of the Culture Ministry regularly bestows a considerable part of its budget on promoting new artists' studios, co-financing renovation of studios undertaken by artists (up to 50% of the total expenditure) and subsidizing urban developers who built artists' studios (between 80,000 and 100,000 FF. for every studio). As Catherine Millet has

pointed out, the contemporary arts-scene in France has evolved from slumming anti-establish-ment art communities to associations of tenants working in subsidized sites (Millet 1994: 280). Happily enough, this growing concern to reintegrate artists back into the heart of our cities seems not to be limited by political or social divides (for specialized literature on studio provi-sion cf. Lansmark 1981; Lipske 1988; Keens 1989; Lawless 1990; Kartes 1993; Colin 1994).

7. A similar conclusion arises, from another perspective, in other studies on urban renewal through the arts (cf. Bianchini 1991; as well as Bianchini and Parkinson 1993).

8. It is surely no coincidence that some of the most successful examples of the 'Cultural Capital of Europe' festival—Glasgow (1990), Antwerp (1993) and Lisbon (1994)—have pro-duced arts-led rehabilitation of decayed waterfronts. The same happened in the old ports of Barcelona and Genoa, two historic art capitals again, whose renewal started after the Olympic games and the Columbus celebrations in 1992 and it is now well-advanced, with brand new aquariums and new museums about to open. To this list we could add the old artistic sea-side colony of St. Ives in Cornwall, which has sponsored a new section of the Tate Gallery since 1993, and the Greek city of Thessalonica, the cultural hub of Macedonia, whose port-quays have featured a Museum of Byzantine Arts since 1994.

9. The solution to this vicious circle might come from a new spirit of collaboration between the arts communities and the public powers, so that instead of just helping creative people to convert leased buildings into studios or galleries, grants would also be directed at helping artists' co-ops obtain affordable mortgages so that they could buy these buildings they have refur-bished. Thus the permanent presence of the art scene in the district would be assured.

10. Proof of this is the fact that artists and artists' organizations have often headed urban revolts. In America, the most notorious case took place two decades ago when passionate cam-paigns for the preservation of New York's SoHo occurred through public demonstrations, political lobbying and anarchist hostility to the law. There are also some well-known Euro-pean cases. In Berlin, during the riots of 1981, artists and young students were featured promi-nently in the world media as the squatters who radically opposed their eviction from the district of Kreuzberg (Colquhoun 1995: 128). Enormous resistence by both artists and scholars has met the renewal of the Temple Bar quarter in Dublin, which has lost its artistic soul and is now a trendy commercial district where most of the new housing is apartments for wealthy singles. Many other famous examples could be quoted, not all finishing with happy endings. Such was the case in London where, recently, artists led the local communities in protests unsuccessfully opposing the transformation of the Docklands into a jungle of office towers (Bird 1993). On these matters, the natural place where art activism belongs is with grassroots movements and communities, not with developers (Felshin 1995). On the other hand, it is quite comprehensible if artists are often diffident and critical towards property developers and urban planners. Nobody would like to be used and abused as an attraction for other tenants, whose presence might eventually outnumber and undermine the initial high concentration of creative people.

References

Arts Council of Great Britain (1989) *An Urban Renaissance. Sixteen Case Studies Showing the Role of the Arts in Urban Regeneration*, London: Arts Council of Great Britain.

Ayard, C. (1988) 'Quartier Nord Malpassé, commande publique,' *La Galérie de la Mer*, n° 1.

Baudouin, T. and Collin, M. (1992) 'Patrimoine et capital portuaire,' pp. 65–70 in *Le patrimoine portuaire*, Le Havre: Association Internationale Villes et Ports (actes de 'Le port et la Ville. Rencontres du Havre,' 16–17 novembre 1992).

Bianchini, F. (1991) 'Urban renaissance? The arts and the urban regeneration process,' pp. 215–250 in S. MacGregor and B. Pimlott (eds.) *Tackling the Inner Cities: The 1980s Reviewed, Prospects for the 1990s*, Oxford: Clarendon Press.

Bianchini, F. (1993) *Urban Cultural Policy in Britain and Europe: Towards Cultural Planning*, Queensland: Griffith University.

Bianchini, F. and Parkinson, M. (eds.) (1993) *Cultural Policy and Urban Regeneration: The West European Experience*, Manchester and New York: Manchester University Press.

Bird, J. (1993) 'Dystopia on the Thames,' pp. 120–135 in J. Bird, B. Curtis, T. Putnam, G. Robertson, and L. Tickner (eds.) *Mapping the Future: Local cultures, global change*, London & New York: Routledge.

Cockcroft, W. R. (1994) *The Albert Dock and Liverpool's Historic Waterfront*, Rainworth: Print Origination Formby and Books Unlimited.

Colin, J.-P. (1994) 'La Cité de la création: et l'art change la ville,' pp. 150–156 in J.-P. Colin and F. Seloran (eds.) *Le mandarin étranglé. Le rôle de l'art dans les transformations sociales*, Paris: Publisud.

Colquhoun, I. (1995) *Urban Regeneration. An International Perspective*, London: B.T. Batsford Ltd.

Dufay, J. P. (1993) 'Vers une défense de l'architecture portuaire,' pp. 109–117 in M. Cantal-Dupart and C. Chaline (eds.) *Le port cadre de ville*, Paris: L'Harmattan (actes du séminaire du même titre organisé par l'Association Internationale Villes et Ports).

Felshin, N. (ed.) (1995) *But Is It Art? The Spirit of Art as Activism*, Seattle: Bay Press.

Gasquy-Resch, Yannick (ed.) (1991) *Marseille-Montréal: Centres culturels cosmopolites*, Paris: L'Harmattan.

Judd, D. and Parkinson, M. (eds.) (1990) *Leadership and Urban Regeneration: Cities in North America and Europe*, Newbury Park, CA: Sage Publications.

Kartes, C. (1993) *Creating Space: A Guide to Real Estate Development for Artists*, New York: ACA Books & Allworth Press.

Landry, C. and Greene, L. (1995) *Revitalising Cities and Towns Through Cultural Development*, Bourners Green, UK: Comedia.

Langsted, J. (ed.) (1990) *Strategies: Studies in Modern Cultural Policy*, Aarhus: Aarhus University Press.

Lansmark, T. C. (1981) *Artists' Spaces: A Study of the Development of Artists' Living and Working Space in Boston*, Boston: Artists Foundation.

Lawless, C. (1990) *Ateliers et artistes*, Nîmes: Editions Jacqueline Chambon.

Lipske, M. (1988) *Artists' Housing: Creating Live/Work Space that Lasts*, New York: Publishing Center for Cultural Resources.

Lorente, J. P. (ed) (1996) *The Role of Museums and the Arts in the Urban Regeneration of Liverpool*, Leicester: Center for Urban History.

Lorente, J. P. (ed) (1997) *Espacios para el arte contemporáneo generadores de revitalización urbana*, Zaragoza: Departamento de Historia del Arte de la Universidad de Zaragoza.

Marks, D. (1993) 'La conservation et la réutilisation de bâtiments portuaires: Albert Dock et Tobacco Dock,' pp. 61–69 in M. Cantal-Dupart and C. Chaline (eds.) *Le port cadre de ville*, Paris: L'Harmattan (actes du séminaire du même titre organisé par l'Association Internationale Villes et Ports).

Millet, C. (1994) *L'Art contemporain en France*, Paris: Flammarion.

Myerscough, J. (1988) *The Economic Importance of the Arts in Britain*, London: Policy Studies Institute.

Paire, A. (1991) *La Vieille Charité de Marseille*, Aix-en-Provence: Édisud.

Parkinson, M. and Evans, R. (1992) 'Liverpool, la restructuration urbaine d'un port en déclin,' *Les Annales de la Recherche Urbaine*, no. 55–56: 45–52.

Remesar, A. (ed.) (1997) *Urban Regeneration. A Challenge for Public Art*, Barcelona: University of Barcelona.

Tellitu, A., Esteban, I. and González Carrera, J. A. (1997) *El milagro Guggenheim. Una ilusión de alto riesgo*, Bilbao: El Correo.

Williams, J., Bollen, H., Gidney, M., and Owens, P. (1993) *The Artist in the Changing City*, London: British American Arts Association.

Zulaika, J. (1997) *Crónica de una seducción. Guggenheim Bilbao*, Madrid: Nerea.

7

The Local and the Global in Popular Music

The Brazilian Music Industry, Local Culture, and Public Policies

Luciana Ferreira Moura Mendonça

Although little is known about the actual impact of the international recorded music industry on local music cultures in developing countries, there is a great deal of speculation concerning its effects. Some scholars assume that the major companies direct and domesticate local cultural production, leading to hegemony and homogenization. Other scholars overestimate the possibilities of "independent" and "original" cultural creation, giving too much weight to the potential of popular culture for resistance and to the capacity of the public to use cultural commodities for their own purposes. Both approaches have their strengths and their limitations.[1] The issue is complicated by the fact that some cultural movements appear to contradict both theses. Though culture industries have enormous resources for achieving their objectives, artists can take advantage of spaces left by these industries to renew and reinvigorate local cultures.[2] One such example is that of the *mangue beat* movement from Recife, capital of Pernambuco State, in the northeast region of Brazil.

In this chapter, I will explore three aspects of the *mangue beat* movement. First, I will consider the characteristics of the international music industry, particularly its capacity to legitimate artists and musical styles. The music industry provides the material and ideological context for the channels through which flow the cultural products of local movements such as the *mangue beat* movement. Second, I will analyze the emergence of the *mangue beat* movement in the context of the creation, production, and recent history of contemporary Brazilian popular music in local and national contexts. Finally, I will examine the *mangue beat* movement in relation to other cultural groups in the same region and to public policies in the area for the arts and popular culture.

The Music Industry: Global, National, and Local Strategies

The international music industry has been dominated by an oligopoly for decades, to the detriment of small producers and independent recording labels. The major companies have pursued an aggressive strategy of expansion in international markets and have occupied the center of power in the transnational music business. In the early 1980s, the industry underwent a crisis brought on by a decline in sales. Beginning in 1985, it changed strategies and started to recover its previous pattern of growth. These companies have frequently changed hands, but the same oligopolistic structure remains. The enormity of their power is incontestible: in 1996 the six biggest groups—Sony Music, Polygram, EMI, WEA, BMG, and MCA—controlled 91 percent of global record distribution, including the distribution of records produced by independent labels.[3] Since then, mergers have reduced the number of major firms to five, reorganizing the concentration of capital, distribution, and marketing decisions. For example, at the beginning of 2000, WEA attempted to merge with EMI, to form the second-biggest record company in the world, but the deal eventually fell through.[4]

On the other hand, these companies maintain a strategy of decentralization of production, by purchasing numerous labels that compete with one another (Lopes 1992). The small labels are often directed toward specialized segments of the market, and some of their products are distributed by the majors. In this manner, the music industry retains its oligopolistic profile but, at the same time, has the possibility (or necessity) of supporting a more open structure, through its association with independent labels. This strategy stimulates the emergence of new types of musical products that meet public demand and replace outdated products (Lopes 1992). As we will see, the success of Brazilian _mangue beat_ bands in the record business occurred because local independent labels could become associated with major companies in the global industry. The valorization of new artists and genres performs an important role in music companies' strategies for overcoming crises in the industry.

Rock and its numerous "substyles" are important aesthetic elements in many local and national contexts, as in the case of the musical movement in this case study. Between accusations of being a form of cultural imperialism and exaltation as a libertarian force, rock has become a global "mediascape," transmitting diverse meanings. In particular countries, it can appear either as an imitation of imported styles or as a stimulus to the creation of hybrid styles,[5] in which musicians blend elements from local musical traditions and add native language lyrics. Thus, rock has an artistic and aesthetic logic that has become autonomous. In part, rock's "autonomy" and "universality" are linked to an international popular culture that is disseminated by the music industry (Ortiz 1994), including sets of practices, a repertory of sensibilities, body expressions, and institutionalized emotions. These features have become a type of cultural capital and a dominant _habitus_ in the field of popular music. As Motti Regev (1997) has said, "The global predominance of rock aesthetics to make local music is a primordial manifestation of the cultural logic of globalization" (p. 137).

Regev argues that the rock aesthetic should be defined as a set of practices in constant transformation; these practices have developed since the 1950s. Some of the principal components are electronic sonic textures, amplification, forms of vocal emission and spontaneous performance, the presence of rhythm instruments, production in the studio, and an eclectic logic that makes possible the application of these elements to many kinds of music. Its meanings include joy and entertainment, challenge and fury, as well as a set of attitudes that leads to certain types of behavior, fashion, and collective forms of appropriation. An important aspect of rock lies in the contradiction between the fact that rock is a mass product but one that also criticizes mass culture and creates an "authentic" public through the same means and processes that are used to establish rock as a product. Its "authenticity"—seen in contrast and in relation to its commercial potential—constitutes a element of tension in the competition among musicians, styles, artists, and records, producing constant innovation in sound, in visual aspects, and in contextual meanings and feelings.

From the point of view of producers and listeners, rock has the capacity to strengthen feelings of local identity and autonomy. It is a form of participation in contemporary and global artistic expression and, at the same time, it is a means of renewing local, ethnic, and national identities. To explain the dialectics between local and global in various forms of rock, Regev (1997) hypothesizes that

> the construction of local styles of rock and their meanings as "local authentic" music is an aesthetic strategy of identity formation that is determined by the "projection" . . . of musicians and public in two spaces or fields of cultural practice: the field of contemporary popular music and the field of national/local identity. (p. 126)

Consequently, in research in local settings, it is important to analyze how the cultural elements are transformed to project new images of identity.

A common characteristic of rock in its various contexts is that people attribute to it, basically, the *same* meaning of a "new" identity that communicates, harmoniously or contradictorily, with "traditional" identities. Often, musicians adapt selectively the elements of rock, which are mixed with local styles of music. Musicians use rock instrumentation and its sonic textures but incorporate instruments, vocal styles, and rhythms taken from the local context to create music that sounds like rock but also like forms rooted in local culture. In this case, there is no need to make a claim that the music is authentic, because it is inscribed in the texture of the sounds.

The Brazilian music market reproduces, to a considerable extent, the general dynamics of the global market, but reflects at the same time the "peripheral" position of the country.[6] In the 1990s, Brazil moved from the thirteenth to the sixth position in the international music market ranking. According to an industry source,

> An increase of 128% has occurred. In global leadership, Brazil comes after the USA, Japan, Germany, Great Britain and France. In 1996, Brazil had sales figures of 891 million dollars, without taking into account the huge market of pirated cassettes. [7]

The number of illegal copies of CDs that are confiscated amounts to almost half the number of CDs legally manufactured in Brazil, totaling 16 million copies in April 1999. By contrast, the pirate industry in the United States controls only 2 percent of the market.[8] The Brazilian Association of Record Producers (ABPD) announced that, from 1997 to 1998, the sales figures for the music industry decreased by 14 percent, from U.S. $1,227 million to U.S. $1,055 million. Consumption diminished by 10 percent. Sales decreased from 117 million copies in 1997 to 105.3 million in 1999. According to the ABPD, the reduction in the market is because of the growth of the pirate market, which corresponds to 45 percent of CDs produced and to 90 percent of the cassettes. Brazil is in the second position on the piracy ranking, representing about 40 million illegal CDs sold annually, which in turn deprives artists of income.[9]

Nevertheless, pessimistic predictions that Brazilian music would be suffocated by massive consumption of foreign music, mainly Anglo-Saxon, have not come true.

> Among about 300 monthly record launchings in Brazil, 60 percent are of Brazilian music, approximately 180 records. Around 80 percent of the songs played on the radio are Brazilian. . . . Among the biggest national markets, besides the USA, Brazil comes after Mexico in terms of the level of local products on the market, and is only behind Japan when considering the performance of the national musical product. It is also interesting to observe that the sales figures of American pop music are not as good in Brazil as they were a few years ago.[10]

The dynamism of Brazilian music production can be attested not only by the music industry figures but through constant music recycling, renovation, and diversification, including a variety of old and recent "genres." Many of the new and hybrid forms cannot be subsumed under the genres predefined by the record industry but fit a wide variety of tastes. However, the matching of particular publics with musical genres frequently happens outside the mainstream, in what has been called the "alternative" market. In terms of the level of capital invested, there is only one Brazilian company that can be placed among the biggest media groups in the world: Rede Globo. Its music division includes Som Livre, Som Livre Portugal, and Globo Group (EUA), responsible for record production and distribution. A couple of years ago, one of the biggest publishing companies in Brazil, Abril Group, which is also involved with other sectors of cultural production, launched a new record label, Abril Music.

In Recife, one of Brazil's biggest cities, where the *mangue beat* movement developed, the structure for music production is inadequate.[11] There are only a few recording studios and a couple of labels and independent record producers. The most interesting initiatives come from two producers: Paulo André Pires and Antônio Gutierrez, known as Gutie. Paulo André produces bands and is the organizer of Abril Pró Rock, one of the biggest rock festivals in the country. Gutie is also a producer of bands and organizes the Rec-Beat festival. It takes place during Carnival and is a showcase for local artists. The restrictions on local music production are mainly economic, because most investment is directed toward southeast Brazil, especially Rio de Janeiro and São Paulo. The Brazilian music market has always been very centralized in these cities, where the headquarters of the major companies and their recording studios are located and the production, distribution, and marketing decisions are made. Until recently, musicians from other regions had to migrate to these centers to develop their careers.

Most of the local record production aims at the "alternative" market, in which consumption is limited, concentrating on local traditional music (various genres), hard rock, and hybrid genres in many different combinations. It is unusual to hear these local bands and artists on local or national radio.

Music Genres, Nationalism, and the *Mangue beat* Movement

Brazilian music is always defined as hybrid. Even "traditional" national genres, like *samba* and *choro* (or *chorinho*), are considered a blend of Iberian and African roots. However, it is important to distinguish these "traditional" genres from the new hybrid genres, because there are always purists on guard to defend and protect "national music" against foreign influences and to claim that some kinds of hybrid genres are "inauthentic" copies of imported models and, as such, "degenerate." This position is based on a conception of culture as something that must be kept isolated or protected to maintain its purity and originality, forgetting that the present manifestations are the result of a historical process of long duration, even in case of "traditional" music.[12] The new hybrid forms attract enthusiastic responses from the rock establishment internationally, probably because of ethnic or local elements that are perceived as exotic and original. They are, most of the time, labeled as world music, along with other styles that are not derived from rock, but from ethnic or national cultures.

Today there is virtually no musical creation in Brazil that is not connected with rock. Rock has been incorporated by composers since the 1960s, when two musical movements—the *Jovem Guarda* and the *Tropicalismo*[13]—took elements from rock to produce different styles. The first essentially produced a copy of rock in the 1950s or early 1960s; the second created hybrid forms with the use of rock textures, instruments, or attitude but with a strong Brazilian accent. Some critics and part of the public of that time saw *Tropicalismo* as an "inauthentic" form, a deviation from the "true" forms of Brazilian song. But rock has achieved greater importance since the 1980s, a period when many bands were created, including some—like Titãs and Paralamas do Sucesso—that have been very successful. This trend changed the nature of Brazilian music, and it is now more difficult to define authentic Brazilian music based on aesthetic elements.

At the beginning of the 1990s, there were few new composers and performers who could be considered innovators on the musical scene. Brazilian music appeared to be in a period of low creativity, at least according to music critics. When the *mangue beat* movement developed in Recife, local newspaper critics and others praised it as a form of musical renewal. This new music became popular with the local public and, after that, with a segment of the national and international public.

Pernambuco State has produced many popular musicians and composers of singular creativity and originality throughout its history, but because they had to leave the state in order to develop their careers and achieve success,[14] their works did not have a strong influence on local culture, except through the mass media that spread their work all over the country. By contrast, the *mangue* movement has affected the entire sector of local cultural production.

The *mangue beat* movement created a vocabulary based on local slang and inspired by metaphors describing the environment of the marshes and their inhabitants, especially the many kinds of crabs. Diversity is one of the most remarkable characteristics of popular culture in northeast Brazil, in general, and in Pernambuco, in particular. Indigenous, African, and Iberian roots are blended in its cultural scope. There are many popular celebrations and many different kinds of rhythms and songs linked to these various celebrations. When they are not located in the context of such popular celebrations, they are intimately linked to songs connected with work, as well as to religious and dramatic traditions. Derived from this context, *mangue beat* is the name of the rhythm created by Chico Science and his band, Nação Zumbi, from the fusion of local rhythms, like *maracatu* and *embolada*[15] and pop genres, especially funk and rock. It created a rich mixture of traditional music with international pop and elements from Brazilian popular music.

The *mangue beat* movement was created around 1991 when Chico Science and his friends—unhappy with the lack of opportunities for artistic expression and enjoyment and involved with cultural production in Recife—started a kind of cooperative to exchange ideas and to support one another. The group consisted of Chico Science, who died in February 1997; Fred 04, composer and lead vocalist of the other important early band in the movement, Mundo Livre S/A; and the journalist Renato Lins. *Mangue beat* became a label, a concept. A *mangue* is literally a marsh, a mud flat, which is an important part of Recife's environment—significant parts of the city were built on marshes. In fact, *mangue* is a metaphor for cultural diversity, based on an analogy with an environment full of diversity. Cultural and economic stagnation were to be overcome by musical innovation, a strong determination to perform their work, and the dynamics of local and global communications. Its symbol is a parabolic anthem on the mud, picking up every bit of interesting information from the international circuit and transmitting creations and ideas from *mangue*. From the outset, the group wanted to produce "an energetic circuit" and to connect "good local vibrations" with the worldwide web of pop concepts and cultural production.[16]

As a concept, the *mangue beat* movement worked (and still works) as an umbrella for a variety of preexisting musical and other art forms (like painting, fashion, movies, and photography). Tightly linked to the urban context in Recife and to the most up-to-date information on globalized culture, the *mangue* movement has been able to spread its ideas among the local population and is becoming well known among young people all over Brazil. In this way, it has helped artists to gain the attention of the public and media. This was a major improvement because there had been plenty of new ideas before but the artists did not have the necessary instruments and structure to develop their work. Material conditions improved when the musicians started to gain attention from national and international critics.

But it is important to add two things. First, rock has been a strong presence in Recife's music scene since the 1970s, so the *mangue* bands were not the only ones to produce this kind of hybrid music. Although *mangue* bands do not emphasize the fact, musicians from the previous generation, who developed their careers in the 1970s, are sometimes seen as precursors of *mangue beat*, because they made songs that blended local rhythms and rock textures. Second, the bands under the umbrella of *mangue* are not restricted to the same beat or style. The most important element of *mangue beat* is its diversity.

Mangue bands moved from amateur status or local restricted careers to professional production in various ways. The first *mangue* band to achieve success was Chico Science's band, Nação Zumbi. The band did a tour in southeast Brazil in 1993 and captured the attention of press and public. Its performance appealed to people from all social classes and education levels because of the song lyrics (based on everyday life) and the band's sound (an original combination of tradition and modernity, emphasizing large military drums and guitar). Nação Zumbi was the first *mangue* band to get a contract with a big record company, and its first record was released by Sony Music in 1994. Two more records were released by Sony but the company terminated the contract after the death of Chico Science. Devotos, a hard-core band whose members live in the poor areas of the highlands of Recife, released its first record on a label associated with a big company—Plug, associated with BMG. Both bands moved to independent labels to launch subsequent records. In both cases, restrictions imposed by major companies on aesthetic expression and the lack of attention the bands received in terms of technical support, marketing, and distribution influenced them to look for other means of production. Other bands produced records through independent labels based in Recife. One example is Cascabulho, which made its first record with Mangroove in 1998 and its second in Europe on a world music label, Piranha Records, in 2000. Some bands have had no opportunities other than local "alternative" production.

Local bands do not always define themselves as *mangue* (although they are seen as such by outsiders). They claim different roots or influences but see themselves as part of the same "scene." What gives some unity to these artists is not cultural or aesthetic homogeneity, but their attitudes toward local and international pop culture. The results are varied, based on different uses of and different emphases on heterogeneous cultural elements.

One of the most interesting effects of the *mangue* movement and its offshoots is that instead of suffocating traditional culture, *mangue beat* is helping local culture to rejuvenate itself. This is what makes *mangue* unique in local history. Local people emphasize this aspect, saying that the *mangue* movement is helping to raise their self-esteem and their appreciation of local traditions.

The "leaders" of the *mangue* movement were influenced to some extent by the punk movement,[17] mainly its valorization of action ("do it by yourself") and of everyday experiences. The discourses and practices of punk made it possible to express local themes that had not been verbalized in collective projects before and contributed to the increasing interest in local culture. Playing traditional local rhythms became fashionable for a certain segment of the middle class. There are indications of greater participation in the *maracatus*—popular organizations that perform important roles in the Carnival parades, but which were formerly in danger of disappearing. Considering the coincidence of time periods, one can assume that the *maracatus* are the object of more interest because of the impact of the *mangue* movement. However, some observers claim that *mangue beat* was not the principal element in the revival of the *maracatus*, attributing their renewal to another organization, formed in the 1990s, called Maracatu Nação Pernambuco, a middle-class group that plays traditional rhythm (Teles 2000:279). In any case, in 1990, there were 61 *maracatu* organizations. In 1998, there were 400.[18]

The impact of *mangue beat* over local culture is not restricted to the renewal of musical tradition. The national and international recognition of the bands influenced the attitudes of the upper and middle classes toward popular culture, specifically toward greater respect for its creativity. As a result, local popular artists—who had been forgotten or who had been known locally but were unknown to large portions of the national public—started to record for the music industry. Some examples are the recent recordings of CDs by Lia de Itamaracá and Dona Selma do Coco, traditional singers of *ciranda* and *coco*, respectively, and of Mestre Salustiano, a *rabeca* player [19] and leader of one of the most important *maracatus* from Recife, cited and celebrated by many contemporary bands. Other examples are the launchings of old Jackson do Pandeiro[20] records, which have also inspired young artists. These examples suggest that cultural industries can have a positive effect on local cultures.

Local Struggles: Public Policies and Cultural Debate

A comparison that can help to clarify the significance of the new emphasis on popular culture is the opposition between the *mangue beat* movement and another cultural movement from Recife—the Armorial movement.[21] Led by the famous author Ariano Suassuna, and consolidated in the 1960s, the Armorial movement searches for the European and erudite roots of popular culture. Members of the Armorial movement research various popular artistic manifestations, looking for the original character of northeast Brazilian popular culture and its Iberian heritage. Research is complemented by creation that includes theater, literature, music, and fine arts. In all fields, cultural products are refined and linked to high culture. The Armorial movement adopts an extremely critical posture against culture industries in general, and particularly against the influence of North American culture. In short, its interpretation of culture can be qualified as elitist, with total disapproval of mass culture. In the music field, for example, groups that were created under the Armorial influence since 1959[22] privileged acoustic instruments (flutes, violins, cellos, etc.) and a repertoire based on research on traditional music or compositions inspired by it. Some compositions sound like medieval music; others, like re-created and refined popular music. They can be located on the boundaries between popular and erudite culture.

Throughout his life, Ariano Suassuna has occupied some public function, and as a result he has been able to develop cultural programs directed toward the valorization of traditional popular culture. Between 1995 and 1998, Suassuna was secretary of culture of the state of Pernambuco. His policies have been oriented toward two goals: the first one "supported . . . activities that were intended to reinforce the cultural identity of Pernambuco, based on the premises of the Armorial movement"; the second, was "functional support to the members of the Historical and Artistic Heritage Foundation of Pernambuco (Fundarpe)," which includes a variety of cultural organizations and museums (Editorial, 'Cultura su Culturas?' 1998). There has been a clear emphasis on initiatives from traditional popular and erudite culture, especially for the Armorial projects. Financial support was available for traditional popular groups, especially the *maracatus*. On the other hand, there was little support for bands linked to the popular music scene. Support for the latter came mostly from Fundarpe[23] or from the municipal secretary of culture.

In 1993, when Chico Science's band, Nação Zumbi, and Mundo Livre S/A did their first shows outside Pernambuco state, in São Paulo and Belo Horizonte, Fundarpe paid their bus tickets. In 1995, when their first record (*From Mud to Chaos*, Sony Music/Chaos 1994) began to be successful and the band did a tour through the United States and Europe—starting from the Summerstage Festival in Central Park, New York—the Fundarpe and the Empetur (State Tourism Company) paid the plane tickets. The state television channel—TV Pernambuco—broadcast the Chico Science and Nação Zumbi concert in Central Park (Teles 2000:296).

Traditional popular culture groups and youth groups that were linked to the *mangue* movement benefited from the campaign "Todos com a Nota" (Everybody with a receipt), in partnership with the State Revenue Service. This campaign resulted in the use of tax money to sponsor music festivals and CD recordings. The possibility of being recorded and distributed was like a prize for some young bands and for popular groups that were outstanding on the local scene.

This campaign is similar to the way cultural activities are supported at the national level. The main initiatives from the federal government are based on tax discounts for companies that invest in cultural products, especially movies. This kind of policy attempts to counteract the attitudes of Brazilian businesspeople regarding culture, which they usually perceive as something secondary, unprofitable, or unimportant. Their mentality favors rapid returns instead of long-term investments in social projects that could benefit people. One can say that there is not a "culture" that defines investment in culture as worthwhile.

Two general aspects of cultural policies in Brazil are unfavorable for popular groups and alternative or *avant-garde* cultural creation and production. The first is that federal and state policies usually give larger amounts of support and more frequent support to recognized artists. Artists receive more financial support when they have already achieved fame and recognition from critics and public than when they are relatively unknown. This is the case in music, movies, and other cultural fields.

The second problematic aspect of culture policies in Brazil is that policymakers are prejudiced against popular culture. They usually favor "highbrow" culture and the formal mechanisms of education, transmission, and recognition of knowledge. One example in Pernambuco was the rejection of a proposal made to the state constitution in 1990 that would have recognized popular artists' knowledge in various cultural areas by providing employment for them in state programs of technical improvement and cultural diffusion (Melo 1990). If it had been approved, the proposal would have generated professional engagement of popular artists with public projects; financial support would have been presented not as a form of aid to "poor people" (a paternalist view) but as a fair reward for valuable services.

On a more general level, Brazilian copyright laws express the same kind of preju-
dice when they fail to define the rights of popular artists or the rights of communities
over the culture they create. Generally, popular culture is seen as something in the
public domain, which means that there is no intellectual property over it. This leads
to the use (and abuse) of popular culture by recognized artists and companies that
take advantage of popular creation.

By contrast, the electric guitars from *mangue*, contradicting what would be expected
by the defenders of protectionist policies, have made traditional popular culture more
visible on the local scene and on the broader circuits of cultural production and consumption, as I have already shown. Beyond the economic aspects, the external recognition of the local culture has benefited social identities, crossing class boundaries and
enhancing local self-esteem. In this sense, *mangue beat* has generated more changes and
is closer to people's needs and aspirations than is the music supported by public funds.

The *mangue beat* movement is closely linked to social criticism. Most bands
denounce the contradictory effects of modernity on the "periphery." In Recife, such
effects can be seen in the pollution of rivers and mud flats, in extreme social class differences, unemployment, a low standard of living, political domination and, last but
not least, little attention to popular manifestations. For example, "From Mud to Chaos"
is the title of a song that is part of the first CD of Chico Science and Nação Zumbi
(which has the same title). The song talks about the perception "that organizing myself
I can disorganize, that disorganizing I can organize myself." It is open to many readings,
but I would like to emphasize one: the song means that, by breaking with traditional
practices, the *mangue* movement could generate a multiplicity of cultural manifestations, a productive "chaos." By jumping into the mud, going *from chaos* (of social reality
and global influences) *to mud*, they found the sources of diversity, rich cultural creation
and alternative ways of production and promotion of local culture.

Notes

This article is a revised and enlarged version of a paper presented at the International Conference for the Sociology of Culture and the Arts, in Barcelona, July, 2000. It is part of a broader
research about the relations between the global and the local in contemporary Brazilian music
production. The research tries to understand, through empirical study of youth cultural movements in Recife (capital of Pernambuco state, Brazil), some issues in the debate on the globalization of culture. It investigates the reorganization of local culture under the influence of
globalization and how "peripheral" cultures achieve some representation in the globalized
market. The methods used included participant observation, qualitative interviews, and
archival research (newspapers and magazines).

1. In fact, this debate is not new. It dates back to the 1950s and 1960s. See Eco 1979.
2. Instead of seeing the popular as an isolated field of cultural production, this conception
considers it as something dynamic and deeply involved with other fields of cultural production. For theoretical works expressing a similar position, see Williams (1997), Hall (1985),
Martin-Barbero (1997), Strinati (1995), among others.

3. *Billboard,* cited in Benhamou 1996. Garofalo (1995:28–29) describes the situation in the early 1990s as follows:

> EMI Records is a division of the British electronic firm Thorn-EMI, which also controls Capitol, Chryslis, IRS and Rhino, among others. Polygram, which includes Polydor, Deutsche Grammophon, Mercury and Decca, as well as the recently purchased A&M and Island, is owned by the Dutch-based Phillips electronic corporation. The German Publishing conglomerate, Bertelsmann, bought RCA Records and its affiliated labels . . . In 1987, Japan's Sony corporation bought CBS Records (now Sony Music) for $2 billion. At present, only one of the top five transnational record companies — (Warner Bros./Elektra/Atlantic), a division of Time-Warner — remains in US hands, and in 1991, Time-Warner entered a partnership agreement with Toshiba and C. Itoh to the tune of one billion dollars. Further, with its $6.6 billion purchase of MCA in 1990, which also included Geffen Records and Motown, Matsushita has also made a bid for a share of the international marketplace.

4. Internet: *CNNfn. The financial network,* February 24, 2000; Kapner, 2001.

5. For a deeper debate about cultural hybridism, especially in Latin America, see Canclini (1997).

6. The record market, as well as other sectors of culture industries, has developed gradually in Brazil, reaching the level of mass consumption only in the 1960s. About these developments, see Ortiz (1988).

7. Internet: On-line magazine *Brazilian Music Up To Date.*

8. Sant'anna (1999). Piracy has more negative effects on mainstream artists than on "alternative" products.

9. Franco (1999): Internet: IFPI. *International Federation of Phonographic Industries;* ABPD. *Associação Brasifeira dos Productores de Discos.*

10. Internet: On line magazine *Brazilian Music Up To Date.*

11. It has been this way for a couple of decades. But in the 1950s and 1960s, Recife's record company, Rozenblitz, was one of the most active in Brazil and the most important company that was supported only by Brazilian capital. It recorded important local and national artists (Teles, 2000:16–20).

12. Some critics and historians of Brazilian popular music defend this posture. Just to mention one name, José Ramos Tinhorão is the best known. These scholars ignore the fact that what is called the "true" Brazilian popular music (MPB) is the result of the canonization of certain song forms which have been recognized on the basis of musicians' practices and of selective valorization by different social actors in the musical field.

13. Representative of these two tendencies in Brazil are, from Jovem Guarda, Roberto Carlos (who continues to have a big success with love songs) and Erasmo Carlos; and from Tropicalismo, Caetano Veloso, Gilberto Gil and Tom Zé.

14. Examples of these musicians (some of whom are no longer alive) are: Luiz Gonzaga, Capiba, Alceu Valença, Geraldo Azevedo, and Lenine.

15. *Maracatu* is one of the most important rhythms from Pernambuco. It appears in various processions during Carnival in Recife and Olinda. There are two types of *maracatu.* The first type is *maracatu de baque virado,* otherwise known as *maracatu nação.* The second one is *maracatu rural,* also known as *maracatu de baque solto* or *de orquestra. Maracatu de baque virado* is more africanized than *maracatu rural* and has its roots in a popular ceremony: the

congada, which shows the coronation of a Congo king and queen, an African tradition reinterpreted in Brazil. Its practices are also related to the Afro-Brazilian religion, called *xangô* in Pernambuco. Historical documents attest to the fact that *maracatu nação* dates back to the beginning of the nineteenth century. *Maracatu de baque solto* or *rural* comes from the sugarcane plantation zone in Pernambuco and exhibits a lot of indigenous influences in the music and in the characters in the parade. In the countryside there is a tradition of popular singers who sing the *emboladas* and *desafios* at street fairs. Both are improvisational forms of singing in which two singers respond to each other. In the *embolada*, while one of the singers improvises the verses, the other plays a tambourine and vice versa. The *embolada* merged with a genre from the coast known as *coco* – giving birth to *coco de embolada*. *Coco* is in the tradition of labor songs. It had its origins in another northeastern state, Alagoas, but spread all around the country. There are different kinds of *coco*, classified according to the instruments used, the region, the kind of verse and so on. See Pinto (1996) and Cascudo (1998).

16. Manifesto *Caranguejos com Cérebro*, in the CD of Chico Science & Nação Zumbi, *Da lama ao caos*, Sony Music 1994.

17. Created in a specific context of few expectations and social criticism in England in the 1970s, the punk movement became very successful. Its principal characteristics were non-professionalism (because of its criticism of the mass media means of production and because of the collective aspect of its creativity), cultivation of an "aesthetics of the ugly and the dirty", transgression, nihilism and furious reaction against social rules and policies. However, in the process of assimilation by the music industry, it lost or changed its original meanings (James 1993). As a result, punk became just one among styles of rock, one more form available for local appropriation. On the other hand, when youth groups incorporate punk influences, it seems that the original critical strength comes back, creating obstacles for media appropriation.

18. According to an estimate by Fundação de Cultura da Cidade do Recife, there were only nine *maracatus de baque virado* and fifty-two *maracatus de baque solto*. The *maracatus de baque virado* had, proportionally, bigger growth.

19. The *rabeca* is a string instrument similar to the violin.

20. Composer and performer who was very successful in the 1950's.

21. For a history of the Armorial movement, see Santos (1999).

22. These groups were composed of different musicians but had almost the same orientation.

23. Fundarpe is an agency associated with the secretary of culture of Pernambuco state. The distinction between the functions of the secretary and Fundarpe is not very clear and can change according to the ideas of each secretary of culture. Generally, the secretary of culture and the president of Fundarpe are the same person. Fundarpe is usually responsible for cultural institutions, such as museums, while the secretary of culture is in charge of projects. During the period when Ariano Suassuna was secretary of culture, the principal activities of Fundarpe were linked to the Armorial project.

References

ABPD. *Associação Brasileira dos Produtores de Discos* (Brazilian Association of Record Producers), http://www.abod.org.br/abpd.htm.

Benhamou, F. (1996) 'Les industries culturelles: livre, disque, cinéma,' pp.63–84 in *L'économie de la culture*, Paris: La Découverte.

Brazilian Music Up to Date, http://www.brmusic.com/uptodate/html

Canclini, N. G. (1997) *Culturas Híbridas*, São Paulo: Edusp.

Cascudo, L. da C. (1998) *Dicionário do folclore brasileiro*, São Paulo: Edusp, 6ª ed.

CNNfn. *The financial network*, http://www.cnnfn.cnn.com/

Eco, Umberto (1979). *Apocalípticos e integrados*, São Paulo: Perspectiva.

Editorial (1998) 'Cultura ou culturas?' (Culture or cultures?), *Jornal do Commercio*, November 16.

Franco, C. (1999) 'Fiera da indústria fonográfica espera movimentar R$ 30 milhões' (Phonographic industry exposition estimates to negotiate R$ 30 million'), *O Estado de São Paulo*, July 22.

Garofalo, R. (1995) The transnational music industry, identity and cultural imperialism,' *Radical America*, 25: 25–38.

Hall, S. (1985) 'Notas sobre la desconstrución de 'lo popular,' pp. 93–110 in R. Samuel, *Historia popular teoría socialista*, Barcelona: Grijalbo/Ed. Crítica.

IFPI. *International Federation of Phonographic Industries*, http://www.ifpi.org

James, D. E. (1993) 'Poesia/Punk/Produção: alguns textos recentes em Los Angeles,' pp.206–234 in E. A. Kaplan (ed.) *O mal-estar no pós-modernismo*, Rio de Janeiro: Zahar.

Kapner, S. (2001) 'With merger deals gone sour, EMI counts its stars,' *New York Times*, May 2: W1

Lopes, P. (1992) 'Innovation and diversity in the popular music industry, 1969–1990,' *American Sociological Review*, 57: 56–71.

Martín-Barbero, J. (1997) *Dos meios às mediações: comunicação, culture e hegemonia*, Rio de Janeiro: Editora UFRJ.

Melo, M. M. (1990) 'Lei recompensa artista popular' ('Law rewards popular artist'), *Jornal do Commercio*, January 9.

Ortiz, R. (1988) *A moderna tradição brasileira*, São Paulo: Brasiliense.

Ortiz, R. (1994) *Mundialização e cultura*, São Paulo: Brasiliense.

Pinto, T. de O. (1996) 'Musical difference, competition, and conflict: the maracatu groups in the Pernambuco Carnival, Brazil,' *Latin American Review*, 17, 2: 97–119.

Regev, M. (1997) 'Rock aesthetics and music of the world,' *Theory, Culture and Society*, 14, 3: 125–142.

Sant'anna, L. (1999) 'CDs ilegais já são metade dos vendidos no Pais' ('Illegal CDs are already half of the total amount sold in the country'), *O Estado de São Paulo*, July 19.

Santos, I. M. F. dos (1999) *Em demanda da poética popular: Ariano Suassuna e o Movimento Armorial*, Campinas: Unicamp.

Strinati, D. (1995) 'Mass culture and popular culture,' pp. 1–50 in *An Introduction to Theories of Popular culture*, London: Routledge.

Teles, J. (2000) *Do frevo ao manguebeat*, São Paulo: Editora 34.

Tinhorão, J. R. (1986) *Pequena história da música popular: da modinha ao tropicalismo*, São Paulo: Art Editora.

Williams, R. (1997) 'Las comunicaciones como ciencia cultural,' pp. 70–81 in J. Martín-Barbero and A. Silva (eds.) *Proyetar la comunicación*, Bogota: Tercer Mundo.

8

Cultural Policy as Marketing Strategy

The Economic Consequences of Cultural Tourism in New York City

Rosanne Martorella

Since World War II, New York City has exercised enormous influence on the economic and cultural life of the United States (Shefter 1993). As a major center for world finance and with the preeminence of Wall Street lawyers, bankers, and financiers, it has maintained its leadership in business. It is also a leading center for fashion, advertising, and publishing industries and for world-famous museums, opera houses, and symphony orchestras.

The 1970s brought serious challenges to New York's role as the most important city in the United States and as a global city for the international business community. A severe fiscal crisis placed the municipal government in receivership, foreign policy experts absconded for Washington, D.C., Los Angeles became the center for a fast-growing media industry, and Tokyo became a leader in world finance. As we now know, however, by the 1990s, New York's preeminent role was reaffirmed. In 1996, the Regional Planning Association published *A Region at Risk* (Yaro 1996) stating that the New York region's leadership in the arts should be viewed as a major element in combating macroeconomic trends affecting the region's decline. This study made headlines by asserting that the arts represent a $11.1 billion industry in New York City, providing an important source of employment and tax revenues. A major strategy that has been used in obtaining funds for the arts has been to highlight the role of the arts in the city's economy. Consequently, the city provides a major example of present dilemmas and contradictions in the use of culture for the economic development of a city. In this chapter, I will discuss the role of economic impact studies and the effects of urban cultural policies that emphasize the economic consequences of arts spending, using New York City as a case study.

Economic Impact of the Arts as a Theoretical Approach

Cultural economists argue that culture is influenced by and, in turn, influences economic factors. They have examined the effects of the arts on urban economies, the effects of public subsidies on the arts, the roles of art markets, and the behavior of consumers and producers of cultural goods and services (Heilbrun and Gray 1993). For example, Lester M. Salamon and Helmut K. Anheier (1996) have shown that nonprofit organizations perform a very significant role within the world economy, accounting for one in every 11 jobs. In the United States, nonprofit organizations represent 6.8 percent of employment. Three-quarters of the income from the sector goes to hospitals and institutions of higher education; social services, culture, and recreation follow. Their comparative analysis clearly reveals the important and understated role that the nonprofit arts play in a country's economy.

Expenditures for arts-related activities are seen as having "multiplier effects," defined as the increase in a community's total income per dollar of direct expenditures. The multiplier effect is a measure of dollar flow related to a specific activity that is created by "turnover" in a defined geographic area before these funds leave the economy or are transformed into savings. The multiplier effect is generally higher in a large city, like New York, than in a smaller city. Studies conducted in the late 1980s estimated a multiplier of 1.6 for arts expenditures in New York. The "export base issue" increases the effects of arts spending. New York's artistic community has national and international influence; because its cultural goods are consumed outside New York, they stimulate other economies as well.

Government Funding for the Arts: National, State, and City Support

If arts organizations are to contribute to the economy of a city or a region, they must be well funded. New York City now provides an environment in which diverse sources of funding are available. This was not the case in the postwar period. The postwar expansion of artistic activity necessitated that arts organizations in general seek new sources of revenues. Expenses were far outreaching their capacity to draw income from ticket sales, endowments were only beginning to become an important source of needed income, and board members' contributions were not enough to offset the rising costs of maintenance and labor. By the 1960s, the government and private foundations had come to the aid of nonprofit organizations. Beginning in the late 1960s, public subsidies grew rapidly. They reached their peak in the 1980s and have been declining since. Currently, private and public sponsorships appear to work in harmony to offset the decline of government subsidies.

In 1974, New York Mayor Abraham Beame appointed the Committee on Cultural Policy, which addressed, for the first time, many of the issues now examined in economic impact studies. The committee's report argued that New York's cultural assets provide the nourishment for a strong economy. This report did much to establish the economic significance of culture in terms of its "multiplier effects" and mandated that the municipal structure is needed to carry out a cultural policy.

Since 1977, New York City's cultural life has been managed by the Department of Cultural Affairs, which provides operational support for major cultural institutions, occupying city-owned buildings or land subsidized through the Arts Commission of the Mayor's Office. With the approval of the city Budget Council, it allocates funds for capital construction and improvement to cultural institutions as well as for school-based cultural events, incorporating arts organizations of all sizes and representing a full spectrum of cultural traditions and diversity. At its peak, 1,400 organizations were included in its jurisdiction. At present, 400 cultural institutions belong to what is now called the CIG group (Cultural Institutions Group) including 34 of the major arts organizations in the city (such as the Metropolitan Museum of Art, the Brooklyn Museum, the New York Shakespeare Festival, Carnegie Hall, City Center) with operating budgets that are totally city funded (New York City Department of Cultural Affairs, 1983–1997).

Over the years, the CIG's annual budget has ranged from $60 million to $90 million. A 75 percent cut in recent years has resulted in the disappearance of many small arts organizations. In addition, the Mayor's Office allocates approximately $100 million each year for the large cultural institutions that receive the bulk of city funds. In 1998, total government funding for organizations belonging to the CIG group amounted to 16 percent of their income, and 13.8 percent of this amount came from the city (Arts Research Center 1999).

One solution to the crisis in funding for the arts has been a program in which grants from the city are matched by private organizations, particularly business organizations. The Cultural Challenge Grant Program, established in 1994, provided New York City arts groups with $10 million in state and city funding. In order to obtain subsidies from the program, arts groups had to raise equal amounts from corporations and individuals as part of a matching program. Based on a strategy of assuring the economic effect of the arts, arts groups benefiting from the program had to show that their activities stimulated tourism and were accessible to people who live and work in New York City.

Capital investments from the city's budget were extensive, amounting to 37 percent of arts expenditures or $313 million over the 10-year period from 1982 to 1992. These investments included tax-exempt bonds issued by New York's Economic Development Corporation, the Industrial Development Corporation, and the Trust for Cultural Resources. In addition, exemptions from real property tax, given on all nonprofit property, save cultural institutions almost $450 million annually. Substantial savings to the arts and cultural institutions are also generated in exemptions from city sales tax for the purchase of machinery and equipment. Between $650 million and $675 million in capital expansion was allocated for the years 1993 to 1998, mostly for nonprofit institutions in New York City and New Jersey. Approximately $20 million of this investment was spent for renovations of commercial theaters (Arts Research Center 1999) The consequences of these partnerships between the city and business have become evident around the Broadway and downtown areas in recent years.

Additional funding for arts organizations in New York City comes from the New York State Council on the Arts (New York State Arts Council Reports, 1982, 1995). In the past, the state council gave large amounts to well-known museums and musical organizations in the lower geographic region of the state (predominantly New York City). During the 1980s, the range of public spending was from $50 million to $90 million. Since the 1990s, there has been a marked shift in priorities with more revenues going to organizations that sponsor culturally diverse programming and reach out to nonelite audiences.

Recently, responding to criticism by taxpayers from the northern regions of the state, the state arts council has redistributed public revenues to include all counties, including the funding of summer festivals in the Adirondack region and of New York City arts groups on tours throughout the state. Approximately 300 performing and visual arts organizations were classified as "primary organizations," allowing these organizations to receive at least 50 percent of the council's funds. About 100 of these organizations are located in New York City. The political climate of arts funding has mandated that "the residents of each county receive arts services proportionate to at least 40 cents per capita of population in each county, except that Council grant standards of artistic quality and administrative competence must be met." For example, although only $600,000 was required by appropriation act mandate for New York City, more than $13 million was appropriated.

From 1988 to 1996, arts funding from federal and state sources declined, but contributions by New York City increased. In 1996, funding for the arts in New York State came from the following sources: 19 percent from the state, 55 percent from New York City, and 6 percent from the National Endowment for the Arts (McKinsey and Co. and Alliance for the Arts 1997: 36). In 1988, the state provided 26 percent, New York City, 26 percent, and the NEA, 17 percent.

The funding policies of the state arts council ensure that no single large and well-known organization absorbs a substantial percentage of state funding. For example, in 1996, an organization such as the Metropolitan Opera Association with a budget of more than $100 million, received only $159,949 of the $2,413,311 allocated to music programs. The Museum of Modern Art and the Metropolitan Museum of Art each received $172,253 of the almost $3 million allocation in the museum program category. In each case, no single arts organization takes away from smaller organizations or those attempting to expand and develop new audiences.

The state arts council is designed to encourage the support of arts activities that appeal to a diverse audience. Consequently, there is consistent support of Hispanic, African-American, and Asian community arts centers and arts activities. In all categories reviewed in the annual report, ethnic and racially diverse groups were represented. For example, both the museum and challenge '96 categories revealed a significant number of grants to arts organizations reflecting ethnic diversity. Art exhibitions at the Bronx Museum, or the Museo del Bario (which received $41,254 in operating support), and at the Museum of the City of New York support art works of Hispanic communities. The state arts council has consistently supported the Dance Theater of Harlem ($71,285 in 1996), and the Alvin Ailey American Dance Theater ($87,603 the same year) because of their appeal to newer, younger, and minority audiences, as well as their attempts at artistic innovation. These organizations would not exist if it were not for strong and consistent funding by the arts council. In comparison, the American Ballet Theater, which has much greater audience support and a larger budget, received $188,947 in the same year—a proportionately smaller contribution from the state from overall dance appropriations of $1,629,214 in 1996.

In summary, the arts council's appropriations attempt to emphasize and ensure statewide distribution, with New York City capturing the bulk of state-allocated dollars for the support of ethnic and racially diverse artistic activities by artists and organizations located there.

Private Sources of Funding and Income Patterns of Arts Organizations

Government policy on local, state, and regional levels has served as a catalyst for privately sponsored programs. Private foundations in New York during the late 1950s along with government-sponsored studies pointed to the need for patronage of the arts. Private and corporate foundations and corporate gift programs have been important sources of income for nonprofit arts organizations. Between 1982 and 1992, private giving to the arts became more important, increasing by almost 67 percent. Foundation support increased by 124 percent, and corporate giving by 103 percent. Total giving by individuals, $147 million in 1992, became the leading category of support to the arts, supplanting local government, the leading source in 1982 (Alliance for the Arts and the Port Authority of New York and New Jersey 1993).

Since private corporations and foundations give a higher percentage of their contributions to organizations in the communities in which they are located, it is not surprising that New York City has benefited from this policy. The Foundation Center (Weber and Renz, 1993) reported that in 1992 New York State–based foundations represented 20 percent of the total support given by foundations to the arts in the United States. (Foundations based in nine other states gave 55 percent, while all other states gave 25 percent of foundation grants.) It is not surprising, therefore, that financial, legal, and technology firms located in New York are its generous patrons (Martorella 1996).

Since New York City is home to thousands of American and international companies, the arts have received direct contributions and grants to its museums and musical events, including corporate sponsorship of major music festivals and the opening of museum exhibits. The McKinsey study (1997:46) reported that 20 percent of all contributions to the arts came from private foundations. Sponsorship by private companies is well publicized and becomes an important component of their public relations and advertising objectives. The Business Committee for the Arts Report in 1998 revealed that business contributions reached a record level of $1.16 billion in 1997 (Business Committee for the Arts 1998). Other arts-related activities include purchasing artworks for headquarters, sponsoring art events at business lunches, and encouraging its employees to volunteer their time to arts organizations. Beginning in the 1980s, real estate redevelopment regulations in New York City have required that corporations include artworks in their lobbies and offices as well (Martorella 1993).

An Arts Research Center report (1999) summarizes the important role that private sources (foundations, corporations, and individuals) play in the income of arts organizations in New York City and state. In 1982, private giving accounted for 25 percent of total cash income of arts organizations. This share grew to 28.3 percent in 1998, an increase of 9.3 percent. Although corporate contributions have increased, their share of total contributions has declined from 1982 to 1999. However, the share of individual giving to nonprofit cultural organizations has been fairly steady as a percentage of total cash income. The Arts Research Center report concludes, "Many arts organizations in New York City have benefited from the prosperity of the times." A strong economy and a rising stock market caused a dramatic increase in the number of new millionaires during the late 1990s. A substantial percent of capital campaign programs by arts institutions continues to be contributed by their trustees. Recent successful fundraising campaigns have included the Metropolitan Museum ($300 million), Carnegie Hall ($70 million), the Brooklyn Academy of Music ($70 million), and the Whitney Museum ($40 million). The New York Public Library's $430 million campaign included 29 donors who gave $1 million apiece, with trustees pledging $100 million. Interestingly, 42,000 contributors gave from $1 to $1,250 for computerizing and digital analyses of essential research documents, and for the renovation of its main building. With more than 39,000 private family foundations in existence (15,000-plus have been created since 1980), arts institutions have benefited from their support (Miller 1997). Since July 1996, tax incentives enabling individuals to donate publicly traded stocks at their fully appreciated value to foundation and nonprofit organizations have encouraged support by individual donors.

Finally, public/private partnerships constitute a major form of art patronage today (American Assembly 1998). Some examples demonstrate remarkable levels of cooperation between different types of donors, both public and private. Since 1991 when a survey showed that two-thirds of New York City schools had no art teachers, a private foundation, with help from three major city museums, has spent millions in arts education to compensate for the decline of school budget allocations in arts education. A grant by the Annenberg Foundation of $12 million pairs schools with orchestras, museums, art studios, and dance groups. The city responded to these efforts in the private sector with $2.5 million, which led to additional private donations. One hundred million dollars has been pledged by the city over the next few years to continue these activities in more than 1,000 elementary schools citywide. One arts administrator commented: "The Mayor has the bully pulpit. He has the ability to try to direct resources in different directions to aid cultural institutions" (Belluck 1997).

Economic Impact of Arts Organizations in New York City

In 1974, at the height of the fiscal budget crisis in the city, manufacturing jobs were being lost and real estate values were declining. However, Lincoln Center had just been completed, and city museums had long-term plans for capital reconstruction and audience development. In the ensuing decade, urban renewal began with the arts as a focus of this revival. During the period from 1983 to 1993, substantial capital investment in arts institutions also benefited the city, as organizations such as the Metropolitan Museum, Lincoln Center, and the Brooklyn Botanical Garden expanded. Out of $1.5 billion in capital investments, New York City contributed $313 million, and private sources covered the remainder. The Mayor's Office continues to serve as a catalyst for private foundations and personal donor support to cultural institutions.

Recent studies have documented the impact of expenditures by arts organizations and have argued that the arts are vital for the economy of New York State and especially for the New York City region (Alliance for the Arts and the Port Authority of New York and New Jersey 1993).[1] These studies document the fact that the largest concentration of nonprofit cultural institutions in the nation and the world are within of New York City. In 1992, the total economic impact of these organizations amounted to $2.7 billion, with direct expenditures of $1.3 billion. Nonprofit cultural institutions also accounted for 26,800 jobs (12,300 full time and 14,500 part time). Museums showed the strongest growth during the ten-year period reviewed by the Alliance for the Arts–Port Authority of New York and New Jersey study (1993), but music, dance, and theater companies all showed an increase in expenditures for this period. During the same period, subsidies from New York City represented $313 million in capital investment.

Since New York City's tourist attractions have a wide appeal, reaching far beyond its municipal borders, the "multiplier effects" of arts-related tourism were examined in a study of the Metropolitan New York–New Jersey area (Alliance for the Arts and the Port Authority of New York and New Jersey, 1993). This study showed that arts activity in general in this area boosted the local economy by $9.8 billion, up 14 percent in a decade. A major source of economic benefit to the city came from visitors who were attracted to the city because of its cultural offerings. In 1992, arts-motivated visitors spent $1.3 billion, an increase of 28 percent since 1982. Visitors accounted for 30,000 jobs and $700 million in wages in 1992. Of the $1.3 billion spent by arts-motivated visitors in 1992, the following industries benefited: hotels ($400 million), restaurants ($400 million), taxis ($96.2 million), and retail ($140 million).

A major study of the economic significance of the arts to the city's economy in 1995 (Alliance for the Arts, Inc., 1997) noted that the five segments examined in the study— nonprofit institutions (dance, museum, music, opera, etc.), commercial theaters, television and film, art galleries, and auction houses, and the businesses that serve the visitors to the region's cultural attractions—contribute to the city's economy in varying degrees (see Table 8.1). In 1995, the economic impact of the arts for New York City was estimated to be $11.1 billion. Employment generated by the arts totaled more than 130,000 jobs. Taxes returned to the city exceeded $221 million. Although the art market has been quite volatile and Broadway theaters and road companies have declined, overall the arts have continued to grow and have become a key element in the revitalized New York economy.

Because of New York's museums, zoos, and botanical spaces have undergone new construction contributing to capital investment in the region, the study also looked at the effects of capital expenditures on the city. This type of capital spending generated a total impact of $170 million. The same study portrayed economic contributions to the arts as representing a "low risk, high return and substantial opportunity" for government and business. The nonprofit theater alone is reported to earn $115 million a year that, in turn, generates an additional $111 million income to the local tourism industry.

With its heavy concentration of galleries, international auction houses, alternative art spaces, and individual artists, New York is a world leader in the exhibition and sale of the

Table 8.1 Economic Impact of the Arts on New York City's Economy by Type of Business, 1995*

Type of Business	Economic Impact	Numbers of Jobs
Motion pictures/TV	$ 3.4 billion	35,068 jobs
Nonprofit arts	$ 3.2 billion	40,723 jobs
Businesses serving visitors	$ 2.5 billion	36,277 jobs
Commercial theater	$ 1.0 billion	10,733 jobs
Galleries/auction houses	$ 823 million	6,211 jobs
Capital spending by Nonprofit organizations	$ 170 million	1,454 jobs
Totals	$ 11.1 billion	130,466 jobs

* Fiscal year.

Source: Alliance for the Arts, Inc., 1997.

visual arts. However, in the late 1980s, many of these organizations were struggling to survive, and a significant number went out of business. In the 1980s, art galleries and auction houses spent a total of $115 million in capital investments (Arts Research Center 1997), but this type of investment was declining at the end of the decade as corporations reduced their purchases, and increases in rents for exhibition space forced smaller dealers out of New York. Art spaces were being taken over by restaurants and retail boutiques. However, in 1992, a study of 500 art galleries revealed that they had an economic impact of $840 million, employing 2,600 full time and 6,700 part time. Since then, there has been an increase in the numbers of galleries in Chelsea, Tribeca, and the East Village.

In 1998, the Museum of Modern Art received $65 million from the city toward its $650 million Capital Campaign. This expansion will double the space for exhibitions and will increase visitors from 1.5 million to 2.5 million by its 75th anniversary in 2004. Trustees David Rockefeller, Donald Marron of PaineWebber, and real estate developer Jerry Speyer, encouraged the mayor to lend his support. Mr. Guiliani justified the city's contribution by saying that the city's investment will be returned in about two years through an increase of almost 2,000 jobs in the museum, hotel, restaurant, and service industries (Dobrzynski 1998).

In 1995, tax revenues generated by arts-related activity in New York State and in New York City were substantial: $480 million for the state and $221 million for the city (McKinsey and Co. and Alliance for the Arts 1997:11). Returns on public arts investments were estimated at 700 percent for New York State and 240 percent for New York City. In other words, federal and state taxes collected from arts activities contribute substantially to government revenues, so government spending in the arts is a good investment. Economic impact studies have done much to gather momentum for political interest groups that lobby for public subsidy.

A Critical Analysis of Arts Economic Impact Studies

Because of their importance to the work of arts advocacy groups and cultural policy planners, numerous economic impact studies have been conducted since the 1970s, documenting the important roles played by the arts in generating revenue for cities across the United States. During the 1970s, at least 28 cities and 17 states sponsored arts impact studies (Cwi 1977). More recently, the New York Port Authority and the State of New York sponsored the arts impact study of the New York/New Jersey metropolitan area summarized above.

These studies created a basis for legitimating the arts and enabled arts advocacy groups to use language understood by business and political leaders in their appeal for government subsidies. Arts impact studies did much to provide an appealing form of argumentation in terms of business terminology. They collected the "hard data" on the income and expenses of arts organizations and the number of artists employed, and they forecast the growth of the arts as an economic phenomenon, using terms such as database, input/output models, real estate spillover effects, employment multiplier, and econometrics. In so doing, these studies established the credibility of the arts in economic terms.

However, economic impact studies have their critics. Some cultural economists argue that they are flawed in their technical analysis because they have exaggerated the "multiplier effects" of arts events and ignored the export base issue. The latter is a problem because both expenditures for arts events and income generated from them leave the local area and affect the economies of areas outside New York as well. Some economists have argued that the arts cannot be compared to a basic industry, and scoff at conclusions that the arts have economic benefits equal to industries such as advertising, management consulting, and computer technology.

Multiplier effects are extremely difficult to assess because all spending circulates around the local economy with numerous and diverse "leakages" possible. Spending involves revenue sources that may have come from other industries within the community, and not from outside funding that could be seen as benefiting the art industry. More important, Seaman (2000) concludes that this overzealous use of impact studies obscures the real essence of arts as public goods. He states that the arts are both "non-excludable" and "non-rival in consumption."

> Effects on a city's image, revitalization of certain neighborhoods, and even increasing worker productivity and emotional health are factors not captured in aggregate spending effects. Yet, these effects would tend to make the arts more like other popularly subsidized activities, such as education, having relevant, unaccounted-for external benefits. . . . In this context, the arts would not have to be exportable to be important. One might suspect that the role of the arts in this overall development scheme would be easily overwhelmed by that of other enterprises. But, at least arts proponents would not have to worry about whether impact studies have established the arts as a basic industry. (pp. 268, 278)

Changing Sources of Income for Arts Organizations

The Arts Research Center study revealed that "the complex job of translating private wealth (primarily created by robust financial markets) into private contributions leads to uneven distribution and over-reliance on one sector of the economy." Museums, for example, receive the largest amount of public funding, and rely more heavily on contributions, both public and private, to offset their expenses. Public funding brings in only 39.4 percent of their income; they must obtain the remaining 60.6 percent through contributions, from their endowments, and from other sources.

A study in 1992 showed that during the previous decade, museums had the largest increases in total real expenditures, seconded by concert halls and opera houses (Alliance for the Arts, Inc. and Port Authority of New York and New Jersey 1993:B1). This growth was attributed almost entirely to the larger organizations: the expenditures of organizations with annual budgets of more than $1.5 million increased 52 percent over the decade.

An analysis of recent trends in the sources of income of arts organizations reveals that they have responded to the decline of public funding by developing marketing strategies to offset their expenses and broadening their audience base to encourage wider consumption of art. Increases in income from admissions, concessions, and gift shops support this argument. Museums, along with performing arts organizations, have the capacities to offset their income gaps with admissions fees and income from concessions and gift shops. Table 8.2 compares earned income sources as a percentage of total income for the period 1982 to 1999 revealing an increasing role for admissions and concessions from 34 percent in 1982 to 45.6 percent in 1998 (Arts Research Center 1999).

In general, small organizations fare less well than large organizations. A report on New York City for 1995 (Alliance for the Arts, Inc. 1997) revealed that organizations with annual budgets exceeding $1.5 million received more income from admissions than smaller organizations. The Metropolitan Museum of Art, for example, is one of the city's most prominent cultural organizations, serving an audience of more than 5 million people annually. However, 75 percent of federal funding for the arts in New

Table 8.2   Arts Organizations: Changes in Sources of Earned Income, 1982–1998

Earned Income Sources as Percentage of Total Income

	FY 1982	FY 1995	FY 1998
Admissions	20.4	25.5	22.8
Concessions	13.95	26.9	22.8
Total	34.3	52.4	45.6

Source: Arts Research Center, 1999.

York City, 57 percent of state funding for the same purpose, and 83 percent of local arts funding go to these large organizations, although smaller organizations rely more heavily on public support for their survival (Alliance for the Arts, Inc. 1997). The economic pressures of the 1980s were felt most severely by small organizations. Among those small organizations that survived, income levels increased by 45 percent, and there was less reliance on public funding in 1992 than 10 years before.

In the future, interest from the endowments of arts organizations will be increasingly important. Endowment interest represented approximately 10.9 percent in 1982, 8.2 percent in 1992, and rose to 13.9 percent in 1998. Given the recent wave of publicity about capital campaigns of nonprofit organizations in New York City, this figure should increase in the millennium (Arts Research Center 1999).

Conclusion

Although New York's leadership position has been challenged as a result of macroeconomic and technological changes, it continues to represent a unique urban center capable of exerting global influence. Cultural factors enhance and contribute to its dominant position. While cultural policies in New York City have tended to focus on establishing priorities with business-related interests, such as tourism, cultural policies in the future will have to include the perspectives of art curators, art directors, and artists to ensure continued innovation and creativity. Using the argument that the arts encourage economic growth in order to justify public support leads to changes in how arts organizations are administered as well as how their influence is interpreted. The consequences of privatization of funding and the emphasis on cultural tourism need to be addressed from a critical perspective.

Art organizations in New York City exhibit a number of contradictory trends that are characteristic of arts institutions in the state and country as a whole. Public funding has steadily declined but has been supplemented to some extent by funding from business and other private sources. Organizations that are better known have been able to offset their expenses by contributions from private sources (Bowen 1994). Large organizations such as museums undoubtedly fare better in this funding environment than small organizations such as art galleries and small theater groups. The latter have particularly suffered from the instability of funding in recent years, leading to substantial losses in artistic innovation that are impossible to calculate. It is not surprising, therefore, that only small performing art companies (such as ballet or experimental theater groups), with substantially lower start-up costs, have been created over the last 20 years. Art forms such as symphony and opera organizations require bigger budgets.

In order to respond to critics who argue that public art subsidies should be allocated to arts organizations that have wide public appeal, arts organizations have increasingly made attempts to reach a broader audience and to overcome the elitism that has traditionally characterized this sector. A recent study of New York City audiences indicates an increase in foreign-born people and contends that the socioeconomic characteristics of arts audiences reflect the ethnic and racial groups of the city. Public subsidies by the state have been redirected toward a decentralization of funding, as well as the establishment and support of arts activities in poorly served areas. The state arts council emphasizes local decisionmaking in its decentralization program, thus supporting more diverse activity. By contrast, New York City's allocations favor highly publicized, well-attended museums and musical events attended by tourists and visitors to the city.

Although museums have been very successful in attracting increasingly large audiences, there may be a tendency to compromise the standards of museum curators. The following advice to heritage administrators is alarming: "If cultural tourism is to become a real learning experience for an increasingly diverse public, museums and heritage sites need to be user-friendly and communicate 'stories' rather than 'messages.' The cornerstone of any policy for visitor care in museum heritage management is, above all, pleasure" (Schouten 1998). Arts organizations have increasingly succumbed to pressures to accept commercial ventures as they scramble for money and are required to expand their audiences in order to receive public funding.

It can be argued that too much emphasis has been placed on the economic impact of the arts. In their attempts to legitimate public subsidies, arts councils have supported studies that show how increases in the number of jobs and tourists contribute to urban renewal and the "symbolic economy" of New York, as well as how they create other multiplier effects stemming from arts-allocated funds. Arts organizations have supported such an ideology linking business and the arts to ensure their access to much needed funds. In so doing, little attention has been given to the purely aesthetic, educational, heritage, or civilizing effects that result when societies deem artistic culture and activity important. More specifically, the allocation of public funds should be based on an understanding of how the arts promote a better society, an awareness of the necessity to extend to citizens arts programs historically denied access to cultural activities, and a commitment to the social contributions of the arts for future generations.

Studies of public subsidies and government support of the arts reveal attempts to "legitimate" the arts by emphasizing their noncultural and utilitarian function. Rather than viewing the arts as integral to the cultural evolution of society, or the importance of their accessibility to all segments of a diverse society, the arts have been evaluated in terms of their contributions to urban renewal and economic growth. Though these economic impact studies have justified public subsidies, they may have altered the relationship between the arts and society, changed the role of the artist in society, and promoted the commercialization and marketing of culture to the neglect of aesthetic considerations.

Note

1. These studies combine local, state, and regional figures, making it difficult to isolate New York City's contributions. This is because the political nature of state and local interest groups must be kept in mind when analyzing figures. The report studied 1,366 institutions in the nonprofit sector. Data were collected from the state arts councils of New York and New Jersey. Data were also obtained from the League of American Theaters and Producers, the Art Dealers Association (including 497 art galleries and major auction houses), the New York City Office of Film, Theater, and Broadcasting, the New York State Department of Commerce, the Division of Communications Industry Development, and the New Jersey Motion

Picture and Television Commission. The studies were executed by the Alliance for the Arts, the Port Authority of New York and New Jersey, New York City Partnership, and Partnership for New Jersey. The report included a survey of Broadway and Off-Broadway theaters conducted by the New York League of Theaters and Producers (Alliance for the Arts 1997).

References

Alliance for the Arts, Inc. and Port Authority of New York and New Jersey (1993) 'Executive summary report,' *The Arts as an Industry: Their Economic Importance to the New York-New Jersey Metropolitan Region*, New York: Alliance for the Arts, Inc. and Port Authority of New York and New Jersey.

Alliance for the Arts, Inc. (1997) *The Economic Impact of the Arts on New York City and New York State*, New York: Arts Research Center.

American Assembly (1998) *The Arts and the Public Purpose*. Report of the Ninety-Second American Assembly, May 29–June 1, 1997. New York: Columbia University.

Arts Research Center (1999) *Trends in Income Sources for New York City Cultural Organizations*, New York: Arts Research Center/Alliance for the Arts.

Arts Research Center, Inc. (1997) *The Economic Impact of the Arts on New York City and New York State*, New York: Arts Research Center/Alliance for the Arts.

Belluck, P. (1997) 'Arts education,' *New York Times*, January 19, p.27.

Bowen, W. G. (1994) *The Charitable Nonprofits: An Analysis of Institutional Dynamics and Characteristics*, San Francisco: Jossey-Bass.

Business Committee for the Arts. (1998) *National Survey of Business Support to the Arts*, New York: Business Committee for the Arts.

Cwi, D. (1977) *Economic Impacts of the Arts and Cultural Institutions: A Model for Assessment and a Case Study in Baltimore: a Report*, Washington, DC: National Endowment for the Arts.

Dobrzynski, J. H. (1998) 'MOMA gets $65 M from the city', *New York Times*, April 24, p. 1.

Heilbrun, J. and Gray, C.M. (1993) *The Economics of Art and Culture: An American Perspective*, New York: Cambridge University Press.

Martorella, R. (1993) *Corporate Art*, New Brunswick, NJ: Rutgers University Press.

Martorella, R. (1996) 'Corporate patronage in the United States,' pp. 18–31 in R. Martorella (ed.) *Art and Business: An International Perspective*, Westport, CT: Greenwood Press.

McKinsey and Co. and Alliance for the Arts (1997) *You've Gotta Have Art*. New York: McKinsey and Co.

Miller, J. (1997) 'Top institutions heat up drives for arts funds', *New York Times*, February 3, Sect. A, p.1

New York City Department of Cultural Affairs (1983, 1984, 1985, 1986, 1987, 1988, 1995, 1997) *Annual Reports*, New York: NYCDCA.

New York Foundation for the Arts (1994) *Annual Report*.

New York State Arts Council Reports (1982) (1995).

Salamon, L. M. and Anheier, H. K. (1996) *The Emerging Sector: The Nonprofit Sector in Comparative Perspective—An Overview*, Manchester, UK: Manchester University Press.

Schouten, F. (1998) 'Balancing the needs of tourism and conservation', *Music International*, 50, no. 4 (October/December): 27–30.

Seaman, B. A. (2000) 'Arts impact studies: a fashionable excess,' pp. 266–285 in G. Bradford, M. Gary, and G. Wallach (eds.) *The Politics of Culture*. New York: The New Press.

Shefter, M. (1993) 'New York's national and international influence,' pp. 1–25 in M. Shefter (ed.) *Capital of the American Century: The National and International Influence of New York City*, New York: Russell Sage Foundation.

Weber, N. and Renz, L. (1993) *Arts Funding: A Report on Foundation and Corporate Grant-making Trends*, New York: The Foundation Center.

Yaro, R. D. (1996) *A Region at Risk: The Third Regional Plan for the New York-New Jersey-Connecticut Metropolitan Area*, Washington, DC: Island Press.

9

Democratization and Institutional Change

A Challenge for Modern Museums

Catherine Ballé

In the past, museums were famous for the quality and the extent of their collections. With their rare objects and historic buildings, they were considered as guardians of our "heritage." Nowadays, most museums are seeking public attention by organizing spectacular exhibitions, reorganizing their permanent collections, and renovating and extending their public spaces as well as financing the construction of outstanding buildings. Since the 1970s, major projects have been carried out: the Guggenheim Museum in New York, the Pompidou Center in Paris, the East Wing of the National Gallery of Art in Washington, the Pyramid of the Louvre, the Getty Museum in Los Angeles, the Sainsbury Wing of the National Gallery in London, the Guggenheim Museum in Bilbao, the unique reorganization of several museums in Berlin, and the modern Tate. These projects have been conceived as media events to attract public notice and ensure public success.

The modern museum, as a "global" phenomenon that transcends national boundaries, has undergone enormous change. Regardless of geographical location, museums in many countries have faced new political and popular demands and have responded with similar solutions: cultural activities, development strategies, and modernized features. The nature and extent of this institutional renaissance raises several questions. Is the focus on the public a new priority, or has such a responsibility always been part of the mission of museums but has simply been neglected for several decades? What influence has public and private investment in culture had on museums' responses to visitors' needs? Has "democratization" contributed to the modernization and development of museums? Is the management of these new parameters the challenge museums will face in the future?

In this chapter, I will show that the nature of public access to museums has been debated since their first appearance in the eighteenth century, during their zenith in the nineteenth century, in the course of their gradual decline in the first part of the twentieth century, and in the midst of their renewal today. Next, on the basis of current empirical data from Europe and the United States, I will analyze the influence of cultural policies on democratization, specifically, on the ways museums have changed their responses to their public. Finally, considering the major features of contemporary museums, I will explore the challenges that museums are likely to face in the future.

An Ambivalent Heritage

The museum's treatment of its visitors is not a new concern but one that has been ignored in the somewhat disembodied approach that has characterized the history of museums, in which attention has been paid mainly to artifacts and collections. More recently, historians of arts and culture have broadened their field of investigation by examining the conditions under which works of art are produced, scientific discoveries made, and either art or knowledge received by the public. This new conception of cultural history has led to a reconceptualization of the activities of museums. Dominique Poulot (1983) writes: "I would like to make it clear that questions about the purpose of museums are not a product of our own age. Nor did they arise with the 'museum malaise' of the post-war years. I would go so far as to say that the ambiguity appeared when the museums themselves were established" (p. 13).

The founding of the first collections was dictated by the values and norms of monarchic societies. According to the same author: "The monarchy perceived its collections as part of the apparatus of dynastic prestige. . . . Putting together a collection was the expression of a certain status to be maintained, and also served to increase the dynasty's inheritance" (pp. 14–15). This concern with prestige was shared by a close circle of collectors—monarchs, princes, ecclesiastics (Pomian 1987) and, in more democratic states such as the Netherlands, political dignitaries or merchants (Schama 1987). These people of high rank had in common a desire to own, show, and compare their treasures. In each country they constituted narrow groups, but on the European scale, across regional and national borders, they belonged to a much wider *milieu* within which numerous artistic, scientific, and cultural exchanges took place.

Wealth and prestige were not the only reasons for setting up a collection. Curiosity about nature, sciences, and techniques, interest in antiquities, and a taste for art attracted a wider community than those who could possess rare objects in their *cabinets de curiosités* and private collections. As a result, public access to royal or princely collections was demanded by these amateurs. Sometimes this right was granted, and sometimes it was negotiated. In France, Roland Schaer (1993) writes, "the Salon was the first 'temporary exhibit' organized in 1667 by the Royal Academy of painting and sculpture; this event took place in 1699 at the Grande Galerie in the Louvre. In 1750, King Louis XV made the concession that one gallery in the Palais du Luxembourg should be opened to the public on Wednesdays and Saturdays" (pp. 44–46).

In the arts, Poulot writes (1983), museums had to fulfill an educational purpose: "The main function of the first European museums, in the seventeenth and eighteenth centuries, was an academic one . . . the work of art is the artist's true master" (p. 15). And demand for museums was growing among nonartists. "There was a growing number of dilettante scientists, would-be writers, scholars and artists, the product of economic growth and the spread of education, demanding access to books, artifacts and paintings" (p. 16). Museums had a similar function in the world of the sciences. For example, in Paris, the Jardin des Plantes and its Cabinet des Drogues—which became the Museum of Natural History in 1793—have had a threefold mission since their creation in 1635: research, extending the collections, and education. As Michel Van Praët (1991) sees it, opening the collections reflected a "decision taken by the politicians to reduce the gap between the learned and the uninitiated in the field of scientific knowledge for economic, social or ideological reasons" (p. 104).

The idea of opening collections to a larger public spread across Europe. In France, there was the plan to open the Grande Galerie in the Louvre in 1779; in Germany, the Elector of Bavaria's collection of pictures was opened to the public in Munich in 1783; in Italy, the Uffizi Gallery was opened around 1780. In Austria, the Belvedere in Vienna was opened "to all visitors, provided their shoes be clean." According to Schaer (1993), "By the eve of the French Revolution, the public museum had become a necessary institution, one whose future across the continent seemed more or less assured" (p. 48). Museums had by then any number of public roles, whether vested in them voluntarily by their founders and advocates, or as a result of pressure from those with interests in the arts, sciences, or culture. By the end of the eighteenth century, a "public" for museums had come into being (Poulot 1983).

The French Revolution codified the democratic concept of the museum as a public institution, encompassing the state's responsibility for its heritage and the museum's obligation toward the citizens. This understanding determined museums' evolution in the nineteenth century. Poulot (1994) writes:

> These two aspects of the national heritage, thus defined, became part of the larger history of the relations between the nation and society after the Revolution . . . In other words, we believe that the status of heritage owes its continuity less to the fact of survival, or to its maintenance as a matter of routine or customary activities, than to the intervention of a public ever concerned with emblems and symbols. (p. 11)

In the nineteenth century, museums maintained their function as guardians of the national heritage (Desvallées 1989). But they also stood for universal knowledge and civic prestige. Their duty toward their visitors was to contribute to their education and to strengthen their identity as citizens (Rivière 1989). Museums—along with libraries, theaters, and opera houses—were built in cities as symbols of their importance as cultural centers (Georgel 1994). They expressed the ideals of the political process remodeling Europe: the progress of society, the power of the dominant classes (Sherman 1989), the prestige of nations, and the supremacy of Western culture (François 2000).

As museums gained a certain independence in their location, they confirmed their status as public places and spaces and, in their new settings, they established specific architectural forms (Von Moos 1999). Of the Altes Museum inaugurated in Berlin in 1830, G. H. Rivière (1989) states:

The neo-classical style of its facade served as the model for many museums in Europe and America in the nineteenth century; its solemn composition served to prepare the visitor in advance for the temple-like atmosphere which is now the cause of so many complaints. (p. 52)

The influence of European museums extended to other continents, as Paul DiMaggio (1982 a, b) has shown for American museums in a study of the Bostonian elite. During the nineteenth century, the museum as a temple dedicated to the arts and sciences became increasingly widespread in the Western world (Bazin 1967).

However, the principle of public access to museums met with considerable resistance, as demonstrated by the innumerable rules and restrictions that appeared. A discrepancy arose between the democratic ideal and standard museum practices. This gap was strongest in the case of art museums intended primarily for artists or connoisseurs and opened to a larger public only on specific days such as Sundays. But in many cities, new connoisseurs and experts appeared on the cultural scene—curators, librarians, archeologists, and archivists. Interest in the arts and sciences was shared and developed through the activities of many learned societies, and these became an essential component of bourgeois *sociabilité*.

About the same time and especially in England, some social projects aimed to introduce culture, science, and technology to a wider public such as the Great Shows of London (Altick 1978). A number of cultural initiatives appeared in favor of the most disadvantaged members of society. One especially significant example was the organization of exhibitions of contemporary paintings from 1881 onward in Whitechapel—the heart of the East End of London—in the parish school of St. Jude's (Koven 1994). In rural England, moral improvement led to the creation of museums in many towns touched by the Industrial Revolution (Clarke 1991). As a result, in the latter half of the century governments at all levels came to accept the social usefulness of museums (Schaer 1993:86–87).

However, the legacy of the nineteenth century—the "golden age" of museums—was ambiguous regarding the museum's obligations to the public. In the twentieth century, the ambivalence broadened to encompass the museum per se. As Madeleine Rebérioux (1991) points out, this ambivalence has been reinforced throughout the century. She writes:

The twentieth century has not treated museums well. Restricted in scope for many years to the fine arts—a development which began before the First World War and which has only been overturned in the last twenty years—they became mere places of amusement for the elite and temples of heritage. (pp. 123–24)

Nevertheless, aesthetic redefinitions, scientific progress, and social developments had an echo in museums, as seen, for instance, in the opening in 1905 of the Deutsches Museum in Munich and, between the two World Wars, the Palais de la Découverte in Paris and the Museum of Modern Art in New York. But, with a few exceptions, museums experienced a dramatic decline. In democratic nations, because of lack of public support and funds, various projects never came into being. In totalitarian and Nazi states, museums assumed a dubious role of propaganda aimed toward political and ethnic discrimination.

By the postwar years—with the destruction of monuments and the dispersion of many European collections—museums were judged to be archaic and conservative. When museums were the responsibility of public bureaucracies, this image was attributed to their inefficient personnel. When they belonged to the private sector, they were seen as privileged and elitist entities. As such, they remained isolated and nearly forgotten in the process of change that brought about the modernization of other organizations—private enterprises or public administrations.

Museums were then forcefully criticized within an intellectual tradition that associated cultural heritage with ruins (Déotte 1994). Some artists, like Jean Dubuffet (1968) even foretold the death of museums. In one of the first sociological studies of museum publics, Pierre Bourdieu and Abin Darbel (1966) set out to prove that museums were not only conservatories of the past but also used by and for the bourgeois elite to maintain their social status. The concept of the museum as a tool of social "distinction" and "reproduction" met with great success. As a result, museums were stigmatized as obsolete and inadequate in societies not only convinced of their democratic and popular values but in search of more open institutions. The upheavals of 1968 and the 1970s only legitimated this social criticism, and museums, along with Western societies, seemed to be overwhelmed by a sense of an impending crisis (O'Doherty 1972).

The Influence of a Democratic Project

During the 1970s in the United States and the 1980s in Europe, a drastic change occurred. Access to culture became a driving force for new policies and contributed to an unexpectedly large-scale process of cultural change (Ballé 1987). The idea of cultural development as a social project first appeared among the experts of the museum world and soon was a keynote theme at the meetings of the International Council of Museums (ICOM). This belief became ultimately an international principle when it figured in article 27 of the United Nations' Declaration of Human Rights: "Everyone shall have the right to take part freely in the cultural life of the community, and to appreciate the arts." The same principle was taken up in UNESCO's subsequent conferences (Daifuku 1998). In 1982, the Mexico report on cultural policy emphasized access as a right: "Access to culture may not be restricted according to origins, social position, level of education, nationality, age, language, gender, religion, state of health or the fact of belonging to an ethnic minority or marginal group." The same orientation was reaffirmed, moreover, by the European ministers for culture in the context of the European Union. The democratization of culture inspired many policies and programs. Nearly 30 years later, one can see that these cultural policies (Girard 1977) have been a major factor in the evolution of museums.

Specific agencies for the administration of culture were implemented in the postwar period, such as the Ministry of Culture in France, the Ministry of Education, Culture, and Social Welfare in the Netherlands, and the Ministry of the Beni Culturali in

Table 9.1   Percentages of National Budgets Allocated for Arts and Culture in the European Community, 1985 to 1995.

Country	1985 (%)	1995 (%)
Belgium	0.5	—
Denmark	0.8	1.2
Finland	—	0.9
France	1.0	0.9
Germany	0.4	—
Great Britain	0.2	—
Italy	0.6	—
Netherlands	0.7	1.0
Portugal	0.4	1.2
Spain	0.6	—
Sweden	—	1.0

Sources: Clarke (1991:284); *Statistiques de la Culture en Europe* (1996:132–43).

Italy. At the national and local levels, cultural administrations expanded considerably even in countries where, by tradition, culture is not one of the state's responsibilities. Museums benefited from meeting the goals of policies set by these new government organizations. As a result, their image gradually changed, and they began to be perceived as a medium to enhance culture and education.

Despite the difficulties of comparing cultural spending by different countries, the increase in national budgets for the arts in Europe reveals that culture had become a public concern (Schuster 1985). Although resources for culture were relatively marginal in national budgets, cultural investment was nonetheless emblematic of a democratic spirit (DiMaggio 1996). Spending for the arts and culture by countries in the European Community is shown in table 9.1.

All over Europe, towns and cities became aware of their responsibilities toward their heritage. Cultural heritage—monuments, museums, natural and historical sites—long considered a burden began to be viewed as an asset for local development and even as a means of social integration. The allocation of public funds for culture was extended to local authorities. After World War II, the participation of municipalities in the improvement of their cultural heritage remained low even though many monuments and other cultural institutions belong to these administrations. In the 1980s, the allocation of national funds to regional and local governments was recognized as unbalanced, leading to decisions by national governments to decentralize their cultural policies. Local authorities began to enter into partnerships with the state for new cultural projects. In France, cities such as Lyons, Lille, Bordeaux, Marseilles, and Nantes undertook important renovations to modernize their old-fashioned museums. In Great Britain, the huge national investment in cultural life in London was questioned. The

Museums and Galleries Commission set up Areas Commissions to allow a more equal distribution of public funds. The new policy favored the cultural development of Greater London, Wales, Scotland, and Northern Ireland as well as many cities—for instance, the Meyerside project in Liverpool.

The renewal of museums is without any doubt linked to these public policies, but private initiatives also were crucial, as many museums are privately owned. In the 1990s, 59 percent of museums in the United States were private (Museums Count 1994:36), 39 percent in Great Britain, and 35 percent in Germany. In Italy, 29 percent of the museums were private, of which 13 percent belonged to the Catholic Church (Primicerio 1991). In the Netherlands, 66 percent were owned by foundations or associations, and 12 percent were private (Ministère de la Culture 1996:10–38). Even in France, according to a conservative estimate, 45 percent of the museums are private (*Museums Count*, 1994). The proportion of private museums increased during the period. More sensitive to financial constraints and economic requirements than the museums in the public sector, private museums tried to transfer and apply management knowledge and managerial methods normally used in businesses to the cultural field.

An Institutional Renaissance

For museums, the increased allocation of private or public resources had a tremendous structural impact: it increased their numbers considerably. Growth in the numbers of museums is difficult to evaluate because of the lack of systematic and comparative measures through time and in each country (Schuster 1996). Nevertheless, between 1960 and 2000, the evolution of museums in western Europe has been similar. In Germany, numbers have risen from 1,000 to more than 4,000 (Institut fur Museumskunde 1998), in Great Britain and France, from around 1,000 to more than 2,000—in both cases this "official" figure is well below the "actual" number of museums, thought to be around 3,000 or 4,000 (Museum Focus 1998; Statistiques de la Culture 1999)—and, in the Netherlands, from around 400 to 900 (Museums in the Netherlands 1997). In the United States, over the same period, the number rose from 2,000 to almost 8,000 (Museums Count 1994).

Growth has not been consistent for all types of museums. There is a marked increase in the number of museums related to the humanities—history, society and civilization—and to science or technology. The number of museums of fine arts have not been affected as much, but with the recent openings of museums of modern and contemporary art, they have also expanded. A Dutch study showed that there were, at the beginning of the twentieth century, about as many fine arts museums as other types of museums (Ganzeboom and Haanstra 1989). Today, only about 20 percent of museums are art museums, and the remaining 80 percent represent other types of collections. Italy is an exception: art museums constitute 31 percent of all museums in the country, and a particularly rich artistic and archaeological heritage is reflected in these museums (Primicerio 1991). The increase in numbers of museums has brought greater specialization by theme and, consequently, diversification of the museum system.

Along with these changes, museums have experienced a significant movement toward modernization. The traditional representation of the museum as a conservatory—or a shrine—for past heritage has tended to fade away. The most striking element of this spectacular change is in museum architecture. Museums became privileged projects for famous architects: Frank Lloyd Wright, I. M. Pei, Richard Meier, Renzo Piano, James Sterling, Norman Foster, Frank O. Gehry. The architectural design of museums began to be a symbol of modernity or postmodernity for cities and countries. Through their connection with the latest developments in science, they also acquired an image of modernity; that is the case, for example, with the Space Museum in Washington, la Cité des Sciences de la Villette in Paris, and the new Museum of Natural History in New York. In the arts, experimental exhibitions in contemporary art earned museums the capacity to add "artistic" value to artists' work and, with a significant *volteface* , to "produce" art (Moulin 1994; Crane 1987). At the outset of the twenty-first century, with modern architectural settings and spectacular exhibitions of contemporary arts, sciences, and humanities, museums seem not only to have regained the status they acquired in the nineteenth century but to have won a preeminent role in society today.

Beyond architectural gestures and blockbuster exhibitions, a less visible but no less important evolution took place. Museums radically changed their activities and favored a broader interest in the relationship between the arts, sciences, and society. Museum events have become more diverse, and now feature exhibitions for the novice or the amateur; scientific and educational programs for the specialist—professional, researcher or university student; programs for children, including teaching exercises and school visits; and a welcome extended to the general public—local and national citizens or tourists from other countries. By renovating their buildings and public space, museums became a place to spend leisure time: cafeterias and restaurants, bookstores, shops, conference rooms, cinemas or concerts, even malls as in the Louvre. All these programs, aimed at bringing in more visitors, have transformed museums into media institutions (Hooper-Greenhill 1988).

This diversity of activities has affected the personnel. Gone is the traditional *face à face* between curators and guards. Museums now present a web of expertise in which jobs have to contribute to many different functions. This evolution has encouraged the redefinition of professional standards (Kavanagh 1994; Caillet 1995). Some professions were transformed as is the case for the new managerial dimension of curatorship (Zolberg 1974; Alexander 1996; Octobre 1999). New professions appeared: museographers, architects, designers, administrators, financial advisers, media experts, marketing specialists, and shop employees (Tobelem 1992; Bayart and Benghozi 1993).

The need to raise funds for their many activities has encouraged museums to develop contacts with private benefactors and government administrators. Involvement in theoretical debates and social issues has contributed to strengthening their ties with the academic community. The obligation to legitimate their cultural policies encouraged them to establish closer relationships with political representatives. Over the years, museums became complex organizations (Ballé 1996).

Museums have tried hard to attract the public and the public has responded by coming in large numbers to museums (Gottesdiener, Mironer, and Davallon 1993;

McManus and Miles 1993). Audience studies have shown a steady increase in numbers of visits during recent decades. Even if the figures have to be treated with caution, data from different countries reveal similar trends. In France, the 33 national museums had 3 million visitors in 1958 (Freches 1979:144) and 14 million in 1998 (Cardona and Lacroik 2000). In Italy, visitors to national museums and monuments increased from 18 million in 1979 to 46 million in 1992 (Ministère de la Culture 1996:25). In the Netherlands, the figures rose from 2.6 million visitors in 1950 (Van Mensch 1989) to 25 million in 1997 (Museums in the Netherlands 1997:8). In the United States, the 1979 Museum Program Survey reported nearly 350 million museum visits and, from 1986 to 1988, this number increased from 541 million to 566 million (Museums Count 1994: 61–63). According to a comparative study on cultural practices in European countries: "The number of visitors doubled, on average, between 1970 and 1990, in every country in Europe. At least one out of three Europeans visits a museum once a year" (Guy 1994:91). The importance of museums' efforts toward their publics as well as their interactions with their social environments can no longer be ignored. Museums have reentered society.

The threat that museums were so neglected that they could cease to exist has been avoided, and the criticisms of the 1960s have lost much of their relevance. Museums are more numerous and more active than ever, the displays of their collections have greatly improved, and the numbers of visitors have risen. As a result of scientific and technical progress, conservation processes have been rationalized. Collections have been consolidated and extended. With the differentiation of skills, staff have become more professional. The multiplication of events and diversification of cultural activities have contributed to modernization. Among all these achievements, the number of visitors has constituted the museums' greatest success. Overall, in the last 30 years, museums have experienced an institutional renaissance.

The Dilemmas of Success

This overall positive process cannot be denied and should not be underestimated. But, despite museums' success—or perhaps because of it—there is still unease and, at times, even deep disagreement among museum professionals, political leaders, public administrators, academics, and art and science lovers. Success seems to have a price, as the conference, Art Museums and the Price of Success, organized by the Boekman Foundation in Amsterdam rightly demonstrated (Gubbels and Van Hemel 1993). If these debates reveal the conflicts within museums at present, they also indicate the challenges to come.

Some specialists find that the focus on cultural activities is prejudicial to the preservation of heritage—the conservation of objects, the development of collections, and the transmission of a material legacy. It is also argued that such activities are intended to popularize culture rather than to transmit knowledge of culture. Moreover, the increase in the number of temporary exhibitions has set a higher value on the ephemeral and on the spectacular. This shift has engendered a particular emphasis on the quality of the display of art and artifacts, to some extent blurring the traditional distinction between art or science as heritage and knowledge and art or science as spectacle. However, the day-to-day organization of these temporary events has had the result of neglecting longer-term objectives and led to the lack of investment required for the improvement of permanent collections. Even if such an approach to museums' activities seems to reflect the taste of the public, as the success of these exhibitions shows, doubts remain about its legitimacy and consequences. Finding a balance between the demands of the temporary and the permanent—complementary in theory, but in practice often conflicting—can lead to professional dissatisfaction and tensions among colleagues.

The extension of cultural activities has required new expertise which has engendered various polemics about what a museum is supposed to be: shrine for the arts, educational institution, cultural center, leisure space, or heritage enterprise. The increased number of museums, along with the new types of museums, has led to greater diversity of cultural conceptions, opinions and choices. Furthermore, variations in size and popularity have led to discrepancies between the few world-famous museums—the Louvre, the National Gallery, the Metropolitan Museum in New York—and numerous smaller units. Reputation, financial investment, and professional training divide the museum world, indicating an uneven process of cultural development.

Within the museums themselves, various frames of reference can be traced through differing strategies and even conflicting policies. In the art museums, especially in the most famous, curators, administrators, education personnel, public relations specialists and commercial professionals follow specific goals and, at times, subscribe to contradictory agendas. In museums that have always had a clear educational mission—notably science museums, ecomuseums, or history museums—these differences are not as apparent, but the current discussions as to their commercial potential show that they exist nonetheless.

Financing is, likewise, a matter of dissent. Having had a minimum of resources for decades, museums today often rely on very substantial means. Gaining access to subsidies depends largely on setting up programs that justify public or private investment. Museums have developed on credit, and, as a result, even the richest and most prestigious undergo repeated financial crises. The new financial situation is both a source of strength and of precariousness. This fragility is particularly obvious when museums depend largely on private funds, as do American museums (Zolberg 1981). In Europe, where public funding has a major role, museum policies depend heavily on the political climate and administrative policies (Benhamou 2000). Also, museums have had to address legal questions linked to the inadequacy of administrative regulations in a transformed context. These problems are seen in the necessity in France of passing new laws to fix the terms of private ventures in public museums or, in the Netherlands, the governmental decision to change the status of national museums in order to give them more legal autonomy to deal with management and personnel matters.

The decisions taken in museums often reflect the difficulty of reaching a working compromise between the demands of heritage preservation, cultural aims, and economic constraints. Responding to the priorities imposed by these parameters calls for various skills such as an eye to the future and a willingness to balance different values. Persuading the representatives of various interests to cooperate is an ability with which many museums are not well equipped and are not yet apt to master. The choices entail substantial risks of misunderstanding and misdirection. In such reassessments, the public appears as an economic challenge and has become both an end and a means.

We have seen that museums have been made accessible to all: they exist for and because of the public. But despite the numbers of visitors, public access remains a major complaint. Culture is no longer out of reach, but it is not yet easily shared by the majority. The way to museums is still narrow, and a number of specialists are convinced that museums contribute to cultural exclusion. With statistics in mind, one might well ask how relevant this assertion is. Visitors' studies show that museums deal with substantial numbers of people but they also suggest that these visitors represent only a limited and stable proportion of the population: one-fifth to a quarter of the population account for all visits to art museums (Schuster 1993; DiMaggio 1996; Donnat 1998). The profile of art museum visitors is remarkably consistent. According to these studies, the art museum public is characterized by a high level of education, social status, and income. However, research carried out in the Netherlands and in France in science museums shows that their publics are more varied (Ganzeboom and Haanstra 1989; Eidelman 1992).

Such criticisms have led to a reinforcement of cultural policies at the national level. In France, cultural democratization is an explicit objective of the Ministry of Culture and Communication. As for the museums, most of them have developed strategies addressed to the entire population. With such a goal, every social category is taken into account and, in a marketing approach, becomes a "target group" liable to become the object of a specific action: children and adults; men and women; school groups, students; local visitors, visitors from the rest of the country and abroad; the professional, middle, and working classes, retired people; members of all ethnic and religious groups; individual visitors, families, and groups. More questions are raised concerning the relationships visitors establish with the artistic or the scientific culture. According to some experts, museums have an inadequate understanding of public behavior, underestimate variation in visiting practices, and neglect—or ignore— notions such as taste, visual experience, and scientific curiosity (Heinich 1986; Smith 1996; Zolberg 2000). Museums' cultural strategies—conceived to ensure and enlarge the audience by responding to the public diversity—may answer some of the difficulties museums encounter in a mass society.

To prove themselves politically, culturally, economically, and socially, museums must be a success with the public. Are the controversies surrounding their social roles transitory? Are they a consequence of changes to which museums have not yet adjusted? Are these debates linked to more substantial and long-term contradictions inherent to modern and postmodern societies, as Daniel Bell (1976) suggested? The future of museums will depend on the capacity of their personnel to manage these contradictions. Preserving the cultural heritage while meeting current cultural goals and ensuring economic viability are, and will be, dilemmas as well as challenges for modern museums and their professionals. But heritage and culture are also the responsibility of political representatives and public administrators on a local, national, and global scale. And, finally, they are also the responsibility of citizens, that is to say, a duty shared by the museum's public.

Note

1. The number of visits in France to national, local, and private museums is estimated at 65 million, of which 22 million are tourists (Ministère de la Culture et da la Communication 2000).

References

Alexander, V. (1996) *Museums and Money*, Bloomington: Indiana University Press.

Altick, R. D. (1978) *The Shows of London*, Cambridge: Harvard University Press.

Ballé, C. (1987) 'Les nouveaux musées, une incidence institutionelle de l'évolution culturelle,' *Brises*, 10 (September): 13–16.

Ballé, C. (1996) 'La modernisation des musées: les paradoxes d'une evolution,' pp. 305–320 in J.-M. Tobelem (ed.) *Musées: Gérer autrement*, Paris: La Documentation Française.

Bayart, D. and Benghozi, P.-J. (1993) *Le tournant commercial des musées*, Paris: La Documentation Française.

Bazin, G. (1967) Le *temps des musées*, Brussels: Desoeur.

Bell, D. (1976) *The Cultural Contradictions of Capitalism*, New York: Basic Books.

Benhamou, F. (2000) *L'économie de la culture*, Paris: Éditions La Découverte.

Bourdieu, P. and Darbel, A. (1966) *L'amour de l'art: Les musées européens et leurs publics*, Paris: Les Editions de Minuit.

Caillet, E. (1995) A *l'approche du musée, la médiation culturelle*, Lyon: Presses Universitaires de Lyon.

Cardona, J. and Lacroix, C. (2000) *Chiffres clés 1999*, Paris: La Documentation Française.

Clarke, R. (1991) 'Government policy and art museums in the United Kingdom,' pp. 271–326 in M. Fieldstein (ed.) *The Economics of Art Museums*, Chicago: University of Chicago Press.

Crane, D. (1987) *The Transformation of the Avant-Garde: The New York Art World, 1940–1985.* Chicago: University of Chicago Press.

Daifuku, H. (1998) 'Musées et monuments: le rôle pionnier de l'UNESCO', *Museum International*, 197, 1 (March): 9–19.

Déotte, J.-L. (1994) *Le musée, l'origine de l'esthetique*, Paris: L'Harmattan.

Desvallées, A. (1989) 'Le défi museologique,' in *La muséologie selon Georges Henri Rivière*, Paris: Dunod.

DiMaggio, P. (1982a) 'Cultural entrepreneurship in nineteenth-century Boston, Part I', *Media, Culture and Society*, 4: 33–50.

DiMaggio, P. (1982b) 'Cultural entrepreneurship in nineteenth-century Boston, Part II', *Media, Culture and Society*, 4: 303–22.

DiMaggio, P. (ed.) (1996) 'Introduction', *Poetics*, 24:81-86.

Donnat, O. (1998) *Les pratiques culturelles des Français: Enquête, 1997*, Paris: La Documentation Française.

Dubuffet, J. (1968) *Asphyxiante culture*, Paris: Pauvert.

Eidelman, J. (1992) 'Qui fréquente les musées à Paris?' *Publics et Musées*, 2: 19–45.

François, E. (2000) 'Les mythologies historiques des nations européennes,' in *Publics et projets culturels. Un enjeu des musées en Europe*, Paris: L'Harmattan.

Freches, J. (1979) *Les musées de France*, Paris: La Documentation Française.

Ganzeboom, H. and Haanstra, F. (1989) *Museum and Public: The Public and the Public Approach in Dutch Museums*. Rijswijk: Ministry of Welfare, Health and Culture.

Georgel, C. (1994) 'The museum as a metaphor in nineteenth-century France,' pp. 113–122 in D. Sherman and I. Rogoff (eds.) *Museum Culture*, Minneapolis: University of Minnesota Press.

Girard, A. (1977) *Développement culturel. Experiences et politiques*, Paris: UNESCO.

Gottesdiener, H., Mironer, L., and Davallon, J. (1993) 'France: un développement rapide avec le soutien du public,' *Museum International*, 178 (vol. 45 no. 2): 13–19.

Gubbels, T. and Van Hemel, A. (1993) *Art Museums and the Price of Success*, Amsterdam: Boekman Foundation.

Guy, J.-M. (1991) 'Les pratiques culturelles en Europe' pp. 23–107 in *Participation à la vie culturelle en Europe*, Paris: La Documentation Française.

Heinich, N. (1986) 'La sociologie et les publics de l'art,' in R. Moulin (ed.) *Sociologie de l'art*, Paris: La Documentation Française.

Hewison, R. (1987) *The Heritage Industry*, London: Methuen.

Hooper-Greenhill, A. (1988) 'Counting visitors or visitors who count?' pp. 213–232 in R. Lumley (ed.) *The Museum Time Machine*. London: Routledge.

Institut für Museumskunde (1999) *Statistiche Gesamterhebung an den Museen des Bundesrepublik für das Jahr*, 1997–1998, Berlin: Institut für Museumskunde.

Kavanagh, G. (ed.) (1994) *Museums: Provision and Professionalism*, London: Routledge.

Koven, S. (1994) 'The Whitechapel Picture exhibitions and the politics of seeing,' pp.22–48 in D. Sherman and I. Rogoff (eds.) *Museum Culture*, Minneapolis: University of Minnesota Press.

McManus, P. and Miles, R. (1993) 'Royaume-Uni: la lot du marché,' *Museum International*, 178 (vol. 45, no. 2): 26–32.

Ministère de la Culture (1996) *Statistiques de la culture en Europe*, Paris:La Documentation Française.

Ministère de la Culture at de la Communication (2001) *Synthèse: Museostat*, No. 5 (avril).

Moulin, R. (1994) 'La valeur de l'art,' in *L'art contemporain en question*, Paris: Editions du Jeu de Paume.

Museum Focus (1998) London: Museums and Galleries Commission.

Museums Count (1994) Washington, DC: American Association of Museums.

Museums in the Netherlands. Facts and Figures (1997) Rijswijk: Ministry of Education, Culture, and Science.

Octobre, S. (1999) 'Profession, segments professionnels et identité. L'evolution des conservateurs de musées,' *Revue Française de Sociologie*, 40, 2: 357–383.

O'Doherty, B. (1972) *Museums in Crisis*, New York: George Braziller.

O'Hagan, J. (1998) *The State and the Arts*, Cheltenham: Edward Elgar.

Pomian, K. (1987) *Collectionneurs, amateurs et curieux, Paris et Venise: XVIe-XVIIIe siècle*, Paris: Gallimard.

Poulot, D. (1983) 'Les finalités des musées du XVIe siècle au XIXe siècle,' in *Quels musées pour quelles fins aujourd'hui?* Paris: La Documentation Française.

Poulot, D. (1994) *Bibliographie de l'histoire des musées de France*, Paris: CTHS.

Primicerio, D. (1991) *L'Italia dei Musei*, Milano: Electa.

Rebérioux, M. (1991) 'Le musée lieu d'apprentissage,' in *Le futur antérieur des musées*, Paris: Editions du Renard.

Rivière, G. H. (1989) Musée et societé, à travers le temps et l'espace, in *La muséologie selon Georges Henri Rivière*, Paris: Dunod.

Schaer, R. (1993) *L'invention des musées*, Paris: Gallimard.

Schama, S. (1987) *The Embarrassment of Riches*, New York: Vintage Books.

Schuster, J. M. (1985) *Supporting the Arts: An International Comparative Study*, Cambridge: MIT.

Schuster, J. M. (1993) 'The public interest in the art museum's public,' pp. 39–75 in T. Gubbels and A. van Hemel (eds.) *Art Museums and the Price of Success*, Amsterdam: Boekman Foundation.

Schuster, J. M. (1996) 'Thoughts on the art and practice of comparative cultural research,' in I. van Hamersveld and N. van der Wielen (eds.) *Cultural Research in Europe*, Amsterdam: Boekman Foundation and Circle.

Sherman, D. (1989) *Worthy Monuments*, Cambridge: Harvard University Press.

Smith, J. K. (1996) 'Museum visitor preferences and intentions in constructing aesthetic experience', *Poetics*, 24: 219–238.

Tobelem, J.-M. (1992) 'De l'approche marketing dans les musées', *Publics & Musées*, 2 (December): 49–70.

Van Mensch, P. (1989) 'Museums in the Netherlands: an embarrassment of riches', *Museum* 41 (2): 120–123.

Van Praët, M. (1991) 'Les musées d'histoire naturelle. Progrès des sciences naturelles et evolution des musées scientifiques,' in *Le futur antérieur des musées*, Paris: Editions du Renard.

Von Moos, S. (1999) 'A museum explosion: fragments of an overview' in *Museums for a New Millennium*, Munich: Prestel.

Zolberg, V. (1974) *The Art Institute of Chicago: The Sociology of Cultural Organizations*. Ph.D. Dissertation, University of Chicago.

Zolberg, V. (1981) 'Conflicting visions in American art museums', *Theory and Society*, 10: 103–125.

Zolberg, V. (2000) ' Richard Peterson and the sociology of art and literature,' *Poetics*, 28:157–171.

Part III

REFRAMING URBAN CULTURES FOR LOCAL AND GLOBAL CONSUMPTION

10

Cultural Policy and the City-State

Singapore and the "New Asian Renaissance"

Kian-Woon Kwok and Kee-Hong Low

"It's about time. Singapore swings." These words blared from the front cover of the July 19, 1999, Asian edition of *Time* magazine next to a picture of a young woman blowing bubble gum that was captioned "MTV Asia's Donita Rose lives it up in the Lion City." The subtitle posed the question: "Can Asia's nanny state give up its authoritarian ways?" The lead story, titled "Singapore Loosens Up" provided an answer: "Nanny state? Hardly. Once notorious for tight government control, the city-state is getting competitive, creative, even funky."

It is not routine for nation-states to be praised for being funky. For years, however, Singapore was portrayed in the Western media as the archetypal interventionist state, with rules that affect almost every sphere of public and private life. Hence, one finds frequent references in foreign media to bans on the sale of chewing gum or sexually explicit literature and to social campaigns for promoting courtesy or toilet flushing. But the *Time* cover story was not simply an indication of a new turn in the perspective of foreign media. Referring to the article during the annual National Day Rally address—the equivalent of the State of the Union address in the United States—in August 1999, Prime Minister Goh Chok Tong suggested that there was nothing inappropriate about Singapore being regarded now as funky. Indeed, he said that "making Singapore a fun place" had long been part of government policy: "People laugh at us for promoting fun so seriously. But having fun is important. If Singapore is a dull, boring place, not only will talent not want to come here, but even Singapore will begin to feel restless" (*Straits Times*, August 23, 1999).

This statement provides a springboard for launching the present discussion of cultural policy in contemporary Singapore. Coming from the prime minister, it summarizes authoritatively the thrust and rationale of cultural policy in the nation-state. The Singapore government is serious about promoting fun as a matter of official policy. This formulation, of course, reduces a complex phenomenon to rather simple terms.

In what follows, we offer a discussion of some of the complexities in the logic and workings of cultural policy in Singapore. First, we provide a brief overview of cultural policy during the decades since Singapore's independence in 1965, paying particular attention to the development of policies designed during the 1990s to make Singapore a "global city of the arts" and the "Renaissance City" of Asia—signaling a new way of imagining the nation-state in the new era of globalization. Second, we discuss how this process translates into a reimaging and reshaping of the city and urban life. Third, we discuss cultural policy as a component of the work of government in an age of transnationalism. Finally, we offer some reflections on the relationship between cultural policy and modernity in Singapore, drawing lessons that may have wider theoretical significance for the study of cultural policy.

Positioning Singapore: "Global City for the Arts" and "Renaissance City"

The period from full-fledged independence in 1965 to the early 1980s was known for government policies geared toward industrial and economic development, with cultural development ostensibly receiving lower priority in terms of policy attention and budget allocation. Periodically, leaders and citizens articulated concerns about Singapore being or becoming a "cultural desert," but there were no significant attempts at developing an overall long-term cultural policy. Since the mid-1980s, however, the growing emphasis on cultural development by the second generation of political leaders became evident, in part as a response to what was perceived as the "coarsening materialistic ethos created by concentration on economic gain or moneytheism" (Koh 1980:239).

After several decades of false starts and unfocused efforts in cultural policy, the watershed was marked by the formation of an Advisory Council on Culture and the Arts in February 1988. The council's report of April 1989 made a series of recommendations, especially the establishment of the National Arts Council (NAC) to chart the direction and policies for the arts scene in Singapore.[1] The following year, the Ministry of Information and the Arts (MITA) was created "to help inform, educate and entertain, as part of the national goal to make Singapore a hub city of the world and to build a society that is economically dynamic, socially cohesive and culturally vibrant." MITA's mission is achieved through developing the following policies:[2]

- *Promoting the arts.* MITA aims to make Singapore an artistically vibrant society and an international center for the arts. The National Arts Council is the main body entrusted with developing a strategy.
- *Promoting appreciation of Singapore's heritage.* MITA helps to preserve and promote appreciation of Singapore's diverse cultural heritage through the National Heritage Board.
- *Developing a well-read society.* The National Library Board oversees the nine branch libraries to promote a well-read and informed society. It taps information technology to provide a modern and efficient library service.

- *Promoting commitment to Singapore.* MITA aims to enhance confidence in and commitment to Singapore. This goal is pursued by emphasizing the shared heritage and core values. The Singapore International Foundation and Contact Singapore are geared toward these aims.
- *Preserving social harmony.* With increasing literacy and greater affluence among Singaporeans, the social environment in Singapore has changed over the years. MITA maintains that censorship standards should move in tandem with social trends. Censorship policies allow for creativity and free flow of information, while preserving racial and religious harmony and a wholesome society.
- *Developing international communications and understanding.* MITA seeks to promote a better understanding and appreciation of Singapore and its policies. As Singapore moves into the next lap, international communications will also become increasingly important. Therefore, the challenge of developing Singapore as a key regional and international information center will go hand in hand with the drive to forge greater understanding and cooperation between Singapore and the rest of the world.

The National Arts Council (NAC) was established under MITA in 1991 with maximum autonomy to hire the people it wanted, raise its own funds, appoint advisory committees, and even set up companies to embark on joint ventures. It set up the Singapore Arts Endowment Fund, a centralized pool of money collected from public and private donations for arts use (*Straits Times*, June 29, 1991). The interest generated by this fund is used to support arts groups and organize arts activities. In addition, the government gave the NAC a grant of S$6.5 million in the first year, S$7.4 million in the second, and S$8.4 million in the third year (*Straits Times*, July 24, 1992). In 1992, prominent artists were appointed as arts advisers to help the NAC serve as a link between the statutory board and the arts community. At the same time, other artists from different arts fields were identified as resource personnel.

In addition to the infrastructure represented by NAC, the government has embarked on the building of a multimillion-dollar arts center, which was announced in 1990. In 1992, the Esplanade Co. Ltd. (formerly known as the Singapore Arts Center Co. Ltd.) was set up to "build a well-designed performing arts center, *The Esplanade—Theatres on the Bay,* on time and at best cost: manage it as a preeminent venue attracting the finest in the performing arts; and contribute to the growth of the arts in Singapore."[3] Comprising a series of performance spaces built on a six-hectare site along the waterfront of the Marina Bay, the arts center has cost a total of S$600 million and includes a 1,800-seat Concert Hall and a 2,000-seat Lyric Theatre. As a subsidiary of the NAC,[4] the Esplanade Co. runs like a corporate company taking care of the business bottom line while at the same time looking into artistic and programming policies for the center. Since its inception, the Esplanade Co. has awarded overseas scholarships in arts management and technical training in preparation for its fully operational status when the arts center opens in 2002.

The biennial Festival of Arts, organized by NAC, is one of the major events in Singapore's cultural calendar and actively promoted by the Singapore Tourist Board. It went "global" when the 1996 festival was launched on the World Wide Web to generate international awareness (*Straits Times*, April 11, 1996). The 1998 festival, which had a budget of S$7.8 million, signaled the last of the biennial series. Beginning in 1999, after much restructuring, it was known as the Singapore Arts Festival and is held as an annual event. Aiming to attain the status of the Edinburgh Arts Festival, the new Singapore Arts Festival, with a leaner budget than the biennial festival, will put a greater emphasis on Asian and local works. However, some international components will remain in order to keep its focus as an international event. A permanent logo of the festival has also been created to project this new identity. [5] To encourage greater visibility for the festival and perhaps also the image of Singapore as an international arts city, recent festivals have also attained increased prominence through beefed-up fringe events, including Festival Parade, a Festival Village, commercial tie-ins, and heritage programs taking place all over the island: at the Mass Rapid Transit stations, refurbished heritage buildings, shopping malls, streets, and even the Changi airport transit lounge, a privilege reserved for transit passengers only (*Straits Times*, May 16, 1998).

What, then, can explain all these policies and plans, which have been designed to turn Singapore into a "global city for the arts"? The catchphrase is the title of a 1995 policy initiative that "hopes to do for the arts what it has done for banking, finance, manufacturing and commerce, and help create new ideas, opportunities and wealth." [6] One key to understanding the thrust of cultural policy in the 1990s, therefore, is that policy makers had by then come to appreciate the economic value of the arts. Consequently, the policy rhetoric has gone beyond the previous preoccupation with justifying the *need* to invest in the arts. It has moved on to questions regarding specific strategies and programs. For example, under the leadership of the Ministry of Trade and Industry, a number of key agencies, namely the Economic Development Board, the Trade and Industry Board, and the Singapore Tourism Board "facilitate the introduction of galleries, dealers, and value-added, export-ready products and productions into the business community, publicizing events at home and abroad, structuring tax incentives and promoting investment" (*Straits Times*, April 1, 1998) (see table 10.1).

The development of the arts as a means of attracting business and talent to the city-state is a strong component of policy thinking. At the 1992 Cultural Awards presentation George Yeo, who then was the minister for information and the arts, argued that "a vibrant arts community would also be a boon for the business community as the arts can help attract talented individuals to come to Singapore to work and live and perhaps even settle here." [7]

However, Yeo indicated that the notion of Singapore as a regional hub that attracts foreign talent is only part of a larger vision of the city-state becoming "one of Asia's leading Renaissance cities in the 21st century." To achieve that, "we must develop a high intensity of information and knowledge, and place ourselves as a hub for commerce, finance, culture, communication and transportation" (*Sunday Times*, May 18, 1997). The government envisions Singapore's future role as being the "cultural and artistic bridge to the world" (MITA and STPB 1995:8).

Indeed, that vision is consonant with an entire body of social research on the political economy of "world cities." John Friedmann, one of the major contributors to this

Table 10.1 An Overview of the Arts Scene in Singapore from 1990 to 1997

The following table provides a general overview of arts development and activity in Singapore for the period 1990 to 1997.

Year	1990	1991	1992	1993	1994	1995	1996	1997
No. of arts activities [1]*	1,900	2,000	2,600	2,100	2,300	2,300	3,000	3,000
No. of ticketed attendances [2]*	721,600	679,000	798,000	798,300	845,200	750,500	705,100	764,200
No. of arts groups [3]	143	155	172	178	181	198	205	215
No. of arts companies [4]	n.a.	n.a.	128	150	159	164	174	167
No. of theater seats [5]*	10,800	10,800	16,200	16,200	16,600	16,600	25,800	25,800
(No. of theaters)	(14)	(14)	(16)	(16)	(18)	(18)	(18)	(18)

*   Figures to the nearest (>00)

Sources: *Arts Figures, Key Arts Data from 1990 to 1995.* Compiled by National Arts Council.
Arts, Cultural and Media Scenes in Singapore. MITA 1999.

1. Comprises ticketed and nonticketed performances and visual arts activities
2. Attendance at ticketed performances
3. Refers to registered arts socieites
4. Refers to registered arts companies
5. Includes most commonly used venues for performing arts events

area of research, recalls in his 1995 state-of-the-art article that he was consulted by the Singapore government in the early 1990s. During the discussions it became clear to him that the senior government officials "hoped to hear from me how their city state might rise to the rank of a 'world city.' The golden phrase had become a badge of status, just as 'growth poles' had been in an earlier incarnation. There was little I could say that the government did not already know. But to me this question pointed to an ongoing competitive struggle for position in the global network of capitalist cities and the inherent instability of this system" (p. 36).

Through prudent and transparent pro-business policies, Singapore weathered the so-called Asian crisis of the late 1990s with an enviable degree of resilience. In 1999, even before substantial economic recovery in the city-state and the region, the rhetoric of this "new Asia Renaissance" had not only not lost its momentum but was quickly gaining ground in cementing Singapore's competitive position as a major player on the global stage. At a time when many governments around the region were engaging in economic cutbacks and reassessing their development strategies, the official support for culture and the arts in Singapore seemed even more significant than it actually was.[8] Indeed, as "global politics is being reconfigured along cultural lines" (Huntington 1996:125), the current emphasis on culture and the arts are necessarily part of a larger project in imagining and imaging the *idea* of Singapore as an important cosmopolis that would "capture the magic of Paris and the majesty of Rome." Prime Minister Gok Chok Tong spoke of Singapore's future as a "world city" in a public address in 1999:

> Our goal is to turn Singapore into a cosmopolis—an attractive, efficient and vibrant city exuding confidence and charm, and a magnetic hub of people, minds, talents, ideas and knowledge . . . Visitors will enjoy the Singaporeaness of our city as captured in the unique blend of old and new, East and West, and the harmony and diversity of its multi-racial society.[9]

In a word, Singapore's cultural policy has everything to do with staying on top as a focal node in the late-capitalist world system of the new millennium.

Reimagining and Reimaging the City

The vision of becoming a Renaissance city has spatial consequences. As part of envisioning the cosmopolitan yet "Asian" character in the image of Singapore (Lynch 1972:9), there has been a rush to transform the cityscape into a signification system that encodes and transmits the narrative of Singapore as a modern city-state that is deeply rooted in the relevant Asian civilizations. This involves marking out spaces for the arts and heritage in the cityscape. In general, the revised concept plan released by the Urban Redevelopment Authority (URA) of Singapore in 1991 aimed to chart the physical development of Singapore in three phases: up to year 2000, to year 2010, and to the year X, when the population size could be considered optimal.[10] From this revised concept plan came the development guide plans that detailed specific changes for each of the 55 areas or zones within the URA's purview. Figured into these developmental plans were steps which helped generate "art scapes" in areas such as the Civic and Cultural District (CCD), which covers the Museum Precinct and Theatre Belt, and the Downtown Core (Part), which includes City Hall (also part of the CCD), Central Business District, Selegie/Bugis (the new "entertainment district"), and Marina Center, where The Esplanade will be located. Within the vicinity of these areas are other zones with their respective development guide plans that have some impact on the issues of the present discussion. Without attempting to cover a broad and detailed canvas, we highlight a number of trends for critical discussion.

Heritage as Spectacle?

Since the unveiling of the conservation master plan in 1986, numerous sites around Singapore have been slated for conservation. [11] As part of the project to revitalize the facade of these architectural "treasures," the concept of "adaptive reuse" [12] has been applied to reintroduce "modern" activities [13] suitable for these locations. One of these new usages is for arts purposes. Significantly, the distribution of these conserved sites for arts use has been concentrated within the area known as the Civic and Cultural District and its vicinity. As the name of this area suggests, some of Singapore's major historical and sociocultural references are located within this zoning area: the Supreme Court, City Hall, Parliament House, Victoria Theatre and Concert Hall (formerly the Town Hall), Empress Place, Fort Canning Hill (formerly Government Hill), and the World War II Memorial Monument. Seen as attempts to revitalize the landscape by adding some "color," "soul," or "spirit," these current efforts serve to counterbalance the bland and clinical buildings that clutter the Central Area.

Interestingly enough, apart from the oft-mentioned civic monuments that "speak" of a colonial past, the Central Area also features a high concentration of vernacular architecture that has been consciously inscribed with an "ethnic" narrative. These former residential-cum-commercial dwellings are now representations of hygienically contained ethnic zones: Tanjong Pagar as Chinese, Kampong Glam as Malay, and Serangoon as Indian. Paradoxically, however, most of these vernacular houses have been effectively "deresidentialized" with the help of the housing development project, through which affordable housing ownership is provided for 86 percent of Singapore's population. Once these areas and houses have been conserved, their subsequent usage is carefully managed, giving preference to commercial or other designated purposes that are in line with the planned narrative of that area. In addition, part of the URA's role is to regulate types of usage for these spaces; any change requires approval by the board. However, other more immediate concerns to former residents and commercial operators of these spaces include the high rental fees that usually plague these locales after the renovation project (for example, an 800-square-foot corner unit shop went from less than S$80 a month to S$5,000 a month ["Life!" *Straits Times*, June 3, 1998]) and that often force tenants to vacate and find alternatives. This has greatly affected older forms of businesses that may not find it viable to coexist with other "modern" activities when the consumer profile utilizing these spaces has also changed or moved elsewhere. In a systematic fashion, the conservation project has inadvertently erased a former landscape that does not fit comfortably with the image of Singapore as a modern and progressive nation-city-state.

At the same time, the old-fashioned desire for "rootedness" has been achieved through a series of simulated historical references, heritage markers, and so-called traditional activities. In a sense, the simulation of history through a process of replication via the conservation project has subsequently brought about the disappearance of the "real" city: the city as chaotic, messy, uncontrolled. It has been replaced by an image of what the city should be like. In developing something like the conservation project, it is a question of *imagining* a cultural past: a specific vision of the country's history, heritage, and tradition, such as, for example, a bustling Chinatown with traditional cuisine, small specialized shops, arts and crafts, and cultural activities. Hence, the concept of adaptive reuse has relied heavily on a notion of a glorious and perhaps vibrant past. An exaggerated idea of what the country used to be or what it should have been has been influential in deciding what should fill the space of adaptive reuse or in even coming up with the concept in the first place.

Arts Housing and Its Implications

As comfortable bedfellows in creating a cosmopolitan cityscape, the URA and the NAC have effectively constructed a series of arts housing districts or "arts hub," a term frequently used in Singapore's cultural policy discourse. Under the "adaptive reuse" for arts purposes, the URA plans for these redevelopments while the NAC's Arts Housing Scheme (launched in 1985 under MCD's Ministry of Culture) serves as manager in the redistribution of properties for local arts groups and organizations. With this scheme, old schools and shop houses are acquired and offered at a subsidized rate (30 percent of the market rates) to both amateur and professional arts groups for rehearsal, administrative, and storage purposes.

The existence of the Arts Housing Scheme implies a degree of dependency of artists on the state. While the arts will always need some kind of institutional support, the present scheme can also lead to dependence by provision. It is perhaps a question of discipline through dependency. Once these arts groups are allocated a space for their use, this is subject to evaluation and renewal every two or three years. Some of the criteria include the level of contribution by the group to the arts scene in Singapore, and perhaps, whether real or imagined, the political image of the group in question. Though established groups may have a track record of reputable works and contributions, younger groups may be at the mercy of these standards since what qualifies as active or inactive, sufficient or insufficient contribution remains subjective and therefore heavily relies on some precedent for reference. In some sense, then, becoming product oriented is part and parcel of accepting help from the Arts Housing Scheme. This has been a subject of contention among artists, some of whom argue for a more important "process focus" in making art.

Hence, the notion of discipline here is not only about pandering to requirements of the arts housing project (i.e., to be product oriented) but, more significantly, it is about creating what an artist and making art means (i.e., being process oriented). These so-called roles that artists see themselves as fulfilling—especially one that allows them to portray some semblance of being able to question the status quo, of being "alternative"—only highlights how the circumstance has effectively circumscribed the imagination of being an artist in Singapore.

The Sanitizing of Urban Streetscape

Ironically, the provision and management of arts spaces is also accompanied by the regulation of street life, where living culture might be found. In Singapore, the maintenance of a clean, green, safe, well-managed, and efficient streetscape has almost become a national obsession. However, the situation in colonial Singapore until the 1960s was quite different. Plagued by bad housing conditions and overcrowding, especially in the central area, this situation at some level also provided Singapore with a lively and interesting street life. Unfortunately, the sanitizing of Singapore's streetscape that began in the 1960s as part of the urban planning and renewal projects led to relocation of the majority of the citizenry away from the densely populated central area into public housing. Beng Huat Chua and Norman Edwards (1992) have suggested that such housing improvements may have inadvertently brought about a decline in street life due to "greater voluntary staying at home, especially when the room density per household is substantially reduced as a result of nuclearization of families" (p. 5). However, under hypermodern conditions, there has been an active reintroduction of some sort of regulated street life free from the "appalling unhygienic conditions" (p. 4) of the past which may not be becoming for a global modem city (Chua and Edwards 1992:4).

For example, in Chinatown, there are plans to bring back street bazaars by converting Trengganu and Pagoda Streets into "pedestrian malls." In a bimonthly newsletter of the URA, the Deputy Chief Planner Koh Wen Gin stated that "now the action is ready to move into the streets. The new malls will allow the return of the traditional street hustle and festivities, but without the chaos and without the hair-raising misses between cars and people, carts and trucks" (*Saline* 1997:9). At the same time, these malls will be encoded with cultural symbols to enhance the ethnicity of the area. Durable clay paving and tiles that feature Chinese motifs will replace the present asphalt road on the 10- to 12-meter-wide malls in keeping with "an ethnic Chinese retail area" (*Saline* 1997:9). This increasing commodification of street life and ethnicity has at some level led to an "erasure of spontaneity" (*Saline* 1997:9). The transformation of public spaces into a highly controlled and managed environment has meant that the natural evolution of the landscape cannot and must not be allowed to become the dominant facade for "nothing is left to the imagination or the unforeseen" (Willis 1995:184). Intensifying the ethnicity of Chinatown is to make it more Chinese than it is. In highlighting the "Chineseness" of the area, existing forms of *hybridized* culture coexisting in the space will not feature prominently in the overall image of Singapore; they are rendered invisible in the simulated version of street life.

The Disneyfication of the Civic and Cultural District?

In June 1995, the unveiling of URA's lighting plan for the Civic and Cultural District (CCD) was a significant move to transform and provide a sense of focus to the design of the Singapore cityscape. The extensive planning and redevelopment within the CCD has aimed to provide Singapore with a visible core that leads the unsuspecting tourist through a series of cultural commodities, ready for consumption—raising the question of whether a process of *Disneyfication* is at work, a process with wide-ranging implications.[14] Lim Hng Kiang, minister for national development, in a speech at the opening of the third International Convention on Urban Planning, Housing, and Design, provided some criteria for making "a city of the next millennium vibrant, attractive, and memorable" which, coincidentally, mirrors Walt Disney's original vision for EPCOT (Experimental Prototype Community of Tomorrow) in Orlando, Florida.[15]

In describing the "Singapore experience" to the participants of the conference, Lim could have been talking about Disney's EPCOT center. On a national scale, most of the urban planning projects have been oriented toward achieving this "great city of the next millennium." One of the major projects is the extensive redevelopment of the Civic Cultural District and its vicinity. The CCD, covering an area of 105 hectares, is one of the five major Conservation Districts identified in the Conservation Master Plan for the Central Area of Singapore.[16]

Like the various thematized "lands" at Disney's theme parks, the CCD's different zones are linked via three separate routes distinctly marked with ambience lighting. Detailed in the *Civic District Lighting Plan Guidebook*, these three pedestrian-friendly pathways are aptly named:

- *Celebration Route.* This provides a short walking tour of architecturally rich buildings and some of Singapore's civic monuments.
- *Heritage Link.* Forming a larger loop, the link will take pedestrians and motorists through the district's key attractions along the Celebration Route, covering also the Singapore River and Fort Canning Park.
- *Historical Trails.* These little trails radiating from the Heritage Link connect the Civic District with the conservation areas such as the Singapore River banks, Chinatown, Little India, and Kampong Glam.

Figured into this whole equation are the arts spaces located amid the conservation and historic buildings. As mentioned, the presence of these spaces is meant to boost the "cultured" image of Singapore. While these sites provide high culture (through the Theatre Belt, Museum Precinct, and the up and coming Esplanade, the recently released plans for Singapore's Entertainment Area to be located within the Selegie/Bugis Area aims to be London's Piccadilly Circus and New York's Broadway in providing popular entertainment. Envisioned as the "focus for future arts and entertainment activities in Singapore," it seeks to transform the cityscape into a sensory-loaded palette of brightly illuminated signs, bustling with street life and year-round fun and festivities, all uncharacteristic of Singapore's previous stiff and sober image.

The Art of Governing the Nation-State in the Age of Transnationalism

Thus far we have examined cultural policy in Singapore from the standpoint of the government's positioning of the nation-state as a world city vis-à-vis other world cities and in the global capitalist system, especially in an economically emergent Asia. However, as Michael Schudson (1994) has argued, cultural policy also has everything to do with "the integration of national societies." Moreover, in the contemporary world, this problematic must be understood in light of the challenges to the nation-state amid the presence of global consumer culture and both transnational and subnational loyalties, calling into question the conventional understanding of the integrative function of culture:

> Culture may be integrative, but it may also be disintegrative at the same time. It may ally acquiescent citizens under a common regime and common symbols, but it may also prove a focal point for division, contention, and conflict. In their cultural policy, nation-states provide not so much cultural unity but an authoritative statement of the terms in which union and division will be negotiated. (pp. 42–43)

It is important, therefore, to also turn attention to understanding cultural policy in relation to the efforts of governments in providing authoritative directions and terms for the negotiation of membership in national societies. In this regard, the case of Singapore provides an unusual perspective on the issue because it is an economically globalized city-state, which at the same time is politically a national society, an independent nation, forged out of a culturally diversified population by an actively interventionist state. In the Singapore case, we suggest, it is instructive to understand cultural policy not just as an instrument of governing but, more fundamentally, as both an instrument and manifestation of Foucault's notion of "governmentality" or the particular form of rationality peculiar to state practices (Burchell, Gordon, and Miller 1991). As Colin Gordon (1991) suggests, "Foucault used the term 'rationality of the government' almost interchangeably with 'art of government.' He was interested in government as an activity or practice, and in arts of government as ways of knowing what that activity consisted in, and how it might be carried on. A rationality of government will thus mean a way or a system of thinking about the nature of the practice of government (who can govern; what governing is; what or who is governed), capable of making some form of that activity thinkable and practicable both to its practitioners and to those upon whom it was practiced."

This is not the place for an adequate treatment of the question of governmentality in Singapore. It may suffice, however, to suggest and illustrate how components of cultural policy serve to implement and manifest the particular rationality of government in relation to the shaping of citizens' lives in two areas: heritage and the arts.

The task of engineering a sense of rootedness needed a centralized body to coordinate the fractured memories and histories of Singaporeans. On August 1, 1993, the National Heritage Board (NHB) was set up "to explore and present the heritage and nationhood of the people of Singapore in the context of their ancestral cultures, their links with Southeast Asia, Asia and the world through the collection, preservation, interpretation and display of objects and records" (National Heritage Board 1996–1997). Under the NHB is the National Museum of Singapore, which oversees the development of the Singapore Art Museum, the Asian Civilizations Museum, the Singapore History Museum, and the National Archives of Singapore. For example, seeking to document "the course of Singapore's history from its humble beginnings as a fishing village to the cosmopolitan hub it is today," plans have been made to renovate the Singapore History Museum building "into a comprehensive museum on Singapore's history dating back to the 1800s" (National Heritage Board 1996–1997: 25–26).

As "keepers of memories," the National Archives of Singapore (NAS) established 30 years ago (1968) set out "to intelligently build a comprehensive documentary heritage of our nation and to become a leading resource center for the research and dissemination of information on the history of Singapore" (National Heritage Board 1996–1997). Though in its early years it was preoccupied with preserving government records, NAS has expanded its role to include outreach programs such as traveling exhibits to schools and shopping centers, production of CD-ROMs, and promotion of awareness of heritage among students. Highlighting the significant role of NAS in informing Singaporeans of their past, George Yeo reiterated during the 30th-anniversary celebration of NAS the need for history in nation building:

> The Singapore that the older generations knew when they were young is very different from that which the young see today. Older Singaporeans, who have lived through upheavals such as World War II, the anti-colonial movement, the riots and strikes of the 1950s, and the traumatic birth of the country in the 1960s, had a stronger sense of how much it has changed in the past 33 years. Younger Singaporeans have a much weaker sense of the past. Without such memories, there can be no independent, self-conscious Singapore nation or people. (*Straits Times*, May 2, 1998)

We may also recall the earlier discussion on the transformation of urban life and the cityscape. Such transformation has parallels with the process of colonization, which, as one writer noted, typically relied on "the myth of the clean slate . . . to wipe out and rewrite history" (Al Sayyad 1992:3) through urbanism. [17] Rooted in modernity itself, these urban planning projects introduced what Hosagrahar Jyoti (1992) calls a "theatre of colonial dominance" through "assignment of roles, the making of symbols, and the interpretation of history" (pp. 83–106). In effect, the use of "spectacle is to make a culture forget itself—forget its own history, the questions it asks of itself in order to get from here to there, even its notions of what here and there are and why we want or need to move between them" (Kuenz 1995:192). Consequently, in attempting to *decolonize* the cityscape in postcolonial times, the independent self-government has also relied on these colonial methods of "rewriting our history." The use of images, symbols, and constructed facades in creating the spectacle of a postcolonial cityscape has been part of the nation-building process, of excavating a heritage narrative for the locals, almost like a "story they tell themselves about themselves" (Geertz 1993:448).

It is not surprising, therefore, that this has also been a process of "Asianizing" social memory—a binary opposite to the colonial project (Geertz 1993:448)—through carefully selected perspectives and objectives in heritage conservation projects.[18] After all, "to lose these architectural assets would be to erase a living chapter of our history." [19] Ironically, memory is not about remembering but forgetting, and in preserving these memories there has been a consequential lapse into some sort of "cultural amnesia." [20]

Hence, *recolonization* is perhaps more accurate than *decolonization* as the postcolonial government institutionalizes its legitimacy as the ruling authority, especially through the electoral process. Nevertheless, this does not imply that citizens accept the "preserved" histories without question. For example, a local study on public reactions to the conservation projects that have occurred in Tanjong Pagar suggests that those who were former residents of the place and those whose life-worlds are only a transient reality vis-à-vis the space in question (i.e., either they work there, or they have been there, but they don't or have never lived there, have different perceptions of the changes (Yeoh and Ping 1995). This highlights the significant implications of these projects because apart from original residents who had some sort of intimate life experiences associated with these places before they were conserved and rebuilt, all the others seem to accept unquestioningly the narratives transcribed onto refurbished spaces.

The art of Singapore's governmentality, like most other modern nation-states, has relied on erasing memory, inventing tradition, and rewriting history to support the construction of a national identity and ensure a loyal and cohesive electorate. In Singapore's case, the most recent strategy has been the development of a national education program targeting all levels of the education system. It was launched on May 17, 1997, in response to the discovery that a large number of young Singaporeans know little about Singapore's past, especially the turbulent circumstances surrounding its history, the struggles of the pioneering generation, and the apparent vulnerability of its current position. Introduced originally for students in Singapore schools, the program has expanded its reach to the general population. Produced at a cost of U.S. $10 million, the National Education Exhibition held from July 7 to 31, 1998, at the Suntec City Convention Hall featured an MTV-style multimedia show that traced Singapore's history from 1819 to the present (*Straits Times*, June 11, 1998).

To encourage visitors to "soak in the history of the nation . . . and remind themselves of the hard times that went before" (*Straits Times*, July 8, 1998), the exhibition made it possible for them to take a piece of history home with them. Replicas of "banana money" and ration cards issued during the Japanese occupation, official letters and records of the merger and separation, personal letters of prominent historical figures, and so on were for sale. In addition, two national education-related publications and a CD-ROM version of the multimedia show were available.[21] Without any doubt, this Disneylike theme park ride (complete with motorized seats that transported the audience through the seven stations of the exhibit) together with appropriate merchandising, is an illustration of the increasing transformation of Singapore's selective history and memories into commodities for easy consumption.

This "politics of forgetting" exercised by the state apparatus is a key strategy in preparing a cultural consciousness that will be susceptible to the efficacy of the "new Asia" rhetoric as a solution to "the problem of 'tradition' in contemporary Singapore" (Kwok 1993).

In addition to playing a role in the new Asian renaissance, the promotion of the arts has also institutionalized a modus operandi in the relationship between government and artists. The reactions to and impact of the increasing degree of institutionalization of the arts and culture in Singapore have been mixed. In particular, the state apparatuses have been extremely active in generating a cultural (arts) policy that tends to emphasize an economic rationale. It is not surprising that those who are at the receiving end of the policies find that of arts development in Singapore is being reduced to a business venture undertaken at the national level.

When NAC was established, this notion of a systematic institutionalization of the arts began with the question of sponsorship. Apart from providing a series of grants under its grants scheme (e.g., theatre, annual, professional artists, seed grants, etc.), the NAC also serves as a matchmaker between corporate sponsors and the artists.

Unlike corporate sponsorship in other parts of the world, such as Britain's Business for the Arts, in which there is a direct link between sponsors and artists, companies in Singapore would rather go through the government in order to gain symbolic capital — a recognition of their civic services, usually through NAC's "Patron of the Arts Awards." Going through the government also indicates a stamp of approval for the benefiting arts group, allowing for good business returns through the strong advertising power based on the perceived clout of the selected group. In this situation, NAC has in a sense become the major canvassing body for arts sponsorship in Singapore, and being a government organization (even if it is a statutory board), there has been some distrust of its criteria for handing out money. Local arts groups of the current generation — practitioners below the age of 40 who have been active in doing experimental works that seek to develop arts of an "indigenous nature" — seem to believe that the government is interested only in commercial large-scale impresario works like *Cats*, *Phantom of the Opera*, *Les Misérables*, and *Joseph and the Amazing Technicolor Dreamcoat*, which at the same time have often been used in ministerial speeches and reports as indications of a cultured enterprise.

The problem of sponsorship is also exacerbated by no apparent consistency in delineating the criteria for choosing a recipient. Even though members of the artistic community sit on advisory panels and resource groups to help provide better links between NAC and the arts community, there is very little transparency in the systematic procedures by which a grant or scholarship is finally approved. Those who might be on the receiving end of sponsorship usually have to resort to hearsay, second-guessing and common misconceptions circulating in the artistic community. Hence, when sponsorship is not forthcoming for a local production, it is usually quickly assumed that either there is no interest in developing local arts or there is a problem with censorship.

In Singapore, the issue of censorship is intimately associated with a concept called "out-of-bounds markers," or "OB markers" for short. Koh has suggested that these markers are often taken, but mistakenly, as vague and shifting; other writers are still skeptical as to the clarity of these boundaries (*Straits Times*, May 19, 1998). Censorship guidelines have been put in place, and according to Koh's argument, there should not be any misinterpretation when the boundaries are transgressed. Even with the guidelines, though, a margin of ambiguity remains. First, there is the ambiguity of terms. For example, for live performances like plays, the scripts are subject to approval by the Public Entertainment Licensing Unit (PELU) and the Drama Review Committee of the NAC before they are allowed for public viewing. Robin Loon and Elizabeth Kaiden (1998) have suggested that the terms and concepts listed in the Censorship

Review Committee's Report of 1992 and the licensing conditions issued by PELU are broad, unclear, and open to interpretation. Second, there is the ambiguity of self-censorship. On the recommendation of the review committee, established theater groups with a good track record have been exempted since 1994 from submitting scripts (*Straits Times*, May 25, 1995). This reliance on "self-regulation" only highlights Foucault's (1979) notions of self-discipline and the microphysics of power. Having to exercise some form of self-censorship, the artist must face a great degree of instability and uncertainty as the limits are negotiated. Third, there is the ambiguity of decision. When it comes down to having a show approved for public performance, the actual process of who and what will constitute the final decision is not clear. As in the situation for disbursing grants, even if fellow artists or individuals sympathetic to the arts sit on the drama review committee, it is difficult for the applicant to have a sense of how significant their role is and the actual processes that produce approval (or disapproval).

Taken as a whole, this zone of ambiguity makes negotiating with the state mechanisms an overly cautious process for artists, thereby creating what we call the "myth of antagonism"—artists tend to assume an adversarial position vis-à-vis the state. By constantly carrying the state in one's head, this becomes a more potent form of circumscribing permissiveness than overt control and creates a sensibility that not only worries about transgressing boundaries but also about what "needs" to be said as a "counterdiscourse" to the perceived dominant prescription for society. Significantly then, this may contribute to a false sense of being able to provide an "alternative" commentary when these so-called alternative spaces are framed within the limited binarism. For example, political theater in Singapore is said not to exist or "rather, no theatre company in Singapore would declare itself a political theatre company or even align itself with any obvious form of political agitation" (Loon and Kaiden 1998:1). As a result, any form of political protest or commentary can exist only in what Loon and Kaiden (1998) call "a field of virtuality" created by this zone of ambiguity. It is virtual in the sense that it "exists only in essence or effect (though not actual fact) and also in the sense that it exists in the mind as a product of imagination" (p. 5) not unlike Marx's notion of false consciousness.

In the last decade, the censorship markers and boundaries have not remained stagnant and they have more or less reflected the changing perceptions of what is deemed morally acceptable in the politically defined Singapore-Asian society. Though many would claim that the changes have been incremental without any major breakthrough, the situation has relaxed a little, albeit on the conservative side. The former minister for the arts and information has also hinted at the need for reevaluating censorship rules when he said that "censorship rules had to be updated if Singapore wanted the arts to flourish here" (*Straits Times*, March 1, 1991). However, the art of governing described above is still being exercised, and overt censorship incidents, major and minor, have taken place over the last few years, reinforcing notions that the government will have the final say in deciding what is deemed within the community's "norms of decency and good taste." Perhaps at one level this is true, for within the bounds of its own defined rationality, the government would view itself as accountable at the end of the day. However, the success of the censorship game cannot be attributed to the state apparatus alone, but needs the cooptation of those subjected to its ambiguous rules.

Conclusion: Cultural Policy and Modernity

If the true modern city is, as John Lechte (1995) proposes, "a city of indetermination" (p. 106), then Singapore is a peculiar modern city in which indeterminacy is subdued, domesticated, and managed through, among other things, the work of cultural policy that has consequences for how the city is imagined, imaged, and lived. Rem Koolhaas (1995) has offered a provocative view of what Singapore uniquely represents:

> In Singapore—modernization in its pure form—the forces of modernity are enlisted against the demands of modernism. Singapore's modernism is lobotomized: from modernism's full agenda, it has adopted only the mechanistic, rationalistic program and developed it to an unprecedented perfection in a climate of streamlined "smoothness" generated by shedding modernism's artistic, irrational, uncontrollable, subversive ambitions—revolution without agony. (p. 1041)

We might, therefore, conclude with an equally provocative response to Koolhaas's critique. There are three key terms here: modernization, modernity, and modernism. Singapore has been an exemplar of late-capitalist modernization propelled by a developmentalist and interventionist state, intervening not only into political economy but also, as we have partially documented here, into the spheres of social memory and cultural life. In effect, Koolhaas has suggested that the Singapore case amounts to one of modernization without modernism, especially without its irrational and subversive impulses. However, the work of the Singapore state may yet be characterized as a deeply *modernist* project. According to Peter Abbs (quoted in Pateman 1991), the idea of an avant-garde is that of "being at the vanguard of the historical process and of serving 'the spirit of the age' . . . To be modern was to be on the crest of historical time: the task was to be loyal to the moment, to the 'just now' [Latin: *modo*] of imminent historic realization of 'the world spirit'" (p. 118). This, too, is an understanding that stems from the "unclouded historical optimism" of Marx and Hegel. Indeed, Abbs also quotes Ernst Gombrich's description of modernist artists as the "business managers of the world spirit . . . [having] . . . to be aware of the necessary next step to be taken. . . . They represent, as it were, the next species which had already been prefigured internally" (p. 118).

In this sense, Singapore's political leadership and cultural policymakers are also "business managers of the world spirit" of the epoch of globalization, already prefigured in the late twentieth century, and requiring a new species of men and women— in this case, Singaporeans who are both cosmopolitan and Asian—in the service of a new global political economy. And not just as business managers but also as *artists*, insofar as the work of government is an art. And in view of the idea of a new Asian renaissance, it is instructive to recall that the opening chapter of Jacob Burckhardt's *The Civilization of the Renaissance in Italy* (1958) is titled "The State as a Work of Art." As rationalistic as the modernism of the Singapore state has been, it has also been *culturally* subversive, having the ambition of, on the one hand, working on the premise of a tabula rasa and, on the other hand, actively projecting the next necessary steps that must be taken into a future that is already present.

Perhaps, therefore, Singapore does not represent a case of "modernization without modernism" but rather "modernization without *modernity*"—without the critical and self-reflexive consciousness of modernity (Berman 1982:143–175). The sphere of culture, especially the arts, is where the problematic of modernity is confronted. We suggest that one aspect of this larger problematic is the question of individualism, which is central to the development of modern art and modernism. To return to Burckhardt (1958:100–127), the development of the individual is a specifically modern idea, that of the individual who is not conceptualized merely as a member of some collectivity. Cultural policy, we suggest, is also primarily concerned with not just collective representations (for example, of the nation-state) but also with constructions of the individual, with what Foucault called the "technologies of the self." In constructing the national body politic within a new globalized order, cultural policy makers also define the role of individual citizens within it.

But it is not the case that governments are the active purveyors and citizens the passive recipients of the effects of cultural policy. It is in the spheres of the arts and social memory, in which such constructions are being developed and contested by individuals—artists, cultural workers, intellectuals, citizens—that the tensions, dilemmas, and costs of modernity are explored and articulated.

Notes

1. The formation of the present NAC was first announced in March, 1990 by the minister for community development, Wong Kan Seng (*Straits Times*, January 14, 1991).

2. Taken from MITA's website: www.gov.sg/mita

3. Mission statement of The Esplanade Co Ltd. Taken from *The Esplanade*'s website: www.esplanade.com.sg

4. Its equity holders are the Ministry of Information and the Arts and the National Arts Council.

5. According to Liu Thai Ker, chairman of National Arts Council in the festival's program message.

6. George Yeo, then minister for information and the arts quoted in the 1995 MITA and STBP brochure, *Singapore: Global City for the Arts.*

7. August 14, 1992. Quoted in the EDB brochure, *Singapore Limited*, June, 1995.

8. Budget 98 (for fiscal year, April 1, 1998 to March 31, 1999) released on February 27, 1998, reflected an increase in both operating and development expenditure. The percentage invested in information and the arts stood as 1.4 percent or S$380.70 million (out of which S$82.8 million was set aside for the arts) of the total budget. The operating expenditure was S$196.76 million, up by 4.45 percent from last year and the development expenditure was S$183.94 million, up 41.44 percent from the 1997 budget (*Straits Times*, February 28, 1998). However, with an expected decrease of 1.5 percent in economic growth registered in the previous year, the 1999 Budget saw a slight dip with a total of S$369.70 million (or 1.3 percent of the total) set aside for information and the arts.

9. Goh Chok Tong in a welcome address at the World Conference on Model Cities. Singapore, April 19, 1999.

10. The original Concept Plan put in place in 1971 saw the need to rapidly redevelop urban space in Singapore. Part of this process involved massive zoning projects that divided Singapore into numerous segments, requiring reallocation of the population. Currently divided into 55 planning areas, the Urban Redevelopment Authority (URA) is in charge of coming up with Development Guide Plans (DGP) to detail the segmental developments.

11. By early 1997, there were 32 monuments and 28 conservation areas with 5,311 buildings that had been earmarked for preservation by the URA and the Preservation of Monuments Board. Some of these projects have been completed while others are still in progress. See Urban Redevelopment Authority, 1995–96.

12. Adaptive reuse is modifying a place to suit it to a compatible use that involves the least possible loss of national, historical, or cultural significance of the place (URA and Preservation of Monuments Board 1993). Interestingly, the principles and objectives are based on a number of sources generated by the international polity. International regimes provide a set of institutional prescriptions and guidelines that have a significant impact on the cultural evolution of developing societies. This suggests the hegemony of the international polity.

13. "Modern" activities here include businesses (small to medium companies/SMCs) in advertising, food and beverage, design, arts and crafts, etc. Interestingly, most of the shop houses in the Tanjong Pagar Conservation Area, for example, are occupied by advertising/design firms.

14. See, for example, Ritzer and Liska (1997), Zukin (1991, 1995), and Sorkin (1992).

15. Walt Disney's vision of a Utopian landscape of the future was that of "a city that caters to the people as a service function. It will be a planned, controlled community, a showcase for American industry and research, schools, cultural and educational opportunities. In EPCOT there will be no landowners and therefore no voting control. No slum areas because we will not let them develop. People will rent houses instead of buying them and at modest rentals. There will be no retirees. Everyone must be employed" (Pawley 1988: 39).

16. Others include Chinatown, Little India, Kampong Glam, and Singapore River (with Robertson Quay, Clarke Quay and Boat Quay).

17. This notion of a "clean slate" has been expressed succinctly by Governor-General Marital Merlin of French East Africa: "When we arrive in these new countries, the ground belongs to no one. . . . The land must be given only to those who exploit it and make it useful." (See Wright 1991: 72).

18. Documented in a series of volumes entitled *Objectives, Principles and Standards for Preservation and Conservation*, the series consists of *Conservation Guidelines* (4 volumes) and *Conservation Technical Leaflets* (set of eight leaflets) containing detailed lists on how and what to preserve, down to specifics, such as the types of replacement tiles and materials allowed.

19. Quoted at the back of the information booklet of the exhibition *Our Heritage is in Our Hands* (Urban Redevelopment Authority and Preservation of Monuments Board,1994).

20. This term has been used by authors on space and memory. See, for example, Powell (1997).

21. Apparently, these proved to be very popular as many rushed to purchase them as souvenirs. One student, 10-year-old Mahamed Rais, was even reported saying: "My father

reminded me to buy one and gave me the money. He told me that it was very hard to get the documents" (*Straits Times*, July 8, 1998).

References

Al Sayyad, N. (1992) 'Urbanism and the dominance equation: reflections on colonialism and national identity,' pp. 1–25 in N. Al Sayyad (ed.) *Forms of Dominance: On the Architecture and Urbanism of the Colonial Enterprise*, Brookfield: Avebury.

Berman, M. (1982) *All That is Solid Melts into Air*, New York: Penguin.

Burchell, G., Gordon, C., and Miller, P. (eds.) (1991) *The Foucault Effect: Studies in Governmentality*, London: Harvester Wheatsheaf.

Burckhardt, Jacob (1958) *The Civilization of the Renaissance in Italy*, translated by S. G. C. Middlemore, New York: Harper Torchbook.

Chua, B. H. and N. Edwards (eds.) (1992) *Public Space: Design, Use and Management*, Singapore: Singapore University Press.

Economic Development Board (1995) *Singapore Limited*.

Foucault, M. (1979) *Discipline and Punish*, New York: Vintage Books.

Friedmann, J. (1995) 'Where we stand: a decade of world city research,' pp. 21–47 in P. L. Knox and P. J. Taylor (eds.) *World Cities in a World-system*, Cambridge: Cambridge University Press.

Geertz, C. (1993) *The Interpretation of Cultures*, London: Fontana Press.

Gordon, C. (1991) 'Introduction,' pp. 1–51 in G. Burchell, Colin Gordon, and P. Miller (eds.) *The Foucault Effect: Studies in Governmentality*, London: Harvester Wheatsheaf.

Huntington, S. (1996) *The Clash of Civilizations and The Remaking of World Order*, New York: Simon & Schuster.

Jyoti, H. (1992) 'City as Durbar: Theatre and power in Imperial Delhi,' pp. 83–106 in N. Al Sayyad, (ed.) *Forms of Dominance: On the Architecture and Urbanism of the Colonial Enterprise*, Brookfield: Avebury.

Koh Tai, A. (1980) 'The Singapore experience: cultural development in the global village,' *Southeast Asian Affairs*, 7: 292–307.

Koolhaas, R. with Mau, B. (1995) *Small, Medium, Large, Extra-Large*. New York: Monacelli Press.

Kuenz, J. (1995) 'It's a small world after all,' pp. 54–78 in The Project on Disney, *Inside The Mouse: Work and Play at Disney World*, Durham and London: Duke University Press.

Kwok, K.-W. (1993) 'The problem of 'tradition' in contemporary Singapore,' pp. 1–24 in A. Mahizhnan (ed.) *Heritage and Contemporary Values*, Singapore: Institute of Policy Studies.

Lechte, J. (1995) '(Not) belonging in postmodern space,' pp. 99–111 in S. Watson and K. Gibson (eds.) *Postmodern Cities and Spaces*, Oxford, UK: Blackwell.

Loon, R. S. Y. and Kaiden, E. A. (1998) 'Singapore political theatre: virtuosity in its virtuality,' paper delivered at CONTACT, London, May.

Lynch, K. (1972) *The Image of the City*, Cambridge, Massachusetts: M.I.T. Press.

Ministry of Information and the Arts (MITA) and Singapore Tourist Promotion Board (STPB) (1995) *Singapore: Global City for the Arts*, Singapore: MITA and STPB.

National Heritage Board (1996–97) *Annual Report*.

National Tourism Plan Committees (1996) *Tourism 21*, Singapore: Singapore Tourist Promotion Board.

Pateman, T. (1991) *Key Concepts: A Guide to Aesthetics, Criticism, and the Arts in Education*, London: Falmer Press.

Pawley, M. (1988) 'Tourism: the last resort,' *Blueprint*, October: 39

Powell, R. (1997) 'Erasing memory, inventing tradition, rewriting history: planning as a tool of ideology,' *Singapore Architect*, no. 196, 94–101.

Ritzer. G. and Liska, A. (1997) 'McDisneyization and post-tourism: complementary perspectives on contemporary tourism,' pp. 96–109 in C. Rojek and J. Urry (eds.) *Touring Cultures: Transformations of Travel and Theory*, London and New York: Routledge.

Schudson, M. (1994) 'Culture and the integration of national societies,' pp. 21–43 in D. Crane (ed.) *Sociology of Culture: Emerging Theoretical Perspectives*, Oxford: Blackwell.

Singapore Arts Federation (1996) *Anniversary Souvenir Magazine, 1966–1996*.

Singapore: Facts and Figures (1997).

Sorkin, M. (1992) 'See you in Disneyland,' pp. 205–232 in M. Sorkin (ed.) *Variations on a Theme Park: The New American City and the End of Public Space*, New York: Hill and Wang.

Urban Redevelopment Authority (1995–1996) *Annual Report*.

Urban Redevelopment Authority and Preservation of Monuments Board (1993) *Objectives, Principles, and Standards for Preservation and Conservation*, Singapore: Stamford Press Pte. Ltd.

Urban Redevelopment Authority and Preservation of Monuments Board (1994) *Our Heritage is in Our Hands: A Public-Private Partnership in Conservation*.

Willis, S. (1995) 'Public use/private state,' in The Project on Disney, *Inside the Mouse: Work and Play at Disney World*, Durham and London: Duke University Press.

Wright, G. (1991) *The Politics of Design in French Colonial Urbanism*, Chicago: University of Chicago Press.

Yeoh, B. S.A. and Ping, L. Wei (1995) 'Historic district, contemporary meanings: urban conservation and the creation and consumption of landscape spectacle in Tanjong Pagar,' pp. 46–67 in B. S.A. Yeoh and L. Kong (eds.) *Portraits of Places: History, Community, and Identity in Singapore*, Singapore: Times Editions Pte Ltd.

Zukin, S. (1991) *Landscapes of Power: From Detroit to Disney World*, Berkeley: University of California Press.

Zukin, S. (1995) *The Cultures of Cities*, Oxford: Blackwell.

11

The Immaterial City

Ferrara, a Case Study of Urban Culture in Italy

Maria Antonietta Trasforini

Because a city, even if we take it as the stage of a loving flânerie, is a damned, elusive and most complicated thing.
— A. M. Ripellino, *Praga Magica*

Ferrara, a small Italian provincial town, has a rich cultural tradition dating back to its role as capital of the Renaissance Estense dynasty. After a long period of obscurity that lasted until the late 1980s, it has returned to the limelight, and once more culture is the reason for it. Thanks to the Great Events (*Grandi Eventi*)—major shows, important concerts, or production and performance of musical works—promoted by the local council (*Comune*) and thanks, above all, to the image of them presented by the media (which have coined the term), Ferrara now seems to have become one of the "cities of culture" in national and international competition. If the image of a city is a framework of meaning within which one can interpret what happens there, Ferrara's image is now that of a producer of art and music of quality—exclusive, unique, and refined. In this respect Ferrara as a city of art and culture, that is, as a cultural object, is a successful product.

In this chapter, I will discuss the public production of culture in Ferrara. In this city of 137,000 inhabitants, the local government has been acting as an entrepreneur, and in the early 1990s the expenditure for culture was one of the highest in Italy. I shall also consider the goals that have been pursued, particularly that of turning culture into an economic investment and of placing Ferrara on the international market of cities of art and culture, thus aiming at a global public. Great Events, the most striking instrument and result of this cultural policy, in fact opened out of conditions present in the 1960s, especially the role of local government in promoting art exhibi-

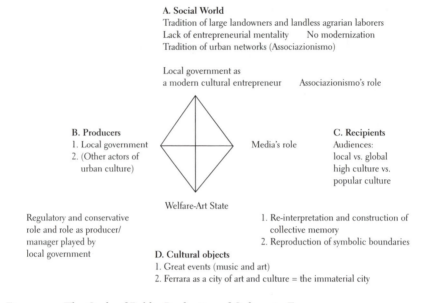

A. Social World
Tradition of large landowners and landless agrarian laborers
Lack of entrepreneurial mentality   No modernization
Tradition of urban networks (Associazionismo)

Local government as
a modern cultural entrepreneur   Associazionismo's role

B. Producers   C. Recipients
1. Local government   Media's role   Audiences:
2. (Other actors of   local vs. global
   urban culture)   high culture vs.
                                                                            popular culture

Welfare-Art State
Regulatory and conservative   1. Re-interpretation and construction of
role and role as producer/   collective memory
manager played by   2. Reproduction of symbolic boundaries
local government   D. Cultural objects
                                              1. Great events (music and art)
                                              2. Ferrara as a city of art and culture = the immaterial city

Figure 11.1   The Cycle of Public Production of Culture in Ferrara
Source: Adapted from Griswold 1994

tions and in fostering preservation and restoration of urban landmarks. I shall consider the entrepreneurial culture in which the local government's activity has taken place, changing from an artisan-communitarian type to a professional-societal one. I shall examine the positive and negative fallout of such activity on the traditional social network of urban culture. The characteristics of the audiences of culture in Ferrara will be outlined, stressing their segmentation and stratification, which echo the high culture/popular culture distinction. I shall finally discuss the drawbacks and advantages of such a model of cultural policy.

Cultural policy is concerned with the process whereby cultural objects are produced (Peterson 1976; Hirsch 1972). Through the mobilization of economic and symbolic resources and of organizational apparatuses, it creates new symbolic boundaries (DiMaggio 1992). Urban cultural policy creates new boundaries between the city and its environment, and inside the city, it builds new audiences and changes the level of stratification in existing audiences.

I will argue that the most important product of Ferrara's urban culture policy is the *immaterial city*, that is the *city of art and culture*. This is at once a real place and a place in the imaginary of global and local culture. There, collective memory is continuously being reinterpreted and reinvented by visitors (tourists) and residents alike. Even though I am mainly concerned with the institutional aspect in the production of culture, I do not underestimate the production of meanings on the recipients' part.

A useful theoretical image for the argument of this chapter is the "cultural diamond" proposed by Griswold (1994), which highlights the strong nonhierarchical relationship among the elements at its four virtual angles. In the case of Ferrara (fig. 11.1), the cultural object includes the city of art and culture and the Great Events; the major producer is, obviously, the local government in its entrepreneurial role; the recipients are the various local and global audiences; the social world, finally, is the economic, cultural, and social environment of Ferrara, her history and traditions. On the various sides of the diamond are listed some of the dynamic phenomena connecting various elements in the figure.

Public Production of Culture in Ferrara: the Welfare-Art State

Because of its traditions of large landowners and landless agrarian laborers, Ferrara never experienced the modernization boom of the 1960s in Italy: it remained a city and an economy in slow motion, cut off from major industrial developments, excluded from the main arteries of communication, off the beaten track with respect to the Via Emilia, the axis and major route of the region of which it is a part. This exclusion did, however, shelter it from the aggressive ravages of modernization. In the end Ferrara was left with neither economic development nor its inevitable effects: environmental degradation and, as a famous Italian author and native of Ferrara said, "the invasion of the 'international' of glass, steel and concrete, cloaking in boredom and conformism all places and all countries."[1]

So, thanks to its recent leap into *postmodernity* by way of a massive investment in culture, today Ferrara paradoxically appears as a model of the postmodern city without ever having been a modern one. By postmodern city we mean a place that lives off *immaterial* production, where cultural goods, that is nonmaterial goods (Hirsch 1972:641) are produced.

Though Ferrara did not attain the national and international stage of music and the figurative arts until the 1990s, the process of reaching this position started in the 1960s. Since then the greatest share of investment and promotion of culture has come from the local government (council and province), which since World War II has been completely under the control of the left.[2] This political identity is one of the sources of that cultural policy, as we shall see later.

Against this background of nonindustrialization, two public actions occurred in the 1960s that are relevant for the development of the Great Events. First, urban preservation and restoration were emphasized: the scenario of the art city was set up by the local government, supported by a part of the local bourgeoisie. Second, Franco Farina, a highly charismatic figure who was then the director of the Gallery of Modern and Contemporary Art in the Palazzo dei Diamanti,[3] organized a number of exhibits of Italian and international contemporary art in a highly original way. Between 1963 and 1993, more than 900 exhibitions[4] have presented an image of Ferrara as a center of culture. Because the public role of education and literacy has taken precedence over the role of private initiative in the arts, a form of protection for the arts has been created, a kind of welfare-art state (vector B-D in fig. 11.1), that has perhaps hindered the rise of other private initiatives.

Other aspects of the Great Events, such as musical offerings, do not show as clear a parallel of public intervention, although we can nonetheless identify a musical tradi-

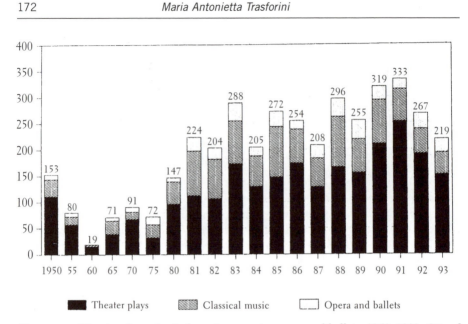

Figure 11.2   Theater plays, classical music concerts, opera, and ballets, 1950–1993. City of
Ferrara
Source: Cultural Statistics (Siae)

tion in Ferrara, both in the past and more recently. This tradition, in which elements of
high and popular culture are interwoven, has prepared the ground for great musical performances. The tradition of wind instruments (oboe, flute, clarinet, trumpet, trombone)
born in the amateur orchestras of the city has provided a substantial number of musicians for professional orchestras in Italy and elsewhere. This popular culture, alive up to
the 1960s, brought music to small towns, spreading music and musical literacy before the
arrival of the compact disc and cassette recorders. The long process of "deprovincializa-
tion" of Ferrara with regard to music finally led to the appearance of avant-garde music
in the 1960s (e.g., Silvano Bussotti) and to the opening of the Teatro Comunale in 1964.

The Great Event as a form of cultural "happening" is thus rooted in these early
events and traditions, but also in a process of transformation that occurred in the 1980s,
namely the boom in the so-called elite arts—theater plays, classical music, opera, and
ballet (see fig. 11.2). The quantitative growth of this type of show preceded the Great
Events and was the context in which they arose.

The Found-Again City: The Culture-Based Investment Strategy

The project of Ferrara as a city of art and culture[5] comes materially into being in the
Investment Plan for the years from 1988 to 1990. This is the instrument by which the
local government aims at turning Ferrara's diversity and lack of industrial development
into a resource. The combination of city of art and city of culture defines a cultural
policy that works along two different yet concomitant lines.

Santagata (1998) distinguishes different goals for the two aspects of the city of art and culture. The city of art "aims at showing itself and at spreading its image. The recipient is the tourist . . . the scholar . . . the cultivated visitor" (p. 168). Those that profit from it are the hotel industry and the shops. The city of culture, on the other hand, "aims at producing cultural goods and at selling its services" (p. 168). This is the city where postmodern production of culture takes place, where the past is used as an imaginary scenario. This combination was fully completed after a decade of debates, and it can be defined as the "found-again city" (*la città ritrovata*).

In the process of construction of the city of art, the first step was the decision that individual cases of urban restoration would cease to be the main focus of attention. Instead, a project took shape of turning the whole city into a museum, as a cultural symbolic complex. Within such a complex, various itineraries were set up: the ancient city, the medieval city, the Renaissance city. An example of this is the project to recover and preserve nine kilometers of the sixteenth-century city walls. The "wall project" was initially promoted in the 1970s by a small group of local bourgeoisie who were concerned with the environment. In the early 1980s it was taken up by the municipal administration, which managed to find funds for it in 1986 at the national (30 billion lire) and European levels. The "wall project" was meant to revive the identity of the place[6] not, the councillor of culture at the time explained, as a historical document from the time past, but as part of the roots on which the city still thrives. It can thus be seen as reconstruction of collective memory, a term that, Richard A. Peterson (1994) has noted, is "often substituted for tradition, acknowledging that the past is continually reinterpreted to fit the changing needs of the present" (p. 183).

As to the city of culture, the project comes into being with the Great Events in the 1990s, but it is already outlined in a statement made by the mayor, Roberto Soffritti (1986a): "We must aim at making Ferrara into a city that produces and consumes culture at the highest level . . . We believe that cultural consumption, even at a mass level, can turn into a source of jobs, of skilled labor, of tertiary activities." Soffritti (1986b) emphasized the entrepreneurial role of local government: "Ours is a municipality capable of investing, of financing, of working and of employing; it is a big machine which can activate relevant productive processes, thus creating new wealth."

For the urban working class such a culture-oriented government activity, though distant from Antonio Gramsci's idea of popular culture, fits in with a left-wing ideology, as it offers new economic prospects. On the other hand, it can secure support from the local *intellighenzia* and from some sectors of the reformist bourgeoisie, thus building a bridge between political and cultural élites. At the same time, it apparently supersedes particular class interests as it promotes a new (Durkheimian) collective representation that binds the city back to its Renaissance past.

Thus, from the second half of the 1980s, Ferrara begins to invest massively in culture, widening its commitment beyond preservation to being a city of art and culture at the level of a quasi-industrial investment, to attract quality tourism and to activate economic synergies at various levels.

Municipal expenditure in culture increased notably between 1983 and 1993, from 6.6 billion lire to 24.7 billion lire (3.4 percent of the city budget in 1983 to 7.6 percent in 1993, with a peak of 8.9 percent in 1990[7]—see fig. 11.3). Compared with other Italian cities, where investment rarely rose above 3 percent, Ferrara's investment is strikingly high.[8] And even among the major cities of the region where Ferrara is situated (Emilia Romagna), only Piacenza, with 6.5 percent, rivals Ferrara, while the other cities' investment in culture rose from 3.4 percent to 4 percent in the same period (see fig. 11.4). Both Ferrara and Piacenza are marginal areas with regard to industry, services, or tourism; the data on cultural investment suggest, therefore, that this is truly an economic investment in the sector of culture.

In Ferrara expenditure increased (more than 200 percent from 1985 to 1993) for preservation and enlargement of cultural institutions such as public libraries, the Gallery of Modern and Contemporary Art, and museums (see table 11.1), and for promotion and organization (+ 58 percent), in areas such as the Great Events or contributions to cultural associations (see table 11.2). Nonetheless, during the 1980s, investment in preservation prevailed.[9] Expenditure on organization and promotion has therefore privileged the activities of the Teatro Comunale, central to the functioning of the Great Events, with a corresponding contraction of resources destined to other local actors like the small or medium-size public and private cultural bodies in the community (e.g. the funds for nonprofit cultural associations decreased between 1985 and 1993 from 36.7 percent to 16.6 percent) (see table 11.2).

In summary, in the 1980s and early 1990s, Ferrara's city council carried out massive investments, preserving its own patrimony while at the same time promoting cultural activity in relatively traditional sectors, such as high-culture music and the figurative arts. It has thus played a regulatory and conservative role alongside its role as a producer/manager (Crane 1992b:155) without, however, producing either real innovation or experimentation, or moving into new fields (vector B-D in fig. 11.1).

Table 11.1   Funds for Cultural Institutions (Preservation) (Percentage Values), 1985–1993 (includes recurring expenses, but not fixed expenses)

Cultural Institutions	1985	1987	1989	1991	1993
Public Libraries	18.0	31.0	30.9	30.0	24.7
Gallery of Modern and Contemporary Art	15.1	11.5	17.7	15.5	21.2
Museums for Ancient Art	29.4	26.5	22.7	25.4	25.5
Historical Document Institute	10.5	11.8	11.8	11.9	10.9
Giovanni Boldini Museum	19.4	12.9	10.2	13.5	15.4
Others	7.6	6.3	6.7	3.7	2.3
Total percent	100	100	100	100	100
Total funds (millions lire)	713.490	927.543	1,365.169	1,355.093	2,121.321

Source: Panizza 1995

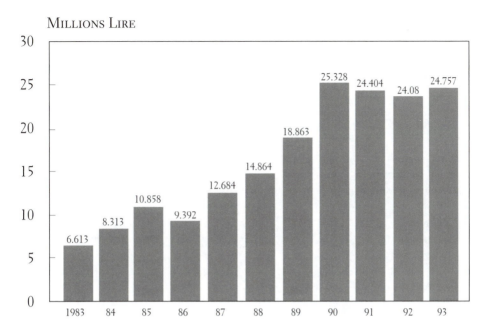

Figure 11.3 Municipal expenditure on culture (recurring expenses and capital expenditure), 1983–1993, City of Ferrara.
Source: Panizza 1995

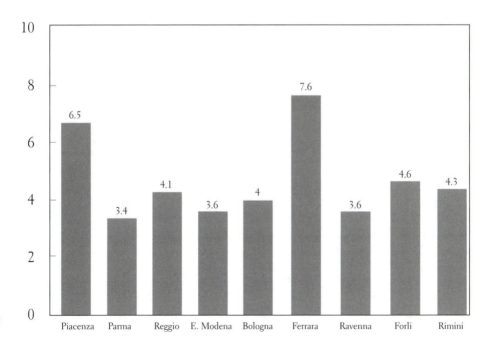

Figure 11.4 Municipal expenditure on culture in the larger towns of Emilia Romagna region (percentage of budget), 1993.
Source: Panizza 1995

Table 11.2   Funds for Cultural Promotion and Production (Percentage Values), 1985–1993 (includes recurring expenses, but not fixed expenses)

Cultural service	1985	1987	1989	1991	1993
Teatro Comunale	63.3	71.4	65.1	83.6	83.4
Cultural associations	5.7	3.7	10.0	2.3	2.9
Other cultural institutions (16)	31.0	24.9	24.9	14.1	13.7
Total percent	100	100	100	100	100
Total funds	3,541.735	4,166.386	5,161.745	4,105.276	5,619.743
(millions lire)	35	86	45	76	43

Source: Panizza 1995

The Cultural Entrepreneur in Ferrara: Between Charisma and Professionalism

The historical lack of an entrepreneurial mentality in the culture of Ferrara and the emergence of charismatic protagonists in its cultural life are two constantly interwoven themes. The first can be traced back to the history of this territory in which landed estates, and therefore large strata of landless agrarian laborers, predominated. Because the great estates allowed their owners to live off rent, they did not stimulate much alternative investment and thus very little entrepreneurial development, while the predominance of landless agricultural laborers produced a labor force unable to develop autonomous initiatives elsewhere. In this vacuum, the lack of action, vision, and entrepreneurship within civil society and the private sector had to be compensated for by the action of public institutions and some associations (see the A-B vector in the cultural diamond—fig. 11.1).

The local government's activity illustrates how the cultural manager evolves from artisan-communitarian forms to professional-societal ones. This means that professionalization of roles is not confined to phases of modernization (Goode 1957), but takes place also when there is an increase in systemic complexity, as indeed was the case in Ferrara. The cultural object is then seen as a competitive and profitable commodity, no longer surrounded by Benjamin's "aura" (1969).

In the 1970s the artisanal cultural entrepreneur who organized quality shows operated in a restricted market, with personal knowledge and relationships at the national and international level, in a climate of limited competition and little organizational complexity. In the words of Farina, then director of the Gallery of Modern and Contemporary Art: "I received funds from the municipality only. I did not spend one cent for advertising . . . I never paid travel expenses for critics . . . who would come anyway . . . I had no public relations office. I never thought of tourism . . . What was important to me was the artist's weight and the fallout on the city. An era has ended with me. Now there is a new one."

In the 1990s the professional cultural entrepreneur is a specialist in selecting and offering products in highly competitive national and international markets, facing high costs and investments in long-term planning and utilizing a complex organizational apparatus. This entrepreneur focuses on media and culture as mass consumption objects and uses culture as a powerful resource that is economic and not just symbolic. His or her rational action aims at producing cultural events according to market logic, and as such it has become progressively autonomous vis-à-vis the bureaucratic –administrative apparatus.

The current director of the Gallery of Modern and Contemporary Art, Andrea Buzzoni, says: "More planning, more coordination, a capacity for short, medium and long-term investments: these are the rules of the game . . . The challenge is to face up to a mass society, to increase its level of quality and to combine quality and quantity. We need a strategy . . . if it can be demonstrated that money can be made (with exhibits), then it is easier to ask local government to invest."

This type of cultural professional already exists in some public institutions and some associations, as well as in private, market-oriented cultural enterprises—such as schools of theater, music, dance, and so on. At the level of urban culture, peopled by small and middling actors, there is still a form of highly personalized, almost charismatic, entrepreneurship, closer to the figure of the community organizer (Santoro 1995:322). In small towns, the increase in professionalism does not seem to lead to a decline in the charismatic dimension, in Weber's sense of the term. In fact, while the role of major entrepreneur and modern manager of culture has been taken by the local government in Ferrara, continuity during the period of transformation appears to have been assured and managed precisely by a charismatic figure: Roberto Soffritti, the left-wing mayor who remained in office for more than 17 years, from 1982 to 1999, and who earned the humorous nickname of "the Duke."[10]

The Great Event: Cultural Superstars and Media Effects

The Great Event of the late 1980s and early 1990s exemplifies the transformation that occurred as a result of the actions of the local government as promoter/producer of urban culture. As such, the Great Event summarizes the passage from a period characterized by artisanal organization, by socially and intellectually restricted circles, by shortages of finance, sponsorship and publicity, to a much larger and more complex structure of production. The transformation is also seen in the organizational structure, now external to the public body: two committees chaired by the mayor were born, Ferrara Arte and Ferrara Musica, which have managerial, organizational, and financial autonomy (see tables 11.3 and 11.4).

Even if it is not possible to attribute a precise date to the origin of the term *Great Event*, what the term refers to is very clear. For music, it means the big shows, the great concerts, and operatic performances produced by the Teatro Comunale of Ferrara, under the direction of Claudio Abbado.[11] Formally they began in 1989 with the

Table 11.3 Exhibitions organized by Ferrara Art Committee from October 1991 to December 1995.

Exhibitions	Number of visitors
Claude Monet and His Friends	232,000
Marc Chagall	182,000
Pictures and Reality	70,000
Spina: Story of a Greek and Etruscan City	185,000
Rossini: Scenery for Operas	6,000
Paul Gauguin and the Russian Avant-Garde	218,000
Luchino Visconti	62,000
Total number of visitors	955,000

settling in Ferrara of the European Chamber Orchestra, conducted by Abbado, and with the reopening of the Teatro Comunale.

In the visual arts, Great Events of that period are a show of Monet's paintings in 1992, and in the same year an exhibition of Chagall, both at the Palazzo dei Diamanti; more recently, in 1996, Gauguin and Klinger shows, and in 1998 one devoted to Pissarro. Between 1991 and 1995 nearly 1 million people visited the exhibitions at the Palazzo dei Diamanti (see table 11.3).

The Great Events are a complicated form of cultural activity, the product of a system of collective action involving numerous actors, organizations, and resources. Behind this complex cultural project stands the collective author described by Becker (1982). It seems to be the result of an organizational "machine" typical of a "cultural industry" as described by Hirsch (1972).

The production of a lyric opera with great stars does not make news in a metropolis, but it does have great media resonance if it takes place in a small town. From the early 1990s Ferrara was increasingly featured in the media not only as a seat of cultural events, but as a place that produced them, and thus as a performer in the cultural field[12] (Grandi 1995). The evolution and complexity of the event are closely covered by the media. Analyses of the contrast between the characteristics of the collective actor, in Becker's sense of the term, and the characteristics of the small town as cultural actor point to a further mechanism at work in the production of public images, one which highlights the role of a Weberian charismatic figure: there is a close, almost intimate, link between Ferrara and Abbado (Bernardelli 1995; Nergaard 1995). In the image presented by the media, Ferrara is in fact transformed into a biographical event of the great performer, and it is illuminated by it. The Ferrara-Abbado link projected by the media produces a kind of David-Goliath effect: it makes Ferrara competitive with the larger Milan (Abbado has chosen Ferrara and not Milan) and it places it next to the Große Berlin (where Abbado conducts the Berlin Symphony Orchestra). The postmodern image feeds off a classical premodern item: charisma.

Table 11.4   Costs and Receipts of Art Exhibitions, Organized by Ferrara Art Committee from October 1991 to December 1995

Contributions from:	Millions Lire	Percentage(%)
Sponsors	1,903.6	14.5
Institutions	611.4	4.7
Ticket sales	7,413.5	56.8
Bookshop sales	2,730.5	20.9
Others	401.0	3.0
Total		100
Total Receipts	13,060.0	
Total Costs	13,677.0	
Difference	− 617	

Source: AEF 1996–1997:127

In the form and in the activity of the Great Event, one notices a complex inter-weaving of the cosmopolitan and the local. Despite the success of the Great Events, public debate in the city about the impact on the local community focuses on two controversial points. On the one hand, there is debate about the distribution of resources between small cultural events and those of the Great Events; on the other, there is concern that the latter may grow outside and at the expense of a healthy "every-day" cultural fabric. The objection, above all from local associations, is that the Great Events may have resulted in the neglect of the local dimension, creating a sense of uprootedness and cultural homogenization and hybridization (Cvetkovich and Kell-ner 1997). Crane (1992a and 1992b) suggests a distinction between *media culture* and *urban culture*: Great Events are, in fact, a hybrid. For their material and symbolic resources, they rely on urban culture, yet they use media culture for global scope and audience. In the epoch of globalization, the Great Event, as a form of cultural policy, makes the tension between the cosmopolitan and the local manifest and extreme: it pushes cultural action outward, beyond the boundaries of the city system used as a stage for a global audience, but at the same time it risks overshadowing actors and activities of the local urban scene.

Consequences of Great Events for Traditional Social Networks of Urban Culture

It is exactly on the local scene of Ferrara, beside the dynamic role of the city council, that *associazionismo*, basically constituted by nonprofit organizations, play a funda-mental role. In general, such organizations are essential to the functioning of urban culture, embodying channels of communication and cultural distribution, and sites of creation and reproduction of socially differentiated audiences and class cultures (Crane 1992b:109). Furthermore, nonprofit organizations have played in Ferrara the important role of interface between individuals and institutions. In fact the shortcomings of civil society in Ferrara, in particular the lack of a strong sense of private entrepreneurship, seem to have been compensated precisely by the way in which people form civic associations (vector A-C in fig. 11.1). In 1994, according to the Provincial Administration of Ferrara, the city had 298 cultural associations distributed as follows: 32.8 percent musical associations, including singing, sound, and video recording; 25 percent recreational circles (associations for leisure, sport, and other cultural activities); 4.7 percent theater clubs; 4.7 percent dance clubs/circles and culture/education of the body. The associations, which range from highly qualified and specialized to amateur groups, constitute urban culture worlds (Crane 1992a:60); they are places for promotion and circulation of events (on average, small ones) produced by different kinds of actors. These organizations contribute to the cultural literacy of their own publics (membership is very well defined) and eventually of a wider audience.

Nonprofit organizations are among the players in the urban cultural network, understood (somewhat in Bourdieu's sense, see 1984:113) as a *field* inside which resources (knowledge and skill) are articulated at various levels: from amateur to semiprofessional and professional. One outcome of this is the construction of an intermediate and mediating culture that acts as connective tissue between the culture of the "base," (i.e., that of the associations, and the "super-amateurs") and the "high" culture of the professionals, which provides information, socialization, professionalization, and entrepreneurship to specific sectors.

Taking into account this aspect of urban cultural activity, we may at this point ask whether and to what extent Great Events in the area of music and arts have in turn become generators of similar networks in the local urban culture—or whether they have hampered their development and increased stratification of audiences.

Today music seems to be the richest sector in structures and initiatives, and to have the most interconnections between the various levels—informative, formative, and professional. It is favored by its multistructured, multileveled complexity: the amateur and the dilettante level of the many musical associations; the formative level of private music schools and the conservatory; the research level at the university; the professionalism of the Sympatheia orchestra,[13] and finally the *high* level of the great interpreters, from Abbado to the Chamber Orchestra. The various genres are also represented: from the classical to opera, concerti, choral, specialized instruments (such as the Plectrum Orchestra), rock music, and dance music. In this context the associations offer circuits of opportunity, and function as filters for young musicians or as places for their performances. In sum, this diffuse musical culture can be seen from a double point of view: as the initial short-term fallout of Great Events, but also as a condition for them. Possibly the Great Events have promoted a partial integration between the worlds of popular music and those of musical high culture.

As for the figurative arts, we have already seen how the local government, through the Gallery of Modern and Contemporary Art, has given rise to a sort of welfare-art state, which, in that respect, has made Ferrara one of the best-served Italian cities. In fact the role played by the private sector in other cities[14] (as shaping and informing about the arts) has been completely undertaken in Ferrara as a public service, with free admission and low-priced catalogs. In the periods preceding Great Events, the gallery collected works by the artists that had exhibits there, including many young ones. "Every artist on show would give us one of his works," says Farina, who was the director at the time. This form of public collecting and cultural accumulation, however, has not been instrumental in promoting the growth of a local cultural/artistic entrepreneurship. This type of cultural policy has been questioned, in fact, because it operated like a "big private gallery," largely preempting the possibility of more and different proposals and suggestions. The lack of a private market of galleries and therefore of an art-buying public—in the past the local bourgeoisie would not buy art, and today it buys outside Ferrara—just as the lack of an academy of fine arts (except for the musical field: an academy of music does exist) has not helped the growth of an articulated field, that is, the circuit of art-related jobs (collectors, dealers, artists, critics, etc.).

A gallery owner noticed that in a public space, like a museum, no one would think of asking the price of a picture, whereas in a private gallery this is normal: "One gets accustomed to the idea that these objects can be bought, otherwise art would not exist. And one realizes that art and culture can actually be a job." The action of the welfare-art state may have had an inhibiting effect on the private art market, producing a kind of economic neutralization of the work of art,[15] obscuring as such the professional dimension of artistic work. As a result, there are no important galleries, and the few places that exhibit art or the few significant events are not so much related to the private sector as to *associazionismo*. In sum, in the visual arts we do not find the dynamism we see in the world of music; furthermore, they remain confined in the symbolic sphere of high culture.

Audiences for Cultural Events in Ferrara: Local vs. Global and High Culture vs. Popular Culture

Who enjoys culture in Ferrara? An answer to this question requires some distinctions, starting from the definition of cultural object and of reception. We have seen that the objects of cultural policy in Ferrara are, at least, two: the city of art and the city of culture, and, on this background, Great (and small) Events. The visitors/consumers of the city of art, often overlapping with the audience of Great Events, produce and reproduce historical and symbolic meanings of the city, and of its past which is thus projected on to the present. As regards users of the city of culture, thus of Great Events, this aspect is less important vis-à-vis ritual elements of social distinction, of reproduction of taste cultures, and hence of construction of symbolic boundaries. Reception, in fact, is not only the end of a communication process, but as Peterson (1994) said, it is "an active process of selection, interpretation, and recombination of elements that can be seen as the 'auto' production of a symbolic world which is meaningful for 'consumers'" (p. 183).

In the following section, having in mind the "interpretative reception of the city of art," I shall focus on audiences segmented on the basis of various types of cultural

Great Events (and professional events) (**High Culture**) (A)	**Urban Cultural Worlds** (B)	**Popular Events** (Popular Culture) (Palio and Busker Festival) (C)
Global Audience	**High Culture Audience**	
A.1 *Restricted Elite* A.2 *Cultivated Nomadic Public*	B.1 *Restricted Elite* B.2 **Associations Audience**	C.1 **Extra Urban Audience**
Local Audience	**B.3 Popular Culture**	
A.3 *Restricted Elite*	**Audience**	C.2 **Local Audience**

Figure 11.5   Dimensions/Proportion of Global/Local and High Culture/Popular Culture in the Audences of Ferrara

offerings: Great Events, events of local urban culture and two significant popular events (see fig. 11.5). I shall consider two relevant dimensions: global vs. local and high culture vs. popular culture.

The wider audience of the Great Events can be characterized as consisting of two segments: restricted elite and cultivated nomadic public (A.1, A.3, and A.2. in fig. 11.5). The restricted elite is a highly cultivated audience, made up of people presumably of the upper-middle class, both local (A.3) and from outside Ferrara (A.1.), who patronize the major musical events. It is a form of attendance that works as a distinguishing practice, a form of social ceremony that underlines one's membership in the "world that counts," and that conforms to "the integrative and distinctive rhythms of the 'society's' calendar," (as Bourdieu put it 1983:282). The patrons are the "happy few," the privileged ones, not only because of the cost of the product, but also because of selection, due to the products' scarcity (the shows are obviously few) and difficulty of access.

In the restricted elite can be included the audience characterized by a strong culture of professional or cultural specialization: these are the scholars of particular subjects, or the passionate lovers of a certain type of cultural product. Apart from some specialized consumers of "great music," we may include in this type of audience the consumers of art who have frequented the *Video Arte* shows, a particularly innovative experimental and research sector, which for many years placed Ferrara on the international circuit of video art experiments. A similar specialized audience is that associated with the Institute of Renaissance Studies. Owing to its international renown, its relationship to the univer-

Table 11.5   Characteristics of Visitors to Art Exhibitions and Museums in Ferrara in 1987 (in percentages)

		%		%		%		%
Sex:	male	55	female	45				
Age:	18–29	36	30–59	35	over 60	29		
Education:	high school	52	university	35	other	13		
Employment:	employed	52	student	20	other	28		
Occupation:	clerical	46	profession	41	working class	5	other	8
Residents of:	Italy	52	Europe	36	Non-Europe	9	Ferrara	3
Source of information:	newspapers, art reviews	22	friends/ other visitors	21	guides	29	other	27
Visits per year: exhibitions	one to five	29	over five	71				
Visits per year: museums	one to two	12	over three	88				

Source: Council of Ferrara 1987 (AEF 1989:300). The size of the sample is not indicated.

sity, and its leading role in organizing international conferences, the institute performs a function somewhat similar to that of a great museum or a great library.

A second type of audience, certainly much larger than the first, is the so-called cultivated nomadic public of the exhibitions (A.2. in fig. 11.5), an expression of a postmodern cultural tourism, "with its particular combination of the visual and the aesthetic" (Urry 1990:87). It is the regional, extraregional and international audience of the major exhibits, which date back to the 1960s and culminated in the Monet and Chagall shows. Of the million or so visitors who attended the seven major exhibitions between 1991 and 1995, less than 10 percent were from Ferrara. It is an audience loyal to the city, coming back again and again, the opposite of destructive tourism. A profile of the people who visited the shows and museum of Ferrara in 1987 has been drawn in a survey carried out that year (see table 11.5).

The cultural capital possessed by these visitors does not inevitably imply a collateral economic capital. There is clearly membership in a well-defined and culturally well-informed social circle (Kadushin 1968) with well-established social rituals and distinctive practices: from 70 percent to 80 percent have visited other museums or shows in the same year.

In view of the crisis of museums of contemporary art (Santagata 1998:178), a comparison with two of the most important museums of contemporary art in Italy (and

Table 11.6　Attendance at Contemporary Art Museums in Italy and France

Museum	Visitors per year (average)	Year
Gallery of Modern and Contemporary Art (Ferrara)	191,000	1991–1995
Castello di Rivoli (Torino)	87,000	1994
Museo Pecci (Prato-Florence)	27,000	1993
Magasin (Grenoble)	20,000	1993–1994
Centre d'Art Contemporaine (Kerguéhennec)	15,000	1993–1994
Centre d'Art Contemporaine (Vassivière)	15,000	1993–1994
Nouveau Musée (Villeurbane)	11,000	1993–1994
Centre d'Art Contemporaine (Tours)	10,000	1993–1994
Consortium (Dijon)	8,000	1993–1994

Source: Santagata (1998:179). For specific exhibits in Ferrara, see table 11.3.

with some French ones) (see table 11.6) suggests that the strategy of the Ferrara gallery has succeeded in identifying and building up its own public.

Another segment is represented by the audience of urban cultural worlds (B.1. and B.2. in fig. 11.5). They are those who attend the local productions and participate in the cultural life of the city, that is, lectures, debates, plays, concerts, and so on organized both by the institutions and by the associations. It appears to be an audience composed largely of people from the same social circles, with shared knowledge and cultural skills, with characteristics of continuity and relative fixity. It includes the local restricted and cultivated elite (B.1 overlapping A.3 in fig. 11.5) who move from one cultural event to another and the faithful members of the cultural associations who attend and support their associations' products (B.2 in fig. 11.5), as a means of confirming their own social identity. With regard to certain areas of consumption and membership of

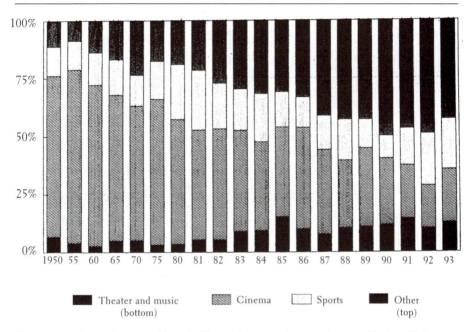

Figure 11.6   Per capita expenditure in Ferrara for types of entertainment, 1950–1993 (in percentages)
Source: Cultural Statistics (Siae)

the associations, it is interesting to note the large number of women involved. This audience seems to confirm Crane's (1992a) hypothesis that "high culture is largely a phenomenon created and consumed in urban settings, transmitted by nonprofit organizations but this represents only a small portion of the forms of culture created and disseminated in urban settings" (p. 71).

With regard to the local audience, the breakdown of their expenditures for various types of entertainment—theater and music, cinema, sport, and other[16]—provides an indirect indication of its characteristics (see fig. 11.6). These data are suggestive of a profound transformation in behavior and culture undergone in Ferrara (as elsewhere in Italy) after World War II. Decreasing expenses for cinema (from 69.5 percent in the 1950s to 22.8 percent in 1993) are paralleled by increased expenses for various other types of entertainment—*other* in Figure 11.6—(from 11.2 percent to 42.9 percent in the same period) and, to a lesser extent, for theater and music (from 6.5 percent in the 1950s to 12.7 percent in 1993). These latter expenses, which refer to both popular and high-culture forms of entertainment, despite having doubled in 40 years, remain within a range that never rises above 15 percent. Even if we cannot infer from this the number of consumers, it is reasonable to assume that they represent a relatively restricted local audience.

Finally, we should not forget that a large audience, both from Ferrara and outside (C.1 and C.2 in fig. 11.5), participates in at least two important popular cultural events that are partially financed by the city council: the Palio (a reenactment of a

Renaissance festival in Renaissance costumes) and the Busker Festival of street musicians. Unlike the Great Events, these events do not boast great stars, they are not part of a project, they do not require a special cultural competence on the participants' part, and they seem to "use" Ferrara as a container or as a fascinating urban scenario for their performances. The latter is of special interest both because it proposes Ferrara as an international meeting place for street musicians from all over the world, and also because of its enormous appeal. In 1996 it drew between 250,000 and 300,000 people. But as one of the organizers observed, it is difficult to define this audience with regard to expectations and behavior: "It's a remarkable atmosphere, the interest of the people even if the musical quality is not that great. . . . The exceptional thing is that the public comes from God knows where, without knowing anything about these musicians. And this is a mystery." Part of the mystery, however, can be explained by the context and its capacity to transform the contents offered into a unique and attractive event.

Conclusions

Our epoch, as David Harvey (1990:295) argues in his discussion on the crisis of modernity, assigns a changing and, in part, contradictory role to the sense of space. On the one hand, we witness the liquidation of space through time-space compression, such as speed of travel, cultural globalization, and creation of the global village; on the other hand, Harvey states, "the active production of places with special qualities becomes an important stake in the spatial competition between localities, cities, regions and nations. . . . It is in this context that we can better situate the striving for cities to forge a distinctive image and to create an atmosphere of place and tradition that will act as a lure to both capital and people of *the right type*" (p. 295).

The role of *spatialization* and a recognizable dimension of *place* are elements in the marketing of the territory that Ferrara has carried out through an exemplary investment in culture.[17] With the recovery of its historical past as a city/museum *en plein air* and with the creation of great cultural performances, it has constructed and promoted a new and recognizable postmodern and postindustrial identity, leaping beyond a modernity that it never actually achieved. Great Event is the cipher, the shorthand formula that in the 1990s defines an activity that is simultaneously modern and postmodern: modern for the complex organization and productive machine it requires, postmodern for the immaterial nature of the product. It is the moment of maximum exposure of the cultural entrepreneurialism of the local council that began in the 1960s, and that continues today to invest in culture-growing resources. It has indeed been an economic investment to attract global and qualified tourism (a goal that has been achieved) and to produce new employment (a goal only partially achieved).

Although Ferrara today can be defined as a postmodern city, it ought not to be forgotten that the modernity missed by Ferrara left her with considerable structural weaknesses, in particular the absence of cultural entrepreneurship in the private sector. Paradoxically this gap has been filled precisely by the city council in its role as a modern culture entrepreneur. But clearly it has not been enough. So the welfare-art state, as productive and protective cultural activity, undertaken particularly in the figurative arts from the 1960s onward by the Gallery of Modern and Contemporary Art, has produced greater cultural literacy among the public, but it does not seem to have encouraged private entrepreneurship in the sector of art. In fact, in the visual arts, the Great Event has not been able to produce a fallout, that is, intermediate culture and a network of arts-related jobs. Even from an occupational point of view, this intermediate culture seems currently stronger in the music sector where there has been for a long time an active interrelationship between forms of popular and high culture.

The Great Event also exemplifies a change in cultural products and in the way of producing them by a small town aspiring to be a global actor: from artisanal works of quality, combining charismatic and personalized initiatives, to more complex cultural products, which must be competitive on a vaster and more demanding market. This qualitative leap has been possible for the small town of Ferrara only through recourse to an alliance, by its nature somewhat a premodern one, with the charisma of the great star Abbado. So, with its provincial dimensions, the small town cannot avoid the intimate and overlapping links in which premodern elements (charisma) mix with the modern (professional entrepreneurship) and the postmodern (culture as production of nonmaterial goods) to outline the complex shape of the immaterial city. The result has been a frame of meaning in which Ferrara has gained an easily recognized "performance" position within the cultural environment. It is precisely from the media stage that Ferrara, as a producer of culture, addresses itself to the virtual audience of the globalization process, an audience only apparently homogeneous but, in reality, strongly articulated. Globalization does not erase the structures of social inequality of reception, but rather it widens and multiplies the urban cultural settings in which the *high-culture model* (DiMaggio 1992) is performed. The Great Event only appears to be inclusive with regard to this audience; in its own way it is indeed strongly selective and, as a result, exclusive in terms of social class and cultural capital. The great musical event attracts a restricted elite to whom it offers social distinction, but it produces enormous interest and apparent accessibility. The great art exhibition attracts the large nomadic public of global tourism and is, as such, accessible, but in fact it draws an audience that is highly selective with regard to cultural capital. Both activities outline symbolic levels of access.

The Great Event develops, finally, a strong dialectic between cosmopolitanism and localism: this cultural strategy uses the city system as a big stage for the external public that it attracts, for the actors that it involves, for the media limelight that it occupies; but, at the same time, it overshadows other actors in the local urban network and drains public resources. It reinforces traditional sectors without producing innovation in other areas. In sum, at the moment in which the small postmodern city becomes a global cultural actor, it also risks, like Saturn, to devour its own children, those small and medium-sized social actors that are the connective tissue of urban culture.

Notes

This chapter uses the results of unpublished research carried out in 1995 on the system of culture in Ferrara. The project was supported by the Fondazione of the Cassa di Risparmio and directed by Umberto Eco. Sixty-seven interviews were conducted with significant figures in the cultural life of the city, followed by an analysis of the press coverage of the major events in Ferrara (Grandi 1995;). I wish to thank Diana Crane for her valuable critical comments and suggestions, Angela Zanotti and Magali Sarfatti Larson for their assistance with the English translation of this article, and my friends, Chiara, Janni, and Lydia for their patience during the preparation of this chapter.

1. The effects of unrestrained urbanization were thus referred to by the well-known novelist, Giorgio Bassani, who was born in Ferrara (*In defense of Ferrara*, Address to the Municipal Council of Ferrara, June 25, 1962). His *Giardino dei Finzi Contini*, about a Jewish family of Ferrara, was made into a film by Vittorio De Sica.

2. Only in the 1990s has the most important local bank (The Fondazione of the Cassa di Risparmio) entered the scene as a sponsor and patron of the *Great Events*. Aside from this initiative, private sector support is small and the role of city government remains strong. On the role of patron played in Italy by business and banks, see Bodo (1994: 111–119), Brosio and Santagata (1992:242), Piperno (1996) and Zambianchi (1996).

3. Palazzo dei Diamanti is the Renaissance palace that houses the Gallery of Modern and Contemporary Art. The name derives from the shape of the stones of the external wall.

4. It is sufficient to cite some of the Italian and foreign artists and the dates of their shows: Emilio Vedova (1968), Andrè Masson (1969), Afro (1969), Piero Manzoni (1971), Marcel Duchamp (1971), Man Ray (1972), Filippo de Pisis (1973), Andy Warhol (1975), Pop Art (1975), Robert Rauschenberg (1976), and Salvador Dalì (1984).

5. In 1995 Ferrara joined the list of UNESCO cities of art as an exceptional example of a Renaissance city.

6. The walls provide an identity by building boundaries around the body of the city. It is the function that the French psychoanalyst Didier Anzieu attributes to the ego-skin (*Moi-peau*): a representation in which the ego uses itself to draw boundaries between inside and outside (Anzieu 1985: 56).

7. These data are inferred from the final balance of accounts (Panizza 1995). On this theme see Bodo (1994: 99).

8. This supremacy reveals itself in 1993 as a rising per capita expenditure on culture: 180.711 lire in Ferrara, 136.740 lire in Piacenza against an average figure for the remaining cities in Emilia between 80.000 lire and 92.000 lire. This figure shows Ferrara is equal to other European cities. In 1990 in France per capita expenditure was 161.000 lire, in Germany in 1989 it was 128.000 lire, while in Italy in 1989 the average was only 24.000 lira (Bodo 1994: 100).

9. From 1983–1993 the expenditure on preservation rose from 3.7 to 16.8 billion lira, while that for promotion-organization went from 2.8 billions in 1983 to 7.7 billions in 1993. These data, unlike the data in tables 11.1 and 11.2, include both recurring expenses and capital expenditures.

10. Almost to evoke the ancient government of the dukes of Este in the Renaissance.

11. Abbado in 1994 conducted Mozart's *Marriage of Figaro* featuring Cecilia Gasdia and Raimondo Raimondi and Rossini's *Barber of Seville* in 1995, while in 1990 he conducted Prokofiev's fairy tale, *Peter and the Wolf*, in which the narrator, unusual for this context, was Roberto Benigni. Such productions are costly. For example, the total cost of producing the *Marriage of Figaro*, about 2 billion lire, was financed as follows: 50 percent (more than 1 billion) from public contributions (ministerial, city council, the theater); 35 percent (700 million) from ticket sales; and finally, 15 percent(300 million) from sponsors (AEF 1994:199).

12. Analysis of the coverage of *Great Events* in the local and national media has been carried out by Nergaard (1995), Bernardelli (1995), Mascio (1995) and Traini (1995).

13. This orchestra comprised of the professional musicians from the city came into being as an effect of the *Great Events*, and in connection with Teatro Comunale.

14. The absence of private galleries does not depend solely on their peripheral location with regard to the art market circuits. In Italy, in fact, information and publicity continues to be undertaken by small qualified galleries in small towns. Of the 310 galleries affiliated in 1993 with the Association of National Galleries of Modern Art, more than 22.3% were situated in places other than the provincial capitals.

15. Bourdieu (1983: 284) underlines the difference between the museum and the gallery: in the first, the objects are economically 'neutralised', excluded from any suggestion of private appropriation in favor of a 'pure appropriation'; in the gallery, instead, the objects are both contemplated and purchased.

16. The category "theater and music" includes different forms of entertainment: plays, dialect theater, opera and ballet, classical music concerts, operettas, musicals, popular music, variety art, puppet and marionette shows. The 'other' includes dancing, fairs and circuses, amusement parks, bowling, and street festivals.

17. On the international cultural competition among cities, see Martorella (1992).

References

AEF (Annuario Economico Ferrarese), CDS, Ferrara, 1985–1998.

Anzieu, D. (1985) *Le Moi-peau*, Paris: Bordas.

Becker, H. S. (1982) *Art Worlds*, Berkeley, CA: University of California Press.

Benjamin, W. (1969) 'The work of art in the age of mechanical reproduction,' pp. 291–353 in H. Arendt (ed.) *Illuminations* (H. Zohn, Trans.), New York: Schocken Books.

Bernardelli, A. (1995) 'Ferrara Musica: Le Nozze di Figaro e I concerti del maestro Roger Norrington,' in Roberto Grandi (ed.) *L'immagine di Ferrara e del suo sistema culturale diffusi dalla stampa nazionale e locale*, Ferrara: Unpublished Research Report.

Bodo, C. (ed.) (1994) *Associazione per l'Economia della Cultura, Rapporto sull'economia della cultura in Italia, 1980-1990*, Roma: Presidenza del Consiglio dei Ministri.

Bourdieu, P. (1983) *La distinzione*, Bologna: Il Mulino (Italian translation).

Bourdieu, P. (1984) *Questions de Sociologie*, Paris: Editions de Minuit.

Brosio, G. and Santagata, W. (1992) *Rapporto sull'economia delle arti e dello spettacolo in Italia*, Torino: Fondazione Giovanni Agnelli.

Crane, D. (1992a) 'High culture versus popular culture revisited: a reconceptualization of recorded culture,' pp. 58–74 in M. Lamont and M. Fournier (eds.), *Cultivating Differences. Symbolic Boundaries and the Making of Inequality*, Chicago, IL: The University of Chicago Press.

Crane, D. (1992b) *The Production of Culture: Media and the Urban Arts*, London: Sage.

Cvetkovich, A. and Kellner, D. (1997) 'Introduction: thinking global and local,' pp. 1–30 in A. Cvetkovich and D. Kellner (eds.) *Articulating the Global and the Local: Globalization and Cultural Studies*, Boulder, CO: Westview Press.

DiMaggio, P. (1992) 'Cultural boundaries and social change: the extension of the high culture model to theater, opera, and the dance, 1900–1940' pp. 21–57 in M. Lamont and M. Fournier (eds.), *Cultivating Differences. Symbolic Boundaries and the Making of Inequality*, Chicago, IL: The University of Chicago Press.

Goode W.J. (1957) 'Community within a community: the professions,' *American Journal of Sociology*, 22: 194–200.

Grandi, R. (ed.) (1995) *L'immagine di Ferrara e del suo sistema culturale diffusi dalla stampa nazionale e locale*, Ferrara: Unpublished research report.

Griswold, W. (1994) *Culture and Societies in a Changing World*, Thousand Oaks, CA: Pine Forge Press.

Harvey, D. (1990) *The Condition of Postmodernity*, Oxford, UK and Cambridge, MA: Blackwell.

Hirsch, P. M. (1972) 'Processing fads and fashions: an organization set analysis of the culture industry system,' *American Journal of Sociology*, 77: 639–659.

Kadushin, C. (1968) 'Power, influence and social circles; a new methodology for studying opinion-makers,' *American Journal of Sociology*, 33: 685–699.

Martorella, R. (1992) 'Global cities and their changing role in cultural production: a comparison of New York, Paris, and Tokyo,' Paper presented at the international conference on *The Arts in the Media Age*, University of Trento (Italy), June 18–20.

Mascio, L. (1995) 'La presenza di Ferrara sui media nazionali,' in Roberto Grandi (ed.) *L'immagine di Ferrara e del suo sistema culturale diffusi dalla stampa nazionale e locale*, Ferrara: Unpublished research report.

Nergaard, S. (1995) 'Ferrara musica : Il barbiere di Siviglia e Pierino e il Lupo,' in Roberto Grandi (ed.) *L'immagine di Ferrara e del suo sistema culturale diffusi dalla stampa nazionale e locale*, Ferrara: Unpublished Research Report.

Panizza, P. (1995) 'La spesa per cultura a Ferrara. Politica di spesa e politica dell'offerta,' in M. A. Trasforini (ed.) *Il sistema della cultura a Ferrara*, Ferrara: Unpublished research report.

Peterson, R. A. (1976) 'The production of culture: a prolegomenon,' *American Behavioral Scientist*, 19: 669–683.

Peterson, R. A. (1994) 'Culture studies through the production perspective: progress and prospects,' pp. 163–189 in D. Crane (ed.), *The Sociology of Culture. Emerging Theoretical Perspectives*, Oxford, UK and Cambridge, MA: Blackwell.

Piperno, S. (1996) 'Sponsorship and patronage in Italy: some regional cases' pp. 131–149 in R. Martorella (ed.) *Art and Business: An International Perspective on Sponsorship*, Westport, CT: Praeger.

Santagata, W. (1998) *Simbolo e Merce. I mercati dei giovani artisti e le istituzioni dell'arte contemporanea*, Bologna: Il Mulino.

Santoro, M. (1995) 'Professionisti della cultura? Identità professionali e carriere nelle organizzazioni culturali del Mezzogiorno,' pp. 281–324 in M. Santoro (ed.) *Fare cultura. La produzione culturale nel Mezzogiorno*, Bologna: Il Mulino.

Traini, S. (1995) 'Ferrara Arte: Claude Monet e i suoi amici e Lucio Fontana' in Roberto Grandi (ed.) *L'immagine di Ferrara e del suo sistema culturale diffusi dalla stampa nazionale e locale*, Ferrara: Unpublished research report.

Trasforini, M. A. (1995) *Il sistema della cultura a Ferrara*, Ferrara: Unpublished research report.

Urry, J. (1990) *The Tourist Gaze: Leisure Travel in Contemporary Societies*, London: Sage.

World Almanac and Book of Facts (1991) New York: World Almanac.

Zambianchi, P. (1996) 'Art patronage among banks in Italy,' pp. 151–158 in R. Martorella, (ed.), *Art and Business. An International Perspective on Sponsorship*, Westport, CT: Praeger.

12

Blackface in Italy

Cultural Power Among Nations in the Era of Globalization

Richard L. Kaplan

The striking prominence of images of African Americans in Italy's public culture raises a question: What is the meaning of this prolific consumption of "blackness"? What can these cultural images tell us about relations of power and culture between nations in the era of transnational communication industries and, more generally, about processes of globalization? This chapter addresses the influence of "globalization" on national cultures. It investigates the particular case of cultural flows between the United States and Italy.

One dominant theory that has engaged with these issues, the theory of cultural imperialism (CI), has presented a forceful, albeit overly simplified, account of the relationship of cultural power between nations. Tying cultural hegemony to economic dominance, CI suggests that culture acts largely as an ideological tool to uphold economically exploitative relationships among countries, and to prevent "dependent" countries from following their own, presumably more balanced, paths to economic growth. Such cultural dominance, CI continues, especially proceeds through the overwhelming presence of U.S. media products in the dependent country. As other critics have argued, cultural imperialism theory offers an ultimately too reductive account of the nature of cultural production and consumption in dependent countries. On the one hand, it misunderstands the nature of power occurring through media messages. On the other hand, it upholds a mistaken nineteenth-century notion of national cultures that promote a largely static, unproblematic conception of the symbolic meanings specific to each country. Through an examination of the case of Italy and its importation of images of American blacks, this essay intends to shed light on the nature and processes of cultural exchange.

African Americans seem widely present in Italy. As tourists they are few, but the average Italian can establish relations of close intimacy with many a figure of American popular culture. She can observe the African American's mannerisms and style, can experience his intonations, even, we might say, enter into the American black's innermost aspirations and desires. It is of course the nature of mass media to permit this imagined communion, this sense of personal intimacy with distant others. John Thompson in his incisive typology of forms of communication has labeled this imagined communion "mediated quasi-interaction." Others have termed it a "para" (or pseudo) social interaction (Thompson 1996:219–25). In fact all media detach communication and social relations from specific space/time locales of face-to-face relations while they establish new forms of communication with others far removed. They extend forms of identification and social relations across the globe and forward in history.

Indeed, it is an essential part of mediated communications that they fundamentally change the nature of social interaction, permitting the establishment of novel relations of identification and power. In James Carey's (1989) formulation, each medium possesses a distinctive "bias" toward specific types of rhetoric, forms of power, and social relations. Furthermore, mass media, by detaching communication from face-to-face forms of interaction—that is, from "folk" cultural production—require the intervention of specialized experts, and tendentially permit the commodification, aestheticization, and massification of communications (Thompson 1996:26–30). What was previously a local folk culture (whether of a class, ethnic or social group) becomes in part stylized by (spatially, socially) distant experts for the consumption by distant (mass) audiences. In other words, local groups lose control over their own culture and public self-presentation. Furthermore, the representations of the local group, in this case African Americans, can be molded to the narrative desires of the receiving audience. Such a process fits almost exactly the broadest figurative meaning of "blackface" as defined by Michael Rogin (1996:18).[1]

The pervasive media provision and purveyance of images of African Americans in Italy is an extensive if typically unnoticed aspect of our contemporary mediated culture. Among the possible litany of examples, let us note the appearance of Bill Cosby's successful hit show on national Italian television networks for many years. Cosby has gone, but has been replaced by other "classics" of the American situation comedy such as The Robinsons or Fresh Prince of Bel Air. Will Smith, the latest instance of the hip, clever, young (nowadays) black hero, approximated media saturation in Italy when his commercial film The Wild, Wild West hit the screens, and his single from the same movie blared over the radio airways and MTV broadcasts. It is typical for Italian variety shows to bring back the classics of American rhythm and blues—Tina Turner comes to promote her latest disc, or Italian comics pretend to be Ray Charles at the piano in self-evidently absurd parodies, or new American star acts arrive to sing their hit singles and make an embarrassed effort at saying "Ciao" to their Italian fans.[2] Meanwhile, the radio is in fact inundated with the beat of rap, rhythm and blues, jazz, and gospel. Partly because of the popularity of dance music and discotheques, American music consistently sells in the top 10 Italian charts. In addition, during the 1999 Christmas season, as workers took a quick bite at the lunch bars in Florence, one could hear gospel choirs providing their version of Christmas muzak. In fact, American gospel choirs make tour stops across Italy, and instruction is available in the proper techniques of gospel singing.

Italy is awash with graffiti that are derived from the States and continually make reference back to their American origins. Of course, traditional Italian graffiti is still present—from slogans of the fascist right, to the denunciation of other cities' soccer teams as *merda*, to avowals of undying love—but specifically American forms of graffiti also have proliferated: "tagging" mars many antique and modern building walls, and murals abound on the cars of the inter-city railroads. Such forms of graffiti are photographed and celebrated in Italian hip-hop magazines, reproduced as brands of knapsacks that are required wear among high school students,[3] and used as background imagery in advertisements for both child and adult clothing.[4] They signify a desirably hip, urban style. (I will discuss later in more detail two further examples of an American black presence in Italy: rap music and a style of clothing that, in its brand names, fashionable cuts, and its advertising makes explicit reference to the denizens of American inner cities.)

We may say that the blacks of America constitute a continual, if somewhat elusive and subliminal, presence in Italy. Like a ghost, they beckon and intrigue many an Italian, but in their mediated distance always elude their grasp. They constitute a type of active figure in the Italian imagination, or at least in Italy's "mediascape" as it is deployed and detailed by the cultural experts in charge of informing, persuading, and entertaining the Italian masses. What is the meaning of this persistent production, consumption, and exploitation of the cultural identity of American blacks? And how can we account for this multifaceted presence of African Americans in Italy?

"Cultural Imperialism": A Theory of Cultural Dominance?

Traditional Marxist theory, and more specifically "dependency theory" and its account of "cultural imperialism," has formulated a strong account of processes of globalization, cultural exchange, and indeed power among nations (Fejes 1981; Tomlinson 1991). Certainly since Marx, there has been diagnosed a general process whereby the far reaches of the globe have become increasingly subsumed into a single economic framework or "capitalist world system" (Wallerstein, 1974). In this account, nations assume the interdependent power-laden roles of economic exploiter and exploited. Countries of the so-called Third World largely provide the raw materials and resources to the richer more developed "core" capitalist countries. As further refined in theories of "cultural imperialism," this economic relation of exploitation and relative backward development is shored up by more modern forces of cultural dominance. Imperial cultural hegemony helps explain the acceptance of market relations, inequality, and impoverishment within a country, and the nation's continued subordinate relation to world economic powers. Such cultural control proceeds, in part, in straightforward terms through the market dominance of imported cultural goods, but also in conscious efforts of elites to impose hegemony. In all this the media products of the U.S. putatively play a major ideological role of justifying exploitative market relationships and in making the attractions of consumerism and capitalism more palpable.

Critics of CI theory note, however, that it doesn't match its progenitor—dependency theory—for sophistication. It largely focuses on external impositions, while ignoring how class relations internal to a country also are crucial for maintaining relations of economic exploitation and, correspondingly, cultural dominance. This criticism can be subsumed under a more general one: CI proposes a too reductive account of processes of cultural production and reception. In Fred Fejes's words (1981), they "view the mass media as primarily manipulative agents capable of having a direct, unmediated effect on the audience's behavior and world view" (p. 287). As I will argue, the Italian case suggests the need to examine how external cultural messages and meanings are appropriated by groups within a country, and to ask what purposes are served by these appropriated discourses.

Since the early 1970s, when CI theory was first formulated, processes of "globalization" have of course advanced. Globalization refers to a set of interconnected, but not necessarily unified, linkages and exchanges among nations. In the last two decades, these linkages have increased both extensively across the span of the globe and intensively, such that nations in some sense can be said to lose their essential autonomy. Furthermore, if theorists of postmodernity or even cultural imperialism are correct, the nation no longer defines a common identity, a common culture, a unified cultural space, but rather is traversed by a series of identities and discourses, which find their locus of origin outside, or transnationally. Social identities and nations no longer map on to each other.

In the arena of culture, two interrelated mechanisms have increasingly enhanced processes of global symbolic exchange. Starting in the 1980s, governments, especially in Europe, liberalized their telecommunication industries. Thus commenced a wave of privatization, competition, transnational merging, and innovation among media industries. Market forces, as Denis McQuail (1995; also Schlesinger 1994) details, achieved a policy hegemony over traditional notions of telecommunications as a matter of public service and state monopoly provision. In addition, advances in telecommunication technology, notably the Internet and satellite broadcasting, seemed to render the notion of national boundaries anachronistic.

"Autonomy" however is a foundational concept of the nation-state, and indeed we might say the notion of a nation as a self-contained, self-determining society is built into the essential theoretical perspectives of classical political science, sociology, and cultural anthropology.[5] Within such a perspective, the nation is seen as a self-governing, culturally self-defining "community of fate" (Castle 1998). Through the apparatus of the democratic state, the nation could supposedly confront the problems that defined its shared fate and legislate its own future.

In the cultural realm (stemming from the ideas of Gottfried Herder and his recuperation of folk culture to underwrite the historical legitimacy of the newly forming nineteenth-century states), nations were defined as unified cultural spaces. This romantic-nationalist theory proposed the nation as a historically shared set of essential values handed down from the past. However, it was necessary to turn to folk or popular culture to find this lineage of organic national values uncontaminated by foreign rule (Rogin 1996:45–46, 53–55).

Such an idea of a nation as a unified cultural space, uncontested internally and uncontaminated by external forces, is also one of the essentially problematic assumptions of cultural imperialist theory (Tomlinson 1991). Leading CI theorist Herbert Schiller, for example, writes that what is at risk with globalization "is the cultural integrity of weak societies whose national, regional, or local or tribal heritages are beginning to be menaced with extinction by the expansion of modern electronic communication" (as quoted in Thompson 1996:169). In denouncing the external cultural control and corruption of the developed capitalist states, CI assumes that each nation is the logical unit for its own cultural identity, and indeed that nations could in some sense be defined as distinct and separate units. By posing such a static and essentialized image of a nation's culture, CI implicitly proposes a spatial model of national cultures—juxtaposing two supposedly distinct societies' cultures. In this manner, the dynamic temporal aspects of national cultures—as contested symbolic spaces, and as traversed by a multitude of forces and identities—are ignored. Here James Clifford's (1988) words are quite salutary:

> [I]f all essentializing modes of thought must be held in suspense, then we should attempt to think of cultures not as organically unified or traditionally continuous but rather as negotiated present processes. (p. 273)

The Media Are American: The Case of Italy

Globalization processes are manifested in everyday Italian life in a multitude of ways: in increased flows and mixes of foreigners; in the increased compulsion of the international markets; in elite policy discourses of disciplining public spending to meet the requirements of competitiveness; and of course in the rampant imported images of other nations, most specifically from the U.S. Let us focus in more detail on American media dominance.

Perhaps the most important, paradigmatically modern medium of the first half of the twentieth century was the cinema. In this context, motion pictures and the United States were almost synonymous. In Europe, the cinema was American, and the cinema defined and glorified America. In Italy since the 1920s, as elsewhere across the continent, at least half the films shown were imports, most typically those of Hollywood. And until the 1950s, the average was 70 percent foreign films. This American dominance or at least Italian openness to imports is evident in other media too. As David Forgacs (1990:29, 69) reports, Italian television schedules since 1980 have been dominated by foreign series. We can also look at other contemporary evidence; examining the music charts for the week ending December 9, 1999, non-Italian albums grab half the top 20 spots, with Anglo-American records racking up 9.[6] Or looking at best-selling fiction books (taking again at random a listing of best-sellers for October 15, 1999) in the top 10, foreign authors take 8 of the slots, although that includes French, German, and Chilean authors—in other words a global mix, not especially dominated by Americans.[7]

In general, American hegemony in the world market has preoccupied and perturbed many intellectual and political leaders from the third world to the first.[8] How could we account for this U.S. dominance of the trade in cultural goods in Italy in particular? In the case of Italy, as cultural historian Forgacs (1990:51–52, 69–70) points out, long-term unequal competition, reinforced by deficiencies in the organization of Italian cultural industries as compared with the vertical integration of American media, fundamentally weakened and rendered noncompetitive Italian film and television producers. For example, Cinecitta', the center of Italian movie production, was forced into various marginal niches in both the domestic and international cinematic markets, for example, various vulgar comedies that the Italian film industry seems to excrete without effort (Stanley 2000).

Economics, however, is insufficient to explain the penetration of American products into the Italian market. We must also examine state policies that open local markets to foreign imports. We need to account for the Italian state's economic liberalism. Even under the totalitarian government of Mussolini, with its proclaimed goal of national autarchy from all foreign dependencies, American cultural goods dominated much of the media market. While the regime denounced the U.S. as a decadent consumerist society, members of Mussolini's own household continued to partake of the pleasures of American light entertainment (Forgacs 1990, chap. 3; and more generally Falasca-Zamponi 1997, chap. 4). In Italy, up to the current era, the state typically combined overregulation with inefficient and arbitrary enforcement, and a corrupt catering to powerful (corporate) interests. All this added up to a form of liberalism that favored large-scale interests (Ginsborg 1990:145–67; Clark 1996:327–37). In the media industries this usually resulted in an alliance of distribution companies (and audiences) that desired cheap foreign products against the interests of domestic cultural industries (Forgacs 1990:27–28, 70).

The case of Italian private television network and media magnate Silvio Berlusconi aptly illustrates this political-economic logic that opens up the Italian market to American products. Until the 1970s, Italy, like most of Europe, maintained a state monopoly over radio and television broadcasting. But in 1976 the Italian constitutional court declared the law restricting audiovisual broadcasting to state agencies valid at the national level, but not at the local. A multitude of private local stations sprang up across Italy. Yet real competition to the state networks (RAI 1-3) for audiences and advertising revenues could occur only if the local stations linked together to supply one standard programming package to viewers and grabbed national advertising. Such networks were manifestly illegal. Yet, Berlusconi, the owner of one network and eventually three major private networks, established an alliance with the leader of the Socialist Party, Bettino Craxi. Craxi, a key player in the ruling coalition, would offer legal protection for Berlusconi's new national stations, and Berlusconi in turn would implicitly supply supportive publicity for the Socialists. Eventually, the government offered postfacto legalization of the established media practices in the so-called "Berlusconi decree" of 1985 (Doyle 1998; Forgacs 1990:141–45, 179–89; Clark 1996: 405–406). Key to Berlusconi's competition with the state networks was the purchase of American media products at substantially cheaper prices than RAI was spending to create original Italian programming. In the year 1981, for instance, RAI continued to produce 80 percent of its own programming, while private stations produced only 10 percent (Forgacs 1990:183).

In addition to such political-economic explanations for Italy's dependence upon cultural imports, Forgacs offers a political-cultural perspective. He asks why the Italian populace does not see Hollywood as an invasion, a challenge to their national autonomy? In a Gramscian analysis, he links this to the historically weak national identity of Italians:

> As a cultural space, . . . Italy has not been strong and effectively hegemonized by a powerful Italian national culture over the last century. . . . There has been an unusually high openness to non-national cultural goods, such as to throw into doubt the existence of cohesive "national" culture from the consumer's point of view. (p. 28)

Italy lacks a coherent "national popular" that is salient and enticing to the average citizen.

The Semiotics of "Blackness" in the United States

Such are the explanations for the impressive degree of U.S. penetration into the Italian entertainment market. These considerations of the nature of media industries are doubtless key to locating the pervasive presence of American blacks in the Italian mediascape. Let us turn for the moment to a rudimentary analysis of the public presence of African Americans in American mass communications, something which cannot be taken for granted and indeed has held notably shifting valences over the last 30 years.

The current prominence of blacks must in some part be due to their own shifting role within the U.S. media industries. In the typical time line, as proposed by Marlon Riggs (1991), African Americans in the twentieth-century mass media went from prominent supporting roles to being virtually invisible in the 1950s and early 1960s. The media's past negative, stereotypical portrayals of African Americans became the subject of controversy and were thus excluded, while at the same time positive portrayals were still unacceptable to a mass audience.

In the post–civil rights era, blacks slowly began appearing in positive supporting roles in American television and film drama. Gradually the corporate industries discovered that a black male lead character was acceptable to white mass audiences, even if black workers were noticeably missing behind the scenes as scriptwriters or executives (Turow 1992). Other factors lent their economic weight to this starring of blacks— the particular attraction of a black star to the sizable audience of African Americans and, with the rise of increasing by segmented markets in television, to youthful audiences in general.

Cultural incentives for the increasing prominence of African Americans upon the electronic and silver screens also need be considered. Blacks, far from losing their supposed group attributes and becoming merely individuals, continue to function as a social category, a complex cultural figure, a walking social signifier. "Blackness" still carries a symbolic charge and an emotional weight in American narratives.

It is necessary to ascertain what that symbolic significance is. Here we offer only a highly truncated accounting of the various valences of "blackness"—a public semiotic of the dichotomous terms black/white. In simplified terms, in nineteenth-century

America (and elsewhere in the Western world), the black man and woman were represented as a deficient Other.[9] By nature, by "race," by their physical corpus, they were seen as not being fully rational participants in the human prospect, as slaves to the demands of their bodies and unable to surmount their desires and instincts. The white *man*, instead, supposedly could exercise the will and reason to control such internal drives.[10] The white man was thought to have the capacity to become more than his body, rather than being governed by internal instinctual drives and desires. In this opposition the black man was expected to accept his subordinate role and become a happy lackey, an Uncle Tom. But if he did not recognize his proper subordination, he became either an ugly physical menace or a buffoon, aspiring to white standards of rationality, but necessarily failing in his immature imitations (Boogle 1993, chap. 1).

The other half of this semiotic dualism—"white"—also suffered its own contradictions, as Richard Dyer (1997) has explicated. The white man supposedly subjected his impulses to a disciplined, rational control. "Will," "spirit," and "character" triumphed over desire and bodily impulse.[11] But in this manner the "white" man became desiccated, lost all color and spontaneity, and became overcivilized, soft, and detached from the harsh realities of the world. American popular culture, in the twentieth century as well as the nineteenth, has consequently been preoccupied with stories about how to recapture the primitive energies and the more concrete social knowledge of the "savages" on our borders—Indians in Westerns (Slotkin 1985)—or those within our borders: African Americans and blackface minstrelsy (Rogin 1996; Roediger 1991; Lott 1993).

The examples of the unfolding of these semiotic terms in mass culture are myriad. Let us cite only one, partly because of its prominence also in Italy and throughout Western Europe: Jack Kerouac's *On the Road*. Numerous members of the 1960s and 1970s counterculture in Europe mentioned Kerouac's formative influence. Kerouac's famous book *Sulla Strada* is published in numerous cheap editions in Italy and distributed as a cut-rate giveaway with such publications as the magazine *La Famiglia Cristiana* [Christian Family] and the newspaper *Corriere della Sera*. (Interestingly enough, Kerouac and the Beatsters maintain their popularity in Italy, much more than in the U.S.) As is well known, in *On the Road* the hero takes his beat-up Chevrolet across America in a sort of replica of Huck Finn's journey on the Mississippi. Such road journeys are typically an escape from the passive, dead-end sterility of middle-class family life. The beatster goes looking for America and freedom from the passivity, conformity, and privatism that is now a cliché characterization of the United States in the 1950s. Beatsters such as Kerouac found one source of a more authentic, more true America in the "Negro" and jazz.[12]

With the onset of the post–civil rights era, these semiotic terms underwent a transformation in the U.S. culture industry. The African American began to be included as a civilized, participating member of American society. His semiotic definition shifted from primitive id to ego and superego, although he still carried traces of his color or, at least, his history. Blackness still counted as an emotionally charged signifier that helped carry the weight of the story forward. Thus, in U.S. detective shows, the boss or superintendent immediately standing over the main hero-detectives is often a man of color—witness *NYPD Blue*'s Detective Clancey and the role of Olmos in *Miami Vice*.

This boss stands for the rule of law, the superego. While he seems to possess an internal anger, a vengeful desire for punishment of wrongdoers, he also holds tight to the iron rule of law and morality in his pursuit of the criminal. What might make a black man especially suitable for the role of superego? One answer would be history: he had to suffer so much to be accepted as a legitimate equal member of American society that he especially recognizes the value of our laws, rights, and morals. A more sinister answer would be color—he is still tied, or burdened, by the weight of his race with its compulsions toward bodily urges and desires; he needs all the more will and discipline to become a rational, controlled moral individual. He thus brings a greater affective charge to the role of disciplining superego.

When an African American becomes the hero, that is, the ego—and today this is more and more common in Hollywood, with such demonstrated money makers as Will Smith, Eddie Murphy, Wesley Snipes, and Denzel Washington—we can ask the same question. What is it about the black man, what about the social semiotics of being an African American, that makes him especially suited for the role of leading protagonist of an adventure/action flick? Ego must of course mediate between the too abstract demands of the superego, and the too great submersion in instinct and nature of the id. The hero must fight back for morality but with knowledge of the tricks and savagery of those he fights.

So what makes the African American especially appropriate for this role of savvy, hip hero? The African American's "history" again supplies a first possible answer. Black Americans have supposedly more often experienced the real roughness of life, life on the streets, life in poverty. They are thus better equipped to go back out on those streets with the hip knowledge and use the tools of the street to fight back. For instance, Eddie Murphy in *Beverly Hills Cops One* and *Two* delights in tweaking the very white, bureaucratic, plodding, clumsy, and naive Beverly Hill cops. Murphy knows what is going down and is not adverse to breaking a few rules, all the while having a laugh or two. We might say, his life back in Detroit—growing up and then working the beat on the Detroit streets, makes him more knowledgeable and more hip about the ways of the world.

The second answer is that the black man is perceived by nature and by race as maintaining access to less rigid, more fluid, more liminal primitive urges. In a sense, as Eric Lott suggests, he is seen as more masculine, more knowledgeable, less constrained by the rules and mythologies of polite civilized society. He is still something of a "trickster," and he is definitely more hip.

From the United States to Italy: The Importation of African Americans

I have offered an evidently blunt sketch of the semiotic complexities of "blackness" in America, the African American being the most prominent racial fantasy infecting our national psyche. The images of blacks as racial primitives, social Others to the American "white," are of long vintage, lasting now almost two centuries as a central part of our commercial popular culture. And it is this popular culture that has repeatedly found entrance into the European, and specifically Italian, mass market. What can a closer examination of the imagery of American blacks in Italy tell us about relations of power and the nature of cultural identities in an era of globalization?

First, we should note that Italy's own production and consumption of an exotic, essentialized image of blacks predates the American imports. The cultural performances of such exotic black Others flow both ways across the Atlantic. Indeed, historians of the original, most profound, and foundational discourse of blackness in U.S. popular culture—blackface minstrelsy—note that minstrelsy was a hybrid cultural creation. It drew upon a diverse range of European and U.S. sources. Such mixed roots confound the notion of an original, distinct, organic culture that purely expresses the folk identity of the nation.

Certainly Italy has developed its own means and manners for depicting Africans. In *Burattini* or Italian marionette puppetry one finds a native theatrical staging of blackness that dates back two centuries and is still performed today as popular children's entertainment. These puppet shows traditionally include in their repertoire the dramatic enactment of conflicts between white Christendom and infidel black Moors. According to Michael Rogin (1996), "These burlesques dramatized feudal war and love or clownish carry-ons between equals rather than the imagined practices of black primitives" (pp. 272–73). Surprisingly enough this Italian harlequinade theater was popular in the United States in the nineteenth century and indeed was one of the sources of American minstrelsy (pp. 19–22).

If the flow of images of exotic Others is any evidence, then U.S. and Italian cultures are hardly autonomous. Rather they should be understood as cross-pollinating and feeding off one another. "National cultures" should be precisely understood as this admixture of elements that are seized and mounted into a ramshackle, contradictory edifice. This commingling of symbolic elements as the melting pot for something new is precisely what theorists of culture have designated by "creolization," rather than a culture consisting in a pure, supposedly uncontaminated, organic expression of the nation's ideas, inner experiences, and general ethos (Hannerz 1992).

Let us now turn to two arenas in the Italian reception of representations of African Americans. We find two key sites where "blackness" is impressively reiterated and reinforced, consumed and produced, as an important social signifier. The first is in youth fashion, and an accompanying set of manufacturers and distributors serving this market. The second is the Italian rap scene. I describe both in terms of a few essential motifs applied to their production of images of blacks, and what these mean in the Italian context. The goal is not exhaustiveness, but rather illustrations of various processes of reception. Both instances—youth fashion and rap—move beyond the case of a mere importation of already constructed mass media texts for the supposedly passive consumption by an Italian audience. Both point to the audience's active role in producing cultural meanings as it receives media messages, and also to the mediation of local industries, which introduce their own selections, emphases, and biases.

Youth Fashion

A significant, perhaps leading fashion trend for the Italian youth market makes explicit references to the "street culture" of urban America. Here I am talking about approximately a dozen lines of clothing and an accompanying circuit of distributors and stores for Italian youth ages 15 to 25. These styles aim to define what is most hip and cool in the youth scene, and consequently become an object of considerable demand among youthful consumers.

Already in their brand names—from "Killah Babe" to "World Tribe" to "gang boy"—some of the clothing companies flag their intended associations with African Americans. In addition, publicity for these brands (as well as others such as Energie, Stussy, Champion, Diesel, Pickwick) often uses blacks as their models, and may situate the models against an urban backdrop of graffiti, busy streets, or rolling subway trains. The clothing styles supposedly draw upon the fashions of the American streets and frequently come labeled with the tag "street culture." For women, in 1999 the style was so-called hip-hop baggy pants, often worn low enough to expose a line of underwear across the belly. For the models, running shoes from Nike or other famous American brands were practically required wear. And among young men, caps pulled down over their ears were standard. Repeatedly—in a variety of ways mythic and symbolic—the companies and their clothes claim to be derived from the styles of America's black youth. Their customers hope to dress themselves in a variety of connotations and significations attached to urban, black Americans.

A series of stores specialize in these brands (at least in Florence where my research took place). These small "boutiques" are usually located outside the elegant and high-rent districts that cater to wealthier, middle-aged customers and tourists. Rather they are situated on seedier streets and closer to where the city youth might circulate, such as near the university. The stores too are typically marked by clichéd signs of African-American urban youth culture. Quite often, a spray-painted mural appears on the store walls in glossy, garish colors, or a collage of American rappers might be pasted on a wall.[13] Logos of the store, as in the case of Arsenico & Batik, might feature a cartoonish black youth. In all, an imagined essence of American blackness is taken as a positive signifier to be appropriated and applied to fashionable clothing.

The line of clothing packaged under the name "Killah Babe" is worth examining in greater detail.[14] Looking at a stores' signs announcing the brand or at its minicatalog, Killah Babe clearly tries to associate itself with an image of forthright, aggressive, rebellious black youth. The name "Killah Babe" itself invokes black slang. Babe's advertising brochure for summer 1999 sports on its front cover a cartoon image of a light-complexioned black woman (see fig. 12.1). She holds aloft a large revolver, as she looks with lowered eyes at the reader. Clichéd insignia of supposed black fashion decorate her body from the pierced nose to her large ruby lips, from her sun glasses to the exposed navel. This cartoonish depiction of a black woman is reproduced in slightly altered form upon various T-shirts and wallets for sale in both summer and winter 1999. In the brochure, a live black model with a tangled cornrow wig is shown in nine poses with diverse outfits. On the back side of the pamphlet is an Asian-looking woman in another ten outfits. Around the borders of each picture are various cryptic or concise phrases in English: "wicked!", "x-rated," "jungle," "ghetto," "phat," among others. All the outfits on display are classified under the label "street culture."[15]

What can we summarize here? First, the lines of clothing, especially those for women, invoke images of an exotic, transgressive Other—sometimes aggressively

Figure 12.1   Publicity for
"Killah Babe" clothing.

provocative and something of a trickster, alternatively more enticing and alluring. In all
they conjure up a traditional Orientalist imagery of blacks (and Asians) as supposedly
more primitive, more in touch with their robust sexual desires and nature. In some
sense we can say blacks are a synecdoche for America, which in turn can be understood
to represent modern "freedom"—consumer freedom, expressive freedom. Here freedom means the liberation of the self from outdated and patriarchal restrictive norms
and social control. Black culture, in the United States as well as outside, has long been
considered a means of access to a less constrained expressiveness, libidinal impulses,
and rapport between internal and external natures. In this context, music is also considered a more authentic, unmediated expression of one's inner impulses and natural
desires. Of course, it has been a long-standing American tendency to turn to blacks as
the bearers of those instinctual energies traditionally displaced and disciplined by Western rationalism (as our earlier discussion of Kerouac illustrates). Furthermore, it has
been an enduring motif in twentieth-century commercial culture to attempt to market
an exotic orientalist Other as more sexual, more in tune with her own sexual desires,
than traditional nineteenth-century pristine and pure Victorian females (Leach 1993).
    Second, the youthful consumer is invited to try on this oriental, exotic Otherness—
black or Asian—literally, by putting on clothes, makeup, hairstyles, postures, and attitudes. Color becomes one more fashion accessory. The individual becomes a flexible

fashionable construction, who can try on Otherness and is no longer tied to fixed physical attributes such as race.[16] Of course, this motif is evident throughout the contemporary fashion industry, most notably with Benetton. In its famous advertisements, Benetton repeatedly juxtaposes whites, blacks, and other people of color as models for the "United Colors of Benetton." In this sense, we can note that many of the lines of clothing make an explicit reference to notions of ethnic pluralism and inclusion. They seem to parody sociological or postmodern jargon with slogans like "meltin' pot," "mixed ethnic look for the summer," "jap style," "world tribe," or elsewhere in the arena of music groups called "mixed blood" [*sanguemisto*] or "black by chance" [*nero per caso*]. Furthermore, tolerant notions of racial mixing and inclusion are also repeated in the rap scene, in its labels and in its explicit leftist-inspired lyrics. Notable is the case of numerous songs by the "soft" rapper Jovanotti. The general love affair of Italian rap for American musicians is reflected in myriad ways in their albums. The group Articolo 31 often incorporates contributions from famed black American artists into its albums.

Michael Rogin has suggested that there are two main evaluative stances toward practices of cross-race identification, or more precisely racial "cross-dressing." Postmodernists celebrate the subversion of given identities and supposed essences through the crossing of racial boundaries. They applaud the disruption of static categories. Modernists instead condemn the caricatured essentialism offered by whites who pose as the racial Other. Relations of sympathetic identification hide the fact that a relation of power still applies and that the singer or designer is appropriating, for his own pleasure and profit, the identity of an essentialized, exoticized Other. An additional negative point against the postmodern appreciation of flexible, transgressive identity construction and pluralistic inclusion is that only some groups have the capacity to choose their identity (Rogin 1996:37, and in general 30–44).

Italian Rap: Articolo 31

When we turn to rap, there is a continuation of the reference to blackness, rebellion, and urban culture. But the connotations of these signifiers come into sharper focus. Of course we need to qualify our characterizations: rap is a complex and heterogeneous phenomenon. It is explicitly "intertextual" and incorporates a multitude of postures and intonations into its own rhythms and rhymes. Here we wish to explore only a few of its rhetorics. These rhetorics make clear that far from being simply force-fed by American cultural industries and absorbed in an undigested form, rap holds a special salience in the Italian context. Rap appears as a "useful discourse"; it is a multiply accented, expansive vernacular that can be molded to the agendas and experiences of diverse individuals and social groups in the Italian scene.[17]

The rhetorical motifs we want to outline are three: first, rap as the voice of the dispossessed speaking out against the dominant powers; a second theme is rap's aggressive masculinity—a reassertion of the masculine individual against those who would deprive him of his social respect; and the third is the posturing and publicity aggrandizing of the supposedly self-made star. These three rhetorics work in complex ways to reinforce and undermine each other. We should also note that they reveal clear limitations to the

Figure 12.2   Album cover for Articolo 31, *Xchè Sí!*

theory of cultural imperialism. In Italian rap, and its identifications with American blacks, Italians are seizing a part of American culture. By their operations they expose the fact that U.S. culture is not a unified capitalist construct. The American media industry does not only export an ideology of consumerism and markets. Rather, media products contain diverse and contradictory ideological strands. Encompassed within U.S. mass culture are diverse class perspectives and social tensions that are exported for the appropriation and conflictual employment by social groups elsewhere across the globe.

We can find these discourses concisely and persuasively portrayed in a series of album covers of Italy's most popular rap group, Articolo 31. On the cover of Articolo 31's latest album, *Xchè Si!*, the rapping duo "J. Ax and DJ Jad" are posed before a television camera in the news studio of one of Italy's major networks ("Studio Aperto" of Canale 5). One is speaking assertively into the camera with microphone in hand, while the other menaces a female news announcer with lengths of cord. The reporter is dropping her script, her mouth open in an expression of exaggerated horror (see fig. 12.2). On the

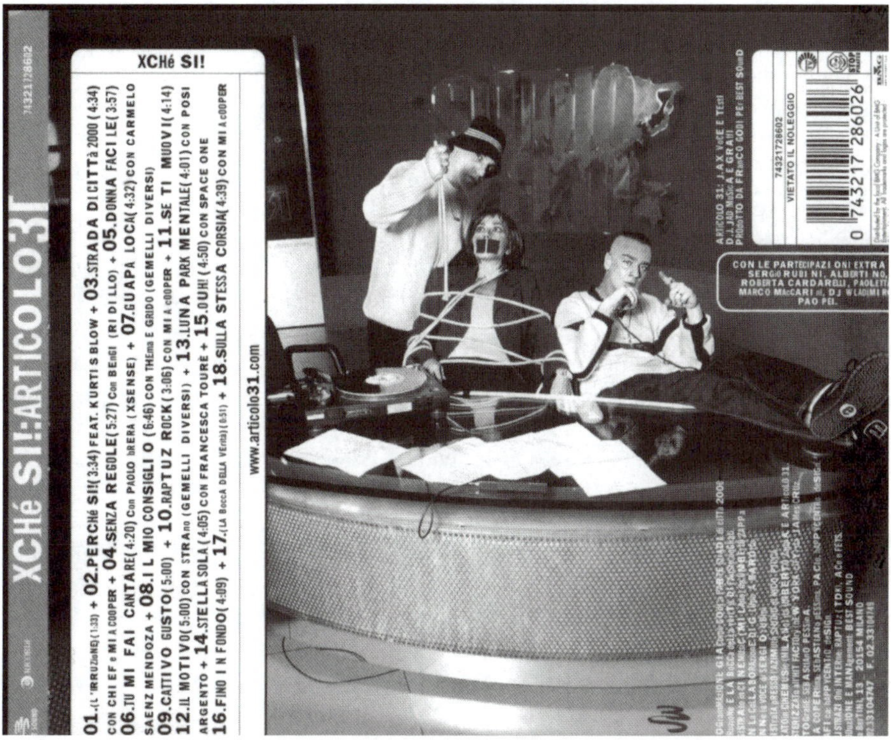

Figure 12.3   Album cover for Articolo 31, *Xchè Sí!*

CD's back cover the woman is bound, her mouth sealed with tape, as the duo look firmly into the album viewer's eyes. They imply their actions are just and proper, and you too should be aware of their force. One of the tools of their musical trade—a turntable for "scratching"—sits on the news desk. In this relatively transparent scene, the duo has shut up the voice of a major media power. They have asserted their own power of speech against those who typically appear as the legitimate arbitrators of the national public identity—the news media. They imply that they—as the voice of the dispossessed—have a more proper authority to speak than the normal interpreters of Italian social life. The CD's title, *Xchè Si!* [Because I say so!], reiterates this message of Articolo 31 as a rebellious counter-authority. In all this Articolo 31 is drawing upon a rather developed imagery of American rap—rap as the recorded voice of the oppressed who in their speech and gestures denounce their oppression. Indeed, I suggest that this is one of the central attractions and allures of rap across a variety of national cultures. To this I should add that Italian rappers typically refer to their American counterparts as angry [*incazzato*], in rebellion. And that in Italy, there is a long-term, persistent left public discourse that describes African Americans as an oppressed minority. Blacks are seen as the historic example of America's bad capitalist faith, notwithstanding its civil rights revolution.

So much we might applaud, but the gendered nature of the disc cover is also brazenly obvious. The rapping duo employ physical (male) force to overwhelm the female employee. It is a woman who is silenced. And she is bound in a way suggestive of sadomasochistic pornography. The very act of rebelling via a violent takeover connotes a marginalized laboring-class masculinity—workers, who once commanded the respect of the world based on their physical prowess and industrial skills, can now engage only in ineffectual and self-defeating acts of rage and rebellion (Dyer 1997, chap. 4). In general, we might add that American rap—with all its paraphernalia of rhapsodizing over the female sex, of grabbing the mike to speak in sharp tones, the cool distant poses of the rapper who glares into the camera with shaded eyes, its blunt movements and forceful gestures that lack all feminine prissiness or elegance—is above all a discourse of masculinity, masculinity reasserted and celebrated.[18]

The third motif is the star as a conscious performer, as a celebrity. In this cultural logic, the rapper has by virtue of his creative artistic talents gained stardom and acclaim. This too has masculine overtones of individual achievement by the dint of his own rough forceful efforts. But in this discourse, all the world has turned into a stage. Its philosophy might be summarized as: I act, therefore I am. I perform well, therefore I am a star. Among rappers, stardom must be held onto against all those forces—establishment power, envious peers, and the dull masses—that would deny and repress their star status. Thus it is no accident that DJ Jad and J. Ax stage their violence in the TV studio. Instead of going out to their public, they seize a central institution of myth-making and organized capitalist publicity (i.e., "the spectacle"). And in their lyrics, they repeatedly vent their anger against the journalists, who are supposedly envious.

Issues of performance may well be generic to members of the human race, which can only "be," through public theatrical displays of who they are (Goffman 1959; Butler 1988). And theatricality may create a series of dilemmas for public performers such as rappers who claim to authentically represent the community at the same time that they mount an elevated public media stage. The quandaries of performance and authenticity are certainly multiplied for all "blackface" performers, such as Italian rappers. After all, the white singer does not really wish to relinquish his white status and assimilate the social position of the black person in Italy, the U.S., or the world. Rather he simply desires to appropriate some of the black person's characteristics. It is a relation of "love and theft," as Lott terms it. In fact the actor demonstrates his power precisely through performance—the conscious and somewhat magical assimilation of the characteristics of the other. But, as I noted earlier, this creates a series of dilemmas: how can one both perform as an Other and still represent the community, the nation?

One finds this dilemma addressed in various ways. The introduction to a volume of lyrics from the soft rapper Jovanotti (1997) declares that Jovanotti "mastered a phenomenon so very American, urban and black like rap and italianized it, rendering it more accessible and giving it a more human face." Meanwhile, Articolo 31 brandishes the slogan "Spaghetti Funk" on its albums and in adorned jewelry. In this manner Articolo 31 comically characterizes its work as a mixed but authentic Italian product. Spaghetti offers an ironic grounding of their identity in an Italian cliché, while funk points to their appropriation of hip American blackness.

Articolo 31's other albums variously elaborate upon these three cultural discourses that refer to, and derive from, black American rap. The previous album, and their most successful to date, continues the motif of the dispossessed commencing immediately with its title, *Nessuno* [No one]. DJ Jad and J. Ax claim a right to speak for all those who are nobodies in the eyes of the powers that be, all those who have been slighted and denied by the normal institutions. This theme is spelled out in the title track "Nessuno" whose lyrics are reproduced in the liner notes. The refrain runs:

> I am No one and represent all those No ones that are around me. Lost in a routine all the same day after day. Upset to the extreme limits. For all you Cyclops, sooner or later we will blind you.
> I grew up having my ears filled with shit. The professor, the television, the politician, the priest. One after another, all screwed me . . .

Nessuno's inside cover is a photo of Quadrifoglio, a working-class neighborhood outside of Milan where the stars claim their origins. The photo shows four giant apartment buildings looking for all the world like an American public housing project. The buildings supposedly form a four-leaf clover, thus the complex's name. The photo constitutes a typical rhetorical strategy of trying to ground the rappers' counterauthority to public speech in a specific locale, in concrete experience, of being real people who know the real Italy and have not departed from their roots. In all this they duplicate the stratagems of American rappers who often invoke their own childhood in the roughest part of the burg, who still know, hang out, and party with the home boys, and so have not broken the ties of black solidarity.

A fist, knuckles forward, fills Nessuno's back cover. It repeats the masculine theme of a blunt physical presence and assertiveness. On one of the fingers is a heavy gold ring—ghetto style—bearing the slogan "Spaghetti Funk."

Articolo 31's other albums have been *Strade di Citta'* [Streets of the city] and *Cosi' Com'e'* [How it is]. Both seemingly promote as their most public themes Articolo's special authority, its particular right to make public pronouncements. These albums assert that Articolo 31 knows "how it is" in all its blunt reality. They know from having experienced the life on the streets firsthand. *Strade di Citta'* bears photos of the duo posing in diverse urban locales and before the insignia of authentic urban life: graffiti-spattered walls. In their stern poses—upright, backs against the walls, glaring directly at the viewer with mouth drawn in a stern line, the musicians invoke both the masculinity of the American rappers, and their public display of themselves as performers. They are dressed here as elsewhere in stylish, prescribed street-derived clothes and jewelry.

Conclusion

The theory of cultural imperialism points to the increasingly foreign sources of national cultures, the global roots of our particular identities. And it suggests we should recognize in these media flows an operation of power in the service of corporate capitalism and the more developed countries. This theory certainly helps to explain important dynamics of cultural circulation in Italy. For indeed much of Italian media content descends from the stars in Hollywood or derives from the studios in New York. The dominance of U.S. industries and Italy's porous cultural borders accounts for a share of the prominence and attraction posed by African Americans to Italian audiences.

Nevertheless, I have argued throughout this essay that CI theory upholds an overly simple image of the production and consumption of culture in general, and the nature of national cultures in particular. As our examples should make clear, cultural rhetorics are often appropriated and redeployed by local cultural producers/consumers for a variety of local motives, derived from their own individual, class and gender experiences. CI theory's blunt opposition between national cultures erases the historically dynamic processes that constituted those national cultures in the first place. Italy and the U.S., as with other nations, cannot so easily be opposed. Cross-national flows have been historically constant, while the internal unity of each nation's culture has been a matter of dispute and debate. CI theory, implicitly holding onto the traditional notion of culture as society's shared ethos, does not recognize this dynamic conflictual, historical dimension to culture.

The images of blacks in America, however mythical and distorted by their journey through the media airwaves and across the Atlantic, constitute a new repertoire for (self-declared) oppositional ideologies and images in Italy. The experience and cultural creativity of African-American performers provide an expansive, open-ended vernacular that has proved itself a rich basis for elaborating upon and defining groups' experiences in Italy in novel and provocative ways. In this context, then, it cannot be the mere defense of supposedly autonomous national cultures from imperialist control and contamination that is at stake. The question is *not* how an internal elite can assume responsibility for a nation's culture and eliminate external control. Rather, the political issue becomes how the culture can be democratized, not insulated.[19]

Notes

I thank Peppino Ortolevi, Richard Letteri, and Simonetta Falasca for their critical comments.

1. It was to this excruciating context, that W.E.B. Dubois was pointing when he described the "double-consciousness" of "black folk" in America. Of course, this expropriation of the production of public images does not depend upon technical media. For most of the nineteenth century, blacks were subject to the ministrations of minstrelsy, that is—a form of oral theatrical presentation.

I don't want to imply that even face-to-face relations are unmediated, direct, and necessarily democratic, contrary to certain formulations in the Hegelian-Marxist tradition. All communication is mediated by historically inherited linguistic systems, cultural meanings, and social norms, and never directly expresses individuals' experiences.

2. Examples are taken from the fall 1999 TV season.

3. In particular the *zaino* "*Murales*" produced by the company Seven for the fall 1999 season.

4. Prenatal, chain store for infants and young children, sets its youthful models against the backdrop of spray-painted murals in its catalog for fall 1999.

5. On anthropology, especially Geertz, see Clifford (1988: 13–16, 233–236, 273–74); and Bourdieu (1990). On sociology see Featherstone *et al.* (1995). In general, we can say the nation was the individual writ large and all the typical contradictions of an individual consciousness-centered "philosophy of consciousness" were reproduced.

6. As reported in "Musica" supplement to *La Repubblica*, December 9 1999.

7. Weekly Listings of the "Libri Piu' Venduti," *La Repubblica*, October 15 1999.

8. France is the case most often cited of fears over the influx and dominance of American mass culture. Cf. Pells 1997; Schlesinger 1994: 31, 33, 38–39. On the third world see Tomlinson 1991; Turow 1992: 221–25.

9. Black/white is one of those essentializing dichotomies that, along with occident/orient and male/female, defined the modern, enlightenment West in its own self-identity and in its conflictual relationships with other cultures and countries. In general see Clifford's presentation of Edward Said's representation of Foucault (1988: ch. 11).

10. Such dichotomous terms, supposedly based in the physical body of social groups—women, children, racial others—emerged as a new legitimating device for justifying inequalities and hierarchy during the Enlightenment (Laqueur 1986).

11. In Susman's time line (1984: ch. 15), the essential cultural ideals of the self change in the early twentieth century. "Character" as an ideal is replaced by "personality," with a focus on expressivity and consumption instead of ascetic, self-control. In this transformation, blacks suddenly acquire new currency, as they represent an "other" who has not subjected an expressive instinctual nature to willful repressive excision. See for instance Erenberg's important book *Steppin' Out* (1981) which talks about the new forms of public behavior such as dance that are strongly influenced by images and cultural traditions of American blacks. But such a timeline is contradicted by novels such as *The Last of the Mohicans* of the 1830s which visibly details in its character Hawkeye the need for an interchange with presumably more primitive instinctual species, i.e. the Indians.

12. On the general relation of bohemia to blackness, see Lott's analysis (1993: 49–55).

13. Spray-painted murals appear on stores, such as Metropole on Via Nazionale and Arsenico and Batik on Via. S. Antonino. A collage of rappers can be found decorating the store Ultra on Via XXVII Aprile.

14. The newspaper *La Repubblica* in its weekend glossy magazine offers an undoubtedly impressionistic study of the diverse strands of Italy's youth culture. Regarding what it labels the "generation of the discotheque," *La Repubblica* states that roughly eight million youths regularly frequent Italian dance halls, within which a distinct subculture is formed of "people of the night". One author provides a gross generalization when she declares that "the appropriate clothes to wear among this group are "large, of the type 'baggy-trousers', or hip-hop. The brand most requested is Killah Babe." Maria Novella de Luca, "Se la notte e' un rifugio," in *Il Venerdi'* supplement to *La Repubblica*, November 26 1999.

15. The models and graphic illustration display some of the main motifs of this style, which we see repeated elsewhere in other brands: the emphasis on both sexual display, a provocative posing—exposed navel, tight T-shirts, revealed edges of underwear—but also another emphasis on relatively adolescent, immature women with small breasts and thin arms, posed in an ungainly posture of the legs and arms.

16. Here we find, as Arvidsson (2000) has recently argued, one more capitalist basis for the post-modern notion of the oft celebrated, flexible reflexive self. Arvidsson's work is especially relevant because it examines the history of Italian twentieth-century culture. However, we

can note that working on the self, styling for fashionable consumption, is a long-term practice among women (Peiss 1996: 320.) Furthermore, we can dispute how free it is, especially in Italy where fashion among youth is notoriously conformist. Fashion, after all, is a display of the self for the approval of others. Fashion can easily be a set of codes to render oneself acceptable to one's peers. And in fact, in Italy an emphasis on proper public appearance—*"fare la bella figura"*—has been a long-standing cultural practice.

17. This exemplifies the widespread turn in media studies from what has been labeled a "media-centric" approach which sees the audience absorbed in the individual cultural texts they consumed, and sees the broader cultural life-world taken over by a media-constructed spectacular culture. Rather, people continue to remain permanently embedded in an overarching cultural life-world, which structures their reception and interpretation of media products. To truly understand either rap, or more broadly images of African Americans in Europe, it is necessary to pay attention to this pragmatic-cultural context of reception.

18. As Lott tells us (1993:49–55), white masculinity was always formulated in dialogue with, and in appropriation of, representations of black masculinity.

19. See Schlesinger's suggestive contrasting of a "Latin-European" conception of "cultural space" against an alternative theoretical tradition focusing on the democratic public sphere (1994:36–38).

References

Arvidsson, A. (2000) *The Making of Consumer Society: Marketing and Modernity in Contemporary Italy*, (Dissertation) Department of Social and Political Sciences, European University.

Boogle, D. (1993) *Toms, Coons, Mulattoes, Mammies, and Bucks: An Interpretive History of Blacks in American Films*, New York: Continuum.

Bourdieu, P. (1990) 'The scholastic perspective,' *Cultural Anthropology*, 5, no. 4: 380–391.

Butler, Judith. (1988) 'Performative acts and gender constitution: an essay in phenomenology and feminist theory,' *Theater Journal*, 40.

Carey, J. W. (1989) *Communication as Culture*, Boston: Unwin Hyman.

Castle, S. (1998) 'Globalization and the ambiguities of national citizenship,' in R. Baubock and J. Rundell (eds.) *Blurred Boundaries: Migration, Ethnicity, Citizenship*, Brookfield, VT: Ashgate.

Clark, M. (1996) *Modern Italy, 1871–1995*, (second ed.) New York: Addison Wesley Longman.

Clifford, J. (1988) *The Predicament of Culture: Twentieth-Century Ethnography, Literature, and Art*, Cambridge: Harvard University Press.

Doyle, W. (1998) 'The rhetoric of communication and the origins of Italy's media deregulation,' Paper presented to the *NCA/ICA Conference* (July 1998) Rome, Italy.

Dyer, R. (1997) *White*, New York: Routledge.

Erenberg, L. A. (1981) *Steppin' Out: New York Nightlife and the Transformation of American Culture, 1890-1925*, Westport, CT: Greenwood Press.

Falasca-Zamponi, Simonetta. (1997) *Fascist Spectacle: The Aesthetics of Power in Mussolini's Italy*, Berkeley: University of California Press.

Featherstone, M,, Robertson, R., and Lash, S. (eds.) (1995) *Global Modernities*, Thousand Oaks, Sage.

Fejes, F. (1981) 'Media imperialism: an assessment,' *Media, Culture and Society*, 3:281–289;

Forgacs, D. (1990) *Italian Culture in the Industrial Era, 1880–1980*, New York: Manchester University Press.

Ginsborg, P. (1990) *A History of Contemporary Italy: Society and Politics, 1943–1988*, New York: Penguin Books.

Goffman, E. (1959) *The Presentation of Self in Everyday Life*, New York: Anchor Books.

Hannerz, U. (1992) *Cultural Complexity*, New York: Columbia University Press.

Jovanotti (1997) *Jovanotti: I Miti Canzone*, Milano: Mondadori.

Laqueur, T. (1986) 'Orgasm, generation, and the politics of reproductive biology,' *Representations* no. 14: 1–41.

Leach, W. (1993) *Land of Desire: Merchants, Power and the Rise of New American Culture*, New York: Vintage Books.

Lott, E. (1993) *Love and Theft: Blackface Minstrelsy and the American Working Class*, New York: Oxford University Press, 1993.

McQuail, D. (1995) 'Western Europe: 'mixed model' under threat?' in J. Downing, A. Mohammadi, A. Sreberny-Mohammadi (eds.) *Questioning the Media: A Critical Introduction*, (2nd ed.) Thousand Oaks, CA: Sage Publications.

Peiss, K. (1996) 'Making up, making over,' pp. 311–333 in V. de Grazia and E. Furlough (eds.) *The Sex of Things: Gender and Consumption in Historical Perspective*, Berkeley: University of California Press.

Pells, R. (1997) *Not Like Us: How Europeans Have Loved, Hated, and Transformed American Culture Since World War II*, New York: Basic Books.

Riggs, M. T. (1991) *Color Adjustment*, Berkeley, CA: Signifyin' Works.

Roediger, D. (1991) *Wages of Whiteness: Race and the Making of the American Working Class*, New York: Verso.

Rogin, M. (1996) *Blackface, White Noise: Jewish Immigrants in the Hollywood Melting Pot*, Berkeley: University of California Press.

Schlesinger, P. R. (1994) 'Europe's contradictory communicative space,' *Daedalus*, 123: 25–52.

Slotkin, R. (1985) *The Fatal Environment*, New York: Atheneum.

Stanley, A. (2000) 'Snub at Cannes has Italy fretting,' *New York Times*, May 25, 2000, B-1.

Susman, W. (1984) *Culture as History*, New York: Vintage Books.

Thompson, J. (1996) *The Media and Modernity: A Social Theory of the Media*, New York: Polity Press.

Tomlinson, J. (1991) *Cultural Imperialism: A Critical Introduction*, London: Pinter Publishers.

Turow, J. (1992) *Media Systems in Society: Understanding Industries, Strategies and Power*, London: Longman.

Wallerstein, I. (1974) *The Modern World System*, New York: Academic Press.

Part IV

REFRAMING MEDIA CULTURES FOR GLOBAL CONSUMPTION

13

Markets and Meanings

The Global Syndication of
Television Programming

Denise D. Bielby and C. Lee Harrington

Although television did not exist at the beginning of the last century, today it is the most common form of visual entertainment worldwide, providing a means of readily accessible and relatively inexpensive entertainment for hundreds of millions of households. Not only is the television industry a major source of revenue for exporting nations, increasingly it is an organizational form of production that spans borders. Each year, four major international conventions bring together members of media industries for the marketing and purchase of television programs. Those gatherings—the NATPE convention, which is organized by the National Association of Television Program Executives and held in the United States every winter; MIPCOM and MIP-TV, which are the Midem Organization of France's annual fall and spring events, held in Monte Carlo; and the by-invitation-only L.A. Screenings, which are held in June in hotel rooms and studios throughout Los Angeles—serve as the international crossroads for the buyers and sellers of television programming. Attendance at each of these venues can number in the tens of thousands and draw participants from every region of the globe. By way of illustration, the number of registered participants at the NATPE convention in New Orleans in January of 2000 exceeded 17,500, including more than 4,300 from foreign countries. Thirty-nine percent of the exhibitors represented countries other than the United States (*NATPE Facts*, February 28, 2000).

The growth of these industry gatherings in the last three decades into major international marketplaces for the exchange of television programs is a direct consequence of the economic robustness of television production in the latter part of the twentieth century. Revenues generated are considerable, and the international market for programs is an extraordinarily lucrative source of profit for major production companies.[1]

In this chapter we analyze the world of American television programming as a cultural product for export abroad, as part of a larger project on global television. We examine the "culture world" of television production, relying upon Diana Crane's

(1992) conceptualization, which expands Howard Becker's (1982) notion of art worlds to include the specific roles of organizations and audiences.[2] To study the American television industry's perceptions of its audiences outside the United States and the ways in which its foreign counterparts perceive American television entertainment, we focus upon the constraints that the world of television production faces as it markets its products internationally. In particular, we analyze factors that affect how and why American television series are modified in preparation for export abroad.

Our approach to this topic is unique in several ways. First, we bring a sociological view to the study of what traditionally has been in the purview of communications scholars. While their research typically focuses on the efficacy and consequence of the communicative process, our perspective addresses the social, organizational, and interpersonal processes that underlie, construct, and inform television as a cultural product. Second, our work differs from most sociological research on the topic. Whereas others analyze television as a market or as an industrial system, we focus upon its micro-organizational accomplishment. In extending the concept of culture world to the international market for television, we consider explicitly how the medium evolved from a domestic product to one that is global in scope, and how collective action is accomplished when participants come from all parts of the world. In particular, we examine how issues of meaning arising in a cross-cultural context shape business strategies, decisions, and outcomes.

We emphasize that our analysis is necessarily restricted to a "snapshot" of the worldwide syndication process, given the frequency and rapidity with which the global television industry transforms. As Muriel Cantor and Joel Cantor noted in 1986, television import/export is a chaotic business in a chaotic market; that statement is even truer today. The workings of the international culture world of television are revealed in myriad ways, and therefore we draw upon multiple sources of information. For this chapter we draw upon interviews with seven executive-level managers, data collected through participant observation at two industry conventions, and observations from continuing fieldwork at companies within the industry.[3] In our analysis, we restrict our focus to television series themselves, forgoing attention to the consequences of new technologies and systems of distribution upon the international marketplace. While those developments are of consequence to the viability of the marketplace for television programming, they have not affected the content of what is produced for export. We focus instead on characteristics of the cultural product itself as part of the business of the international marketplace.

The Domestic Television Industry and International Television Flows

Communications scholars have led the study of exported television. Consistent with their interest in understanding the exchange and impact of information, their scholarship has focused largely upon identifying the flows of programming from one country to another and the major national exporters in the global arena (see Mohammadi 1997).[4] The earliest attempts at systematic documentation of exported television programming revealed that by the early 1970s, the United States, Britain, France, and the Federal Republic of Germany were leaders in its origination (Nordenstreng and Varis 1974). According to that research, the United States led this group with an estimated 150,000 hours of programming per year, followed by the United Kingdom and France, estimated at 20,000 hours each. West Germany exported approximately 6,000 hours.[5]

To some extent these statistics merely reflect the number of hours of airtime that needed to be filled in newly emerging national television systems.[6] For the most part, the leaders in exported programming sent their programs to countries whose broadcast systems were sufficiently developed to have schedules to fill, or who shared the same language. Moreover, by no means did the number of hours reported indicate that programming from any one exporter dominated the globe. In the early 1970s, for example, the United States exported programming primarily to Canada, Australia, Japan, and Western Europe (Varis 1974). Programming from the French commercial group went to Europe, North America, Japan, and 10 French-speaking African countries, with Zaire and Tunisia being the major receivers on that continent. West Germany was a major exporter within Western Europe but had limited presence beyond that sphere because German is spoken in relatively few countries.

While these nations were the largest exporters, several other countries were major producers of programming for international distribution in other regional markets. For example, programs from Mexico were widely distributed throughout Latin America and in areas of the United States where Spanish is widely spoken, and Lebanon and the United Arab Republic were major producers for the Middle East. Analyses of flows among non-Western countries published a decade after Nordenstreng and Varis's first major study show that among Third World countries there was no substantial change in the use of foreign programming (Varis 1986). Among those flows was, however, a trend toward greater intra regional exchange, especially among Arab countries and also within Latin America. Countries with large internal markets, such as Brazil's television and India's film industries, now supply not only their own markets but also send exports internationally (Varis 1984).

Still debated among scholars is the question of whether expansion of international media flows is a mechanism for both economic and ideological cultural domination, specifically by the United States (see Schiller 1991). The so-called cultural imperialist view refers to "the domination of one country's system of symbolically producing and reproducing constructed realities over another's production and re-production of self-identity" (De la Garde 1993:27).[7] The most significant opposing view has come to be known as the "active audience" perspective, which argues that the response of actual viewers to imported products is complicated and nuanced, which problematizes any straightforward notions of "domination." According to Ien Ang, "it is hard to distinguish . . . between the 'foreign' and the 'indigenous,' the 'imperialist' and the 'authentic': what has emerged is a highly distinctive and economically viable hybrid cultural form in which the global and the local are inextricably intertwined" (1996:154; see also McAnany and Wilkenson 1992; Schwoch 1993). Research has addressed the cultural domination thesis at a number of different levels, though this focus is beyond the scope of the analysis reported here.[8]

Relevant to the debate over cultural dominance is the ratio of imported to domestically broadcast programming. Nordenstreng and Varis's 1974 UNESCO report relied upon questionnaire data collected from more than 50 countries to analyze the general content and percentages of imported versus domestic programming.[9] In this study, the first ever of the direction of exported television, the authors revealed that American programming prevailed in the global market, followed by British programming, and that entertainment programming comprised a greater portion of the imported product than did other forms, such as news.[10] In a more recent study of Latin American television broadcasters in Mexico, Peru, Argentina, Brazil, and Venezuela, Livia Antola and Everett Rogers (1984) argued that examining "audience-hours" (i.e., the number of hours divided by size of audience for each program) provides a more realistic assessment of exposure to imported programming and demonstrates that it is substantially lower than proponents of the dominance thesis imply. Within Mexico in 1982, the year of Antola and Rogers' study, the 50 percent of programming hours filled by imported programs translated into one third of the total possible audience-hours of viewing. Moreover, of four available channels, only two carried a high proportion of imported programs.

The significance of these figures for Mexico was borne out in interviews conducted by Antola and Rogers with Latin American television broadcasters in Venezuela, Brazil, Argentina, Chile, Mexico, and Peru regarding viewers' preferences for domestically produced versus imported programs. According to the executives interviewed, audience preferences ranked in the following descending order: locally produced programs, imports from other Latin American countries, and last, programs from the United States (which was the source of the greatest percentage of imported programs). Lina Davis (1997) found a similar pattern of viewing preferences in Ecuador, a smaller and less developed country than those studied by Antola and Rogers. These findings support notions of a cultural discount, or "cross-border reduction in value." As Hoskins and Mirus suggest, "A particular programme rooted in one culture, and thus attractive in that environment, will have a diminished appeal elsewhere" (1988:500; see also Straubhaar 1991). The discount is less in entertainment genres than in other categories, which Hoskins and Mirus argue is the single biggest reason why entertainment-based programming (rather than education- and/or information-based) dominates international flows (1988:501).

Tamar Liebes and Eliku Katz (1990) suggest that some genres originating in Western cultures, such as serialized dramas, have an inherent cultural power that makes them accessible and appealing in almost every region where they are imported. Serials are believed to have a unique ability to "explore apparently global themes in more specifically local ways" (Barker 1997:93; see also Borchers 1989; Liebes and Katz 1990; Lopez 1995). Their narrative structure, which leaves them open to a wider variety of cultural readings than other forms of programming, also contributes to serials' success on the global syndication market (Allen 1997). While U.S. viewers are most familiar with serials in the form of daytime soap operas (originating on radio in the 1930s and moving to television in the early 1950s), there is an astonishing diversity of serial narratives worldwide (Allen 1997; McAnany and La Pastina 1994). Today, Latin American serials (or telenovelas) are the most exported television products in the world, with Brazil the most prolific producer and exporter (O'Donnell 1999:3; see also Allen 1996).

While much of the literature on serials' global success focuses on content or genre characteristics, recent scholarship indicates that concrete and local programming practices may actually be more instrumental in shaping viewing preferences. For example, Stuart Cunningham and Elizabeth Jacka (1994) identified factors other than genre that accorded success in the United Kingdom of the Australian soap import *Neighbors*. On one hand, they found that certain cultural themes (e.g., the youthfulness and "whiteness" of the cast, and the historic ties between Australia and Britain) resonated with the audience. On the other hand, they emphasize that crucial to the success of *Neighbors* were aspects seemingly as mundane as placement on the network schedule (early and late afternoons, five days per week) and reaching the target demographic (the "youth" audience). In this instance, specific programming strategies were successful in placing the series before an audience that would both find it and appreciate its meaning.[11] Conversely, *Neighbors* failed to catch on with U.S. viewers for reasons partly related to content/genre (e.g., the show's "nonexceptional realism"), but mostly due to factors such as "gridlock" scheduling and the brevity of the show's run (Crofts 1995:112).

While issues of genre continue to be relevant, these findings underscore the importance of focusing primarily upon "middle-range" factors in understanding how and where imported programming comes to dominate audience preferences. Cantor and Cantor (1986) advocate this strategy in the conclusion of their exploratory study of the international marketplace of American television. They noted that "the production and distribution of American programs abroad is a complex and intricate process, involving many players both in the United Sates and abroad—including the audience." They go on to conclude that "the time has now arrived for communication researchers to move away from a model of direct, single-centered, and worldwide influence to one that functions as interactive, multicentered, and regional" (Cantor and Cantor 1986:518).

Research on exported media identifies numerous factors that potentially affect the direction and extent of its flow and may occur either in production or distribution of a media product (Mowlana 1997:34). We follow the lead of Mowlana and of Cantor and Cantor by exploring in detail the production and distribution of internationally syndicated U.S. programming in the context of specific marketplaces, taking into consideration that the market is shaped by formal, legal, and technical constraints on the one hand, and by informal rules and understandings rooted in culture and ideology on the other. Below we discuss some of these factors, organized by topic so that we are able to emphasize national or cultural variation across countries or regions of the globe.

Issues in Production and Distribution for Syndication to Foreign Markets

Language, Translation, and Culture

As we noted above in our discussion of the initial UNESCO report on television flows (Nordenstreng and Varis 1974), exports were constrained by language from the very beginning. At first, U.S. exports, for example, exports went to other English-speaking countries, with the exception of Japan. Language differences can be surmounted by subtitles or dubbing, but a fundamental consideration for both buyers and sellers is literacy rates of purchasing countries. Literacy is a precondition for subtitling, of course, but not for dubbing. A representative from China to the 1998 NATPE convention told us that imported programming is always dubbed because 25 percent of the country is illiterate; translations and dubbing are done in China.[12] A related factor affecting the decision to subtitle versus dub (which may be the determining factor in whether a program can be purchased) is economic cost. Dubbing, though necessary for some purchasing countries, costs 5 to 10 times as much as subtitling (Van der Weel 1990:23).

Antola and Rogers's (1984) study of Latin American countries, discussed above, reported that Mexico was the gatekeeper for translations of all products sold to Latin American countries. According to their research, Mexico inherited that role from Cuba, where nearly all dubbing for Latin America was conducted until the 1959 revolution. Because of Mexico's established film industry, it possessed the organizational infrastructure and talent to take over the task. Mexico's role as gatekeeper eventually grew in importance because more often than not individual countries were unable to provide sufficient revenue to exporters that would also cover the cost of dubbing products into Spanish.[13]

One reason for the vested interest among Latin American buyers in maintaining the location of dubbing and translation in Mexico (Mexico City, to be exact) is that it makes censorship easier. At the time of Antola and Rogers's research, cultural policy was that certain types of stories were not allowed in imported products (for example, kidnapping, references to guerrillas, and depictions of certain types of sexual behavior); episodes with this program content were simply edited out. In addition, certain English words are censored in their Spanish translation. Indeed, a coordinator of acquisitions for the Fox Latin American Channel told us that to this day, buyers from Latin America are surprised ("shocked" was her term) at the vulgarity in American television and struggle with whether potential acquisitions can be made acceptable to their audiences.

As the above examples illustrate, at some point the constraints on preparing an exported series for airing extend well beyond technological considerations and into matters of cultural adequacy in the broadest sense. One of us, while traveling in Italy in 1999, learned firsthand some of the more subtle ways in which a series is adapted to local cultural interests. In that instance, it was the prime-time sitcom "The Nanny" (which first aired in the United States on CBS and is distributed internationally by Columbia Tristar International Television). As an import it was dubbed; Fran Drescher's "fingernails on a chalkboard" voice was closely mimicked (as was just about every other American actor's voice in television and films imported to Italy, including many former stars like James Cagney and Humphrey Bogart). What came as a surprise, however, was learning from Italian viewers that Drescher's character was not Jewish as it is in the original American version; instead, she was Sicilian and her voice was dubbed into a distinctly Sicilian dialect. Indeed, local viewers informed us that Sicilian accents are dubbed for any character who is considered to be "a gangster" or otherwise a foil for cultural propriety.

Italian voice-over artists take pride in being among the most professional and expert in the world. The country's 1,050 dubbers, representing 80 companies, are unionized, with the best becoming "stars in their own right" within Italy (Boudreaux 1998). In their case, participation in the culture world of internationally syndicated programs contributes in crucial ways to the meaning of imported programs for Italian audiences. Dubber Mario Paolinelli explained, "For viewers, hearing our voices is like having close friends at home. If the characters speak a different language, they're not friends anymore" (Boudreaux 1998). When successful, this kind of intervention literally transforms the product into one that genuinely incorporates local cultural meaning.

A melding of technical and cultural considerations happens in other ways as well. For example, audio dubbing is done "split track," which breaks out the voice track from the musical track. This is done because buyers in some countries wish to retain the American music as a feature of the imported production, which their audiences actively seek out as a reason for viewing. The program buyer from Lithuania whom we spoke with at the 1998 NATPE convention explained that her country dubs its programming but preserves the original soundtrack and sound effects, "whose quality is valued and should not be sacrificed." Even this approach to music is complicated, as a senior project manager at Paramount who oversees distribution of programming to Europe pointed out to us: because lyrics are the focal point of some songs, they are often left untranslated and are heard in English.

Entertainment and Cultural Limits

As noted earlier, entertainment-based (rather than information- or education-based) programming dominates international television flows (Hoskins and Mirus 1988), though countries vary in the proportion of network schedules devoted to entertainment. In 1974, Nordenstreng and Varis showed that entertainment programming typically predominates when a network is commercially owned and operated rather than noncommercial or state owned. In Japan, for example, where both network forms exist, Nordenstreng and Varis showed that commercial stations devoted 80 percent of airtime to entertainment programming, in contrast to the noncommercial NHK, which allocated just one-third of its total time to such programs (1974:17). A more recent example is the current shift in the European television system (beginning in the 1970s and 1980s) away from a public service tradition toward privatization and a market economy (Owen and Wildman 1992). According to Ole Prehn and Else Jensen, "While the emphasis in the U.S. is on entertainment and large audiences, the European tradition has been to offer people a variety of programs, which may not always attract large audiences but nevertheless are of cultural and political importance. During the last decade, this tradition has been challenged both by the proliferation of channels and by the political climate favouring a market oriented approach" (1993:221). In short, entertainment television is on the rise throughout Europe.[14]

Although critics of the effects of the international market often presume such products are immutable and exported without modification, we find otherwise. Indeed, those involved on the production and distribution side of international syndication as

well as buyers in receiving countries recognize that many aspects of television programming, like any other cultural product, do not necessarily translate across borders
and must be adapted to do so. As a result, some genres of programs are selectively marketed to specific regions, producers and syndicators often allow buyers to control editing and other modifications for their markets, and producers sometimes avoid certain
themes and language in anticipation of the decisions of gatekeepers in foreign markets. For example, Bradley Bell, the executive producer and head writer of *The Bold
and the Beautiful* (CBS), the most popular U.S. soap opera in the world, explains, "I
am definitely aware of our international audience when I develop story lines . . . I stay
clear of long, drawn-out trials because I think that international viewers may get bored
with endless details of how the American legal system works. . . . Romance—the focus
of our show—is the international language" (quoted in Museum of Television and
Radio 1997:161).[15] Below, we show some of the ways that export constraints are taken
into consideration by producers, sellers, and buyers.

Demand for particular genres like action-adventure or telenovelas, for certain forms
such as feature-length films, or for programming of a given quality may motivate a purchase, but the ways in which a given series will actually be used by the purchasing
country varies.[16] In the previous section, we discussed how the placement of a series
on a network's schedule reflects the targeted foreign audience regardless of the domestic audience for which the series was originally intended. But adaptations can go far
beyond that. For example, telenovelas are an extremely popular form of programming
around the globe (see Barker 1997; Lopez 1995; Matelski 1999; O'Donnell 1999).
Countries as diverse as China and Turkey are frequent buyers because they find the
stories compelling; other countries purchase telenovelas because of the popularity of
actors cast in various roles.[17] A director of international sales from Carolco (a major
Colombian producer of telenovelas) who attended NATPE informed us that Colombian firms typically produce series of 100 to 120 episodes.[18] However, importing countries, including China, may purchase only 90 or 100 episodes. Economics explains
some of those decisions: in many developing nations, with hours of television programming to fill but relatively small budgets to acquire all genres, it is difficult to afford
long-running serials. In the case of China, state politics was perhaps the most important factor shaping decisions about imported programming. Until very recently, Chinese television stations were prevented from purchasing programs with more than 40
episodes; this government mandate kept both U.S. and Latin American serials off Chinese television for many years (Hornik 1996).[19]

In the United States, there is widespread concern among some groups about explicit
depictions of sex and violence (Montgomery 1989), and we expected to hear similar
commentary readily voiced by those who buy and sell programming for the international marketplace. In fact, few addressed the topic in conversation unless we introduced it, although once we did, representatives from other countries almost without
exception indicated that they found such aspects problematic, regardless of where programming originated. For example, the Lithuanian buyer we spoke with identified
German programming as the most problematically explicit, and American program-

ming increasingly so, but imports from both countries were manageable. In her country, all programs with sex or violence are scheduled to be broadcast after 11 P.M.

China manages the matter of violence differently. The representative of the government organization that handles imports of foreign programming told us at NATPE that action adventure imports from Hong Kong are problematic for buyers from China because of frequency, not kind. Violence cannot exceed a certain number of occurrences within a given interval, and it "has to be justifiable." As the government representative explained, there are two levels of censorship, one prior to or at the time of purchase, and one after acquisition, which can prevent the purchase from airing. If the series is rejected at that point, the supplier is obligated to supply another series in its place. How this is enforced is unclear, but it was represented to us as "a way around" problematic situations. The impact of China's policies on those who export programming to that country is illustrated by the following, which appeared in a *Wall Street Journal* article about Encore International, Inc., the China division of the International Channel cable network:

> To avoid alarming Chinese authorities, Encore's executives screen 1,200 hours of programming a year to select 500 hours they think CCTV [China Central Television] will find acceptable. In the U.S., a broadcaster might buy a TV series after seeing one or two episodes; Encore screens every hour of every show, wary of a single episode on a homosexual affair or child molestation that would sink the whole series. (Chang 2000:B-4)

These examples illustrate that for exchanges to work, many different types of accommodations are made in response to the cultural context of the importing country.

Foreign buyers new to the international marketplace sometimes find their assumptions about quality and popularity challenged. A producer in the satellite broadcast operation of the Korean Broadcasting System who was visiting the United States to learn more about American programming explained to us that as a legacy of her country's traditional practice of airing only acclaimed foreign documentaries and films from sources such as the BBC, PBS, or NHK, it was presumed that the increased presence of imported entertainment programming for Korea's two commercial networks could be of a similarly high (i.e., "educational") quality. Consequently, series sought for importation were expected to impart culture and knowledge, and those, she explained, are identified and defined as ones that have achieved "high ratings" in a prime-time schedule. On this first visit to the United States she found to her surprise that many of the series that did well in that market were unacceptable by Korean standards because of their preoccupation with money or their questionable taste. To her, shows such as *Jerry Springer* (produced and distributed by Universal Television Group/USA Networks, Inc.) and *Change of Heart* (Telepictures Production/Warner Brothers Domestic Television Distribution) are "improper for a Korean audience." Learning of these series' success in the global marketplace, she was confronted with the reality that concepts such as popularity, taste, and value, which in her view coincided in Korean culture, might not do so elsewhere.

In sum, buyers and sellers adapt in numerous ways to regional and local needs and expectations, often based upon informal understandings and arrangements that are the outcome of cultural practices. In a final example, we examine some of the ways in which constraints can arise in the context of joint production ventures between countries. This kind of co-production was devised as a business strategy to manage complications from cultural prescriptions or policy regulations. For example, co-production intended for the European market may be produced in France by a division of a larger international corporation in order to meet French programming quotas (Carveth 1992).

As an illustration, consider the 1998 NATPE seminar titled "On Your Marks in Germany!" in which selected U.S. production company representatives interested in developing co-productions with that country pitched concepts for hypothetical series to German media executives and critics. The seminar was designed to show industry participants how to approach opportunities for joint ventures. The title of a hypothetical action-adventure series was G-5, produced by Michael Mann from *Miami Vice* with Luke Perry as an "attached star." A key feature of the series would be the high-tech G-5, described as "the most sophisticated and elaborate aircraft available today." The story setup is organized around two former successful "top gun" pilots who are best friends and who relied upon unorthodox methods while in the military. With the fall of the Soviet Union, each left the service and went to work for himself. During the course of an attempt to steal jewels previously stolen by the Soviet Union, they encounter a U.S. agent who presses them into service for the U.S. government in exchange for their freedom and who keeps them from being sent to prison for their deed. "There will be considerable humor, but the jeopardy is real," and because of the humor and appeal to a younger audience, it is not a "10 o'clock" show (i.e. intended for adult audiences and dealing with mature themes). One lead role is open, as is the part of the government agent. A flight attendant part is also uncast, and the U.S. producer is considering a popular German actress for the part.

Reactions from the German critics emphasized a variety of local factors that needed to be considered in developing the series for broadcast in their country. Only one executive gave it a favorable reaction. He noted that the mix of action and humor was similar to several currently successful shows in Germany, and commented that there is a big demand for "high-class" productions in Germany, such as one like this. He noted, however, that it would need popular German actors cast in all the unfilled parts.

Of the critics who were less interested, one found the plot too complicated, and said that German audiences "don't want to see the Secret Police again because we've already had all that stuff." This German executive also emphasized that securing financing for an expensive production such as this would be a major stumbling block. Following up on that comment, another German critic noted that competition is already very strong in prime time and that imported and co-produced series are not doing well. He added that this kind of action series is expensive to produce if it is to be done well and that, given its similarity to existing series, it would be unlikely to attract a German investor. Finally, one representative from a German network announced that his company would take a show with a concept and features as proposed, but *never* one that deals with any foreign characters. Noting a trend that has evolved over the past two years, he observed that every German broadcaster with assets prefers to produce series by himself. While acknowledging that local productions should "look American" in quality, he emphasized that the content must be entirely German— locations, actors, and story settings.

Traditionally, the media industry has relied upon a "concentration" strategy for the production and export of media content. Under this approach, all production activities take place within the domestic environment, and the products are exported to other countries. This model prevailed at the time of the 1974 UNESCO report. However, changes since the 1970s in the structure and function of international media institutions required countries to adopt a "dispersing" strategy (Porter 1990), in which production and distribution are spread across participating countries in order to take advantage of resources unique to each of the locations of participating partners. Its intent as a business strategy is to standardize marketing. From Hollywood's vantage point, "such a strategy would allow the United States to overcome host country language, cultural, and institutional barriers by tailoring media product to suit local needs" (Carveth 1992:718). As we saw illustrated above, this would appear to be far easier said than done.

From what we observed at the NATPE seminar, it appears that macro-organizational adaptations such as co-productions must still accommodate middle-range factors if they are to succeed. Whether cultural considerations are anticipated at the time of development or at the time of sale seems to make little difference. Speaking more generally about attempts to standardize global marketing strategy, Akaah (1991) found that consumer characteristics and behavior, the nature of corporate ownership, and the orientation of the corporation all present challenges to the success of such strategies. Although a manager at Paramount told us that as of early 2000, co-productions in foreign countries are accounting for an increasing proportion of international sales, given what we observed at the NATPE seminar, producers still must adapt to local or regional conditions; otherwise they may not be able to get beyond a pitch in efforts to sell to a country with an established locally based industry.[20]

Interestingly, a concept that seems to have achieved considerable success is the newer form of international export known as foreign licensing, which entails the selling of a domestic program concept, such as game shows or "magazine" series. As an international program, the licensed version contains domestic segments but with the buying country's "frame" wrapped around them. Programs like this sell internationally, according to the manager at Paramount, in his view because there is always a demand for United States television programming. Similarly, an international version of MTV sells well abroad, but in this instance a "frame" is created by the United States that allows for "inserts" of the buying country's local artists (but see Banks 1996). While these are considered exports, in content they accede to local interests.[21]

Conclusion: Observations about the Culture World of International Television

Our examination of the international market for television considers how the business and regulatory environment in the early years of the domestic U.S. industry created incentives for program suppliers to seek new sources of revenue in domestic syndication and foreign markets. Pursuit of those alternatives to domestic network markets set events into motion that launched an international industry and, subsequently, a significant scholarly and policy debate. Our analysis takes a "middle-range" approach (Cunningham and Jacka 1994) by using Diana Crane's concept of a culture world to explore the cultural frames that organize the business decisions of buyers and sellers in the international market. In this final section of our chapter we address implications of our analysis for sociological work on the culture of marketplaces and for the cultural imperialism debate.

Examining the international industry of television as a culture world enables us to go beyond strictly business considerations such as risk, transaction costs, and profit, and instead focus upon the forms of cooperation and patterns of collective activity that create television as a cultural product and render it available and accessible to audiences worldwide. To economists, a television series is merely "an asset consisting of a bundle of broadcast rights" (Owen and Wildman 1992:181), but it is clearly much more than that, given the debates that surround the medium. Television is a product that embodies cultural substance reflecting interests and values. It originates in the creative process of writers, and it is evaluated by critics and audiences who apply aesthetic criteria that ultimately determine the fate of individual series. Although those in the business are motivated by profit, a central feature of this culture world is the ways collaboration among individuals with disparate understandings about the cultural product shape its production, distribution, and reception globally.

Our examination of the "production" side of the culture world of international television does not support the contention that the exporting of domestic series from the United States (or other countries, for that matter) to foreign markets readily finds an audience and "naturally" propagates dominant cultural themes and values. If anything, the uncertainty over what does and doesn't work, and what is and is not accepted by audiences in domestic markets (see Bielby and Bielby 1994; DiMaggio 1977), is magnified when attempting to sell a U.S. production to a foreign audience. Our examination of this industry suggests that similar circumstances prevail as well in other exporting countries. Moreover, our work takes current understanding about market uncertainty a step further and reveals how efforts at managing that uncertainty transform the product itself, how it is exported, and how it is received. In a study of the U.S. industry almost 15 years ago, Cantor and Cantor (1986) concluded:

> [we could not] support the thesis that the network of domestic production and syndication ending with overseas distribution is tightly controlled and manipulated by the government, nor for that matter by anyone or any one group. Rather we found a marketing environment that charitably could only be described as chaotic, unruly, and unpredictable, with no one really in charge and no one knowing, for example, why certain programs sell one year and do not move off the shelves the next. (p. 514)

Since then, the international market has become even more diverse and unpredictable. Always underlying any collaborative effort among those in the television industry is a major source of uncertainty—a series' popularity with the audience. However, our study puts us one step closer to understanding the implications of that kind of uncertainty for the cultural content of what gets exported.

Though new institutional arrangements such as co-productions and licensed concepts have proliferated since the Cantors' study, those formats are not always viable. In addition, as nations successfully develop their own industries, preferences for local productions take hold, complicating the export market even further. More than two decades ago, Pool (1977) asserted that audiences would prefer their own domestic productions over imported fare to the extent that a country has an economic base to afford it (see also Straubhaar 1991). That claim, made in the midst of the raging debates over cultural imperialism, proved prescient. In the meantime, analysts who try to make sense of the global marketplace of television have a formidable task ahead of them because of the wide variation in types of programs that are exported, the systems of broadcast in the purchasing countries, cultural differences across those countries, and national policies regulating imports.

In our future research, we need to explore in greater detail how participants in the international marketplace organize their understandings of the business and cultural contexts in which they operate. For example, to what extent are established genre categories useful tools for labeling types of series that are successful in some regions but not others? Are specific genres important in opening new international markets, and are they supplanted by other kinds of programming as the market matures? What local cultural considerations, if any, are made in tailoring packages of exported products to specific countries or regions? How does critical feedback from the international market, including audiences, influence concepts for new series and those already in production? Who do organizational decision makers rely upon for creative and aesthetic judgments about the global market? What control, if any, do exporters have over audience use of products abroad? In sum, as we seek to understand the social construction of the business of exported media, we need to clarify how the properties of the cultural products themselves shape and are influenced by the global market.

Notes

1. For example, in 1998, Disney, which owns ABC, generated $3.8 billion, or 17% of the company's overall revenues, through its international business (McClellan 1999). In contrast, in 1957, foreign distribution for the entire U.S. industry grossed a mere estimated $14 million (Seagrave 1998: 36).

2. Becker (1982) defines art worlds as cooperative action among specialized personnel oriented toward the production of a cultural form. According to Crane (1992: 5, 112), study of popular culture and the arts is best approached through a synthetic model that integrates the study of class culture, media culture, and production of culture. Her model of a "culture world" is comprised of five components: (1) culture creators and their support personnel; (2) conventions or shared understanding about what cultural products should be like; (3) gatekeepers who evaluate cultural products; (4) organizations within which or around which cultural activities take place; and (5) audiences whose taste preferences affect the availability of cultural products.

3. Those from other countries with whom we spoke held titles such as "deputy manager, sales"; "coordinator, acquisitions"; and "head of foreign relations/acquisition." Each had major responsibility for acquiring programs for a network in their country of origin.

4. The first international exchange of television programs took place between the United Kingdom and France in 1950 (Nordenstreng and Varis 1974).

5. Statistics refer to the number of hours of airtime filled in the destination markets. That is, if 20 episodes of a one-hour series are sold in 100 markets, that series accounts for 2,000 hours.

6. A variety of factors prevent developing nations from producing their own programs, thus rendering them dependent on imports. Those factors include "low income resources, lack of industrial infrastructure, lack of support by weak governments, inappropriate models for production, and lack of trained personnel" (Straubhaar 1991: 45; see also Hoskins and Mirus 1988).

7. According to leading proponent Herbert Schiller, the primary assumptions of the original 1960s version of the cultural imperialist theory were: first, that media/cultural imperialism was but one subset of a larger system of imperialism; second, that "what is regarded as cultural output also is ideological and profit-serving to the system at large"; and third, that in the late 20TH century, the corporate economy is increasingly dependent on the media/cultural sector (1991: 14). Schiller argued that the cultural domination that exists today, while still heavily focused on the U.S., "is better understood as transnational corporate cultural domination" (p. 15).

8. See, for example, research on the economic model of television program flows (Hoskins and Mirus 1988; Wildman and Siwek 1988) which builds upon the work of Pool (1977), and the importance of "cultural proximity" (Straubhaar 1991) in explaining patterns of regional program trade.

9. We discuss the 1974 UNESCO report at some length because, though now more than 25 years old, it quickly became a primary source in subsequent scholarly, policy, and cultural critiques of the preeminent presence of American programming abroad. We also believe that many of its key findings have been overlooked by scholars.

10. In a study published two years later, William Read (1976) revealed that two-thirds of the foreign sales of American programs at that time went to countries with the most receivers and the largest audiences, in particular Canada, Australia, Japan, and the United Kingdom. Read's study reconfirmed that the principal direction of programming flow was from the U.S. to the other seven countries. Although it is uncertain whether all countries had an equal opportunity of being included in Read's study, given that its focus was on information from dominant countries, it was, nevertheless, revealing of the regional domination of countries with strong export programs.

11. This strategy is followed even among newly emerging commercial networks. When asked specifically about soap operas, the head of programming acquisition at a Lithuanian network whom we interviewed at the 1998 NATPE convention explained how her network was broadcasting some popular imported soap operas during daytime and others in the evening, depending on the intended audiences.

12. Deputy manager, sales, from the China International TV Corporation, Beijing, China.

13. Antola and Rogers also found that series were not sold to other countries until Mexico purchased the rights.

14. That imported entertainment programming prevailed in so many countries only heightened concern for its effects upon local culture (see, for example, Schiller 1979). The UNESCO report itself notes, however, that "in the selection of most entertainment programs, ideological considerations do not play much of a role, but many countries exercise greater selectivity in purchasing information-type programs" (Varis 1974: 107). Further, since release of the UNESCO report, considerable scholarship on the extent to which audiences are active, critical readers of television-as-text has demonstrated that the mere presence of a particular cultural good does not automatically have profound cultural or ideological effects on local audiences. In their meta-analysis of the effects of imported programming on television audiences, Michael Elasmar and John Hunter (1997) conclude that, "At most, foreign TV exposure may have a very weak impact upon audience members" (64; see also Ware and Dupagne 1995; Yaple and Korzenny 1989).

15. Indeed, Pierre Juneau (1993) argues that "the overall success of the American audiovisual industry rests on its ability to produce a type of entertainment that appeals to large, anonymous, undifferentiated audiences and that is unencumbered by forms of cultural content that might be an obstacle to portability" (p. 19).

16. Telenovelas are the Latin form of the U.S. daytime serial (soap operas). Each consists of a long-running serial narrative that can be traced back to prior melodramatic forms, that both originated in and were sponsored by U.S.-based companies producing domestic products (Lopez 1995). However, whereas soap operas are open-ended and potentially limitless, telenovelas have a specific number of episodes, achieving narrative closure through definite endings (see Barker 197).

17. Unlike U.S. soap operas, telenovelas typically organize their advertising campaigns around popular actors cast in lead roles (see Harrington and Bielby 1995; Lopez 1995).

18. Most Latin American telenovelas are 100–150 episodes long, in contrast to the "endless middle" characteristic of U.S. soap operas (see Allen 1985; Lopez 1995).

19. While the mandate has been lifted, a representative to NATPE from China International TV Corporation informed us that Chinese buyers today prefer telenovelas over U.S. soap operas. In their view, American soaps "don't work" because "they focus too much on the individual, and not the 'dynasty'" (i.e., family; see also Hornik 1996). For that very reason, the former prime-time American series *Dynasty* has been very popular in China.

20. Co-productions were launched in the 1980s as a viable approach to foreign markets. Although they have been characterized by one observer as a "low-volume, mid-budget business" (Grantham 1999), they continue to proliferate because they are an effective means of responding to rising production costs and the complicated constraints involved in exporting a solely U.S.-owned and produced product to foreign markets. Precise statistics on the prevalence of co-productions are not available. However, their increasing popularity is evidenced by the attention devoted to them by industry seminars and international law firms that specialize in organizing such deals. Coverage of new co-production deals has become a regular feature of industry trade publications (see, for example, Leventhal 1997; Williams 1997; Edmunds 1996).

21. An interesting failure in the export of existing program concepts was observed when Telemundo attempted to revamp its prime-time programming in order to attract a younger, more Americanized Latino audience. One of its failed series was an adaptation of *Charlie's Angels*, that had a hip young Latino cast but relied upon old scripts for its plots. Though the audience's rejection was in part a reaction to the dropping of Telemundo's highly popular prime-time mainstay, telenovelas, from its evening fare, another reason for the failure was

that the series' concept proved to be of little interest to the targeted audience. One high-level industry source from a rival network who is familiar with the Latino market also suggested to us that the overly sexualized female characters were seen as offensive by some sub-populations of the Latino audience. The reasons for the failure of this series underscore the subtle ways in which cultural constraints operate, even for those within the cultural system (see, for example, Faber, O'Guinn, and Meyer 1986).

References

Akaah, I. (1991) 'Strategy standardization in international marketing: an empirical investigation of its degree of use and correlates,' *Journal of Global Marketing*, 4, 2: 39–62.

Allen, R. C. (1985) *Speaking of Soap Operas*, Chapel Hill, NC: University of North Carolina Press.

Allen, R. C. (1996) 'As the world turns: television soap operas and global media culture.' pp. 110–127 in E. G. McAnany and K. T. Wilkenson, (eds.) *Mass Media and Free Trade: NAFTA and the Cultural Industries*, Austin: University of Texas Press.

Allen, R. C. (1997) 'As the world tunes in: an international perspective,' pp. 111–119 in The Museum of Television and Radio, *Worlds Without End: The Art and History of the Soap Opera*, New York: Harry N. Abrams, Inc.

Ang, I. (1996) *Living Room Wars: Rethinking Media Audiences for a Postmodern World*, London: Routledge.

Antola, L. and E. M. Rogers (1984) 'Television flows in Latin America,' *Communication Research*, 11, 2: 183–202.

Banks, J. (1996) *Monopoly Television: MTV's Quest to Control the Music*, Boulder, CO: Westview Press.

Barker, C. (1997) *Global Television: An Introduction*, Oxford, UK: Blackwell.

Becker, H. (1982) *Art Worlds*, Berkeley: University of California Press.

Bielby, W. T. and Bielby, D. D. (1994) '"All hits are flukes": institutionalized decision-making and the rhetoric of network prime-time program development,' *American Journal of Sociology*, 99, 5: 1287–1313.

Borchers, H. (1989) 'Watching US-produced soap operas in Germany: on some implications for cross-cultural understanding,' pp. 268–286 in P. Funke (ed.), *Understanding the USA: A Cross-Cultural Perspective*, Germany: Gunter Narr Verlag.

Boudreaux, R. (1998) 'Actors may have the last word in strike by Italian dubbers,' *Los Angeles Times*, September 19: A9.

Cantor, M. G. and Cantor, J.M. (1986) 'American television in the international marketplace,' *Communication Research*, 13, 3: 509–520.

Carveth, R. (1992) 'The reconstruction of the global media marketplace,' *Communication Research* 19, 6: 705–723.

Chang, L. (2000) 'Cracking China's huge TV market,' *Wall Street Journal*, August 1: B–1,4.

Crane, D. (1992) *The Production of Culture: Media and the Urban Arts*, Newbury Park, CA: Sage.

Crofts, S. (1995) 'Global neighbors,' pp. 98–121 in R. C. Allen (ed.) *To Be Continued: Soap Operas Around the World*, London: Routledge.

Cunningham, S. and Jacka, E. (1994) 'Neighborly relations? Cross-cultural reception analysis and Australian soaps in Britain,' *Cultural Studies*, 8: 509–526.

Davis, L. L. (1997) 'Prime-time in Ecuador: national, regional television outdraws U.S. programming,' *Journal of American Culture*, 20, 1: 9–18.

De la Garde, R. (1993) 'Dare we compare?' pp. 25–64 in R. de la Garde, W. Gilsdorf, and I. Wechselmann with J. Lerche-Nielsen (eds.) *Small Nations, Big Neighbor: Denmark and Quebec/Canada Compare Notes on American Popular Culture*, London: John Libbey & Co., Ltd.

DiMaggio, P. J. (1977) 'Market structure, the creative process, and popular culture: toward an organizational reinterpretation of mass culture theory,' *Journal of Popular Culture*, 11: 433–51.

Edmunds, M. (1996) 'Co-Prods targeted to connect internationally,' *Variety*, 364 (9), September 30:171.

Elasmar, M. G. and Hunter, J. E. (1997) 'The impact of foreign TV on a domestic audience: a meta-analysis,' *Communication Yearbook*, 20:47–69.

Faber, R., O'Guinn, J. T. C. and Meyer, T. P. (1986) 'Diversity in the ethnic media audience: a study of Spanish language broadcast preference in the U.S.,' *International Journal of Intercultural Relations*, 10: 347–359.

Grantham, B. (1999) 'The changing international television marketplace: co-production opportunities for American producers,' Paper presented at the Sedona Conference, Sedona, Arizona, March 25–26, 1999. <www.rmslaw.com>

Harrington, C. L. and Bielby, D. D. (1995) *Soap Fans: Pursuing Pleasure and Making Meaning in Everyday Life*, Philadelphia: Temple University Press.

Hornik, S. (1996) 'Soaps get big in China.' *Soap Opera Now!*, January 15:3.

Hoskins, C. and Mirus, R. (1988) 'Reasons for the U.S. dominance of the international trade in television programmes,' *Media, Culture and Society*, 10: 499–515.

Juneau, P. (1993) 'Prologue: overview of issues in culture and national identity,' pp. 15–21 in R. de la Garde, W. Gilsdorf and I. Wechselmannn, with J. Lerche-Nielsen (eds.), *Small Nations, Big Neighbors: Denmark and Quebec/Canada Compare Notes on American Popular Culture*, London: John Libbey & Co. Ltd.

Levanthal, L. (1997) 'Cable nets look abroad for profits, partners,' *Broadcasting and Cable*, December 8: 105–6.

Liebes, T. and Katz, E. (1990) *The Export of Meaning: Cross-Cultural Readings of Dallas*, New York: Oxford University Press.

Lopez, A. M. (1995) 'Our welcomed guests: telenovelas in Latin America,' pp. 256–275 in R. C. Allen (ed.), *To Be Continued . . . Soap Operas Around the World*, New York: Routledge.

Matelski, M. J. (1999) *Soap Operas Worldwide: Cultural and Serial Realities*, Jefferson, NC: McFarland & Co., Inc.

McAnany, E. G. and A. C. La Pastina (1994) 'Telenovela audiences: a review and methodological critique of Latin American research,' *Communication Research* 21: 828–849.

McAnany, E. G. and Wilkenson, K. T. (1992) 'From cultural imperialists to takeover victims? Questions on Hollywood's buyouts from the critical tradition,' *Communication Research*, 19: 724–748.

McClellan, S. (1999) 'Iger takes on global duties,' *Broadcasting and Cable*, March 1: 12.

Mohammadi, A. (1997) *International Communication and Globalization*, London: Sage.

Montgomery, K. C. (1989) *Target Primetime: Advocacy Groups and the Struggle over Entertainment Television*, New York: Oxford University Press.

Mowlana, H. (1997) *Global Information and World Communication*, 2nd edition. London: Sage.

Museum of Television and Radio (1997) *Worlds Without End: The Art and History of Soap Opera*, New York: Harry N. Abrams, Inc.

Nordenstreng, K. and Varis, T. (1974) 'Television Traffic—A One Way Street?' *Reports and Papers on Mass Communication* No. 70, Paris: UNESCO.

O'Donnell, H. (1999) *Good Times, Bad Times: Soap Operas and Society in Western Europe*, London: Leicester University Press.

Owen, B. M. and Wildman, S. S. (1992) *Video Economics*, Cambridge, MA: Harvard University Press.

Pool, I. (1977) 'The changing flow of television,' *Journal of Communication*, 27, 1: 139–149.

Porter, M. (1990) *The Competitive Advantage of Nations*, New York: Free Press.

Prehn, O. and Jensen, E. F. (1993) 'Public service and the television marketplace: the case of the Nordic countries in a changing European television landscape,' pp. 217–235 in R. de la Garde, W. Gilsdorf, and I. Wechselmann with J. Lerche-Nielsen (eds.), *Small Nations, Big Neighbors: Denmark and Quebec/Canada Compare Notes on American Popular Culture*, London: John Libbey & Co., Ltd.

Read, W. H. (1976) 'Global TV flow: another look,' *Journal of Communication*, 26 (Summer): 69–73.

Schiller, H. I. (1979) 'Transnational media and national development,' pp. 21–32 in K. Nordenstreng and H. I. Schiller (eds.) *National Sovereignty and International Communication*, Norwood, NJ: Ablex.

Schiller, H. I. (1991) 'Not yet the post-imperialist era,' *Critical Studies in Mass Communication*, 8:13–28.

Schwoch, J. (1993) 'Cold War, hegemony, postmodernism: American television and the world-system,' *Quarterly Review of Film and Video*, 14, 3: 9–24.

Seagrave, K. (1998) *American Television Abroad: Hollywood's Attempt to Dominate World Television*, Jefferson, NC: McFarland & Company, Inc.

Straubhaar, J. D. (1991) 'Beyond media imperialism: asymmetrical interdependence and cultural proximity,' *Critical Studies in Mass Communication*, 8: 39–59.

Van der Weel, A. (1990) 'Subtitling and the SBS audience,' *Media Information Australia*, (May, No. 56):22–26.

Varis, T. (1974) 'Global traffic in television,' *Journal of Communication*, 24, 10: 102–109.

Varis, T. (1984) 'The international flow of television programs,' *Journal of Communication*, 34: 143–152.

Varis, T. (1986). 'Patterns of television program flow in international relations,' pp. 55–65 in J. Becker, G. Hedebro and L Paldan (eds.), *Communication and Domination: Essays in Honor of Herbert I. Schiller*, Norwood, NJ: Ablex Publishing.

Ware, W. and Dupagne, M.. (1995) 'Effects of U.S. television programs on foreign audiences: a meta-analysis,' *Journalism Quarterly*, 71:947–959.

Wildman, S. and Siwek, S. E. (1988) *International Trade in Films and Television Programs*, Cambridge, MA: Ballinger.

Williams, M. (1997) 'Kirch programming spans the world,' *Variety*, 365 (10), January 13:122.

Yaple, P. and Korzenny, F. (1989) 'Electronic mass media effects across cultures,' pp. 295–317 in M.K. Asante and W.B. Gudykunst (eds.), *Handbook of International and Intercultural Communication*, Newbury Park, CA: Sage.

14

Globalization of Cultural Production

The Transformation of Children's Animated Television, 1980 to 1995

David Hubka

Many of the discussions about the nature of globalization, such as the extent of cultural homogenization or heterogeneity that results from globalization (Featherstone 1990; McChesney 1999) and the nature of the process itself as a form of cultural imperialism or as a syncretization of local and global processes (Robertson 1992), are very general and only superficially informed by knowledge and understanding of the actual activities, relationships, and processes involved in economic and cultural transactions between global actors in specific culture industries and institutions. Theorists writing about the globalization of culture have called for a substantive focus on the practical instances of globalization, through which processes of cultural integration and differentiation operate (Featherstone 1990). Notably, Roland Robertson (1992) argues that globalization is best understood through a mapping of actual intersocietal and intercultural encounters and that these should deal with the "processes of cultural syncretization—more specifically . . . the ways in which problems of particularism and universalism have been addressed" (p. 41).

The case of children's animated television provides an opportunity to examine both economic and cultural factors that led to an intensification of cross-national collaboration in this form of television production as well as the strategies that resulted in innovations in programming that were compatible with consumer tastes in countries that were culturally very diverse. The complexity of the global networks in this industry, which includes both large and small companies from large and small countries, means that these networks cannot be characterized in terms of a simple center-periphery model. Analysis of these materials also shows that elements of homogenization and heterogeneity may exist in the same segment of the industry.

Though much research on cultural production tends toward reductionism or overdetermination, prioritizing, for example, industrial, regulatory, or content features, the current model I will discuss assumes that cultural production is best understood through examination of the intersections of the various spheres (regulation, production, consumption, representation, and identity). My analysis here focuses on production strategies but tries to place these in a context of regulatory conditions and patterns of consumption. Such important research questions as the specific comparative readings or interpretations of program content made by different individuals and different audiences are beyond the scope of this chapter.

Children's animated television[1] in the 1980s and early 1990s, as shown in the sections below, was characterized by an intensification of international production and distribution, substantial growth in the industry worldwide, and the development of new production and programming strategies for new global markets. Though the international production and trade of animated television began as early as the 1950s,[2] changes that occurred between 1980 and 1995 can be seen as marking a new period of globalization for the industry and its consumers. In addition to the increased complexity of international trade relations centered on this type of television programming, innovations in production strategies, such as international co-production, and new methods of producing alternate versions of programs for different markets led to improvements in the cultural "fit" between globally distributed programs and local audiences.

The case of animation is distinct from that of other types of television production, since the production and representational features of animation make it more adaptable to international postproduction techniques. For example, voice dubbing is considerably more effective with animation than with live action; animation allows for more consistent continuity and provides for more effective editing and potential resequencing of scenes. The numerous stages of animation production are more easily divided across national labor markets, providing a better basis for such production innovations as international co-productions, which grew from uncommon to commonplace through the 1980s and mid-1990s. As a result, though transnational corporations tended to dominate the international trade of animated television before and after the 1980s, smaller producers were in many cases able to participate in and benefit from global trade. Co-production arrangements involving new and varied forms of creative collaboration were an important mechanism in this change. Moreover, globalized trade and distribution in this instance did not involve a strict homogenization of cultural production, but rather the development of additional strategies that worked to mediate the needs of producers and consumers in different ways.

The current analysis focuses on the types of strategies employed by animated television producers in the course of expanding and competing for global markets in the 1980s and 1990s. This includes a review of some of the different contingencies of local consumer audiences that provided motivations for producers to seek new production and content strategies for children's animated television. The first section describes some of the pressures and barriers faced by distributors, including differences in consumer preferences for certain program features, government regulation in the form of quotas, and increasing competition. The discussion then turns to some of the strategies that producers developed to accommodate differences in consumer markets, with a focus on the rise of international co-production partnerships for children's animated television programs. Finally, I look at the development of program versioning—the production of alternative versions of programs, which differed according to the specific requirements of each consumer market.

Barriers to International Distribution of Animated Television Programming

Though international production and consumption of television animation increased in the 1980s and early 1990s, these processes did not replace local with imported programs and consumer practices. In many cases, persistent barriers to importing programs remained because of critical differences in consumer cultures regarding television and children's programs. These barriers included the existence of relatively narrow schedules for children's programs in several markets, and differences in consumer preferences for such features as faster or slower pacing, as well as other characteristics attributed in many cases to local, traditional styles of animation. Regulation played a significant and complex role in the globalization of children's television during this time. Government regulation and industry attempts at self-regulation have had various influences on each instance of importing television into a national market. With respect to children's programs, government regulatory bodies and pressure groups tended to focus on content issues such as violence, but also worked to protect local production of all forms of television through, for instance, broadcast quotas for local production.

Scheduling Differences in Different Markets

Trade sources noted difficulties in distributing children's programs into certain markets, as a result of relatively fewer opportunities to broadcast. For instance, in 1983, Group W Promotions (the full owner of Filmation in 1983) reported that Britain's ITV had bought the entire inventory of He-Man programs, making the sale the largest importation of television animation to date in the United Kingdom, "a rare bulk purchase for any foreign network" (*Variety* 1983a:40). However, the company reported that:

> ITV won't strip He-Man the way American stations that have taken it into syndication will . . . because stripping is alien to the British way of programming . . . so while American stations have agreed to take eight runs of each of the 65 half-hours over two years (on a barter arrangement; no cash will change hands), ITV has purchased eight runs of each episode over five years. (p. 40)

This difference in scheduling represented significant differences in the way in which British children consumed He-Man; though this involved regular scheduling, viewing was far less frequent. Similarly, *TV World* noted limitations in broadcast practices within the South Korean television broadcasting industry in 1979, reporting very limited telecast hours—daily broadcasts began in the late afternoon, and a few hours earlier on Sundays and holidays; broadcasters provided only one hour of children's programs per day. For the most part, programs (variety, quiz shows, action serials) were locally produced by a single production team; broadcasts were supplemented with U.S. or Japanese cartoons dubbed into Korean (Constant 1979:30).

Another barrier to international distribution of children's programs was the mixing of child and adult audiences. In some nations, for instance, the fragmentation of child and adult audiences was less straightforward because domestic viewing habits included the entire family, or parents allowed children to stay up later than in U.S. markets. For instance, in 1979, *TV World* reported on the problems with scheduling for children's television in Hong Kong and described the findings of a local research group:

> Separate children's programs are largely meaningless in Hong Kong, where half the primary school children are at school in the morning, and the other half in the afternoon . . . The half-hearted attempts to set up children's programs in Hong Kong are . . . an example of paying respect to an ideal imported from elsewhere. We all know good BBC children are in bed by eight o'clock and that adult viewing can safely begin . . . In Hong Kong children and young people do not live in a world separate from adults. . . . [They] see their television right through prime time (ending 10:30–11 P.M.) every evening. (Tillman 1979:24)

Again, in 1985, *Variety* reported on difficulties accessing Asian television markets by U.S. producers, noting, for instance, that Thailand had invoked a television broadcast blackout between 6:30 and 8 P.M. "in the interests of children and families" (Murdoch 1985:46). Malaysian state restrictions also limited the broadcast of certain episodes of children's programs such as *The Hardy Boys* and some cartoons because they included dancing (p. 46).

Differences in Consumer Preferences

Aside from practices and regulations of scheduling, persistent consumer preferences for local production and animation styles occasionally presented barriers to international distribution. Consumer tastes and preferences for domestically produced animation programs remained strong in several important markets, such as the United Kingdom and Japan. And *Variety* reported in 1990 that animation production in Europe was booming and noted that there was a major trend favoring classic European animation over U.S. style or globally acceptable products:

> It's unlikely that these new European products will supplant the likes of Mickey Mouse or the Teenage Mutant Ninja Turtles (on course to rake in 22 million United Kingdom pounds in paraphernalia sales throughout Europe this year, according to one industry analyst) in the hearts and minds of European children, but the hope is that some of them at least will be explicitly European. (Hardy 1990:55).

Similar shifts in consumer preferences with respect to U.S. programs in Asia occurred in the mid-1980s. In 1985, *Variety* reported that sales of U.S. programs to Asia were softening, as local production was on the increase. Australian MCA's Pal Cleary argued that since U.S. programs were produced for U.S. audiences, it was surprising that they had sold abroad in the first place. Paramount's George Mooratoff noted that U.S. programs sold abroad at costs that were low relative to original production and had served as a platform for broadcasters to venture into local production: "With one or two exceptions, and excluding Japan, US product internationally does subsidize local production" (Murdoch 1985:46). Therefore, in some cases, consumer markets for local animation programs were supported by the markets created by the global distribution of television animation.[3]

In 1986, *TV World* described DIC's animation style as having a "Euro-look," even though most of the programs were produced in the United States and Japan. These variations in international consumer demands in terms of stylistic features persisted in some markets. For instance, *TV World* reported on the continued failure of Japanese television animation to obtain distribution in the United States. Its success was limited by what North American programmers saw as the inappropriate content of much television animation in Japan. A spokesperson for Tohoku Shinsha noted that the company had not succeeded in selling Japanese animation programs to the United States because:

> Americans don't want their children to watch the kind of animation in which there are machines which are destructive or where there is cruelty to animals or violence involving human beings. Somehow, these things are accepted in Japan, but they are certainly not seen in the same light overseas. (De Stain 1986:22)

Preferences in the features of children's animated television also varied widely from one market to the next (e.g., violent vs. "soft" content). One of the most often mentioned was pacing, usually cited as a problem for those who wanted to sell programs in the U.S. market.

In 1979, *TV World* quoted Mary Alice Dwyer, director of daytime and children's programs for NBC-TV: "I'm not sure that foreign packagers understand our marketplace," and noted that foreign programs often lacked the pacing required for commercial broadcast in the U.S. (1979a: 52). In 1979, *TV World* also noted that U.S. and Latin American markets required faster pacing than France (1979b). In 1983, Paul Talbot of Fremantle noted that U.S. audiences "demand fast involvement" and advised European producers to drop the theatrical tradition of slow openings (Friedman 1983:58). In 1988, *Variety* reported differences in the requirements of program pacing in Germany:

> While the slow pacing of most Tuetonic tot television eliminates chances of sales to America, West Germany's largest purveyor of children's programming, Hamburg-based Igelfilm Productions, managed to get a foot in the door with livelier offerings to Nickelodeon. (Gill 1988:121)

The trade magazine also quotes the head of Igelfilm Productions, Christian Lehman:

> All of the slow-paced animation or live-action pieces that Europeans seem to thrive on are rejected out of hand by all the US buyers I've ever encountered. Step up the pace and you've got a chance in the American market. (Gill 1988:122)

The obverse was also true in that the features associated with U.S.-style animated programs kept them out of certain markets. In 1991, *Variety* reported on one of the "toughest markets to crack" for U.S. animation producers and distributors, quoting Brian Lacey, marketing director for Zodiac Entertainment:

> In Singapore, FBC is the only broadcaster, the only game in town. The German market, which is much bigger since reunification, has a very high standard for children's programming. They really take a critical look at everything—storyline, theme, color. Scandinavia is very difficult for cultural reasons. They like story-driven kids programs. In their eyes, a lot of American product comes up short in pacing and content, or they feel the cartoon's humor is too fast-paced for their children. (1991b)

Changing Regulatory Pressures and the Encouragement of Co-Production

Regulation of television broadcasting for children was not a new phenomenon in the 1980s. Hamelink (1995), for instance, notes that the key policy orientation of the 1980s worldwide was toward deregulation. The trend was away from a regulated, public-service orientation, and toward a market-driven environment for the commercial trade of these services. This trend, furthermore, worked to create global tensions between the perceptions of children's programs as a public good and their use as a means of commodifying child audiences, and between the views that television was a mechanism for developing citizenship and political community and a mechanism for developing consumerism and economic community. By the late 1980s, however, the trend toward the global deregulation of commercial television worldwide had resulted in expanded broadcast hours, expanded hours of broadcast for commercial programs, and an increased demand for children's programs that had often to be filled with imports.

On the other hand, deregulation did not involve a straightforward opening up of foreign markets for all products. While commercial broadcast hours expanded and non-commercial public broadcast declined, local content quotas tended to remain in place. This type of regulation, in turn, contributed directly to the rise of co-production partnerships. For instance, according to Westinghouse Broadcasting's director of international sales and marketing, the international marketing of *Teenage Mutant Ninja Turtles* in 1991 was affected strongly by quota regulations. As a result, he noted:

> We really look at it in terms of co-productions . . . we definitely spend a lot of time thinking about it. You can't move a show otherwise. We really quiz them on what they need before we produce. (Busby 1991:70)

Production quotas also changed in response to the rise of co-production partnerships. For instance, in 1989, *TV World* reported on the globalization trend in television animation, and the effects on the Canadian animation industry: "The animation market—as other markets—is changing substantially with rationalization taking place on a global level" (Lavers 1989b:27). Following the trend toward the international division of labor around television animation, the Canadian Radio and Television Commission

(Canada's broadcast regulator) devised a point system to evaluate qualifications for Canadian content. A point each was given for Canadian direction, scriptwriting, first or second voice, design supervision, layout and background, camera operator, music composer, and editor. A total of six points, as well as the key animation being done in Canada, would qualify a program as Canadian (Lavers 1989b).

Government and public advocacy organizations encouraged and assisted in the creation of co-production partnerships. For instance, the demand for children's programming was addressed in 1988 by the Australian Foundation for Children's Television, a public advocacy organization that worked to improve children's programs by developing international co-production as well as marketing partnerships for existing programs. The organization's strategy evolved in response to government regulations in the form of tax incentives. Dr. Patricia Edgar, the director of the organization, noted:

> I don't believe we can raise a presale of 70% (needed under current government tax subsidies for production investment) so we're looking at international ways of co-financing with people with common interests. [Children's program producers] are disadvantaged in the market. The foundation has been able to make up the difference with overseas sales, but prices are down, so we've got to look for partners that are compatible to help defray costs. (*Variety* 1988a:118)

In 1994, *TV World* reported on the formation of the European Children's Television Centre, an international organization focused on the increasingly commercial environment of children's television that worked to develop a less commercial, international co-production series, *Teensat*, a teen magazine program (Akyuz 1994). Government organizations also worked to develop co-production partnerships as a form of economic stimulation. For instance, in 1991 *Variety* reported on the television animation boom in Wales, describing the positive influence of EVA, "an animation development and production venture with partners in Belgium, Germany and France. It was set up under the auspices of the European Community's Media 92 project" (1991b:71).

Variety attributed much of the boom in the European international trade in animation to Cartoon, part of the Media 92 program launched by the European Commission in 1989. Cartoon was dedicated to creating a European producer-buyer forum to enhance financing of animation production, and, as *Variety* noted, "it has also established a comprehensive pan-European animation data-base, and encourages animation studios to form multinational European Economic Interest Groups to undertake substantial projects" (Hardy 1990:55). Cartoon's greatest success was in television animation; it secured financing for 27 projects (135 program hours) from European broadcasters (p. 55). *Variety* quoted BBC Enterprises executive Michael Shields as saying about Cartoon: "This is good for the producers. Its teaching them how to present themselves to their international partners, and that is really needed" (Williams 1991:66). According to *Variety*, Cartoon was created to encourage and support small-scale production in an industry in which marketing efforts require great sophistication and resources: "Throughout the 1980s, European animation was largely a cottage industry of artisan-run companies unfamiliar with the requirements of producers and programs outside their own territory" (p. 63). Cartoon supported small and medium-size produc-ers to form European Studio Groupings that would make cross-border activity easier to conduct. One Spanish producer commented on the success of the ESGs: "All you need is for the BBC to know your British partner in a grouping, and you find yourself involved in work for the main British network . . . work that otherwise you might not have had access to" (p. 66). The Cartoon forum also provided links between publish-ers and merchandisers, such as Per Grubert of the Danish-based international media company Gutenbergus Group, who approached La Frabrique regarding *Souris Souris*, suggesting that the concept might transfer to publishing.

The international trade in children's animated television in the 1980s and 1990s saw global expansion of markets, but broadcast schedules were not uniform, and consumer preferences for certain styles and features of animation persisted. Some audiences maintained strict preferences for local programs, and provided some of the motivation for producers to seek new ways of producing programs that would appeal to diverse global audiences. The changing environment for producers included a need to attend to regulatory pressures in order to be better able to enter new markets. These factors were all critical in the rise of international co-productions.

Strategies for Overcoming Barriers to International Distribution

International Co-Production

The globalization of children's animated television led to decreased importance of national consumer markets and an emphasis on producing for international distribu-tion. The president of Hearst Entertainment Distribution noted in 1991 that the indus-try could no longer assume that the sale of product to the primary U.S. networks was the greatest source of profits; now, "everyone knows that the secondary market is where you make your profit" (Busby 1991:41). Financial incentives to access foreign markets motivated important developments in international production strategies, most notably an intensification of the international division of labor. Animation production is par-ticularly well suited to an international division of labor, since the various stages of production can easily be carried out in different international locations. This flexibility allowed producers to develop international production strategies earlier and more extensively than producers of other types of television programs.

Co-productions were often developed as a means of enhancing the marketability of programs by incorporating, through shared creative control, an improved fit between product and consumers from different markets. The following section describes the financial motives for international co-production partnerships, which often, but not exclusively, involved access to U.S. financing and markets. Motives for co-productions often included the collaborative cross-marketing of animation and toy products, and the potential to access popular characters. But the sharing of creative control was also a secondary motive related to financial concerns, since access to international markets required specific attention to different cultural conditions.

The Financial Push for Co-Production

Internationally, the rise of co-production partnerships in the 1980s and early 1990s was due in large part to cost benefits and increased profit returns. For instance, in 1987, Guider reported in *Variety* on increases in international television co-production arrangements: "In the English-speaking world, new alliances are being forged that were unthinkable five, even two years ago" (p. 3). They noted that the increases were due to shrinkages in field operations of the three U.S. networks, the increases in numbers of private broadcasters in Europe and dramatic increases in production costs worldwide. Smaller producers were taking advantage of the deals for financial reasons, as well as in order to increase their prestige worldwide (Guider 1987:547). Similarly, in 1988, *TV World* noted that Canada's Cine Group had been kept viable almost exclusively through animated television co-productions with France (*Sharky and George*), Belgium (*Ovide and the Gang*) and Yugoslavia (*The Little Flying Bears*) (Lavers 1988).

In the early 1980s, the financial incentives for co-production partnerships were complex, but often stemmed from differences in labor supplies. For instance, in 1981, *Variety* reported on the co-production agreement between BRB International of Spain and Nippon Animation of Japan to produce *The Three Musketeers* — BRB would hold world distribution rights, excluding the Far East. Manager Claudio Biern Boyd noted:

> At first, we considered doing the series in Spain, but Spanish animators are simply not equipped for this kind of large-scale project. You need art directors, animators, a whole professional team. It took another company two and a half years to produce *Don Quixote* and that's just too long. On *The Three Musketeers*, budgeted at $3,000,000, the Japanese will deliver one segment a week. If you did it in Spain, the series would take four years to produce. There are good animators in Spain, but they are lacking the infrastructure for doing big jobs. (p. 44)

Different financial conditions contributed to the tendencies of national producers to seek international co-production partnerships. On the other hand, the rise of alternate television broadcasting systems in the United States, which initially had smaller budgets than network producers, provided motivation for seeking co-production partners. For example, in 1988, *Variety* noted that basic cable service Nickelodeon had to keep its costs down and sought international co-production for alternate sources of production funding (e.g., *Count Duckula* and *Dangermouse* were co-produced with Thames Television in the United Kingdom) (*Variety* 1988c:115).

Similarly, a lack of nationally based investment funds was a common motivation for developing international co-productions. In 1990, *Variety* reported that the animation industry in France was booming: three times more animation was produced in 1989 than in 1988. However, the greatest problem in animation production in France in 1990 was identified as production costs. Pierre Sissman, animation president for Walt Disney France, which opened in 1989, estimated that production costs in 1990 were 150 percent of those in the U.S. As a result, French animation producers tended to use foreign subcontractors. Jacques Peyrache, head of Pixbox and president of the Producteurs du Film d'Animation (a group with 19 French producers as members, aiming to promote French animation) estimated that only 5 percent of French animation had been produced entirely within French borders (Kindred 1990:58). Moreover, rising costs led increasing numbers of French producers to turn to international co-productions (largely with European partners).

The desire to access the U.S. market, in which broadcast opportunities were proliferating, was an important motivation for co-production partnerships with the United States. Moreover, while U.S. animated products tended to dominate international markets both prior to and after the 1980s, the preference for them was not universal, even in the United States.[4] Throughout the 1980s, animation from other locales gained access to U.S. consumer markets.[5] For instance, Gaumont (a French production-distribution multimedia international conglomerate) gained access to the U.S. Saturday morning schedule in 1981 through an international television co-production with Hanna-Barbera based on Gaumont's already internationally popular Smurfs. In 1983, DIC Enterprises, a division of Audiovisuel Enterprises of France, became the first overseas company to sell an animated series directly to a United States network. *The Littles*, based on a Scholastic Books line, was in production for distribution on ABC's Saturday morning schedule. DIC also produced the syndicated *Inspector Gadget*, which had landed Kellogg sponsorship in the United States, and represented Kellogg's largest media buy for the year. DIC, according to *Variety*, was beginning to play an important role in U.S. television, driving a wedge into the control exercised by the major U.S. Saturday morning animation television producers: Hanna-Barbera, Marvel, and Filmation. DIC had created its own merchandising division and had closed 10 licensing deals on *Inspector Gadget* (Hollinger 1983:61). This trend continued through the 1980s, as various producers of television animation expanded sales beyond their home markets.

Large-scale U.S. producers like Marvel were also more interested in working with collaborators to improve their own domestic and international sales. *Variety* reported that the 1983 MIP (Market for International Programs—an important annual international television trade conference) was marked by an increase in development contacts for co-productions among smaller independent producers (Loftus 1983:92). Later, in 1986, *Variety* reported on the success of a series of co-production projects between U.S. Sunbow Productions and Marvel Productions (*GI Joe, My Little Pony, Transformers, Inhumanoids* and *Jem*—all highly successful) (Gelman 1986). The success of Sunbow and Marvel productions was enormous in the 1980s: "Sunbow's shows are currently on the air in almost every European territory and are also transmitted on Pan European channels including Sky Channel, Superchannel, The Children's Channel and Tele-5" (Friedman 1988:60). After only three years of operation, Sunbow's international distribution arm had sold programs in more than 80 territories (p. 60). Speculating on the reasons for these successes, *Variety* noted: "The strength of the relationship has been such that they've been able to talk well with and to each other, and each brings a lot of expertise to the table" (Gelman 1986:81).

The desire to access U.S. markets through co-productions with U.S. producers was not an attractive proposition for everyone in the business. For instance, Nelvana (a Canadian firm) head Michael Hirsch noted that international television co-productions were "more expensive than productions done for the US" (Ayscough 1990:64). The Nelvana/ Cinar (of France) co-production of *Babar* cost between C$350,000 and C$400,000 per episode, while each episode of *Beetlejuice* (a U.S.-Canada co-production) cost about C$300,000. On the other hand, co-productions tended to sell better in Europe, and, *Variety* concluded, "while the production price tag is significantly higher for [European] co-productions, the long-term profits can be greater too" (Ayscough 1990:64). As a result, Nelvana had several programs in development, and intended to "stick to its European co-production structure for up-coming series *Rupert Bear*" (YTC in Canada, TVS in the United Kingdom, and Ellipse in France) with no U.S. presale (p. 64). Similarly, Montreal-based Crayon, a subsidiary of Cinar Group of France, had been engaged in several co-production projects with French producers and had largely avoided U.S. sales, using money from the European presale to finance production (p. 64).

In another instance, the Children's Television Workshop (producer of *Sesame Street*) engaged in a series of international co-production partnerships in the 1980s and early 1990s as a means of developing exclusively non-U.S. markets. This included an exchange of program segments between all national partners, as well as locally tailored "inserts." The new trend toward co-productions was described by the Children's Television Workshop as not strictly a means of keeping costs down, but also as a means of improving the cultural fit between programs and consumers (Woodman 1986:19).

While lower production costs and co-financing were an important motivation for seeking international co-production partnerships, an interest in increasing profits by gaining rights to use popular animation characters was also evident from the early 1980s. For example, in 1980, *Variety* described the continued prestige of Disney characters in feature distributorship internationally, as well as increases in co-production arrangements to access popular characters. In 1980, Toei of Japan was in negotiation with Marvel Comics for an equal co-production partnership in developing television and feature animation around *Spider-Man*, *The Incredible Hulk*, and *Captain America*. Toei was willing to make an unprecedented initial investment of $5 million for the lead-in co-production (Werba 1980:38).

Co-Production and Creative Collaboration

However, while better financing and greater access to markets, as well as the enhanced marketability of programs, provided primary motives for co-production partnerships, an important, related, secondary motive was the desire to include a cultural collaborator in the creative process to help create a product that would appeal to consumers in other markets. International co-productions rose in popularity in the 1980s as a means of increasing the capacity of animated television to better articulate the expectations of a variety of global consumers. For example, in 1987, *Variety* reported on new attempts by British producers to develop co-production ties with U.S. producers. A shift in attitude had occurred among British producers: previously they had preferred to develop programs locally and then, after the fact, attempt to sell them to U.S. broadcasters, who would often "shoot down their ideas or pitch them back with requests for a more international approach" (Variety 1987a:99). The willingness to co-produce came after program costs continued to soar, and domestic markets in Britain continued to shrink. Though financial concerns were an important initiating factor, the problem of producing programs with cultural relevance remained and were perceived to be resolvable through co-production partnerships.

Moreover, some nations were perceived to be better at achieving the cultural relevance sought through co-productions. Sometimes this was because of common traits in the two cultures represented in the partnership. For example, in 1987, *Variety* reported that Turkish broadcaster TRT was developing international co-production ventures for the first time. The project, titled Heritage, was an Islamic culture project initiated with Jordan TV (*Variety* 1987b:358). Conditions in Canada that allowed for a variety of cultural links with other countries contributed to its success as a co-production partner. In 1989, *TV World* reported on increases in the volume of international co-production deals, identifying Canada as "the world's greatest co-producer." *TV World* ascribed the prevalence of co-productions in Canada to the presence of government subsidies and internal pressures:

> The small size of the Canadian domestic market is often cited as a reason for Canadian companies to look outside the country for necessary financing, but co-productions are also increasingly a mark of Canada's heterogeneous and multi-cultural national character. (Lavers 1989a)

Some linkages were influenced by the presence of an existing relationship. For instance, in 1987, *Variety* reported that attempts to increase co-production ties between CBS and Australia's Nine Network had followed from an already close relationship between the two broadcasters (Murdoch 1987). Similarly, in 1988, according to Rome's RA-1 Scaffa, while "some US producers [had] gone to Korea, and their presence there [had] already increased the cost of production beyond [RA-1's] possibilities," RA-1 had avoided rising costs by cementing long-term relationships with NTV and Tokyo Movie (*Variety* 1988b:120).

Therefore, the cultural 'fit' between co-producers was an important factor, suggesting that local cultural differences represented a mediating factor in the development of co-productions as intercultural processes of production. These co-productions tended to take advantage of the potential in animation production for flexible specialization, which supported the production of different versions of programs for different international markets. As a newly developed set of institutional and production arrangements, co-productions therefore represent an important mechanism whereby producers were better able to link the production process with the various international consumer markets for television animation. The development of international co-production schemes was motivated primarily by considerations of cost and marketability, although closely related secondary reasons included the development of culturally relevant programs that met consumer expectations in international markets. Evidence suggests that producers sought co-production partnerships as a means of enhancing the marketability of their programs abroad, both through marketing partnerships and creative collaboration.

Strategies for Dealing with Differences in Consumer Tastes in Global Markets: International Versioning

Though co-production arrangements seemed a promising way to develop internationally appealing programs, the process was often difficult. Co-producers were faced with problems associated with the varying tastes of the different audiences. Bruce Johansen, senior vice president and director of program development for Multimedia Entertainment, noted some difficulties in an interview with *Variety* on U.S.-European TV co-productions: "The problem is the show. The deal is always easy to put together. But storylines that work in one culture don't always work in another" (Lipmann 1988:56). Although U.S.-European live-action co-production partnerships lowered production costs, the use of British writers and locations tended to give programs a European flavor, which was not popular with U.S. audiences (Lipmann 1988).

Language Dubbing

Large U.S. producers such as Hanna-Barbera, however, had considerable success marketing their characters abroad prior to the 1980s. This established appeal carried well into the 1980s and early 1990s. In 1989, for instance, *Variety* reported that Worldvision (the international distributor for Hanna-Barbera since the company had been acquired by Taft Broadcasting in 1979) was aggressively marketing more than 3,000 hours of Hanna-Barbera animation available for international buyers of television programming (p. 64). Worldvision Vice President Bert Cohen announced the creation of a new program: the European *Hanna-Barbera Hour*, which had already been sold in Italy, West Germany, and Belgium, and which featured a mixture of U.S.-developed Hanna-Barbera characters: the Flintstones, the Jetsons, Yogi Bear, Huckleberry Hound, and Quick Draw McGraw. *Variety* said in its story:

> Hanna-Barbera creations are liked by adults as well as by children. 'They're not violent; they're characters everyone can relate to, even though they can get into mischief, they're happy characters. Cohen doesn't agree that Fred Flintstone, with his joyous cry of Yabba dabba doo, or Yogi Bear are quintessentially American. All Hanna-Barbera creations are "universal characters," he maintains. (p. 64)

However, this international appeal of certain characters had been mediated by variations in personalities established through voice dubbing. Cohen noted that because Hanna-Barbera had no central marketing theme until recently, Hanna-Barbera characters had adopted different personalities in different countries and certain characteristics were more successful in some markets than in others: "The Flintstones are very strong in the United Kingdom; Scooby Doo is liked by the French; Italy is in love with

Yogi Bear. [I]n fact, Yogi is an up-market character in Italy, a spokesman for all kinds of causes" (Busby 1991:70). As Cohen's remarks indicate, dubbing had been an after-market addition to children's animated programming prior to the 1980s. While this was true of most programming sold in foreign markets, the importance of dubbing to foreign sales became more apparent in the 1980s as distributors noticed that formats most amenable to dubbing were also the most successful.

Although international markets began to demand dubbing to greater degrees through the 1980s, some evidence exists that U.S. child consumers had specific preferences for U.S. accents prior to this point. For instance, in 1979, *TV World* reported on efforts by television animation producers in France to create a greater market for their products internationally. They noted that the only dubbing by French producers in postproduction was for English-speaking markets, and the dubbing in this case was done in the American version, because British audiences were more likely to accept U.S. English dubbing than were U.S. audiences to accept British English dubbing (*TV World* 1979a).

In 1983, *TV World* reported that U.S. media buyers emphasized the need for U.S. English dubbing, rather than subtitling, which was accepted more readily by audiences elsewhere. Dick Harper, president of Harper Associates, defended the U.S. audience preference for U.S. English dubbing, indicating that particular dubbing needs were in place in other markets as well: "France does not accept shows dubbed in Montreal; Mexico does not take shows dubbed in Spain" (Friedman 1983:58). In 1988, Nayeri reported in *Variety* that the French networks broadcast extensively to children, but used mostly foreign-produced programs. French cartoons were very expensive to produce: while a 26-minute Japanese animated program cost approximately $10,500, including dubbing, a French program would have cost 10 times this amount to produce (p. 190). As a result, more than 80 percent of children's programs carried on one of the leading French channels (TF1) in 1988 were produced in either the United States or Japan (Nayeri 1988:190). This suggests that appropriate language dubbing was a central consideration in the global distribution of television programs. In fact, consumer expectations for the local vernacular extended beyond the need for appropriate language, to include the need for locally appropriate dialect and accent.

In the 1980s, television producers in and outside of the United States began to develop postproduction dubbing as a means of boosting foreign sales. Evidence suggests that they began to favor more easily dubbed types of programs such as animation. For instance, Studio Hamburg in 1983 launched a foreign sales drive aimed at English-speaking markets, focusing on the more easily dubbed types of television programs, such as documentaries, puppet shows, and animated cartoons (*Variety* 1984a). In 1987, *TV World* reported on the success of Studio Hamburg's attempts at English versioning with *Around the World in Eighty Days*, which had been sold in Australia and Scotland. Sales officer Axel Pult noted that the sales would not have been made without pre-made English versions (*TV World* 1987:31). U.S. producers also began to develop postproduction dubbing of foreign programs for the non-U.S. market. For instance, in 1983 *Variety* noted that Western World TV Enterprises, a distributor of television programs (e.g., those produced by the BBC and Time-Life) in Latin America was reporting increases in trade. The publication noted that Western World had begun to dub programs with Spanish-speaking voice-overs, for example *Nick and Pick* (a children's puppet show) from SRC (Canada), for distribution in Mexico (1983b).

In 1986, *Broadcast* noted that, while older, previously produced live-action programs such as *Lassie* and *The Lone Ranger* were enjoying widespread popularity, the most exportable shows were animated children's programs:

> Most programmers maintain that animated programming does so well at home and abroad because it's easy to dub and cheap to produce—they estimated that the average half-hour program cost approximately $285,000 to produce . . . Almost all today's successful domestic shows are sold abroad, most dubbed into a number of languages, including French, Italian, Portuguese, Japanese and something called "neutral Spanish." (Woodman 1986:19)

Sesame Street, which combined live action with animated sequences, was partly dubbed, and partly produced in conjunction with foreign producers, who inserted locally produced versions of puppet sequences This included new characters that, as described by Children's Television Workshop's Fran Kaufman, "are culturally more acceptable to the children who are watching, or street scenes filmed in their countries" (p. 19). Moreover, evidence also suggests that language-appropriate dubbing became increasingly popular throughout Europe in the 1980s as cable channels proliferated. For instance, *Variety* (1988d:121) reported on the creation of KinderNet (Dutch for Children's Television), which carried mostly subtitled, and post-synchronized foreign material. It was also the first all-Dutch cable channel.

Story and Sequence Editing

The postproduction process was not limited to dubbing of voices and sometimes included reediting for form and content. In 1986, Canada's Cinar purchased and developed postproduction work on a Japanese television series (25 hours)—*The Wizard of Oz*. The program was developed as an Anglo-U.S. television series (50 half hours) and was edited to create three theatrical features. Dubbing was done with mostly Canadian voice and musical talent (*Variety* 1986:81). In 1985, *Variety* noted that Thames Television of Britain had had the greatest impact of British producers on U.S. television through format importing (most notably U.S. sitcom copies *Three's Company, The Ropers*). However, *Variety* also noted that animated programs were not copied, but rather versioned for U.S. markets. For instance, *Danger Mouse* had been distributed on Nickelodeon in the original 10-minute versions but was being postproduced in the U.S., and developed into a half-hour format for Saturday morning network broadcast (1985a:134).

This greater demand and potential for the development of international versions of animated programs, and the ultimate heightened success of animation when compared to live-action formats, were increasingly acknowledged throughout the 1980s and into the 1990s. For instance, in 1991, *Variety* described the international marketing of *Tiny Toons* as involving a very careful process of postproduction for voices, picking the right voice, and developing the right character depending on the country of distribution. The senior vice president and general manager of animation at Warner Bros. noted, "In the past, dubbing has been handled in a haphazard fashion sometimes. You can end up with some weird, unusual voices. We want the characters to have the right attitude and youthful qualities" (Busby 1991:70). *Variety* reported consistently through the 1980s and early 1990s that international buyers for television animation had become more sophisticated over the past few years, expecting more quality programs, as the market had begun to fill with internationally produced television animation.

In some cases, moreover, the development of versions of foreign programs by U.S. producers for distribution in the United States required not only dubbing but radical alterations to the original visuals. For instance, in 1984 *Variety* described a Turner Program Services licensing agreement for animated feature films (a total of 10 by that point), originally produced by Japan's Toei, for dubbing and redistribution in Anglo-U.S. markets. They estimated a profit of $1.5 million to $2 million for Turner, and described an upcoming deal in which Turner would purchase *Draemon*, 150 seven-minute cartoons, for postproduction into 50 half-hour shows for distribution in the United States. (*Variety* 1984b: 61). The reformatting in this case was extensive, involving radical alterations in dialogues and story lines. Similarly, in 1985 U.S. producer Kidpix began to capitalize heavily on international sources of existing children's programs through an intensive process of postproduction. The process, described in *Variety*, began with raw animation from a series of segments from foreign (mostly Japanese) animated television series. The segments were then rescripted with a new chronology and story line. U.S. voice actors were used and six original songs were scored to a stereo soundtrack to complete a 90-minute feature film for television and video release with a U.S.-oriented title. The budget for each film in 1985 was less than $1 million, considerably lower than full-production films. *Variety* reported in 1985 that Kidpix had closed three separate deals for U.S. distribution (Tusher 1985).

Wrap-around Live Action

Another common form of international versioning that involved considerable alterations was the use of locally identifiable live-action hosts in sequences that would "wrap around" or be inserted before and after animated sequences (much like that developed by *Sesame Street* producers). For instance, the executive vice president of marketing at Buena Vista Television (Disney's television distribution arm) in 1991 attributed the international success of Disney television programs to the development of local-market programs called "clubs," and the insertion of alternate local sequences: "Our shows are molded into Disney club packages in each country. They're formatted with a new form of Mickey Mouse, a live-action character that interacts with other characters who are nationals from that country" (Busby 1991:70). Similarly, *Variety* (1988c) reported that U.S. producers were considering new ways to tailor programs in order to draw foreign audiences:

Worldvision is discussing with broadcasters in Italy, Spain, West Germany and Latin America the concept of a children's hour that would blend 30 or more minutes of Hanna-Barbera animation with programming centered around a local personality. Such a hybrid could include a studio audience and a locally produced game. (p. 115)

This use of wrap-around host sequences for international versions was also developed specifically through international co-production schemes in the 1980s and early 1990s. For instance, *TV World* (1990) reported on a new Disney co-production project involving five foreign partners: United Kingdom's ITV, France's TF1, Italy's RAI-1, Germany's ARD, and Spain's Catalonia TV3. The Disney European Christmas Special would be shown to at least 15 other broadcasters. The program was set in the Italian village where the story of Pinocchio took place, and in a Bavarian fairytale castle. It included Tom Jones and Ruth Pointer singing Disney film songs, and clips from Disney cartoons. Each co-production partner provided a different presenter-host in order to customize the program for each market. Etienne de Villiers, president of Buena Vista International, noted: "We think this is an innovative way to meet each individual broadcaster's needs whilst providing them with production values that could not be achieved on an individual basis" (p. 4).

Wrap-around live-action hosting was an important feature of the highly popular and broadly internationalized *Sesame Street*. In 1989, *TV World* reported on the success of the international co-production of *Sesame Street*. Joan Lufkano, director of international production and senior producer of adapted series, noted that 50 percent of the program was produced by the Children's Television Workshop, and the other 50 percent included local production of the live-action street scenes and wrap-arounds. The co-productions often involved negotiations over creative decisions on program content: "We consult them on their 50 percent and sometimes find ourselves saying things like 'That's not something we would do . . .' and telling them why" (Friedman 1989:32). Once a co-production arrangement was made, a production advisory board was named and foreign producers were brought to New York for a two-week intensive workshop.

A conflict arose with the Israeli co-producers who wanted to include religious inserts. Children's Television Workshop refused, and in the working out of a compromise, the street sequences were developed to include a number of different characters who were shown to coexist: religious and nonreligious Jews, Ashkenazi, Sephardic, and Oriental ethnicities, and an Arab was included as a regular cast member.

Similarly, another popular co-production, *Fraggle Rock* (between the Canadian Broadcasting Corporation and Jim Henson), involved extensive versioning that included production of alternative international live-action sequences, which were incorporated into the story line around puppet sequences. *Variety* (1983c) reported that the CBC had been doing well in the U.S. cable market, beginning with the sale of *Fraggle Rock*: "a program which has become an important staple of HBO's schedule, but is somehow overlooked as a CBC co-production" (p. 54). This program later became a successful project for dubbed versioning. Harriet Yasky, executive vice president at Henson Associates reported that a segment of *Fraggle Rock* was being produced for different markets: in North America, a live character was a retired inventor, in England a retired lighthouse keeper, and in France a retired chef (*Variety* 1988c:115).

Again, it should be noted that program versioning, especially language dubbing, was a common feature of the international television animation trade prior to the 1980s. However, the beginning of the 1980s marked an intensification of versioning, most notably, the integration of versioning into all stages of production, including production planning. Whereas alternative language dubbing of programs produced initially for, and released into, U.S. markets prior to the 1980s was carried out mostly in postproduction, by the mid-1990s it had become commonplace to produce multiple language versions as part of the production process, prior to the point of sale or distribution. As well, the rise of international versioning included such innovations as sequence editing and alternate international inserts with localized appeal. Overall, these types of strategies became increasingly popular in the international trade of television animation throughout the 1980s and 1990s, and eventually became commonplace.

Conclusion

Some of the strategies involved in the production and distribution of animated television in the 1980s and early 1990s were relatively new, while others were intensified or more complex versions of strategies pursued prior to the 1980s. Producers of animated programs were faced with varying pressures in the form of persistent preferences for program features such as local animation styles, content, and pacing, as well as distinctions in patterns of television consumption. While such innovations as co-production partnerships were seen as tactics to survive in the place of changing financial conditions and government regulations that supported local production, they were also viewed as important new ways to improve the fit, through a sharing of creative control, between programs and local audience expectations. Another important mechanism for accommodating differences in consumer cultures, which intensified during the 1980s and 1990s, was the coordination and simultaneous production of multiple versions of animated programs. This involved language dubbing, alterations in story and character features, as well as host inserts of programs featuring local personalities. Overall, these strategies worked in significant ways to localize the content features of globally distributed programs, and remain today as important features of the processes that constitute a new and distinctive period of globalism with respect to animated television.

The changes that occurred in this period can be characterized as globalization. However, in order to better understand the concept, much more information is required on the inner workings of the media industry, and, specifically, the historical and economic context within which changes in the television animation industry took place. Major developments in animation production during the 1980s and 1990s included the diversification and consolidation of operations around animation production and ancillary businesses such as character licensing and toy manufacturing and distribution. Similar changes also characterize the broader economic situation of the media industry, especially with respect to changes in and intensifications of the global activities of transnational media corporations. Comparative analysis needs to focus on the timing of these changes, as well as the particularities and similarities between the case of animated television and other cultural industries and sectors.

Moreover, since the conditions affecting the international television business continue to evolve, localized production strategies will continue to play an increasingly important role. For instance, developing the argument that the globalization of media industries has involved the integration of local with global media industries, Robert W. McChesney (1999) cites global news media mogul Rupert Murdoch's address to a United Nations conference on television in 1997. Murdoch stated, "The right mix for Western media is taking the best international programming and mixing it with local content. Localization is playing an increasingly crucial role" (p. 106). As McChesney concludes, the globalization of media industries, including the concentration and conglomeration of global holdings and operations worldwide, is not a process that can be encompassed by a traditional notion of cultural imperialism (p. 106). As the focus of this chapter on animated television has sought to demonstrate, the production process has not been characterized by an exclusive, straightforward global homogenization of product, but has rather incorporated in increasingly central ways various strategies of localized production.

A greater emphasis on comparative analysis is needed to better understand the specific ways in which television animation can be characterized as more or less amenable to localized strategies of production when compared to other television formats and media products. As opposed to the more easily identifiable nationally prescribed features of live-action television characters (such as those in *Dallas*), animation often has the benefit in global markets of fantasy-based characters without readily identifiable national characteristics (e.g., Yogi Bear, Mickey Mouse, Smurfs). [6] However, many of the strategies discussed were similar to those used by producers of live-action programs. For instance, versions of game shows for children and youth were produced independently through format copying. *Variety* reported that the success of Nickelodeon's children's game show *Double Dare* had led to a number of internationally licensed versions using a local personality and local contestants (*Variety* 1988a: 115). Also in 1984, *Variety* noted that a strong demand for music features in Japan, combined with the high cost of well-known U.S. pop stars, was leading some of the smaller Japanese broadcasters to seek co-production partnerships with Western producers. This was a unique situation in Japan, since a robust domestic interest in investing production money had previously limited the need for international production funding (Segers 1984).

To fully understand the cultural dimensions of globalization with respect to audiences, more research is needed on the relationship between the ways people consume global programming, and what has become accepted by some as central to the conceptualization of globalization—what Roland Robertson (1992) terms "the intensification of consciousness of the world as a whole" (p. 8). In order to understand the ways in which the everyday experiences of television programming are global or local, analysis is required on other levels, including, for instance, studies of how programs are read or understood in similar or distinct ways by different groups, and according to different cultural identities (see Ang 1985; Liebes and Katz 1990). The differences between child and adult viewers of television in different countries need to be addressed. While children's programming is a distinct industry category, some studies have shown that children, like adults, consume television programs in ways that articulate their own social relationships and identities (e.g., Hodge 1989; Moores 1993; Nava and Nava 1996).

A review of industry trade sources reveals the importance of localization for selling television animation in global markets. Between the early 1980s and mid-1990s, this entailed specific changes and innovations in strategies of production and in content. In these cases, rather than creating a straightforward global sameness, companies working in the international business of animated television were able to accommodate in different ways the various expectations of consumer groups located in countries in many parts of the world.

Notes

This paper benefitted from suggestions and comments of Wallace Clements, Chris Dorman, John Jackson, Rob Shields, and Will Straw—and especially those of Diana Crane, John Harp, and Emer Killean. Many of the ideas are theirs; all of the errors are mine.

1. Industry definitions of animation include a relatively indistinct range of programming (e.g., adult animation vs. children's animation, scientific/educational, as well as puppetry). For the purposes of the current study, animation is taken to include both animation and puppetry, but is limited to dramatic programming, as opposed to advertisements or program separators, station identification inserts, and so on. Although some recent cartoons have been developed for adults, the vast majority of television animation has been produced for children. Therefore, most of the present analysis deals with children's programs. Though the review also includes puppetry, the production of these types of programs has been less frequent than animation. A notable exception is *Sesame Street*, which incorporates live action and puppetry with animation.

This analysis relies on information provided in international industry trade journals (especially *Variety*, but also *TV World* and *Broadcast*). The initial review included more than 1,000 articles, including references to international activities regarding television production and distribution. These journals relate developments in production and distribution practices as well as developments in consumer markets regarding the globalization of animated television in the 1980s and early 1990s. This chapter focuses on changes that began in the early 1980s, when production strategies such as international co-productions began to gain popularity. For instance, *Smurfs* was the first international co-production resulting in a prime-time U.S. program, in 1981. By the mid-1990s, production strategies such as co-production and intensive versioning were well-established.

The sources used tend to have a "pro-industry" bias, especially in reporting on the efforts of regulators and industry pressure groups. However, information provided by trade journals is seldom entirely one-sided in support of producers and distributors. They present the views of a wide range of actors (such as advocacy trade groups and trade unions) involved in the television industry and related organizations, although they tend to represent some voices better than others. Moreover, trade journals are, in many instances, the only sources of information on some industry events, trends, and activities. They often tend to be the most complete sources in that they provide detailed and focused records of industry activities. The chapter attempts to chart changes in production strategies, for which trade journals are a rich and important source.

2. For instance, small-scale producer Herb Klynn used production studios and labor in Korea to produce *The Gerald McBoing-Boing Show* and *Mr. Magoo* for U.S. network television in 1956, and was soon followed by large-scale producer Hanna-Barbera.

3. This distinction also exists with programming other than animation. The Broadcasting Research Unit, an independent unit partially funded by the BBC, described the relationship between U.S. television and United Kingdom audiences as "unique and peculiar to the United Kingdom". Head of acquisitions for the BBC-TV suggests: "US programming provides variation in the pacing of entertainment . . . British producers have learned from this in the past 10 years, especially in acknowledging the high entertainment values and escapist values of such material" (Baker 1984: 74). He also noted that British and American tastes are not identical: "The success of an American TV series lies in the tension generated between invention and convention, and whenever the latter dominates over the former, the series has usually exhausted itself" (p. 74). *Dukes of Hazzard*, for instance, lost half its audience between 1979 and 1983 (Baker 1984).

4. The practice of importing to the United States was an important feature of the globalization of animated television during the 1980s and 1990s. By the early 1980s, U.S. producers and distributors had already recognized the international marketability of children's programs and were interested in finding programs abroad that would be successful in the U.S. (Abrahams 1979:14).

5. Scholars have also begun to note this shift. Mike Featherstone and Scott Lash (1995) identify studies of cultural Americanization, but also identify attempts to define and study processes such as Europeanization, Japanization, and Brazilianization.

6. Evidence for this appears, for instance, in a 1989 report by the *New York Times*, which described the global boom in animated character-driven advertising promotion. Bernard Shine, owner of a Los Angeles Disney memorabilia gallery, noted of Mickey Mouse: "He's become a corporate logo. He used to be an adventuresome, comic character. He's now become a pitchman, a generic logo that fits every product" (McGill 1989: 35). McGill notes: "The fact that these are cartoons and not real people adds to their desirability, many advertisers say" (p. 37).

References

Abrahams, J. (1979) 'United States: Pressure groups bring gradual change,' *TV World*, April, VII/4:12,14.

Akyuz, G. (1994) 'Rikakli's baby,' *TV World*, October, XVII/8: 74.

Ang, I. (1985) *Watching Dallas: Soap Opera and the Melodramatic Imagination*, (translated by Della Couling), London: Methuen.

Ayscough, S. (1990) 'Canadian animation on the rise, too,' *Variety*, November 5, 341:64.

Baker, B. (1984) 'British audiences are watching 30 hours of peaktime U.S. TV,' *Variety*, October 17, 316:92.

Busby, S. (1991) 'Yanks wrap toons to go,' *Variety*, May 27, 343: 41, 70.

Constant, N. (1979) 'South Korea: Maverick economy with stable stations,' *TV World*, April, VII/4: 30–31.

Currie, J. (1998) 'Impact of globalization on Australian universities: competition, fragmentation and demoralization,' Paper presented at the International Sociological Association 1998 World Congress, Montreal.

De Stain, I. (1986) 'Cost keeps US looking east,' *TV World*, March–April, IX/3: 22.

Featherstone, M. (1990) 'Global culture: introduction,' pp. 1–14 in M. Featherstone (ed.) *Global Culture: Nationalism, Globalization and Modernity*, London: Sage.

Featherstone, M. and S. Lash (1995) 'Globalization, modernity and the spatialization of social theory,' pp. 1–24 in M. Featherstone, S. Lash and R. Robertson (eds.) *Global Modernities*, London: Sage Publications.

Friedman, A. J. (1989) '20 years on,' *TV World*, August, XII/6:32.

Friedman, A.J. (1988) 'Sunbow shifts into live action gear,' *TV World*, October, XI/8: 60.

Friedman, A.J. (1983) 'Co-production key to US market?' *TV World*, February, VI/2: 58–96.

Gelman, M (1986) 'Sunbow takes to Marvel like duck to water in animation,' *Variety*, September 17, 324: 81.

Gill, E. (1988) 'German kid TV programming has outgrown its baby shoes,' *Variety*, April 27, 331: 120.

Guider, E. (1987) 'Co-productions in a new role for international TV,' *Variety*, October 21, 328: 3, 547.

Hamelink, C. T. (1995) *World Communication: Disempowerment and Self-Empowerment*, London: Zed Books.

Hardy, P. (1990) 'Europeans animated by cartoons boom,' *Variety*, November 5, 341: 55.

Hodge, B. (1989) 'Children and TV,' pp.158–171 in J. Tulloch and G. Turner (eds) *Australian Television: Programs, Pleasures and Politics*, North Sydney: Allen and Unwin.

Hollinger, H. (1983) 'Europe-based DIC Enterprises sells cartoon series to ABC,' *Variety*, June 22, 311: 61.

Kindred, J. (1990) 'Germans drawing as fast as they can,' *Variety*, November 5, 341: 58.

Lavers, D. (1988) 'Canadian group goes the animation route.' *TV World*, August, XI/6:39.

Lavers, D. (1989a) 'Worldwide worries, Canada's concern,' *TV World*, March–April, XII/3:24–25,27.

Lavers, D. (1989b) 'Ahead of the pack,' *TV World*, October, XII/8: 67, 69.

Liebes, T. and E. Katz (1990) *The Export of Meaning: Cross-Cultural Readings of Dallas*, Oxford: Oxford University Press.

Lipman, J. (1988) 'Intl. TV co-production on the increase,' *Variety*, October 26, 333:1, 56.

Loftus, J. (1983) 'CBS eyes Latin market via deal with Globo TV,' *Variety*, February 9, 310:1, 92.

McChesney, R. W. (1999) *Rich Media, Poor Democracy: Communication Politics in Dubious Times*, Urbana and Chicago: University of Illinois Press.

McGill, D.C. (1989) 'Mickey sells; is he now oversold?' *New York Times*, May 20, 138:35, 37.

Moores, S. (1993) *Interpreting Audiences: The Ethnography of Media Consumption*, London: Sage.

Murdoch, B. (1987) 'Aussie Nine net old CBS partner,' *Variety*, September 30, 328:112.

Murdoch, B. (1985) 'US product going soft in Far East and Asia; local production is up,' *Variety*, August 7, 320:46.

Nava, M. and O. Nava (1996) 'Discrimination or duped,' pp. 126–134 in J. Corner and S. Harvey (eds) *Television Times: A Reader*, London: Arnold.

Nayeri, F. (1988) 'French nets don't neglect kids, but do pass over native products,' *Variety*, April 27, 331:190.

Robertson, R. (1992) *Globalization: Social Theory and Global Culture*, London: Sage Publications.

Segers, F. (1984) 'Japanese suppliers set to absorb broad range of video programming due to robust domestic market,' *Variety* , October 10, 316:38, 46.

Tillman, S. (1979) 'Hong Kong: Problems of improving the programs,' *TV World*, April, VII/4:24.

Tusher, W. (1985) 'Kidpix consummates worldwide distribution deal with 4 Star,' *Variety*, July 17: 43.

TV World (1990) 'Disney's festive European co-production,' *TV World*, January, XIII/1: 4.

TV World (1987) 'Versioning is working,' *TV World*, March–April, X/3:31.

TV World (1986) 'Euro-look from DIC,' March/April, IX/3:9.

TV World (1979a) 'A very particular market,' *TV World*, April, II/7:51–53.

TV World (1979b) 'Looking for foreign appeal,' *TV World*, April, II/7:61, 63.

Variety (1991a) 'Four tough markets to crack,' *Variety*, May 27, 343:75.

Variety (1991b) 'Cardiff a contender as a cartoon capital,' *Variety*, January 21, 342:71, 74.

Variety (1989) 'Hanna-Barbera and Worldvision can keep the characters all in the family,' *Variety*, July 12–18, 335:64.

Variety (1988a) 'Kid TV foundation of Australia seeks development paths,' (Perspective children's TV) *Variety*, April 27, 331/1:116, 118, 120.

Variety (1988b) 'RA-1 to spur family viewing by moving kid fare to 7 p.m. parents joined for "Golden Coin",' (Perspective children's TV) *Variety*, April 27, 331/1:120.

Variety (1988c) 'Kidvid going international, co-production deals form many new partnerships,' (Perspective children's TV) *Variety*, April 27, 331/1:114.

Variety (1988d) 'Kindernet caters to Dutch pre-13s,' (Perspective children's TV) *Variety*, April 27, 331/1:121.

Variety (1987a) 'Changing economics bring down barriers to U.K. co-production,' *Variety*, October 14, 328:99.

Variety (1987b) 'Foreign sales, co-prod deals on TRT slate,' *Variety*, February 25, 326:358, 376.

Variety (1986) 'Canadian animation for TV series is now in high clover,' *Variety*, November 26, 325:81, 84.

Variety (1985a) 'Thames making waves in US by exporting its TV formats,' *Variety*, January 16, 317:134.

Variety (1985b) 'Worldvision's $90-mil sales year sees more than half from o'seas,' *Variety*, March 13, 318:75, 104.

Variety (1984a) 'Youth market tunes into SIN as programming mix widens,' *Variety*, April 18, 314:50.

Variety (1984b) 'Turner sees lotsa loot in Japan-made cartoons,' *Variety*, October 31, 317:61.

Variety (1983a) 'British ITV web, Aussie 7 net grab "He-man" from group W,' *Variety*, June 1, 311:40.

Variety (1983b) 'Western World business fine; looks brighter,' *Variety*, March 30, 310:90.

Variety (1983c) 'CBC cracks US cable market, wraps up Australia TV sales,' *Variety*, March 23, 310:54.

Variety (1981) 'Spain's animated "Musketeers" borrows Japanese know-how,' *Variety*, September 30, 304:44.

Werba, H. (1980) 'Animation in Japan nears $1-bil mark,' *Variety*, June 4, 299:5, 38.

Williams, M. (1991) 'Euros go global at toon meet,' *Variety*, October 7, 344:63–66.

Woodman, S. (1986) 'Fickle gluttons,' *Broadcast*, December 12, 18–19.

15

From Western Gaze to Global Gaze

Japanese Cultural Presence in Asia

Koichi Iwabuchi

A dominant image of Japan is of a faceless economic superpower with a disproportionate lack of cultural influence upon the world. Japan has money and technologies but cannot diffuse its culture. The culture of Japan that is considered worth appreciating is usually something traditional which is to be put on exhibit to show its irreducible uniqueness (Hannerz 1989). Contrary to this assumption, however, Japan has long been exporting cultural products overseas, particularly to Asia. The Japanese cultural presence in Asia is becoming increasingly conspicuous in the 1990s. This chapter explores the nature of Japan's cultural presence overseas.

While acknowledging that textual analysis and audience study of Japanese popular culture are indispensable for obtaining a comprehensive understanding of the Japanese cultural presence overseas, I will focus here on the marketing strategies—both by Japanese and local cultural industries in Asia—that direct its distribution.[1] One reason for the comparative invisibility of Japan's cultural presence in Asia is Japan's peculiar position in the global audiovisual market as an exporter of what may be called "culturally odorless" products, that is, products which, in contrast to American export icons, such as Coca-Cola or McDonald's, do not immediately conjure images of the country of origin in the minds of consumers. Increasing economic power in Asia and the proliferation of media space in the region has dramatically increased the export of Japanese popular culture. However, Japanese cultural industries still tend to be less concerned with the direct export of Japanese cultural products than with selling the know-how of "indigenizing" the West, particularly America.

At the same time, the Japanese cultural presence is becoming increasingly conspicuous in the 1990s as local industries of other parts of Asia now find commercial value in promoting Japanese popular culture in their local markets. This local initiative also gives Japanese cultural industries more confidence in the exportability of Japanese products. I will suggest that the ascent of a Japanese cultural presence in

Asia not only shows that Japanese cultural industries have become key players in media globalization; but also testifies to the emerging currents of transnational cultural flow brought about by globalization processes.

Culturally Odorless Products and Glocalization

In July 1997, a Japanese television news reporter covering an ASEAN meeting in Kuala Lumpur joked that there were three requirements for becoming a member of ASEAN (Association of South East Asian Nations). First, one must play golf; second, one must love karaoke. Compared to these cultural practices, which are not particularly Southeast Asian but are common in the male-dominated business circles and the middle class in many parts of Asia, the third requirement is very much Southeast Asian: last but not least, the reporter continued with a faint smile, one must be able to eat durian, the delicious but pungent-smelling fruit of Southeast Asia.

This joke brings to mind a distinctive feature of the nature of Japanese cultural presence in Asia, the transnational cultural flow of Japanese influence in general, and particularly of its audiovisual products: Japanese cultural presence tends to be "culturally odorless" and its cultural products are destined to be localized in overseas markets. That playing golf for business and enjoying karaoke are even jokingly considered requirements of membership of ASEAN points to Japanese cultural influences in Southeast Asia, and no doubt elsewhere in the region. However, these activities do not evoke images of Japan and thus of Japanese cultural presence, as they have been fully localized, incorporated as integral parts of business culture and the everyday life of the middle classes in the region to an extent that they represent consumer modernity in Southeast Asia. At the same time, as the punch line of the joke reminds us, such common signifiers of modernity in the region are not enough to articulate distinctive local identities. No matter how karaoke and golf signify common business practices and the preferred leisure activities of an emerging, affluent middle class in the region, it is not the localized cultural products of foreign (Japanese) origin but the fruit with an insuppressible local odor that ultimately confers the Southeast Asianness of ASEAN.

The difference between the presence and the influence of foreign cultures and the significance of local odor is a key to understanding the strategies behind Japanese exports of media/audiovisual products. The major audiovisual products Japan exports overseas may be characterized as the culturally odorless three Cs: consumer technologies, such as VCRs, karaoke and the Walkman; comics/cartoons (animation); and computer/video games. I use the term cultural odor to focus on the way in which the cultural presence of a country of origin and images or ideas of its way of life are positively associated with a particular product in the consumption process. Any product may have various kinds of cultural associations with the country of its production, but it is when the image of the lifestyle of the country of origin is strongly evoked as the appeal of the product that the cultural odor of cultural commodities concerns me. The way in which the cultural odor of a particular product becomes fragrance—a socially acceptable smell (a desirable smell)—is not determined simply by the perception of the consumer that something is made in Japan. Neither is it necessarily related to the functions, influences, or the quality of a particular product or image. It has more to do with discursively constructed images of the country of origin that are widely disseminated in the world. The influence of McDonald's throughout the world, for example, is enormous in terms of the bureaucratization and standardization of not only food but also other everyday life activities such as education and shopping (Ritzer 1993). But no less important to its international success is its association with an attractive image of an American way of life. As Mike Featherstone (1996) argues,

> It is a product from a superior global center, which has long represented itself as the center. For those on the periphery it offers the possibility of the psychological benefits of identifying with the powerful. Along with the Marlboro Man, Coca-Cola, Hollywood, Sesame Street, rock music and American football insignia, McDonald's is one of a series of icons of the American way of life. They have become associated with transposable themes which are central to consumer culture, such as youth, fitness, beauty, luxury, romance, freedom. (p. 8)

McDonald's of course does not inherently represent America. It is the discursive formation of the latter that confers McDonald's symbolic meanings. In contrast, the dominant image of Japan, constructed by a Western Orientalist discourse and reinforced by a self-Orientalizing discourse in Japan, is mainly concerned with traditional and particularistic cultures and, more recently, high-tech sophistication (Iwabuchi 1994). The Sony Walkman is also an important cultural commodity which has various influences on our everyday life. Paul Du Gay et al. (1997) chose it as the cultural artifact most suited to the multilayered analyses of cultural studies. The Sony Walkman, they argue, may signify "Japaneseness" in terms of miniaturization, technical sophistication, and high quality. Such Japanesenesses are analytically important but not especially relevant to the Walkman's appeal at a consumer level. The use of the Walkman does not evoke images or ideas of a Japanese lifestyle, even if consumers know it is made in Japan and appreciate Japaneseness in terms of its sophisticated technology. Unlike American commodities, as Featherstone (1996) points out, "Japanese consumer goods do not seek to sell on the back of a Japanese way of life" (p. 9). As Wanling Wee said, they lack any influential "idea of Japan."

The cultural odor of a product is also closely associated with racial and bodily images of a country of origin. Japan's three Cs are cultural artifacts and present an imagery in which the bodily, racial, and ethnic characteristics are erased or softened. This is particularly evident in Japanese animation where the characters, for the most part, do not look Japanese. Such non-Japaneseness is called *mu-kokuseki*. This literally means something or someone lacking any nationality, but also implies the erasure of racial or ethnic characteristics and any context which would embed the characters in a particular culture or country. Internationally acclaimed Japanese animation director Oshii Mamoru[2] suggests that when Japanese animators and cartoonists are sketching attractive characters, they *unconsciously* choose not to draw realistic Japanese figures (Oshii, Ito, and Veno, 1996). In his case the characters tend to be modeled on Caucasian types.

Even if Japanese animators do not consciously draw *mu-kokuseki* characters in order to export their animations overseas, it is no accident that Japan has become a major exporter of animations and computer games. Japanese animation industries always have the global market in mind and are aware that the non-Japaneseness of characters works to their advantage in the export market. Since Tezuka Osamu's *Astro Boy* in the early 1960s, Japanese animation has long been consumed overseas. Japan routinely exports animation films. Animated films constituted 56 percent of all television exports from Japan in 1980 and 1981 (Stronach 1989) and 58 percent in 1992 and 1993 (Kawatake and Hara 1994). While other film genres are mostly exported in the original Japanese language, only 1 percent of animated exports were in Japanese. This implies that animation is routinely intended for export (Stronach 1989:144). Similarly, the producers and creators of game software *intentionally* make the characters of computer games look non-Japanese because they are clearly conscious that the market is global (Henshûshitu 1995). Mario, the principal character of the popular computer game Super Mario Brothers, for example, does not evoke an image of Japan. Both his name and appearance are Italian. Consumers and audiences of Japanese animation and games may be aware of the Japanese origin of these commodities, but they perceive little Japanese bodily odor.

Sony, from the outset, has also had a strong policy of becoming a global company. The name of the company and its products, such as Walkman, are in English, the world language. At the same time, what characterizes Sony (and Japanese manufacturers in general) as a significant global company is its marketing strategy, which is committed to local market differences. This global marketing strategy is another of Japan's significant contributions to the world of commodities. It is best expressed by what Sony calls "global localization" or "glocalization." In order to penetrate different local markets at once, global companies try to "transcend vestigial national differences and to create standardized global markets, while remaining sensitive to the peculiarities of local markets and differentiated consumer segments" (Aksoy and Robins 1992:18; see also du Gay et al. 1997). This strategy is not an exclusively Japanese practice. The term "glocalization" has apparently become a marketing buzzword of the global business world. Its entry in *The Oxford Dictionary of New Words*, however, acknowledges its origin in Japan:

> modeled on Japanese *dochakuka* (deriving from *dochaku* "living on one's own land"), originally the agricultural principle of adapting one's farming technique to local conditions, but also adopted in Japanese business for global localization, a global outlook adapted to local conditions. (Quoted in Robertson 1995:28)

It is indeed an interesting question why the term "glocal" was originally used by Japanese companies, but we should not regard the act of *dochakuka* (indigenization) as a unique cultural essence of Japan (Iwabuchi 1998). What should be borne in mind, however, is that cultural borrowing, appropriation, hybridization, and indigenization are, as the ASEAN joke suggests, common practices in the global cultural flow. What is more relevant to my topic is how Japanese companies *imagine* Japan's position in the global cultural flow when they develop strategies of glocalization. Behind such developments we can discern the engagement of Japanese companies in efforts to suppress Japanese "odor" in order to market their products overseas.

Of particular importance here is that although originally deployed by manufacturers of consumer goods, globalization strategies can also be discerned in Japanese music and television industries attempting to enter Asian markets. Their marketing strategies appear to be based on two assumptions. The first is that Japan's successful indigenization of foreign (Western) cultural influences presents a prototype for other Asian countries to follow. Since World War II, Japanese popular culture has been deeply influenced by American media. There has been no policy of imposing any quota on foreign popular culture in the audiovisual market since the war. Japan quickly localized these influences by imitating and partly appropriating the original, rather than being dominated by American products and "colonized" by America. Although Japanese television programming relied enormously upon imports from Hollywood in the 1950s and early 1960s, for example, since the mid-1960s, the imbalance has drastically diminished. Since 1980 just 5 percent of television programs have been imported (Kawatake and Hara 1994). Japan is now the only country, besides the United States, with a domestic television program market that is almost self-sufficient. This is not to say that no foreign popular culture is consumed in Japan, but testifies to a widely discerned empirical tendency that locally produced media products tend to be more popular than imported ones, even though they may entirely imitate the products of foreign origin (Lee 1991; Straubhaar 1991). What the Japanese experiences teach Japanese cultural industries is that this empirical tendency can be marketed in other parts of Asia.

At the same time, the question of the universality of Japanese cultural products and of Japanese cultural hegemony also has much to do with Japanese originality in developing glocalization. Until recently there has been no strong impetus on the part of Japanese cultural industries to export popular culture to other countries. There are several reasons for this, including the existence of an affluent Japanese market and the historical obstacle of the memory of Japanese colonialism in exporting Japanese culture to other parts of Asia. But it can also be argued that low exports are explained by the notion of "cultural discount" (Hoskins and Mirus 1988). This concept explains the diminishing attractiveness of a particular television program in other cultures due to cultural differences based on style, values, or beliefs. Cultural prestige, Western cultural hegemony, the universalism of the United States and the prevalence of the English language are advantageous to Hollywood. However, Japanese TV industries themselves seem to believe that their products would suffer a high cultural discount overseas. If "culturally odorless" products consciously or unconsciously lack Japanese bodily images, the imagery of television programs and popular music is inescapably represented through living Japanese bodies. While Japanese cultural industries have been unsure of the exportability of distinctively Japanese products, they are confident that other Asian countries will follow the same path as Japan in terms of a rapid indigenization of foreign (American) popular culture.

Finding Local Pop Stars in Asia

Despite the economic and currency crisis, Asia became the hottest market for global media industries in the 1990s. In the Asian market, localization has become a key word for the success of global media industries. For example, Rupert Murdoch's STAR-TV struggled with cultural and linguistic differences in Asia. The lesson STAR-TV has learned is that exporting English-language programs produced in Hollywood is no longer enough; thus Murdoch has announced, "We've committed ourselves to learning the nuances of the region's diverse cultures" (*Asian Business Review* 1994). Rather than broadcasting pan-Asian programs in one language, STAR-TV switched its strategy to localizing programs by finding local partners (*Far Eastern Economic Review* 1994).

The growing Asian audiovisual markets have also made Japanese cultural industries keen to do business in the region. Japanese cultural industries are conscious of the significance of localization, but in a different way from STAR-TV. In 1994, Dentsu, the biggest advertising agency in Japan, organized a committee to promote the export of Japanese audiovisual products and submitted a report to the Ministry of International Trade and Industry. The report clearly saw the great possibility for Japanese products being further accepted in Asian markets and suggested the necessity of developing more export-oriented production systems, including market research and language dubbing, to expand exports. However, many members of the committee also pointed out the likelihood of Japanese cultural products soon being superseded by local ones and emphasized developing other strategies for entering Asian markets, such as co-production and format trade, which sells the concept of television programming. This view corresponds with my own research. In November 1994, I interviewed many cultural producers in Japan concerning the popularity of Japanese products in Asia. Interestingly almost every producer thought that Japanese products would not be well received in the Asian market for long. As a long-term strategy, instead of exporting Japanese products, they prefer to produce "local" products in various Asian markets by indigenizing Western (American) popular culture.

In this respect, a 1993 Japanese film about the Japanization of Asia is suggestive of how Japanese cultural industries imagine the global cultural flow. The film *Sotsugyô Ryokô: Nihon kara kimashita* [My graduation trip: I'm from Japan], is about a Japanese male university student who becomes a pop star in a fictional Southeast Asian country when he travels there. The country is in a phenomenal "Japan boom," and he is scouted by a Japanese agent. He wins a star search audition and quickly becomes a national hero. Putting aside the depiction of a Japan boom in Asia, which the director himself acknowledged was not realistic, the interesting issues dealt with in this film are the status of American popular culture and the circulation of Japanized Western popular culture in other parts of Asia. The film begins with a scene in Japan in 1979 in which the hero as a child is earnestly watching a Japanese star singing a Japanized version of the song "YMCA" by the American pop group Village People.[3] The child dances along with the star on the screen. Symbolically he later performs the same number as a pop star in an Asian country. The premise appears to be that the basic model of Japanese popular culture is American and that Japan can provide a model for localizing strategies.

What the film does not show is the endless simulation of American pop in Asia through a second-generation simulation of Japanese pop music which is "homegrown," although unquestionably owing a debt to American trends. Japanese popular music, much of which is deeply influenced by American popular music, has been popular in Hong Kong, Taiwan, and Singapore, but there is little awareness of this in these places because most of the songs are sung by local singers in local languages. For example, Chinese audiences listening to Hong Kong popular music are unaware that a song is actually a cover version of a Japanese song because they do not know the Japanese original (cover songs might well constitute a fourth 'C' of Japanese culturally odorless products). In a 1994 TBS "News 23" report[4] on Japanese cultural industries in Shanghai, both the owner of a record shop and a customer said that the local people knew very few Japanese songs. They also said Japanese songs were not popular in China and that Japanese record companies should develop a more subtle marketing strategy. But this was followed by a Japanese narration observing that people listen to many Japanese songs in China without realizing their origin, because the songs have come to Shanghai via Hong Kong or Taiwan.

Japanese cultural producers are obviously aware from their own experience that Japanese cultural commodities are destined to be indigenized/localized and/or differently appropriated in each locale. It is, they seem to believe, through the process of indigenization of the foreign (West) rather than the export of the product per se that Japan can capture the attention of people in Asia. For example, the Japanese music industries that are most active in entering the Asian market use Japanese popular music production know-how to seek out "indigenous" pop stars rather than exporting Japanese stars directly. The film *Sotsugyô Ryokô* is suggestive in this respect as well. The hero achieves fame through an audition, which gives audiences the feeling that anyone in Asia can be tomorrow's star.

A televised star search audition was in reality the basis of the development of the Japanese pop idol system—the processes by which media industries manufacture pop stars—in the 1970s and 1980s. In the early 1990s, Japanese cultural industries tried to export the system to other parts of Asia. Many auditions were held in Asia, particularly in China, by Japanese talent agencies and recording companies such as Hori Production and Sony Music Entertainment. Also, a Japanese television station has been co-producing a talent quest TV program, *Asia Bagus*, with Singapore, Malaysia, and Indonesia since 1992.[5] In this strategy for producing local pop stars in Asia, Japanese cultural industries are not trying to export Japanese cultural artifacts but rather to market the process whereby local contestants and audiences can appropriate and consume products of foreign origin. This is the element of Japanese "originality" in glocalization—to incorporate the viewpoint of "the dominated" (who in this case have long learned to negotiate with Western culture) in the local consumption of media products. The Japanese strategy of localization tries to create local zones by gauging the practices of local media centers and their dynamic indigenization processes. Indeed, this dynamic is exactly what the Japanese cultural industries are trying to produce in the Asian markets.

In this strategy, Japanese cultural industries attempt to become interpreters of the West for Asia. A Japanese cultural producer stressed in an interview with me in 1996 that the strength of Japan is its 50 years of experience and accumulated know-how of "American education." He, like other Japanese producers, seems to believe that Japan is the most successfully Westernized country in the world. However, Japanese cultural industries share with other economic sectors a pessimistic view of the country's standing, as the world shifts from Japan-bashing to Japan-passing and now to Japan-nothing. Behind the confidence of Japanese music industries in their know-how in terms of indigenizing the West, there is also a fear that other Asian countries are now bypassing Japan and indigenizing the West directly. The same producer also emphasized in my interview that Japan has to be fused (*yûgô suru*) with other parts of Asia:

> Japanese cultural industries have a misconception that Japan is more advanced than any other Asian country in terms of popular culture, but what is happening is that other Asian countries are rapidly absorbing American culture. I think an Americanization of Asia cannot be avoided. Japan has to be involved in this process in order not to be left out of the prosperous Asian markets. I would propose the acronym "USA," to stand for the United States of Asia. Like the United States of America where many different cultures are fused, our USA should fuse different cultures so something new emerges from Asia.

What he was stressing is that Japan must be fused with other parts of Asia, particularly the Greater China cultural bloc. Japanese music industries suspect that this is the only way for Japan not to be left out of transnational popular culture in Asia. They are struggling with how to be involved in the rise of cultural industries in other parts of Asia before it is too late.

Another consideration to be borne in mind is that the strategy of localization is effective mainly in a relatively immature market such as China, not in mature markets like Taiwan and Hong Kong, where Japanese popular culture has long had an influence. These countries have imitated and indigenized the Japanese idol system, and there is not much space for Japanese cultural industries to tell them how to indigenize the West (Ching 1994).

This does not mean that Japan no longer has a cultural influence in these areas. Contrary to the expectation of the Japanese cultural industries, Japanese television programs and popular music are becoming more popular in such mature markets. While the export of the Japanese idol system is still sporadic, the circulation of Japanese television programs and popular music in Asia has become widespread. There are some markets in Asia where Japanese popular culture products rate highly, despite the embodiment of their textual appeal in living Japanese actors and musicians, but the interests which are promoting such products in those markets are more often local than Japanese. This is particularly the case with Taiwan. The ascent of Japanese popular culture in Taiwan has not occurred through active promotion by Japanese cultural industries. Rather it is the local cable channels, STAR-TV, and local music industries that have been actively selling Japanese products. In other words, the localization of Japanese popular culture in Taiwan has less to do with Japanese promoters disguising the content with local odor than with local marketing strategies that subtly turn the attention of audiences to the fragrance of Japanese popular culture.

Japan in Taiwan: Local Promotion

Japanese popular music occupies a mere 2 to 4 percent share of the Taiwanese market (Chinese pop constitutes 75 to 80 percent, and international 15 to 20 percent), according to my interviews with figures in the Taiwanese music industries in 1997, although there are no reliable figures available. However, Japanese popular music has gradually increased its presence in Taiwan in the last three to four years. In the week of March 25 to 31, 1997, five Japanese songs were in the top 10 of single-CD sales figures, according to the IFPI Taiwan hit chart.[6] This is an amazing phenomenon, despite the fact that local artists do not issue single CDs and thus the single-CD chart is almost entirely made up of international single CDs. What is noteworthy is that Japanese popular songs are becoming common in Taiwan and are released there soon after their appearance on the hit chart in Japan. A significant factor in the recent popularity of Japanese popular culture in Taiwan is the Taiwan government's removal at the end of 1993 of a ban on broadcasting Japanese-language television programs and songs. Along with the liberalization movement, what has also been important in facilitating the influx of Japanese popular culture in Taiwan since the late 1980s is the development of communications technologies and the expansion of entertainment markets in Taiwan. This has both exposed the audience in Taiwan to more information about Japanese popular culture, through newspapers, magazines, and television, and has given the local industries a better appreciation of the value of Japanese popular music, thus encouraging them to invest a good deal of money in promoting it in Taiwan.

During the period of my field research in Taipei in 1997, two local companies, Magic Stone and Sony Music Taiwan, were particularly interested in selling Japanese artists in Taiwan. Neither is controlled by Japanese companies. Magic Stone distributes Japanese popular songs from Avex Japan, a company that had not, until recently, established branches in Asian capitals but promoted its CDs by licensing. Licensing allowed this small independent company to avoid the high cost of maintaining an office and employees.[7] Magic Stone has supported the Japanese dance music of Komuro Tetsuya (the most popular and influential artist and producer in Japan) in becoming "cool" in Taiwan. Taiwanese record companies usually spend freely on publicity for the new albums of local artists, but relatively little for international artists. The managing director of Magic Stone boasted to me that his company had recently invested the same amount of money in publicizing Japanese artists in Taiwan as it had in publicizing local artists.

A similar arrangement can be seen in Sony Music Taiwan's promotion of Dreams Come True. It was Sony Music Taiwan, not Sony Music Japan, that took the initiative in deciding which Japanese artists to sell in the Taiwanese market. Sony Music Taiwan had cautiously planned to promote Dreams Come True in Taiwan over a two-year period and finally succeeded in inviting the group to Taiwan in 1996. According to the vice president of Sony Music Taiwan, the company spent a considerable amount of money on promotion in Taiwan, almost 10 times the average for international artists, resulting in sales there of more than 200,000 copies of Dreams Come True's CD, a phenomenally successful figure for foreign artists.

The managing director of the Taiwan office of a Japanese recording company lamented in an interview with me the difficulty he had in convincing the Tokyo head office of the importance of spending money on publicity to sell CDs in Taiwan:

> Japanese companies naively assume that Japanese know-how is completely transferable to other Asian markets, but they do not understand how media environments vary and systems work differently. In Taiwan, TV is a medium that sells spot commercial time, and recording companies have to pay for using it, even when the record is the theme song from a TV drama. This is common practice throughout the world, as far as I know—so it is Japan that is different. The Japanese system is too self-contained to extend its power overseas.

These comments show some of the difficulties that Japanese music industries face in selling Japanese artists as well as in the enterprise (mentioned earlier) of exporting Japanese know-how to Asian markets. It is possible for the Japanese music industries to be self-contained because Japan is the world's second-biggest economic power and consumer market. Japanese cultural industries do not have to risk investing huge sums of money in other Asian markets where profits may not be very attractive to them. The same is true with Japanese popular musicians. For them, Japan is no doubt the most important market, and they cannot sacrifice it to visit less profitable markets.[8] Avex's strategy of licensing suits the Taiwanese market. Japanese companies do not risk their own money, and Japanese artists do not have to go on frequent tours to promote themselves. The manager of Magic Stone was emphatic that the promotion of Japanese popular music in Asian markets can be done effectively only in conjunction with the marketing strategies of local industries.

The same can be said of Japanese television programs. Recently Japanese dramas have attracted a larger, young (particularly female) audience in Taiwan than either locally produced, Hong Kong, or Western/American dramas (Hattori and Hara 1997; Ishii et al. 1996). A news reporter from Taiwan whom I interviewed observed that Japanese dramas are now one of the most common topics of everyday gossip for high school and university students. Apart from their textual appeal, Japanese television programs in Taiwan benefit from the maturity and expansion of the local television market, which has forced local companies to recognize the capacity of quality Japanese TV dramas to find a niche market in Taiwan.[9]

A Taiwanese programming officer for STAR-TV told me that they programmed Japanese dramas in order to attract a large Taiwanese audience. Japanese programs are clearly indispensable to STAR-TV's strategy of localization in Taiwan. An important factor to consider in the recent popularity of Japanese television programs in Taiwan is the rapid development of cable television. Cable TV emerged as an illegal business in the 1980s. After a long battle between the government and the cable operators, the government changed its policy from prohibition to regulation. The 1993 Cable TV

Law legalized cable television, but even before it came into force about 50 percent of households were watching cable (known as "the Fourth Channel"). Under the Cable TV Law, levels of viewing have continued to rise; in 1998 nearly 80 percent of households watched cable television, and Taiwan has the most developed cable television system in Asia.

The Cable TV Law requires that at least 20 percent of the programs of the cable channel be locally produced, but it is obvious that many cable channels do not abide by this condition. Most channels are buying entire programs from overseas, mainly from the United States, Hong Kong and Japan. Lewis et al. (1994) have argued that the development of cable television in Taiwan facilitated "re-Americanization" after a period when the people's preference for local programs reduced the number of American programs on the air; ESPN, HBO, Discovery, and CNN are some of the leading program packages in this "re-Americanization" of Taiwan. However, the dramatic increase in Japanese television programs in Taiwan has been another significant trend of the last few years, particularly since the end of the ban on Japanese-language TV programs. In 1997 there were five Japanese cable channels in Taiwan. [10] One channel broadcasts its own programs by satellite almost simultaneously with Japan, but the other four buy entire programs from Japanese commercial television stations for local rebroadcast. In addition, the free-to-air channels and STAR-TV all regularly broadcast Japanese programs. In 1992 the total export of television programming from Japan to Taiwan was about 600 hours (Kawatake and Hara 1994). There are no accurate figures available on Japanese program exports to Taiwan after 1993, but in 1996 the commercial TBS network alone exported 1,000 hours of programs to Taiwan, according to my interview with TBS.

The popularity of Japanese popular culture in Taiwan has an impact on the export strategies of Japanese cultural industries. Taiwan's case suggests to the Japanese cultural industries that a Japanese cultural odor does sell. A manager of Dentsu who promoted format sales of Japanese quiz shows in Asia also mentioned this shift. He said in an interview with me that what has been made clear is that Japanese television programs have gained a certain universal appeal. In 1997 Sumitomo Trading Co. Ltd. launched JET as the first Japanese pay TV channel with TBS, whose profits from selling programs overseas are the highest in Japan. JET supplies nine Asia-Pacific countries (Taiwan, Hong Kong, Thailand, Singapore, Malaysia, Indonesia, the Philippines, Australia, and New Zealand) with a channel of exclusively Japanese television programs in four languages—Japanese, English, Mandarin, and Thai—by satellite uplink from Singapore. In its advertising, JET declares:

> People with an eye for trends have their eyes on Japan. On its fashions, celebrities, and
> hit products—anything that's new and fun. Today, trend-conscious viewers throughout
> Asia can enjoy up-to-date programs from Japan 24 hours a day: on JET TV.

The emphasis on the attractiveness of Japanese popular culture has clearly become a key to the export strategies of Japanese TV industries in Asian markets.

Another interesting example is that of the music producer Komuro Tetsuya, whose entry into Asian markets was aided by foreign media, specifically STAR-TV. Komuro and News Corporation established a joint company, TK NEWS, in December 1996. The purpose of the company was not only to promote Komuro's music but also to popularize the Komuro Family as a music group in Asia. When the family had two concerts in Taipei in May 1997, they attracted more media attention than global pop star Whitney Houston, who happened to be giving a concert two days before the Komuro Family. TK News also produced a TV program to find local artists for the Komuro Family; a thirteen-year-old Taiwanese female singer called Ring made her debut with them in April 1998. This sounds like the familiar strategy of finding a local star, but the crucial difference is that Komuro is not only an artist but also a capable producer. Although Komuro announced his willingness to learn about News Corporation's conceptions of local sound and localizing marketing strategies which had been developed for Asia (*Nikkei Shimbun* 1997), what was important for TK News was not localizing Komuro's sound so much as his fame. The selling point was that the local artist had been produced by the best producer in Japan. As a result, Ring's first single went to the top of the IFPI Taiwan single-CD chart immediately after its release.

According to a former director of STAR-TV's music channel, Channel V, the Japanese music market is more sophisticated than other Asian markets in terms of the absorption and indigenization of a wide variety of Western popular music. In his opinion, Japanese music, though a new taste for the Taiwanese audience, is similar but easier for them to relate to than Western popular music. He also said that Channel V is more local than MTV Asia. "If MTV can be compared to McDonald's, Channel V is a dimsim." When I asked whether Japanese popular culture and music are dimsims, he answered "yes." Elsewhere, he has predicted that "being Japanese will be fashionable in the twenty-first century" (*Aera* 1997). I was also told by the managing director of a Taiwan record company that Japan should be confident of its own popular culture, and that the 1990s were a turning point for Japanese popular culture which is taking over the symbolic role of American popular culture in Asia: Japanese popular culture is becoming another object to which young people in Asia will aspire. To what extent these scenarios materialize remains to be seen, but since the predictions were made by people in managerial positions, they must be, to some extent at least, self-fulfilling prophecies.

From Western Gaze to Global Gaze

The Japanese cultural presence is becoming more visible and discursively more articulated. The discursive manifestation of the cultural presence of a foreign country usually happens when that presence seems either to be a threat to national identity or national interest, or to be an object of yearning in the recipient country. In either case, the presence of a foreign country marks its cultural hegemony. It was Sony's purchase of Columbia in 1989, and Matsushita's purchase of MCA (Universal) in 1990 that dramatized the ascendancy of Japan as a global cultural as well as economic power by making the Japanese presence in the United States visible. The merger of hardware and software by Japanese media companies shocked the United States, which had previously disdained Japanese capacity to produce culture. Although Matsushita retreated from Hollywood and Sony struggled to make a profit (even though Columbia finally achieved phenomenal box-office sales in 1997), the ascendancy of Japan's culturally odorless presence in the global audiovisual market continues to attract academic and media attention.

Undoubtedly the emergence of discourses on the popularity of Japanese culturally odorless products in the world reflects the fact that Japanese cultural industries play a substantial role in globalization processes. Japanese cultural power finally matches its economic dominance. What is particularly significant in the discursive manifestation of Japanese cultural presence is that Japanese cultural products are now appreciated even by dominant Western countries. An animated film, *The Ghost in the Shell*, was premiered simultaneously in Japan, America, and Britain. Disney is distributing Miyazaki Hayao's animated films globally. Computer games are dominated worldwide by three Japanese manufacturers, Nintendo, Sega, and Sony. The popularity of Japanese game software is exemplified by Super Mario Brothers. According to a survey, Mario is a more famous character among American children than Mickey Mouse (Henshûshitsu 1995). A question arises: If Sony's purchase of Columbia articulated Japanese cultural and economic power as a threat to the United States, what kind of hegemony or images of power does the popularity of Japanese animations and computer games overseas confer on Japan?

Japanese animated culture and imagery evoke, to a certain degree, both a sense of threat and a yearning overseas. On the one hand, the global circulation of Japanese animated culture causes a fear of cultural invasion and decadence in Western countries, and discourses of "techno-Orientalism" in Western countries present new, dehumanized high-tech images of Japan (Morley and Robins 1992). At the same time, we see the emergence of *otaku*, obsessively devoted fans of Japanese animations in Western countries whose mania makes them wish they were born in Japan. To them Japan "looks more cool" than the United States. Okada (1995) compares this Western passionate consumption of Japanese animation to Japan's—and his own—experience of yearning for America through the consumption of American popular culture. Paradoxically, Okada seems to argue, Western audiences appreciate a Japanese way of life which is embodied in the *mu-kokuseki* (racially, ethnically and culturally unembedded) imagery of animation. If the Japaneseness of Japanese animations is derived from their active erasure of bodily Japaneseness from the visual imagery, the object of yearning is an animated virtual Japan. In this respect, Okada's argument at least serves to remind us that a sense of yearning for a particular country evoked through the consumption of cultural commodities is inevitably a monological illusion since it is little concerned with the complexity of 'real' culture.

Another way of making sense of Japanese cultural power is to look at the issue of cultural power—and hegemony which is articulated through the cross-cultural circulation of products—in a different light. It does not seem entirely contingent that the manifestation of Japanese cultural hegemony has occurred in the last decade. This is a period when the globalization of culture has been accelerated by several interconnected factors: the global integration of markets and capital by powerful transnational corporations, the development of communication technologies that easily connect all over the globe, the emergence of an affluent middle class in non-Western countries, and the increasing number of people moving from one place to another by migration and tourism. What has happened to cultural flows under these conditions is that the variety of images and commodities—most of which are still from the West, though non-Western countries such as Japan are increasing their share—are simultaneously circulating in urban spaces all over the globe. While this makes Western modernity ubiquitous, at the same time the original ownership of images and commodities becomes increasingly insignificant and irrelevant. To put it in an exaggerated manner, images and commodities tend to become culturally odorless because origin tends to be subsumed under local appropriation. The specificities or "authenticity" of local cultures, as Miller (1992) argues, are to be found "*a posteriori* not *a priori*, according to local consequences not local origins" (p. 181). By appropriating, hybridizing or indigenizing images and commodities of "foreign" origin, even American culture is conceived of as "ours" in many places. McDonald's is so much a part of their own world that it no longer represents an American way of life to Japanese or Taiwanese young consumers.

What disappears in this process is a sense of derivative modernity, that "our" modernity is borrowed from modernity that happened elsewhere (Chakrabarty 1992). Ubiquitous modernity, in contrast, is based on a sense that our modernity is the one that is simultaneously happening everywhere. To put it differently, the Western gaze that has long dominated the material and discursive construction of non-Western modernity is now melting into a global gaze that subtly resists either a condemnation of cultural imperialism or cultural domination or admiration for (Western) cultural superiority. This shift is therefore as much about our interpretive framework as about reality. The age of Americanization, in which cross-cultural consumption was predominantly discussed in terms of the export of a way of life and ideas of a dominant country, is over. It is the shift from a Western gaze to a global gaze, I would suggest, that Japanese cultural hegemony thrives on. Although commodities and images are dominated by a small number of wealthy countries, including Japan, and many parts of the world are still excluded from enjoying global cultural consumption, their presence and uneven distributions are becoming more difficult to demarcate.

The point is most clearly elucidated when we look at Japanese cultural presence in Asia. Fifty years would seem long enough for former colonies to become more tolerant toward, if not to forget, the legacy of Japanese imperialism.[11] It is not totally an accident that the ascent of Japanese cultural presence in Asia coincides with the decline in the dominance of a discourse on cultural imperialism.

Even in the age of the global gaze, the local odor still finally matters. Moreover, the desire to become at once modern and different is one that the global gaze generates (Hannerz 1996). It is this desire that lets durian articulate the modern local identity of Southeast Asia; and it is the same desire that is increasingly exploited by transnational corporations. The Japanese market is not immune from the transnational cultural industries' strategies of glocalization. Miwa Yoshida, the female vocalist with the pop group Dreams Come True appeared on the cover page of the October 14, 1996, issue of *Time Asia*. The issue's cover story was the "Divas of Pop." Yoshida was one of the divas, along with Celine Dion, Gloria Estefan, Whitney Houston, Mariah

Carey, Alanis Morissette, Tina Arena, and Faye Wong. In Japan this was reported in major newspapers, and sales for the issue almost tripled. But Yoshida was only on the cover page of the Japanese version of *Time Asia*. In other Asian countries, including Taiwan, the cover page carried the picture of Faye Wong, a Beijing-born Hong Kong singer. No matter how well received in other parts of Asia, it will not be easy for the sweet scent of Japanese popular culture to overpower the deodorant of global cultural industries, which are the main force for promoting uneven distributions, organizing cultural diversity, and selling cultural odor to local markets.

At the same time, it cannot be denied that Japanese cultural odor has gained momentum in Asian markets. In this chapter, we have seen this trend in the promotion of Japanese popular culture in Taiwan, where a new word has emerged to describe young people who love to consume things Japanese.

This testifies to another trend—that of the globalization process promoting intraregional cultural flow among non-Western countries. While what Japan can export to Western countries is still limited to well-recognized culturally odorless products, much broader selections of Japanese TV programs and popular music are increasing their presence in Asian markets. This chapter has focused on marketing strategies, but the ascent of Japanese TV dramas and popular music in Taiwan also has much to do with their textual appeal. In my research in Taipei and Hong Kong, many young viewers said they found Japanese TV dramas more attractive and easier to relate to than American dramas, because of both cultural and bodily similarity and textual subtlety. This is not to say that Japan has become an object of yearning in other parts of Asia, nor that a priori cultural proximity generates regionalization. Rather, under globalizing forces, cultural similarities and resonances in the region are newly articulated. It is also an emerging sense of coevalness based upon the narrowing economic gap, simultaneous circulation of information, the abundance of global commodities, and the common experience of urbanization that has sustained a Japanese cultural presence in East Asia.[12]

It is often argued that the beauty of Japanese traditional culture was discovered by the West, and that this in turn made Japan conscious of the Western gaze when claiming its cultural uniqueness. In the case of contemporary popular culture, it is neither Japan nor the West but modernized Asia which has discovered the commercial value and cultural resonance of Japanese popular culture. What tends to be emphasized in traditional culture is Japan's irreducible difference; but, for audiences in East Asia, Japanese popular culture represents cultural similarities and a common experience of modernity in the region that is based on an ongoing negotiation between the West and the non–West-experiences that American popular culture cannot represent.

Non-Western countries have tended to face the West to interpret their position and understand their distance from modernity. The encounter has always been based upon the expectations of difference and time lag. Now, however, some non-Western "modern" countries are facing each other to find neighbors experiencing and feeling similar things and the temporality of East Asian vernacular modernities via America-dominated cultural globalization. The image of Asian youth, at least in marketing terms, might be defined as one of consuming hybrid: youth who have material power and passion for consuming fashionable cultural products and who do not care about the origin of those consumer items or media products. Nevertheless, preferred cultural products are not without East Asian flavor, as those are reworked in the Asian context by hybridizing various fads from all over the world. Affluent Asian youth are keen to consume things which are inescapably global and (East) Asian at the same time. If Japanese popular culture tastes and smells like dimsim and kimchi by Hong Kong, Taiwanese, and South Korean media industries and consumers, it might be because it clearly represents the intermingling of global homogenization and heterogenization in the East Asian context.

However, it should be stressed that increasing intra-Asian cultural flows highlight uneven power relations in the region. The active construction of meanings takes place under the system of global capitalism in which Japan has a major role. People's freedom of negotiation at the receiving end of the global cultural flow operates under unambiguously asymmetrical relations. Only through the careful analysis of intraregional cultural flows can we understand how the newly articulated time-space configurations and asymmetrical cultural power relations are tilted with Japan's transnationalist desire for Asia, which strongly reflects Japan's imperial legacy in the region.

Notes

An early version of this paper was presented to the international symposium *Media Globalization in Asia-Pacific Region*, Taipei, May 20–22, 1997. My research in Taiwan and Hong Kong was conducted between December 1996 and January 1997 and in May 1997, with the support of a Toyota Foundation research grant.

1. For a comprehensive analysis of Japanese TV dramas and popular music in East/Southeast Asia, see my forthcoming book tentatively titled as *Transnational Japan: Media Globalization, Localization and Asianization*, forthcoming.

2. This chapter follows the Japanese convention that family names precede personal names.

3. The Japanese version, unlike the original song, has no gay culture subtext; instead, it features an 'original' dance.

4. October 6, 1994; TBS is one of Japan's national commercial television networks.

5. I have written about this in more detail in Iwabuchi (1995).

6. Including two songs of Amuro Namie (one of which became number 1), two songs of Globe, and one song of Dreams Come True.

7. One disadvantage of the system is that the artists whom Avex wants to sell do not necessarily attract licensing partners and the amount of money spent on publicity is totally decided by the partner. However, this licensing strategy has been successful in Taiwan.

8. Chage & Aska, who toured Asia twice, were exceptional in this regard and were also unusual in becoming popular overseas.

9. There is no doubt that STAR-TV has been the pioneering player in diffusing Japanese television programs to Asia, particularly to Taiwan. STAR-TV started broadcasting in August 1991 and the "Japanese Idol Drama Hour" has been the most popular program on the Chinese channel since 1992. Although STAR-TV has been discussed widely in terms of its pan-Asian satellite broadcasting and of its possible penetration into China, it should be

remembered that Taiwan has been a major target, too. This is particularly true with STAR Chinese Channel and Music Channel V (which replaced MTV in 1994). Recently STAR-TV launched a new Chinese channel, Phoenix, for the mainland Chinese market and STAR Chinese Channel is now broadcast exclusively in Taiwan. Japanese programs, particularly dramas, are occupying the prime time slots on the STAR Chinese Channel.

10. NHK Asia, Gold Sun, Videoland Japan, Po-Shin, and JET (Japan Entertainment Television).

11. As mentioned above, Taiwan removed its ban on broadcasting Japanese-language TV programs and music in 1993 and the president of South Korea has publicly announced his intention of ending the restrictions on importing Japanese cultural products.

12. For a detailed analysis of the consumption of Japanese TV dramas in Taiwan, see Koichi Iwabuchi (2001).

References

Aera. (1997) January 20.

Aksoy, A. and Robins, K. (1992) 'Hollywood for the 21st century: global competition for critical mass in image markets,' *Cambridge Journal of Economics*, 16: 1–22.

Asian Business Review. (1994) May.

Chakrabarty. D. (1992) 'Postcoloniality and the artifice of history: who speaks for "Indian" pasts?' *Representations*, 37: 1–26.

Ching, L. (1994) 'Imaginings in the Empire of the Sun: Japanese mass culture in Asia', *Boundary 2*, 21, 1: 199–219.

Far Eastern Economic Review. (1994) January 27.

Featherstone, M. (1996) *Undoing Culture*, London: Sage.

du Gay, P., Hall, S., Janes, L., Mackay, H., Negus, K. (1997) *Doing Cultural Studies: The Story of the Sony Walkman*, London: Sage.

Hannerz, U. (1989) 'Notes on the global ecumene,' *Public Culture* 1, 2: 66–75.

Hannerz, U. (1996) *Transnational Connections: Culture, People, Places*, London: Routledge.

Hattori, H. and Hara, H.-Y., (1997) 'Tachanneruka no naka no terebi to shichôsha: Taiwan kêburu terebi no baai' (The proliferation of television channels and audiences: a study of Taiwan cable television), *Hôsô Kenkyû to Chôsa*, February, 22–37.

Henshûshitu, A. (1995) *Sekai shôhin no tsukurikata: Nihon media ga sekai o sesshita hi* (The Making of World Products: The Day when Japanese Media Conquer the World), Tokyo: Parco Shuppan.

Hoskins, C. and Mirus, R. (1988) 'Reasons for the US dominance of the international trade in television programmes,' *Media, Culture and Society*, 10: 499–515.

Ishii, K., Watanabe, S. and Su, H., (1996) *Taiwan ni okeru Nihon bangumi no shichôsha bunseki*. (Analysis of viewer data for Japanese programmes in Taiwan), Discussion Papers Series No. 701, Tsukuba: University of Tsukuba.

Iwabuchi, K. (1994) 'Complicit exoticism: Japan and its other', *Continuum* 8, 2: 49–82.

Iwabuchi, K. (1995) 'Return to Asia? Japan in the global audiovisual market,' *Media International Australia*, 77, August: 94–106.

Iwabuchi, K. (1998) 'Pure impurity: Japan's genius for hybridism,' *Communal Plural: Journal of Transnational and Crosscultural Studies*, 6, 1: 71–86.

Iwabuchi, K. (2001) 'Becoming culturally proximate: the a/scent of Japanese idol dramas in Taiwan,' in B. Moeran (ed.) *Asian Media and Advertising*, London: Curzon.

Iwabuchi, K. (forthcoming) *Transnational Japan: Media Globalization, Localization and Asianization*, Durham, NC: Duke University Press.

Kawatake, K. and Hara, Y. (1994) 'Nihon o chûshin to suru terebi bangumi no ryûtsû jôkyô' (The International Flow of TV Programmes From and Into Japan), *Hôsô Kenkyû to Chôsa*, November, 2–17.

Lee, P. S.-N. (1991) 'The absorption and indigenisation of foreign media cultures. A study on a cultural meeting point of East and West: Hong Kong,' *Asian Journal of Communication*, 1, 2: 55–72.

Lewis, G., Slade, C., Schapp, R., and Wei, J.-H. (1994) 'Television globalisation in Taiwan and Australia,' *Media Asia*, 21, 4: 184–189.

Miller, D. (1992) 'The young and restless in Trinidad: a case of the local and global in mass consumption,' pp. 163–182 in R. Silverstone. and E. Hirsch (eds.) *Consuming Technologies: Media and Information in Domestic Spaces*, London: Routledge.

Morley, D. and Robins, K. (1992) 'Techno-Orientalism: futures, foreigners and phobias,' *New Formations*, 16, Spring: 136–156.

Nikkei Shimbun. (1997) January 10.

Okada, T. (1995) '*Anime bunka wa chô kakkô ii*' (Animation culture is super cool), *Aera 2*, October: 43–44.

Oshii, M., Ito, K., and Ueno, T. (1996) '*Eiga to wa jitsu wa animêshon datta*' ('Film was actually a form of animation'), *Yuriika*, August: 50–81.

Ritzer, G. (1993) *The McDonaldization of Society*, London: Sage.

Robertson, R. (1995) 'Glocalization: time-space and homogeneity-heterogeneity,' pp. 25–44 in M. Featherstone, S. Lash and R. Robertson (eds.) *Global Modernities*, London: Sage.

Straubhaar, J. (1991) 'Beyond media imperialism: asymmetrical interdependence and cultural proximity,' *Critical Studies in Mass Communication*, 8, 1: 39–59.

Stronach, B. (1989) 'Japanese television,' pp. 127–165 in R. Powers and H. Kato (eds.) *Handbook of Japanese Popular Culture*, Westport: Greenwood Press.

Wee, C.J.W.-L. (1997) 'Buying Japan: Singapore, Japan, and an "East Asian" modernity,' *The Journal of Pacific Asia*, 4: 21–46.

Contributors

CATHERINE BALLÉ, Director of Research, Centre National de La Recherche Scientifique and Centre de Sociologie des Organisations, Paris; author of numerous journal articles, *Sociologie des Organisations* (1990), and coauthor (with Dominique Poulot) of *Musées en Europe, une democratisation inachevée* (forthcoming).

ALISON BEALE, Associate Professor, School of Communication, Simon Fraser University, Burnaby, BC; coeditor of *Ghosts in the Machine: Women and Cultural Policy in Canada and Australia* (1998) and author of numerous journal articles.

DENISE D. BIELBY, Professor of sociology, University of California-Santa Barbara; author (with C. Lee Harrington) of *Soap Fans: Pursuing Pleasure and Making Meaning in Everyday Life* (1995) and numerous publications on the sociology of culture, media, and gender.

DIANA CRANE, Professor of Sociology, University of Pennsylvania, Philadelphia, PA; author of several books including *The Transformation of the Avant-Garde: The New York Art World, 1940–85* (1987), *Production of Culture: Media and Urban Arts* (1992), and *Fashion and Its Social Agendas* (2000), as well as numerous articles in journals. She is the editor of *Sociology of Culture: Emerging Theoretical Perspectives* (1994).

C. LEE HARRINGTON, Associate Professor of sociology at Miami University, Oxford, OH; author (with Denise D. Bielby) of *Soap Fans: Pursuing Pleasure and Making Meaning in Everyday Life* (1995) and numerous journal articles on the sociology of culture and the sociology of law.

DAVID HUBKA, Ph.D. in sociology, Carleton University, Ottawa; Ph.D. dissertation, *Globalization of Cultural Production: The Case of Children's Animated Television, 1978–1995* (1998).

KOICHI IWABUCHI, Assistant Professor of media and cultural studies at International Christian University, Tokyo; author of *Transnational Japan: Media Globalization, Localization, and Asianization* (forthcoming), and numerous journal articles in English and Japanese.

SACHIKO KANNO, Program Coordinator, Planning Office, The Japan Foundation, Tokyo. She has a diploma in the history of decorative arts. Her research interests include cultural policy, activities of culturally oriented nonprofit organizations, and government support for nonprofit organizations.

RICHARD L. KAPLAN, lecturer, Department of Sociology, University of California-Santa Barbara; author of *Politics and the American Press: The Rise of Objectivity, 1865–1929* (forthcoming).

KEN'ICHI KAWASAKI, Professor, Department of Cultural Sociology, Komazawa University, Komazawa, Tokyo, Japan. Editor of several volumes on cultural policy and author of numerous journal articles in English and Japanese.

NOBUKO KAWASHIMA, formerly Research Fellow, Centre for the Study of Cultural Policy, University of Warwick, Coventry, UK; now Department of Economics, Doshisha University, Kyoto; author of *Museum Management in a Time of Change: Impacts of Cultural Policy on Museums in Britain, 1979-1997* (1997) and *The Making of a Programme Diary: A Study into the Programming of Arts Presentation at Arts Centres in Britain* (1998) and several journal articles.

MARI KOBAYASHI, lecturer, Faculty of Cultural Policy, University of Shizuoka Culture and Arts; researcher on cultural policy and law.

KIAN-WOON KWOK, formerly Professor, Department of Sociology, National University of Singapore; now directing a company that brings together technology and the arts; author of journal articles and a forthcoming book on cultural policy in Singapore.

JENNIFER LINDSAY, formerly Program Officer at the Ford Foundation in Jakarta, Indonesia; now Professor of performance studies at the University of Sydney, Australia; author of *Javanese Gamelan* (1992), *Cultural Organisation in Southeast Asia* (1994), and translations of Indonesian essays and literature.

J. PEDRO LORENTE, permanent lecturer in the Department of Art History, University of Saragossa, Spain; author of *Cathedrals of Urban Modernity: The First Museums of Contemporary Art, 1800–1930* (1998) and editor of *The Role of Museums and the Arts in the Urban Regeneration of Liverpool* (1996). He is working on a forthcoming book on the recent history and urban impact of museums of contemporary art.

KEE-HONG LOW, formerly research scholar, Department of Sociology, The National University of Singapore, Singapore; author of journal articles and active practitioner in the Singapore theater community.

ROSANNE MARTORELLA, Professor, Department of Sociology, William Paterson University, Wayne, NJ; publications include *Corporate Art* (1993), and *Art and Business: An International Perspective on Sponsorship* (1996), and numerous journal articles.

LUCIANA FERREIRA MOURA MENDONÇA, a Ph.D. candidate in sociology, teaches anthropology in the School of Sociology and Politics of São Paulo and the Santo André Foundation in Brazil.

STEFAN TOEPLER, Associate Research Scientist, Institute for Policy Studies, Johns Hopkins University, Baltimore, MD; author of *Culture Financing* (in German) (1991), coeditor of *Private Funds, Public Purpose: Philanthropic Foundations in International Perspective* (1999); contributing author of *Global Civil Society: Dimensions of the Nonprofit Sector* (1999); and guest editor of a *Journal of Arts Management, Law, and Society* issue called "Arts and Culture in Post-Communist States" (spring 2000).

KUNIYUKI TOMOOKA, Ph.D. candidate, Department of Sociology, University of Tokyo and part-time lecturer at Tsuru University, Rikkyo University, and Shibaura Institute of Technology; coauthor of *Kyosei Syakai No Bunka Senryaku* (Cultural strategy for coexistence) (1999).

MARIA ANTONIETTA TRASFORINI, Associate Professor, Department of Human Sciences, University of Ferrara, Ferrara, Italy; author of *The Psychoanalyst as a Professional* (1991) and editor of *Arte a parte: donne artiste fra margini e centro (Art Apart: Women Artists In and Out of the Mainstream)* (2000).

ANNETTE ZIMMER, Professor of social policy and comparative politics, Department of Political Science, Wilhelms-University of Münster, Münster, Germany. She has published extensively on social policy, the nonprofit sector, and cultural policy. Her publication credits include: *Das Museum als Nonprofit Organisation: Management und Marketing* (Nonprofit Museums: Management and Marketing) (1995), *Der Dritte Sektor in Deutschland* (The Third Sector in Germany) (1997), and *Krise des Wohlfahrtsstaates—Zukunft der Kulturpoltik* (The Crisis of the Welfare State—The Future of Cultural Policy) (1997).

Index

Abbs, Peter, 164
African Americans, 191, 192, 193, 197, 198, 205, 211
  as hero, 199
  and youth culture, 201
Ang, Ien, 217
Anheier, Helmut K., 119
animation, 234, 254n
  Japanese, 258–259, 268
  and consumer preferences, 234
  and dubbing, 234
    in international markets, 245–247, 248
  and editing, in international markets, 248, 249, 250
  and international co-production, 249, 255n
  and international versioning, 248, 250
    role of local hosts in, 248
  and localization, 252
  and postproduction, in international markets, 248
  and television producers, 234
  see: childrens' animated television
Antola, Livia, 218, 220
Anzieu, Didier, 189
Appadurai, Arjun, 2–3
Archambault, E., 35
artists, 97, 98, 99, 100, 104n, 105
  in Singapore 156–157, 161, 163, 164
  see also: cultural policy, Singapore and
arts, 93, 105, 118
  funding in New York, 120–122
  and cultural policy in Singapore, 150, 151
  and economic value of, in Singapore, 152
  and modernity, 165
  and urban economies, 119
arts communities, 97, 104n
arts expenditures
  and multiplier effects, 119, 124, 126
arts organizations, 119, 121, 129
  changing sources of income of, 127–128
  economic impact of, in New York City, 123–125
  in New York City, 128
  see also: nonprofit organizations
Arvidsson, A., 210
Asia, 6, 7, 8, 9, 19, 150, 159
audience(s), 2, 5, 9, 16, 17, 86, 129
  active, 200, 217
  effects of imported programming on, 232n
  foreign, 21
  global, 21
  Italian, 221
  reception, 211,
  resistance, 11
  responses, 11
  studies, 140
  for television, 216
  in Ferrara, 170, 180, 181, 182–183, 184–185, 186, 187
  expenditures of, 185, 190n
  in Southeast Asia, 71, 75
  and global programming, 251
  see also: public
Australia, 15, 18, 73, 74, 84